THE DEATH AND RESURRECTION OF THE SOUL

A Training Manual for Counselors

DEDICATION

This book is being published as a tribute to my wife, Judith Giesing, on the occasion of our 60th wedding anniversary. I want very much to let her know how much I love her and also, how much I respect what she has done for her Lord and the many "daughters" she has counseled, mentored or just plain loved.

She has done a lifetime of ministry without charge to anyone and has received little recognition for it. However, she is rich and famous in my eyes and in the eyes of her Lord Jesus.

—Joseph Giesing

JOSEPH GIESING

A TRULY REMARKABLE BOOK

This book is a treat for the mind, emotions and spirit! It brings a wealth of experience and understanding that is required for the healing of the whole person. It is a blend of technical knowledge, spiritual power and an exciting series of personal experiences in the field of soul healing.

It is essential for those who want to understand how the human heart is healed after being hurt or devastated. Pastors will find this book "must reading" to assist them in understanding and shepherding their flocks. Professors can use this book to add a dimension to their students' education that they could never find anywhere else.

The Author deals with an extensive range of issues including; communication problems, personality disorders, psychoses, neurosis, physical, emotional, and sexual abuse, abortion guilt, satanic ritual abuse, and many other issues.

Also, the book draws on many sources, which are documented, not the least of which is the Bible. Jesus and the Holy Spirit working with the counselor are the main sources of power for the inner healing of the wounded lambs who come for healing.

As such, the Author has headed a ministry entitled "**Wounded Lamb Ministries**" which seeks to mentor others who feel the calling to minister to the "walking wounded."

TESTIMONIES

How do I put into words the value that Judy and her ministry of inner healing has had on my life? I was a basket case when I met Judy, dealing with the results of abandonment as a child, and abuse suffered both in childhood and as an adult. I sat through many hours of counseling with Judy dealing with inner healing, or soul healing. At times I wanted to give up, but through Judy's love and sincere desire to help, I was always drawn back. Today, as I look back, I don't recognize the person I was those many years ago, and I thank God for Judy and her ministry of inner healing.

—Patti A.

I met Judy in 1982, and at that time, I had been deeply traumatized from molestation, wife beating, put in the hospital from the same and chased by the Costa Mesa Strangler. Judy then took me through de-victimization and inner healing and brought me to a place where she brought my mind and soul to restoration. Over the years, she helped me with healing and financial assistance.

So, to sum it up, I would say, with the help of the Holy Spirit, Judy has truly made a difference in my life.

—Pastor Renee Leetch

My name is Pat, Patricia Learn. Judy Geising took me through many years of inner healing. I had suffered from much abuse of every kind. I was born on October 20th, 1943 in upstate New York to an Italian family.

Because of this abuse, I suffered years of mental breakdowns where I would become psychotic and had to be hospitalized. It started at age fifteen. I came to the Lord in 1977 when we came to California and I met Judy shortly after at Teen Challenge. I needed counseling for my hyperactive twin boys. Then Judy prayed with me for Inner Healing. Judy spent a long time with me. I had years of abuse and breakdowns, but the Lord healed me.

It has been almost twenty years since I had a breakdown. My psychiatrist has taken me off all the psychotropic medication, except one pill at night. I have lost all my weight and am trying to stay as healthy as I can. The Lord used Judy in a mighty way in my life. SHE IS STILL A BLESSING TO ME!

—PATRICIA LEARN

I can hardly testify without coming to tears about how Judy laid down her life for me at a time when I was so in need, vulnerable & sick. I was first concerned about getting what is called "inner healing" because my mom had been into New Age.

But God showed me clearly her help is what I needed. Judy came every week & spent 2 to 3 hours with me. Holy Spirit was so strong when we would pray to see what He wanted to do to bring healing.

The anointing on Judy was so full of God's love that I would easily get visions for what he wanted to do & visions that helped heal my wounded soul, that then enabled me to forgive the most horrible of experiences.

There's no way I could thank her enough. She & Joe have helped me also in every possible way.

Forever grateful,

—PRISCILLA VAN SUTPHIN BS, MN

These are the things that I have been delivered from:

1. 11 personalities (mostly children of various ages);
2. Psychological drugs to cope;
3. In and out of mental hospitals;
4. I was having flashbacks of being raped by my dad and brother on camping trips when I was very young. My mother confirmed this before she passed away.

However, now:

1. I only have one personality;
2. I no longer take psychological drugs to cope;
3. I only go to mental hospitals to visit women who have been abused and need help.

My husband, Bob, has needed caregivers and still has one. Every caregiver we have had has been abused in every way imaginable. The Lord brought them here to heal.

Thank you, Jesus. Thank you, Mom (Judith). You will never know how you and Jesus have helped me; what I have learned from you and Jesus and are able to minister to these precious "wounded lambs."

I thank you and they thank you.

—SHARON

The DEATH *and* RESURRECTION *of the* SOUL

A Training Manual for Counselors

JUDITH GIESING

M.S. Pastoral Counseling and
M.A. Marriage, Family & Child Counseling

Wounded Lamb Ministries

Wake-Robin Press
2020

Opinions expressed are solely the author's.
Printed in the United States of America.

First Edition: August 27, 2020
ISBN 978-1-946970-04-6
Library of Congress Control Number: 2020914876

Published by
Wake-Robin Press
An imprint of redbat books
La Grande, OR 97850
www.wakerobinpress.com

Text set in Mrs Eaves OT Serif

Cover Images:
David White photo—*Dawn Breaking Over Everest*
Romany Fawzy art—*Jesus Hugging Lamb*

Cover Design & Book Layout by
redbat design | www.redbatdesign.com

TABLE OF CONTENTS

NOTE: *Most scripture references are taken from the New American Standard Bible (NASB) unless otherwise noted.*

PREFACE

When I began counseling in 1975, I had no concept of the vast number of people who had been deeply wounded and scarred emotionally due to severe rejection, abuse and deprivation. I continue to be astounded by how many lives have been devastated by sexual molestation, child abuse, divorce, violence, incest, and even satanic ritual abuse. If our society continues to shut God out of its homes, schools and institutions, turning instead to Secular Humanism and the occult for answers, we can expect the number of casualties to increase dramatically.

As Spirit-filled believers, we are all waiting anxiously for the last great revival to stem this tide. Many believers have found, however, that accepting Jesus as their Savior did not automatically erase the emotional pain they were suffering, nor did it change their attitudes and behavior. Nor were they able to "lay aside the old self with its evil practices" which resulted from their inability to forget what lay behind.

The cry of our heavenly Father's heart is to bind up the brokenhearted and set the captives free from their past lives. The desire of my heart is to then see these sanctified saints go forth to heal and deliver others with God's love and truth. Thus, I have attempted to compile the wisdom and knowledge acquired through my own and others' experiences in a manual designed to train laymen to heal wounded souls.

My fervent prayer is that many believers will get the burden and become anointed vessels of God, led by the Holy Spirit, through whom Jesus' healing love and power can flow. My impassioned plea is that all who read this book will also hear and answer the desperate cries of a wounded world by choosing to become instruments of God's healing love, power and truth!

—Judith Giesing

The DEATH *and* RESURRECTION *of the* SOUL

> "I can't rewrite the first chapter one more time!" I sobbed. The little girl in that chapter is hurting too badly, and I don't know how to comfort her. I can see her cowering in a corner of the basement behind a stack of boxes. Her little body is naked and trembling. I can hear her whimpering. "God, I'm hurting bad enough! It just isn't fair that I have to go back and hurt for that little girl, too! I don't want to feel her pain. I can't write any more about her. I just can't! So, don't ask me to!" I had begun to relive the events of that horrible afternoon, and there was no stopping the memories. "Go away!" I yelled at the little girl. "I can't help you. I can't take care of you! Just go away!" But her frightened whimpering just grew louder and louder...

This heart-rending excerpt is taken from Lauren Stratford's astonishing book, *Satan's Underground*. This precious saint was begging God not to make her relive the horror of the sexual and satanic ritual abuse she had suffered during childhood because the pain was too excruciating. Even though Lauren knew Jesus as her Savior and had made Him her Lord, the "little girl inside her" was still suffering the unbearable pain of the searing wounds inflicted upon her.

Each of us has rooted in his subconscious an "inner child of the past," whose most cherished desire is to have an intimate relationship with someone who will love and accept him exactly as he is, thus giving meaning and purpose to his life. Many times, however, the inner child of a person has been subjected to extreme rejection, abuse and deprivation which has left deep wounds and scars on his soul and spirit. Since only God is perfect, only His perfect love and acceptance can heal this individual's emotional wounds and give him the intimate love union for which his whole being longs. "There is no fear in love, but perfect love casts out fear" (1 John 4:18).

The inner child of a person is also controlled by the manner in which his parents or parental figures raised him. Therefore, not only must the inner child's wounds be healed, he must also be set free from the "programming" of his "internal parent of the past." "For as he thinks within himself, so he is" (Prov. 23:7 NAS 1977). Since only God is perfect, only He possesses the truth which will free a person's inner child from the control of his parental programming. "You shall know the truth and the truth shall set you free" (John 8:32).

I believe the "mandate" God has given me for the body of Christ is to help train and equip lay counselors to "bind up the brokenhearted" with God's love and "set the captives free" with God's *truth.* These chosen saints are called to be the vessels used by God to help each wounded believer receive emotional healing, enabling him to develop an intimate love relationship with His heavenly Father and to rebuild his life firmly grounded in His truth.

Healing and deliverance of a person's soul and spirit takes place as the Holy Spirit reveals the painful memories that need to be healed, and the judgments, inner vows, soul ties, and curses that need to be broken. After Jesus heals his wounds and scars through the soul healing process, the counselee's inner child will finally be able to see his parents and others through Jesus' eyes and forgive them with His agape love. This sincere forgiveness from the heart will enable him to believe that God truly does love him, since he will no longer view the Lord in the way that he saw his parents—condemning, abusive, controlling, unreliable, etc.

This truth will free him so that he will now be able to discover his real identity in the security of God's love and the freedom of His truth. The counselee will now be able to trust God to fully develop his potential in Jesus Christ, giving true meaning and purpose to his life.

Thus, the objective of this training manual is to teach lay counselors how to let the Holy Spirit lead them through the soul healing process, allowing Jesus to bring about these goals in the lives of His wounded lambs. For a counselor to accomplish this task effectively, he must have some knowledge of how each person's soul is uniquely programmed by his interaction with his parents and others.

Therefore, the first section of this book is devoted to describing how an individual's soul develops, resulting in certain behaviors, attitudes and characteristics. The second part portrays how the soul healing process takes place—healing, purging and purifying the heart which leads to the death of the soul (self). The third section depicts how the soul is then resurrected in Christ, sanctified and changed into His image, through reprogramming the internal parent with God's love and truth (renewing the mind).

Part I. DEVELOPMENT *of the* SOUL

The development of each individual's soul is distinctly unique, comprised of the sum total of his inheritance—physical, spiritual, emotional—and his environmental experiences from the moment of conception on. The most significant influence in forming a child's personality is his interaction with his parents, although interaction with significant others and number and position of siblings in his family are also important factors.

Since this interaction begins at the moment of conception, attitudes and actions of the parents may wound the soul and spirit of their child even in the womb. Dr. Thomas R. Verny in his book, *The Secret Life of the Unborn Child*, reports that personality traits and attitudes are formed in a baby as a result of prenatal or birth trauma. For example, a baby may refuse to bond with its mother after birth as a result of her rejection of her baby in her womb. Thus, interaction between parent and child begins in the womb.

Another important factor is that the temperament of a child, formed by genetic determinants, often has a significant influence on the parents' method of interacting with him and on how he perceives and reacts to this interaction. Thus, a child who is very quiet and sensitive usually evokes a much different reaction from parents than one who is aggressive and strong-willed. For example, when my daughter was small, she would cry if I frowned at her, while her older brother never cried even when he was spanked!

A. EGO STATES.

About eighteen years ago, God led me to thoroughly study one of the secular theories of personality development, "Transactional Analysis," which was developed by Dr. Eric Berne and made popular by the book, *I'm OK—You're OK*, written by Dr. Thomas A. Harris. Although this theory has no lasting answers for treatment, it can be used as a tool to help us understand the development of our souls, as well as our interactions with others, through the use of a particular set of concepts involving ego states. Thus, it helps us understand the basis of human behavior, attitudes and feelings.

In his book, Harris describes an experiment conducted by Wilder G. Penfield, O.M., C.C., C.M.G., M.D., LL.D., F.R.S., in which he probed different parts of the temporal lobe of the brain with an electrode. He discovered that the electrode evoked specific memories along with the feelings associated with past events. The memory could not be evoked without the associated feelings. Thus, the evoked recollection was a reproduction of what the patient saw, heard, felt, and understood.

Recollections are evoked by the stimuli of daily experience in much the same way that they were evoked by Penfield's probe. Involuntary recollections may be described as a "reliving" in which we experience spontaneous feelings but cannot remember the event causing them. Much of what we relive we cannot remember!

Harris relates an example depicting this fact which concerned a female patient who heard a song which produced an overwhelming melancholy in her. She was gripped with an unbearable sadness! Later she had a flash of remembrance in which she saw her mother sitting at the piano and heard her playing the same song she had heard her playing when she died. She had relived precisely the same feeling which was recorded when her mother died!

Thus, we can conclude that the brain functions as a high-fidelity recorder, putting on tape every experience, locked together with its associated feelings, from the time of conception until death.

These recorded memories and related emotions are available for replay today in as vivid a form as when they happened. We cannot only remember how we felt, we can feel the same way now!

1. CONTENT OF EGO STATES.

Transactional Analysis makes the assumption that three internal ego states exist within people—Parent, Adult and Child.[1]

The contents of P-A-C, modified, are:

Recordings in the brain of parental beliefs and behavior along with child's perceptions and resulting judgements of these beliefs and behavior (BELIEF SYSTEM)

Computer which makes decisions after examining information received from three sources: Parent, Child and data gathered from the outside world by the Adult. (THOUGHT SYSTEM)

Recordings in the brain of emotional reactions of child to parental behavior along with his resulting inner vows. Also natural drives, free & self-will, desires, rights, creativity, curiosity, the "real self" (MOTIVATION SYSTEM)

Figure 1. EGO STATES

a. PARENT. Parental opinions, judgments, dogmas, laws, rules, morals, standards, values, etc., plus the parental patterns of how to do different things, are recorded in the Parent data. Nurturing experiences, such as hugs, looks of pride, coos of pleasure, etc., are also recorded in the Parent, as are memories of rejection, abuse, trauma, and deprivation.

Since the ability to reason is undeveloped in a child, the data in the Parent is recorded straight without any editing on the child's part. Thus, the sight of his usually loving father verbally abusing his mother is recorded in the child's mind without including the fact that his father was drunk because he had just lost his job. Many

1 When referring to a particular ego state, the words "Parent," "Adult" and "Child" will be capitalized throughout this book. More about analyzing transactions will be discussed later. The contents of the three ego states are summarized in Table 1. Tables and illustrations have been placed in the back of this book so that the flow of the text will not be interrupted.

such inconsistencies and contradictions may be recorded in the Parent. For instance, parents often say one thing and do another. Also, the father may be hostile and the mother loving, producing an inconsistent parental image.

There may also be conflicting images from one parent, e.g., a mother who smothers her son with kisses, but when he asks for a drink, she shoves him away. The little guy is caught in a "double-bind" in which he is hurt, no matter what he does. If he accurately discerns his mother's behavior, he must accept the fact that she does not seem to be able to love him. But if he discerns inaccurately, he might request her love and be rejected.

Thus, due to his lack of reasoning ability, many of a child's perceptions are distorted, leading him to draw many false conclusions regarding parental behavior. From these inaccurate conclusions, he then forms many beliefs or judgments which are recorded in the Parent data. For example, the daughter of "yuppies" (young, upwardly mobile, professional people) might conclude falsely, "My parents only love me because I perform well." This belief (judgment) becomes a vital part of the "belief system" which will determine her attitudes and behavior in adulthood. Some of the most common judgments made by children are: "Parents are always right," "It is dangerous to disagree with parents," and "If I want to be accepted, parental approval is mandatory."

The more the beliefs and behavior of his parents line up with reality, the more computer time is freed up for a Child to pursue creativity, pleasure, development of talents, etc. However, many children are preoccupied much of the time with the conflict between their parents' beliefs and behavior and what they see as reality. If a child's parents are too threatening to him due to his judgments, he may give up and quit trying to inquire into areas of conflict. In this case, he will accept his parents' beliefs, reinforced by their behavior, as true without checking them out with reality. Thus, he may believe many incorrect, biased, parental opinions, judgments, myths, etc., which are then stored in the Parent data as "prejudice."

The parental beliefs accepted by the Child, both accurate and inaccurate, plus his perceptions of parental behavior, both accurate and inaccurate, along with the resulting judgments which he makes, form the belief system which programs his attitudes and behavior as an adult. This belief system which the Child creates, being the affective part of the Parent data, will be referred to as the Parent.

b. CHILD. The Child may be thought of as being subdivided parts: the Adaptive Child and the Natural Child. The wounds resulting from a child's judgments of his parents' behavior create feelings of rejection, anger, fear, etc., which are recorded in the Adaptive Child data. A Child may decide to express his feelings directly in anger or repress them and respond in fear. Anger or fear, therefore, become the primary feelings which drive him to make controlling inner vows, also recorded in the Adaptive Child data. These inner vows will then determine his attitudes and behavior as an adult.

While judgments are decisions about what a child believes (perceives to be true), inner vows are decisions of his will involving action. Using the previously mentioned example, fear of rejection might drive the daughter of "yuppie" parents to make the inner vow, "I will always perform superbly," resulting from her judgment, "My parents will love me only if I perform well."

Many things happen to us today which recreate the situation of childhood and bring on the same emotions which we felt then. These experiences "trigger" the Adaptive Child and cause a replay of the original feelings of rejection, anger, guilt, etc., which then reinforces our inner vows. When a person's negative feelings dominate his reasoning, his Adaptive Child is said to be "hooked" and in control.

Unfortunately, negative feelings far outweigh the positive ones contained in the Adaptive Child data. There is a constant demand for a child to give up his desires for the reward of parental approval, which can disappear as quickly as it appeared. Thus, the predominant by-product of the frustrating, civilizing process is "not OK" feelings, even if the parents are "good."

Recorded in the Natural Child are good feelings, such as those generated by warm milk, mother's cuddling and rocking, touching a kitten, etc. Also located in the Natural Child are the free will, as well as goals, dreams, talents, and positive natural drives, such as creativity and curiosity—the desire to explore and know and the urge to touch and experience. Self-will and negative natural drives, such as power, greed and envy are likewise recorded in the Natural Child. The Natural Child may, therefore, be selfish, demanding, lazy, impatient, and jealous, as well as carefree, spontaneous, creative, and happy. Thus, we might theorize that the Natural Child is that person who really is—the "real self," the "inner man."

In adulthood, the Adaptive Child adapts to the dictates of the belief system (Parent) through anger or fear. Thus, anger or fear become the Adaptive Child's prime motivating force. This force then drives him to compel the Adult to carry out the inner vows which were made in childhood. In some cases, the Parent is so weak that the Child does not feel forced to adapt to its demands. Since then, the Parent does not exercise direct control over him, the Natural Child is free to exercise his own will. This freedom allows his natural drives to become his prime motivating force. It should be noted, however, that the Parent does not control the Natural Child indirectly, since he is still in bondage to the programming of the Parent.

We might conclude, then, that the motivating force which to think and act in a certain way is either anger or fear (Adaptive Child) or natural drives (Natural Child). This motivation system will be referred to as "The Child." Thus, it appears that the Adaptive Child is motivated through anger or fear to make inner vows which cause him to think and act according to a belief system which he himself created! Simply stated, the Adaptive Child has created his own Parent which now controls him!

The good news is that, the Child being analogous to the heart in many ways, the Lord Jesus is able to free the Adaptive Child from himself by healing the broken heart (Child) of a person with His love and "enlightening the eyes of his heart" (Parent) with His truth!

c. ADULT. The main function of the Adult is to reason and make decisions after it has analyzed data from the Parent and the Child and compared it with information from the outside world. To perform this function accurately, the Adult compares the data in the Parent with reality to see whether or not the contents are true and still applicable today. The Adult then compares the data in the Child with reality to see whether or not the feelings stored there are appropriate to the present or are in response to outdated Parent data.

An individual whose soul is relatively healthy might possess an Adult strong enough to make the decision to discard both the Parent data and the corresponding Child emotions if he decided that they were false and no longer appropriate. More often than not, however, since most of us function with damaged souls, a person possesses a weak Adult who succumbs to the demands of his Adaptive Child. These demands usually consist of inner vows made as a child which his Adaptive Child is now being driven by anger or fear to enforce. The Adaptive Child controls the Adult by forcing it to think and act according to them. The person with a powerless Parent also possesses a weak Adult who usually gives in to the demands of the Natural Child who is controlled by his natural drives—usually negative ones.

An example of obsolete Parent data still in control concerns a woman who never put a hat or coat on a table or a bed. If she forgot or her children broke this rule, she overreacted. Finally, she asked her mother why she had made this rule. She replied that some neighbor children had been infested with lice, so she instructed her not to put her hat or coat on their tables or beds. We can see why this recording of Parent data, along with its corresponding emotions, replayed with its original urgency!

2. IDENTIFICATION OF EGO STATES.

The language of 'Transactional Analysis' is also useful in helping us analyze our transactions, each of which consists of a stimulus by one person and a response by another. This response becomes a new stimulus to which the first person responds. Using Berne's language, we can discover which ego state of each person—Parent, Adult or Child—is originating each stimulus and response. The clues which help us identify whether a stimulus response is Parent, Adult or Child include, not only the words, but also the tone of voice, facial expressions and body gestures used.

a. PARENT. Verbal expressions helpful in identifying the Parent state are: "How dare you!" "Now what?" "If I were you, I would," or

"Not again!" "Always" and "Never" are usually Parent words which reveal the limitations of an archaic system closed to new data. Many evaluative words, whether critical or supportive, signify the Parent state because they make judgments. Examples are lazy, stupid, shocking, naughty, ridiculous, nonsense, absurd, crazy, worthless, poor thing, disgusting, cute, sweet, adorable, lovely, precious.

"Should," "ought" and "must" usually indicate the Parent, although they can also be used by the Adult. The automatic, unthinking use of these words, together with body gestures and tone of voice helps us to identify when a person is "coming on Parent" in a transaction.

Physical gestures characteristic of the Parent state are hands on hips, pursed lips, furrowed brow, pointing index finger, sighing, arms folded across chest, tongue-clucking, foot-tapping, patting another on the head, and head-wagging. I am sure most of us will have no trouble identifying when someone is functioning in the Parent state!

b. CHILD. Verbal expressions which identify the Child state are: "I want," "I wish," "I don't care," "I guess," "I don't have to," "I must have," "I have a right," and "I need." Many superlatives, such as bigger, biggest, better, and best indicate the Child state since they are used to impress the Parent and overcome the "not OK" feelings.

Since a Child's earliest responses to the external world are nonverbal, the most readily apparent clues indicating the Child state are seen in physical expressions. Any of the following signal the involvement of the Child state in a transaction: tears, quivering lip, tantrums, high-pitched, whiny voice, shrugging shoulder, downcast eyes, delight, teasing, laughter, squealing, squirming, or giggling.

c. ADULT. The Adult state may be identified by words signifying data processing, such as: who, what, when, where, why, how, in what way, true, false, possible, I think, I see, I feel, in my opinion. Although physical clues representing the Adult state are more difficult to recognize than those of the other two states, listening with the Adult may be identified by an interested facial expression and by continual movement of the face, eyes and body. The Adult also lets the curious, excited Natural Child show its face.

3. PROGRAMMING OF EGO STATES.

a. JUDGMENTS AND INNER VOWS. As pointed out previously, the belief system (Parent) of a person is composed primarily of judgments, i.e., beliefs which he formed as a child in response to his perceptions of his parents' behavior. As a child is growing up, parents draw many conclusions, i.e., make many judgments, about a child's behavior, personality, appearance, etc., which they continually reinforce through words and actions! Many examples of these judgments or "word curses" come to mind: "You are so stupid," "You are slow as molasses," "You are a plain Jane," "You are too fat," "too lazy," "too bratty," etc. By reinforcing their negative judgments, parents unknowingly write the "script" which their child "acts out" in life.

Since a child usually forms judgments that his parents are always right and that he must have their approval, he has no choice but to agree with them. Thus, he accepts their judgments that he is stupid, lazy, ugly, etc. Bound by self-deception, he then makes an inner vow, i.e., a life-controlling decision, which assures that the judgment or word curse which he made against himself will come to pass. "The heart (Child) is more deceitful than all else, And is desperately sick; Who can understand it?" (Jer. 17:9). We are bound by the vows which we make as children, usually before the age of five, because they are so strong that they control our lives as adults. "For as a man thinks within his heart (Child), so he is" (Prov. 23:7).

Examples of self-judgments and the resulting inner vows are: "Since I am stupid, I will probably fail at everything I do (self-judgment); therefore, I am not even going to try (inner vow);" "Since I am ugly and nothing can be done about it (self-judgment), I won't try to improve my appearance (inner vow);" "Since I am fat and always will be (self-judgment), I will eat just as much as I want to (inner vow)." Parents generally reinforce their child's low self-esteem by constantly confirming these negative judgments: "See, didn't I tell you that he would never amount to anything!" Thus, they create self-fulfilling prophecies by programming their children to reject themselves and to ask for and expect rejection from others!

On the other hand, in some cases, instead of rejecting and expecting too little of their child, parents idolize and expect too much of him. These "expecting" parents program their child with "good" judgments which are as binding as the bad ones. Examples of so-called good judgments are: "You are so smart," "so pretty," "such a good boy," etc. Self-judgments and the vows which follow are: "Since I am smarter than other kids, I must never fail if I want be accepted;" "Since I am so good, I must be perfect to be accepted;" and "Since I am so pretty, I must always stay thin if I want to be loved."

These "positive" vows are just as damaging, of course, as negative ones, since the child making them is always trying to "meet the mark." He puts impossible demands on himself as he tries to please a parent who will never be satisfied with his performance but will always expect more. Conversely, he may just give up because he knows that he will never be able to meet their expectations. Thus, he also suffers from rejection because he never feels accepted just as he is. A schizophrenic condition may result when a child has both a "rejecting" and an "expecting" parent, since he is not sure which "script" he should follow.

Judgments and inner vows are as numerous as people. The most binding judgments and vows usually concern relationships with parents. Many times, little girls are crushed when their daddies are too busy or preoccupied to notice them. Feeling ignored and rejected, they may make the judgment that all men are insensitive and uncaring; therefore, men will never be able to meet their needs or make them happy. As a result, they will vow that they will never share their inner selves with any men!

A small girl who is molested makes many judgments and vows: "Men are nasty, cruel, dirty;" "Men use and abuse you, so I will never trust them;" "I hate men and will never become intimate with any man." All judgments and vows concerning men usually include God also since He is believed to be a man by little girls.

Many times, little boys are devastated when their mothers pry into their affairs and share their most intimate secrets with everyone. Feeling betrayed and exposed, they make the judgment that all women are "nosy, manipulating gossips" who will betray their confidence sooner or later. As a result, they vow that they will never become intimate with women because they cannot be trusted.

Little boys and girls alike judge their parents to be controlling, dominating, unreliable, unpredictable, cruel, weak, etc. All of these judgments and vows must eventually be broken during soul healing if the Child is to be freed from the control of the Parent.

b. CONSEQUENCES OF JUDGMENTS. In the spiritual realm, when a child makes a judgment against his parent, he plants a "seed of bitterness" which takes root in his soul. For example, the first reaction of a small child who is beaten by his father is judgment that his father is cruel, followed by anger, hatred and rebellion. But fear quickly follows the initial anger arousal when he perceives his helplessness. Thus, fear is the alternative response to anger when a child is hurt, rejected or deprived and he realizes that he is powerless to change the situation. Feeling helpless, he represses his original judgment along with the resulting anger, hatred and rebellion, and responds in fear.

Even though, as an adult, this person has long since forgotten the "bitter root" judgment which he made against his father as a child and then repressed, the "law of judgment" was put into effect. "See to it that no one comes short of the grace of God; that no root of bitterness springing up causes trouble, and by it many be defiled" (Heb. 12:15). Since his judgment dishonors his father, even if his judgment is true, Deut. 5:16 ensures that life will not go well with him in the area in which he judged.

Also, when a child judges his parent, the law which declares that the measure which a person metes out he must receive, goes into effect. "For in the way you judge, you will be judged; and by your standard of measure, it shall be measured to you" (Matt. 7:1,2). So, this child must receive harm in the same area in which he judged his father. Lastly, his judgment was a seed sown which someday had to be reaped. Just as a tiny mustard seed grows to produce a large tree, so a seed of judgment sown increases the longer it remains unrecognized and unrepented of. "Whatever a man sows, this he will also reap" (Gal. 6:7).

Bitter root judgments, according to John Loren Sandford and Paula Sandford in *Healing the Wounded Spirit* are the most common, most basic, most unrecognized, and unrepented of sins in all our lives! Since this child's bitter root judgment was that his father was cruel, this seed planted has to be reaped in adult life either in actual, perceived or self-inflicted cruelty. **Table 2** depicts that if this child does not repress the anger, hatred and rebellion resulting from his original judgment, he will retaliate against others and make an inner vow to punish them. In this case, he will become a cruel victimizer like his father and portray some or all of the symptoms on the left side of the chart. Although a victimizer, he is still a victim of his parental programming.

If he decides that it is not safe to express the anger, hatred and rebellion resulting from his original judgment outwardly, he will repress them, turning them against himself. In this case, he will rationalize that since it is not safe to disagree with his parent, he will agree with him that he is at fault and deserves to be punished. His reaction will be one of fear and guilt. Therefore, he will vow to punish himself and become a victim, either of himself or others and manifest symptoms on the right side of the chart. Thus, he will punish himself and attract people who are cruel or perceive people to be cruel.

In the latter case, as an adult under stress, he may be flooded by the same fear of brutality which he had as a child to the extent he is convinced that the salesman at the door is going to kill him—a paranoid delusion. This type of delusion is an extreme case of domination by the Child which occurs when present-day occurrences trigger feelings stemming from obsolete experiences which are then inappropriately externalized.

Therapists using Transactional Analysis as a helping technique believe that the revelation that the original threat to the child no longer exists is all that is necessary to liberate the Adult and eliminate a paranoid delusion. They believe that when the client understands that the archaic feelings stem from outdated experiences stored in the Parent, he will be able to "get into the Adult" and "turn off" these outdated feelings in the Adaptive Child. But even though the Adult may understand that the Parent is no longer a threat to the Child because the Parent data is obsolete, the Child only knows that he is still hurting and afraid!

So, using willpower to turn off his archaic feelings will not work, no matter how strong the client's Adult is, because the root cause of his feelings has not yet been dealt with. Healing of memories is intensely powerful because Jesus removes the original threat to the Child—the root cause of his feelings, by healing his soul, wounded and scarred by his father's cruelty. The Child of this person can then forgive his father, "dig up" and remove his bitter root judgment. Jesus is then able to cleanse away the child's guilt and replace his anger, hatred and bitterness with acceptance of love and compassion for his father, himself and others.

Of course, we must be aware that whenever a person makes judgments and vows or harbors bitterness, anger, hatred, etc., he opens the door for demonic spirits to deceive, confuse, oppress, and/or possess his mind. The spirits then have permission to fuel and intensify the symptoms outlined in **Table 2**, although they did not cause them. The more a person believes and nurtures the lies the demons are telling him, the deeper his root of bitterness grows, the stronger his symptoms become and the more he loses touch with reality. This, in turn, may open the door for demons to come in and take up residence in his soul.

Thus, the person experiencing a paranoid delusion—in all probability, demon-possessed, has so completely succumbed to Satan's lies that he is convinced everyone's main goal is to kill him. When Jesus heals this person's wounded soul, he will be able to repent of his judgments, forgive his parents, break his inner vows, and begin to realize who he is in Christ. The demons will then no longer have permission to harass him because he has "fallen out of agreement" with them. Since they have lost their foothold, they will leave voluntarily, having been "starved out."

c. SOUL TIES. Having studied the powerful effects that judgments and inner vows and their consequences have on a person's life, we can readily understand that parental programming "ties" the soul of a child to his parents in an almost unbreakable bond. The Bible gives us a descriptive picture of how remarkably strong a soul tie can be. As stated in 1 Samuel 18:1, the "...soul of Jonathan was knit to the soul of David, and Jonathan loved him as himself."

When a woman knits a garment, the yarn is interlaced in such a way that it becomes interlocked, requiring great strength to rip it apart. When the parts of a fractured bone knit together, they become cemented so firmly that they will not fall apart. Thus, souls that are "knit" together are interlocked or cemented into a firm bond that cannot easily be broken.

Jonathan gave David his robe, arms, sword, bow, and belt. He would have done anything for David, even lay down his life for him. Jonathan made a covenant with David, swearing to him in the name of the Lord, saying, "...The Lord will be between me and you, and between my descendants and your descendants forever" (1 Sam. 20:42). The soul tie formed by Jonathan and David is an example of a "godly" soul tie.

The parent who loves and accepts his child unconditionally, respecting his worth and uniqueness while encouraging him to develop his full potential in God, forms a godly soul tie with his child. This parent knows how to lovingly discipline his child, yet allow him the freedom to make choices, indulge his curiosity and express his creativity. Consequently, this child will gain a sense of security, self-acceptance and confidence from the godly soul ties formed with his parents which will sustain him the rest of his life. Also, the example of loving, accepting parents will usually lead him to form many more godly soul ties during his adult life.

Unfortunately, due to our parents' behavior and our consequent judgments and vows, many of us have formed "ungodly" soul ties with our parents. As we have seen, a rejected and abused child believes his parent's judgments that he is "no-good," "lazy," "will never amount to anything," etc. The distrust, insecurity, self-rejection, and lack of confidence developed by this child from the ungodly soul tie formed with his parent will lead him to "fulfill" his parents' "prophecies," ultimately destroying his life.

Sadly, the more rejection and abuse a child has received, the more he longs for acceptance, causing him to form many more ungodly soul ties throughout his life. This longing for love often drives people, especially women, to form ungodly soul ties through fornication and prostitution. Men are often driven to find this missing love through many forms of aberrant sexual behavior.

Compulsion for acceptance drives hurting individuals to search for love in all the wrong ways and places, causing them to form ungodly soul ties with all kinds of fleshly indulgences. Common substitutes which people use to attempt to satisfy their unrequited parental love are alcohol, drugs, food, sex, work, sports, material goods, even the occult. By substituting these sinful gratifications for God's love and acceptance, their souls become tied to them. These substitutes for God's love will be discussed further when the subject of symptoms is considered. All soul ties not sanctioned by God must, of course, be broken during the course of soul healing.

4. DOMINATION OF EGO STATES.

As we have seen, parents or parental figures are the people predominantly responsible for programming the attitudes and behavior of children, thus forming the different characteristics which will dominate their lives as adults. Therefore, it would be helpful to discuss some of the basic patterns which people employ to Parent their children, along with the resulting personality characteristics which the children develop. Also included in the following discussion will be the corresponding ego state which dominates each personality type.

In his book, *The Liberation of the Soul,* Lawrence E. Nielson, Ph.D., describes eight basic patterns of parental programming from which develop eight different attitude and behavior patterns in the child. These patterns of parenting and the resulting characteristics formed in the child are adapted from Dr. Theodore Millon's description of eight basic personality types, given in his book, *Disorders of Personality: DSM IV and Beyond*. Millon's personality types are given in parentheses after "personality of child." Nielson lists four parental patterns under "overcontrol," two under "under-control" and two under "rejection."

a. DOMINANT INTERNAL PARENT (OVERCONTROL PATTERNS). In the overcontrol pattern, the "expecting" parent imposes too much control on the child which inhibits his natural impulses (Natural Child) and his choices (Adult). He is overly conscientious and concerned that the child always does the right thing. He only loves the child conditionally, on the basis of living up to his expectations. Since his parent is so controlling, the child must adapt to his demands by conforming or rebelling. Since he has a strong desire to win his parent's acceptance, fearing his rejection, he usually conforms. As a result, he becomes very performance-oriented and overly concerned about what others think of him. His self-esteem depends on whether he is accepted or rejected by others.

The child with an overcontrolling parent makes many judgments which form his belief system (Parent). Repressing the anger, hatred and unforgiveness resulting from his judgments, he conforms to his parent's demands through fear of rejection by making inner vows which will determine his attitudes and behavior the rest of his life. Thus, as an adult, his Internal Child will be predominantly Adaptive Child programmed by the demands of his Internal Parent through fear of rejection. His Adult will then be programmed by his Adaptive Child to think and act according to the inner vows which, as a child, this person was driven to make in response to his own judgments. Judgments and inner vows common to each parental pattern are listed in **Table 4**.

The Parent, therefore, becomes the dominant ego state in the overcontrol pattern. In the following figure, the Parent's strength is shown by its large size, while the weakness of the Adult and the Child is depicted by their smaller sizes. The Parent's control is portrayed by its large overlap onto the Adaptive Child (shaded area). The extensive control of the Adult by the Adaptive Child is depicted by its large overlap onto the Adult, while the Natural Child's weakness is shown by its small overlap onto the Adult. A description of each of the four overcontrol patterns of parenting follows the figure:

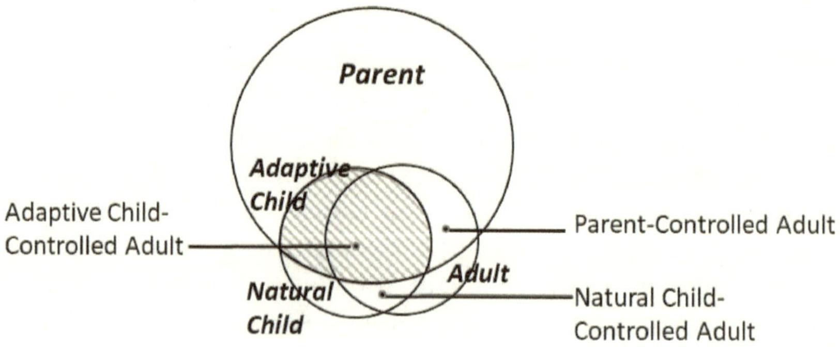

Figure 2. DOMINANT INTERNAL PARENT

(1.) Authoritarian. In the authoritarian pattern, the parent enforces his power on the child in an attempt to make him conform in order to preserve his security with him. The parent is dominating, judgmental, strict, legalistic, and impatient with failure. He inhibits love, spontaneity and freedom in the child. This is the only overcontrol pattern in which the child, especially if his temperament tends to be extraverted, does not conform through fear. The parent is so strict that the child's anger often overcomes his fear. As a result, he expresses his anger outwardly according to **Table 2**, becoming a victimizer.

Adults with this personality type seek power and have to be in charge, examples being an aggressive, vindictive army sergeant and a slave-driving corporate head who uses cut-throat tactics to get ahead. Although an angry victimizer, the Adaptive Child of this type of person is still conforming to the internal parent's demands, trying to earn acceptance by outperforming everyone else. We might say that he is so insecure and desperate for approval that he overdoes it, striving to be the best or win the game of life at any cost.

Another interesting point is that he has become, due to his judgments, very much like the Parent whom he judged. People who are products of the other three overcontrol parental patterns also tend to become like the parent whom they have judged. The child of an authoritarian parent, often a girl, who has a more introverted temperament may repress her anger and conform through fear. In this case, she develops a personality type more like the passive ambivalent, to be discussed later. She will, most likely, attract someone like her father, a victimizer, for a husband.

Usually the authoritarian pattern develops because of the parent's own insecurities, i.e., he must have control of the child to feel secure about himself. Also, he may enforce obedience to feel good about himself or control may even be seen as a biblical principle with which he feels he must comply.

Personality of the Child: (active independent)—competitive, insensitive, hostile, dogmatic, impatient, defensive, self-disciplined, strives for superiority and power, performance-oriented, vindictive, absolute conscience—thinks in blacks and whites.

*(2.) **Over-Coercion.*** The over-coercive parent is constantly telling the child what he should and should not do. He is constantly nagging, questioning, debating, and criticizing the child's behavior. He behaves erratically, shifting from hostility to reassurances of love, so the child can never predict the outcome of his behavior. Although he is obedient, conforming through fear, the child develops an internal resistance pattern, resulting in negativism, procrastination and indecision. As an adult, this person is very uncomfortable to be around because of his changeable moods. He may be very compatible and charming and then, for no apparent reason, become irritable, defensive and even hostile.

The parent in this pattern is extremely insecure and uncertain about his ability to parent his child properly—anxious about enforcement, yet anxious for the Child to do the right thing. He is always in an internal conflict which results in inconsistent, ambivalent and irritable behavior toward the child.

Personality of the Child: (active ambivalent)—resistant, stubborn, negativistic, moody, irritable, vacillating, defensive, pessimistic, passive-aggressive, distrusting, compulsive-impulsive, conflicts between guilt and anger, discontented, conflicted conscience—confusion as to what is right and wrong.

*(3.) **Perfectionism.*** In this pattern, the child is constantly urged to do better. Regardless of how well he does, he could have done better. Since he can never please the parent, he lives in constant fear of failure and rejection, resulting in insecurity and low self-esteem. He strives for performance rather than building relationships and punishes failure with guilt. As an adult, this person is always striving to perform, so he will take on whatever task he is asked to accomplish; he can never say "no." Although a "do-gooder," he is often impatient and critical of himself and others. Ministers, counselors and community workers are often this personality type, as are individuals suffering from anorexia nervosa.

The perfectionist parent is very common in our culture which places a high value on achievement and competition. This parent may be compensating for his own sense of failure through his child's accomplishments or he may be extending his own ego by idolizing his Child and thus, trying to make him perfect.

Personality of the Child: (passive ambivalent)—conforming, inhibited, submissive, obedient, competitive, guilt-prone, fearful, anxious, defensive, responsible, orderly, compulsive, inflexible, dogmatic, over-sensitive conscience—punishes failure with guilt.

(4.) Overprotection. The overprotective parent is excessively concerned about his child's health, safety and welfare in general. He protects the child from normal interpersonal conflicts so that he remains dependent and feels inadequate to cope with the demands of life. As a result, he condemns himself and lacks the confidence and discipline necessary to make decisions or develop his own potential.

As an Adult, his security and satisfaction depend on the attention and support of others. A "clinging vine," he often attracts very dominating people who enjoy his dependence on them. But his attachments can make demands on others who eventually pull away, causing him much pain.

In this pattern, the parent may be using the child to supply his emotional needs in an effort to compensate for his own deprivation of love. The child may have a sickness or handicap that brings out the parent's protective qualities or the parent may have suffered the loss of a loved one and is consoling himself by becoming too emotionally involved with his child.

Personality of the Child: (passive dependent)—dependent, needs support, approval, and reassurance, cooperative, fear of rejection, anxious, submissive, feelings of inadequacy, guilt, self-pity, indecisive, magnifies failures, lacks self-discipline, relative conscience.

b. DOMINANT INTERNAL CHILD (UNDER-CONTROL PATTERNS). In the two under-control parental patterns, parents give in to the child's natural impulses more than is warranted. Thus, inadequate discipline and too much attention cause the child to become self-centered, demanding and unable to respect the rights of others. As a result, he sustains an unrealistically high opinion of himself and is unable to cope with the frustrations of life. Without the inner constraints of fear and guilt, he fails to develop self-control and self-discipline.

Since his parent does not control him, at least directly, the child is not required to conform to his demands. Judging his parent to be powerless and ineffective, he vows that he will do whatever he wants to. Since he has no anger, fear or guilt as a result of his judgment, he is free to exercise his own will and allow his natural drives—usually negative ones, to have free rein.

Although in the under-control patterns, it appears that the child controls his parent, the parent is still in control of the child indirectly because he "writes" the child's "script," i.e., programs his attitudes and behavior from the moment of conception. Thus, as an adult, as long as his Internal Child is "acting out" his Internal Parent's script, this person is in bondage to the programming of his Parent.

But, since the Parent has no direct control, it is powerless. Thus, his Internal Child will be predominantly Natural Child with very little Adaptive Child. Therefore, in the under-control pattern, the Natural Child becomes the dominant ego state, exercising control over the Adult who is too weak to withstand its demands. In the following figure, the Natural Child's strength is shown by its large size, while the weakness of the Parent and Adult is depicted by their smaller sizes. The Parent's powerlessness is shown by its small overlap onto the Adaptive Child. The extensive control of the Natural Child is shown by its large overlap onto the Adult, while the Adaptive child's weakness is shown by its small overlap onto the Adult. A description of each of the two under-control patterns follows the figure:

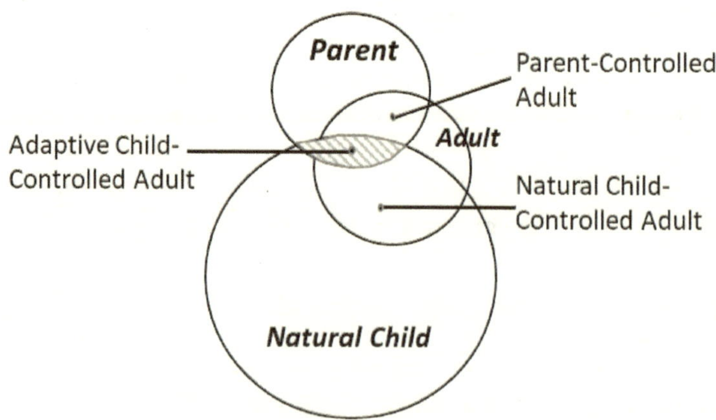

Figure 3. DOMINANT INTERNAL CHILD

(1.) Over-Submission. In this pattern, the parent submits to the child's will, and the child learns to manipulate the parent into getting what he wants. Through pleading, temper tantrums, being cute, withholding love, etc., the child's will prevails. He learns to do things for social recognition rather than personal satisfaction. Competence is measured by how others react to him rather than by achievement. As a result, he becomes irresponsible, impulsive and undisciplined.

As an adult, he is the "life of the party" type who revels in "being in the spotlight," "showing off" and entertaining everyone with his theatrics. He refuses to be held accountable for his actions or take responsibility for anything. A woman with this type of personality tends to be very manipulative, seductive and flighty, exhibiting her emotions and opinions which vary dramatically.

The over-submissive parent may be reacting to an overly harsh childhood; he may have a desire for his child to be popular; he may be afraid to discipline his child because he might be rejected, or he may feel inadequate to discipline appropriately.

Personality of the Child: (active dependent)—manipulative, aggressive, extraverted, attention-seeking, unpredictable, impulsive, dramatic, easily frustrated, superficial relationships, lacks self-discipline, irresponsible, carefree, relative conscience.

(2.) Overindulgence. In this pattern, the parent pampers and indulges the child who learns to expect others to wait on him. He just expects to get his way and gets angry if he does not. Unlike the child of an over-submissive parent who actively manipulates to get his way, the "spoiled," overindulged child passively expects things to come his way without any effort. Since there is no discipline, he develops few skills for achievement, assuming responsibility or interacting with others.

As an adult, this person would, of course, be very egotistical and narcissistic, exploiting and taking advantage of people, expecting them to wait on him and demanding that the world revolve around him. Examples of this personality type might be certain movie and rock stars, political leaders and athletes—people in the spotlight.

The indulgent parent may be overcompensating for a childhood of deprivation; he may be afraid his child will reject him, or excessive guilt may prevent him from disciplining; he may have succumbed to "spoiling" the youngest or an only child.

Personality of the Child: (passive independent)—superiority feelings, ungrateful, exploits others, self-seeking, resists authority, self-confident, undependable, few anxieties, easily frustrated, lack of motivation, over-rates achievement, absent conscience.

c. DOMINANT INTERNAL PARENT & CHILD (REJECTION PATTERNS). As we have seen, even the child of "good" parents experiences some rejection. But rejection which deeply scars a child's soul exists when a child is not valued, loved, wanted, or considered important. This traumatic rejection may be expressed by treating the child harshly and cruelly, belittling him, making excessive demands on, or withholding love from him. Rejection, being the opposite of acceptance, always results in insecurity, low self-esteem and lack of confidence and self-control in the child.

The rejected child has no hope of winning his parent's acceptance through obedience or manipulation, so his only choice is to rebel or withdraw. Therefore, he may decide to express the anger, hatred and rebellion resulting from his many negative judgments directly, vowing to dominate and use others. Alternatively, he may choose to repress his feelings and withdraw in fear and guilt, vowing to avoid others because they might hurt him. Often, severely rejected children decide to oscillate between rebellion and withdrawal. Thus, they will move against people or away from them, but never with them. Rejection has, therefore, the most destructive effect on the personality of all the parental patterns.

In adulthood, the Internal Child of the rejected person is largely an Adaptive Child who adapts to the Internal Parent's dictates either by rebelling in anger, becoming a victimizer, by withdrawing in fear and guilt, becoming a victim or by alternating between the two. Although his child is controlled by the programming of his Parent, the behavior of this person is dominated by the Parent when he is withdrawing and by the child when he is rebelling. Thus, both the parent and the child are dominant ego states in the rejection patterns. By enforcing the many vows he made as a child, the Adaptive Child of the rejected person controls the extremely weak Adult, who has great difficulty coping, making decisions or interacting with others.

The following figure shows the strength of the Parent and the Child by their large sizes and extreme weakness of the Adult by its small size. The extensive control of the Parent is shown by its large overlap onto the Adaptive Child. The extensive control of the Adaptive Child is shown by its large overlap onto the Adult, while the Natural Child's weakness is shown by its small overlap onto the Adult. A description of the two rejection patterns follows the figure:

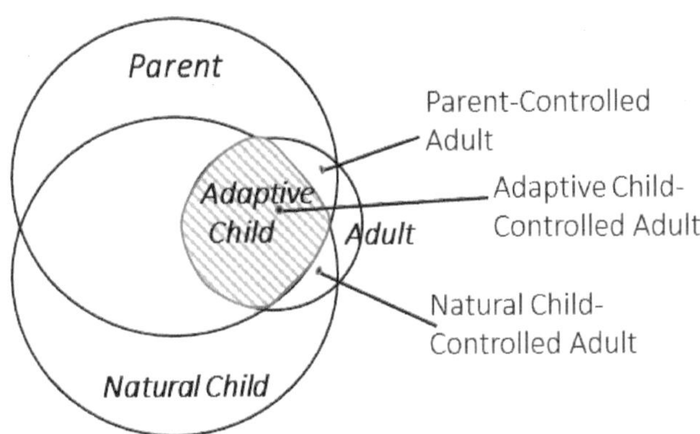

Figure 4. DOMINANT INTERNAL PARENT & CHILD

(1.) Active Rejection. In the active rejection pattern, the hostile parent treats the child harshly and punitively. Anger is communicated directly as the child is belittled, criticized or even physically abused. He may be made to feel stupid, inept, ugly, etc. The child may react by building defenses to protect himself from the emotional pain and also by angrily fighting back. Insecurity, hostility and suspicion characterize his relationships.

In adulthood, unlike the active independent personality type who expresses his anger within the confines of society, the active detached type rebels against society by breaking its laws and hostilely destroying both property and people. Examples of this personality type are "street kids" who grow up in the ghetto, becoming members of gangs, drug pushers, Mafia members, hard-core criminals, etc. Referred to as sociopaths, they dedicate their lives to victimizing the society which they feel has victimized them.

The actively rejecting parent may be reacting in hostility to a devastating childhood, or he may be emotionally disturbed—in all probability, demon-possessed.

Personality of the Child: (active detached)—avoidant or aggressive, feelings of rejection, hostility, anxiety, suspicious, defensive, insecure, guarded, lonely, vigilant, introspective, lacks empathy, self-centered, self-rejecting, isolated, hardened conscience.

(2.) Passive Rejection. In this pattern, the child is not wanted and is looked upon with disfavor. His emotional needs are neglected, and he may even be deprived of physical necessities. This pattern wounds and scars a child more deeply than any other because it leaves a void, an emptiness in the child's life. In the active rejection pattern, there is a relationship between two people, albeit a negative one. But, in the passive rejection pattern, there is no one with whom to interact. This lack of relationship often results in a lack of personal identity in the child. He has difficulty in every aspect of life—communicating, achieving, changing, understanding others, etc. As a result, he is often victimized.

As an adult, this type of person is usually not able to take an active role in society since he is so withdrawn, unresponsive and passive. He just drops out of society and lives a lonely existence within himself in his own small, isolated world. Examples of this personality type are "loners"—spinsters, hermits, drifters, people who live on the streets, or inhabit mental institutions.

Passively rejecting parents are either emotionally disturbed, totally inadequate socially or completely self-absorbed.

Personality of the Child: (passive detached)—aloof, withdrawn, emotionally unresponsive, apathetic, lonely, isolated, feelings of rejection and fear, passive, lacks motivation and initiative, colorless, autistic, avoids relationships, undeveloped conscience.

After studying these methods of parenting and the consequent behavior and attitudes that develop in children, we can see that, by far, the most significant influence in shaping our personalities is our interaction or lack of it with our parents. We can usually spot right away which personality profile is ours.

Since two other factors, such as our temperament and birth order position also influence the development of our souls, our personality characteristics may be a combination of several profiles. Usually, however, the strongest parent "writes" the child's "script," i.e., determines the method of parenting that will be predominant. A summary of the eight parental patterns and the consequent personality profiles of their children is given in **Table 3**. Some of the judgments and inner vows which a child might make in response to each of the styles of parenting are given in **Table 4**.

My own developmental history consists of a controlling, critical mother and an extremely passive father. Thus, my mother set the style of parenting for our family which was perfectionism. My mother was poised, self-assured and outgoing—a classic extrovert. She always dressed in the latest fashion, had impeccable manners and in my mind, was the epitome of elegance! Her charisma and style drew people to her like a magnet. She tried for five years to become pregnant; I was her first child and only daughter.

As a child, I thought that I always had to "be on my best behavior," exhibiting perfect manners. I felt like I was her little "doll" whom she enjoyed "showing off." It is clear to me now that she idolized me as an extension of her own ego. Thus, I believed that I had to be just like her to be accepted. This was, of course, devastating to me because my personality is the opposite of hers. I am shy, sensitive, self-conscious—a classic introvert! So, I was always striving to be like my mother so she would accept me—an impossible goal for me to reach!

My judgment was that my parent was critical, controlling and impossible to please. My inner vow was, "I must perform perfectly. I cannot afford to fail because this will put me to shame, making me unacceptable." The fear of being put to shame was programmed into me because my mother's favorite rebuke was, "Shame on you!"

It must be pointed out that knowing our parents' particular method of parenting cannot be used as a justification of our own undesirable behavior and attitudes. Our parents, for the most part, are just products of their parents' programming, so we cannot place any blame on them. Neither should we excuse ourselves from changing by deciding that since we were programmed a certain way, there is no hope for us.

On the contrary, the more we understand about our unique developmental history, the more the Lord holds us responsible for change. "And from everyone who has been given much shall much be required" (Luke 12:48 NAS 1977). The revelation of the judgments and vows which we have made, i.e., the script which the Internal Child in each of us is still acting out, gives us the opportunity to choose to receive soul healing so that God can "rewrite our scripts!"

5. EXCLUSION OF EGO STATES.

In addition to domination, there can also be exclusion of an ego state which results in a more pathological condition. The exclusion of the Natural Child in a person usually results in a neurotic condition. Exclusion of the Adult results in psychosis, while a psychopathic state is the consequence of parental exclusion. It must be noted that the term "exclusion" is used relatively in the sense that an ego state cannot actually be completely excluded.

a. EXCLUSION OF NATURAL CHILD. Typical of the person who has excluded his Natural Child would be a "workaholic" who strives continuously to succeed, trying to outperform everyone else. He is usually rigid, legalistic and ritualistic, trying always to keep everything in his life firmly under control. He often neglects his family and does not allow himself or even know how, to have fun, play and enjoy life.

His overcontrolling parents, undoubtedly rewarded him for perfect conformity, diligent effort and doing exactly as he was told. Probably employing the authoritarian or perfectionist method of parenting, they were so dominating, stern and duty-bound that he decided that the only safe way to live was to turn his Natural Child off completely. As a consequence, he has very little happiness, fun or freedom recorded in his Child.

In childhood, this person probably judged his parents to be dominating, controlling and rigid. He is now reaping this seed sown in like measure because his Adaptive Child perceives itself to be completely controlled by the strict, dominating Internal Parent which he is still trying so desperately to please. The life-controlling inner vow which he made might have been, "I must perform perfectly and succeed at any cost because I will not be accepted if I fail."

His Adaptive Child conforms to the demands of his Parent through fear and guilt if he is the passive ambivalent personality type or through anger if he is the active independent type. His Adaptive Child then controls his Adult through the inner vows which he made as a Child. "For as he thinks within himself, so he is" (Prov. 23:7). In the following figure, the extensive control of the Parent is shown by the fact that it has completely engulfed the Child, producing a totally Adaptive Child with no Natural Child. The extensive control of the Adult by the Adaptive Child is shown by its eclipse of the Adult. The small sliver of Adult depicts direct control by the Parent through the prejudice which is recorded in the Parent:

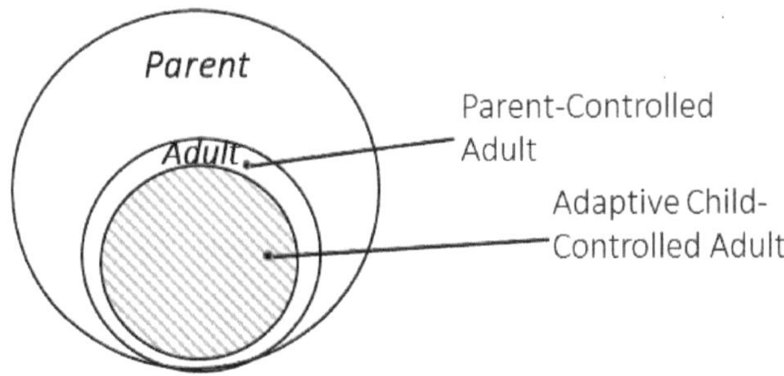

Figure 5. EXCLUSION OF NATURAL CHILD ("workaholic")

Many businessmen, political leaders and professionals, including pastors, fit into this category. Thinking that they are obeying and pleasing God, many pastors are controlled by the dominating Internal Parent; thus, they are still striving to please their fathers, many of whom were also ministers. The demands for high performance usually being the greatest on first-born children, they also have a strong tendency to exclude the Natural Child.

In general, a counselor can help this type of person by employing the soul healing process through which Jesus heals his wounds, enabling him to forgive his parents, and break his judgments and inner vows. Specifically, his main objective is to assist in freeing the counselee's Adaptive Child from his overcontrolling Parent. His Child would then be able to give his Adult permission to let Jesus create a happy, spontaneous, fun-loving Natural Child in him.

Through faith visualization, guided by the Holy Spirit, the omnipotent love of Jesus will transform the counselee's stern, authoritarian parents into happy, carefree, loving ones who encourage him to make his own decisions, be creative, have fun and enjoy life! In addition, visualizing Jesus cutting the umbilical cords, symbolizing soul ties, which attach the counselee to his parents frees him to become the person whom Jesus created him to be.

Thus, during soul healing, Jesus will recreate the counselee's childhood to be the way it would have been if He would have been allowed to be present. This process of reparenting the counselee's Child is possible because the Lord is not bound by the time element and because imagined experiences can be as real as ones that actually happened. After the wounds in his Child have been healed by Jesus' love, the counselee's Parent can be reprogrammed with the truth that, it is okay, and even essential, for him to learn how to have fun and enjoy life. He can instruct the counselee to use his Adult to give his Child permission to be free, spontaneous, playful, and thus, resist the badgering and guilt heaped on him by his Parent.

As his Child continually resists his Parent, developing a nurturing, loving Parent instead, the boundaries will be re-established between his Parent, Adult and Child, and his new-found freedom in Christ will begin to take hold. His Adult will be able to hear the Holy Spirit more and more clearly because he will no longer view God in the same way that he viewed his father—controlling, strict and legalistic. His liberated Natural Child will be able to enter into an intimate love union with his heavenly Father and eagerly and joyously embrace the dreams and goals which He has for him!

b. EXCLUSION OF ADULT. As we might suspect, not having a working Adult is a much more serious matter than being without a Natural Child. The person with the latter problem is able to function quite well in society, while the individual with the missing Adult, having lost touch with reality, is usually confined to a mental institution.

His rejecting parents may have treated him harshly and cruelly by emotionally and/or physically abusing him. Or, they may have ignored him completely, neglecting his emotional and spiritual needs and even depriving him of physical necessities. Their behavior may have been totally inconsistent—loving and nurturing one moment, abusing and neglecting the next. The child's action may have brought him rewards one time, but condemnation the next, which caused him great distress since he never knew what was expected of him. In some cases, one parent may have loved and accepted him, while the other abused and rejected him.

This unpredictable parental behavior may have produced such an intense internal conflict in the Child that he vowed to give up and quit trying to make sense out of things. Thus, he may not have developed a functioning Adult. The inaccurate perceptions (delusions) which he derived from his conflicting parental images caused him to make many negative judgments which formed his belief system (Parent). Intense, opposing feelings of anger, hatred, guilt, self-condemnation, fear, etc., arising from his judgments, drove him to make contradictory inner vows which then determined his attitudes and behavior for life.

Thus, as an adult, this patient is at the mercy of severe, contrasting feelings and inner vows which drive him to exhibit ambivalent behavior. Unable to decide whether to punish others or himself, he vacillates between venting his anger, hatred, bitterness, etc., directly, on the one hand, and repressing his feelings and turning them against himself on the other. Thus, he may viciously attack and make excessive demands on others one moment and express contrition and feelings of fear, guilt, worthlessness, and self-condemnation the next. Oscillating between displaying stubborn resistance and hostility one time and self-destructive submission another, his responses are made in the Parent or the Child ego state, usually the Child.

Thus, as in the rejection patterns, the Internal Child of the patient is predominately Adaptive Child, programmed to react to the punitive Parent's demands by alternating between rebellion and withdrawal. Although his Child is controlled by his parental programming, his behavior is dominated by the Parent when he is withdrawing and by the Child when he is rebelling. Therefore, both the Parent and the Child are dominant ego states, the Adult having been excluded. The following figure shows the excessive strength of the Parent and the Child by their large sizes. The expansive dominion of the Parent is portrayed by the fact that the Child is engulfed by the Parent, producing a pervasive Adaptive Child, while excluding the Adult:

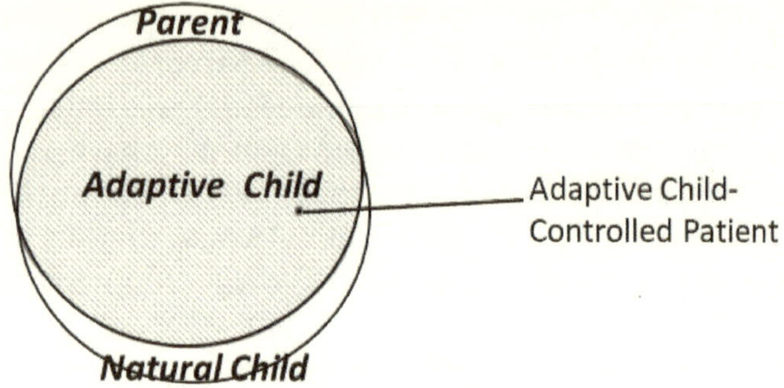

Figure 6. EXCLUSION OF THE ADULT (psychotic)

In cases of severe psychosis, the Internal Parent and Child of a patient "come on straight," frequently in a jumbled replay of early experiences that do not make sense because they did not make sense to him when they were recorded. An example of this concerns a female hospital patient whose singing of tent-meeting hymns (Parent) was interspersed with obscenities related to bodily functions (Child). The content was bizarre but seemed to replay an old Parent-Child conflict between good and bad—"shoulds" and "should nots," salvation and damnation.

We might conjecture that this patient's parents were loving and accepting at times, but then for no apparent reason turned on her, abusing and rejecting her. Thus, she might have received many contradictory messages. These "double-bind" messages may have created a conflict so severe that her Adult, deciding that the struggle to make sense out of them was too difficult, made an inner vow to give up. Giving up did not solve the problem, however, as she still suffered with the same terrifying feelings which had plagued her as a child.

When the Adult gives up, the "door" appears to be open for demons to enter a person's soul and, we might say, appropriate his identity. For example, if a patient's Internal Parent-Child conflict becomes severe enough, his Adult may cease functioning, allowing his personality to split into two or more identities through which demons are then allowed to operate. The supposition that evil spirits take on the characteristics of a person's internal conflict is readily affirmed by observing a patient suffering from the dissociative neurosis–termed "multiple personality," which will be discussed later. For example, a patient's personality might consist of two identities which demons appear to control: Dave, the quiet, shy, reclusive one and Sam, the loud, obnoxious one who throws violent fits of rage.

Demons may also set up a complex, intricately woven system of fantasies in which a patient lives. This is graphically illustrated in the description of the bizarre activities taking place in a young psychotic's mind in the book, *I Never Promised You A Rose Garden*, a novel by Joanne Greenberg. This book describes how a psychiatrist entered the patient's fantasy world in an attempt to bring her back to reality.

The first step in treating a psychotic is to quiet down the Parent-Child conflict going on inside of him. Drugs are most often used for this purpose. Calming a patient's inner conflict through the use of drugs seems to rescind the permission of the demons to display their more overt behavior. He will often state, "The voices inside my head have quieted down." Thus, it should be easier to "hook his Adult." But often, the person is in such a drug-induced stupor that he has trouble responding at all.

A much more effective way to get the Adult functioning again is to become the loving, nurturing, accepting, understanding "parent" which the patient never had. A psychotic is trapped in a state of unreality; thus, he is extremely lonely and is yearning to establish a relationship with someone. When he is confronted with someone who loves, respects and accepts him as he is, this is a new and intriguing experience. When he learns that he is so special and important to Jesus that He would have died for him alone, he begins to gain hope, and his Adult begins to respond.

When his Adult can begin listening, understanding, processing data, etc., the healing process can begin. Working with a psychotic to establish a working Adult is, of course, a long, slow process requiring much love, patience, support, and encouragement. With man's limited love and resources, helping psychotics begin operating in society again would be impossible. But with God's all-encompassing love and infinite power, all things are possible!

c. EXCLUSION OF PARENT. Excluding the Parent is an even more serious matter than blocking out either the Natural Child or the Adult. The person with an excluded Parent probably had actively rejecting parents who were so brutal and terrifying that the only way to preserve life was to block them out completely. But the problem with eliminating the painful Parent is that what little "good" there is in the Parent—laws, values, morals (conscience)—is also thrown out.

Therefore, this type of person breaks laws, destroys property and abuses and uses people solely for his own purposes. The only consequence with which he is concerned is whether or not he will be caught, not whether he has hurt anyone. He is totally absorbed in himself and the gratification of his needs and desires. The Child of an individual with a working Parent will experience shame, remorse, guilt, etc., when he does something wrong, For example, if a person arrested for child-molestation expresses no feelings of guilt or remorse apart from the fact that he was caught—it is safe to assume that he has no functioning Parent.

The severe hurts and wounds which he experienced as a child caused the person with a blocked-out Parent to judge his as being brutal and vicious. Intense feelings of anger, hatred, bitterness, rebellion, etc., arising from his judgments, caused him to make many hostile inner vows such as, "I will do whatever I want;" or "Whoever gets in my way will be sorry!" His feelings of anger and hatred being so strong that they overrode any feelings of fear, he decided to express his anger, hatred, rebellion, etc., directly against others, Thus, as an adult, he is reaping the "seed of bitterness" which he sowed as a child by becoming a cruel victimizer the same as or worse than his parents.

Even though he has excluded his Parent, this person is still adapted to the programming of the Parent through anger. Therefore, although his Internal Child is primarily Adaptive Child indirectly controlled by Parental programming, his behavior is dominated by his Child since he is rebelling in anger and bitterness.

The following figure shows the strength of the Child by its large size. The extreme control of the Child is shown by the fact that the Adult is engulfed by the Child, who has excluded the Parent:

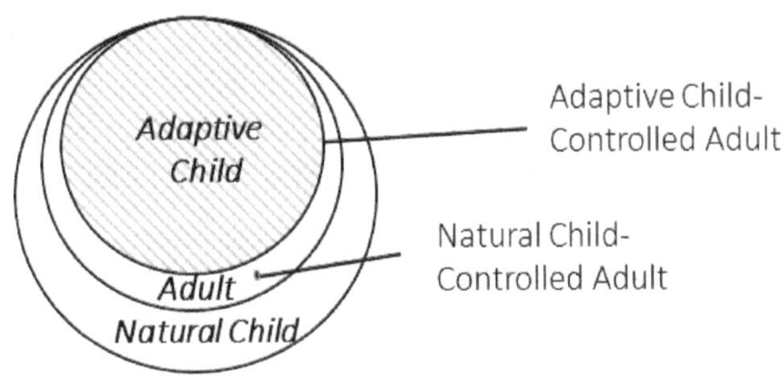

Figure 7. EXCLUSION OF THE PARENT (psychopath)

An extreme example of a person with a totally blocked-out Parent would be the psychopath. This person is apparently able to hurt, even kill, others without experiencing any shame or remorse whatsoever. In recent times, news accounts of psychopathic killers and their horrendous deeds have multiplied. David R. Wilkerson, in his book, *The Vision*, prophesied in 1974 that there would be increasing anger, hatred and violence among young people. We are witnessing the fulfillment of this prophecy in the increasing gang violence and brutal killings in Los Angeles, New York and other cities.

Studies have recently shown that beginning with the time when God was "banned" from the schools, rebellion, destructive behavior, breakdown of morals, violence, crime, etc., have increased dramatically among young people. Thus, it appears that we are reaping what we have sown by producing a generation of youth who have blocked-out the Parent and, as a consequence, have no working consciences. The fact that we will continue to reap this frightening harvest is affirmed by Rick Joyner, Joe Brandt and others, who recently prophesied that huge mobs will be roaming the streets, viciously attacking and destroying everything in their paths in the coming years.

The tremendous difficulties inherent in counseling a person without an operating Parent are obvious since he has no conscience. Not only will this person's deep wounds and scars have to be healed by the Lord, He will have to help him create a loving, nurturing, accepting Parent filled with God's truth. Since the Child of the psychopath trusts absolutely no one, only God's grace, infinite love and supernatural power has a possibility of reaching him!

6. BALANCED EGO STATES (BIBLICAL PARENTAL PATTERN).

Since we live in such a sinful world, our study has dwelt upon negative parental programming and consequent development of unhealthy souls. Thus, it would be appropriate to include in our study of soul development a discussion of the positive Biblical pattern in which the parent balances discipline and freedom with agape love—the basic ingredients necessary for the formation of a healthy soul (see **Figure 8**).

The emotionally healthy parent's Inner Child is secure enough in his Father's love and acceptance through Christ that he is able to exercise loving control over his offspring's self-centered desires. He is able to balance correction, instruction and encouragement so that the child develops self-control, responsibility and self-direction. The godly parent teaches the child respect and concern for others, the consequences of sin and his need for forgiveness.

Discipline of the youngster will be balanced with freedom to express feelings, needs, desires, and to develop his unique individuality and God-given potential. The child will be given the freedom to make choices, enjoy pleasure, express his creativity, and indulge his curiosity to explore. Only through freedom can a child learn to impose restrictions upon himself, developing self-discipline without coercion from the parent.

The righteous parent will exercise discipline and freedom with agape love which accepts the young person unconditionally and respects his worth and uniqueness. He will be able to understand, communicate and give unselfishly of himself for the child's well-being. Agape love develops security and self-esteem in the youngster, enabling him to control his emotions, cope with stresses and successfully achieve his full potential in God, finding fulfillment in life.

The child who is blessed with such a parent will form a strong, healthy personality in which all three ego states are balanced. The loving, nurturing, liberating Parent of this young person will contain truth and his Child will feel loved and accepted and free to express his feelings, desires and creativity. His Adult will be able to think and reason wisely because his Parent contains truth and is supplying his Child's needs for love, acceptance, etc.

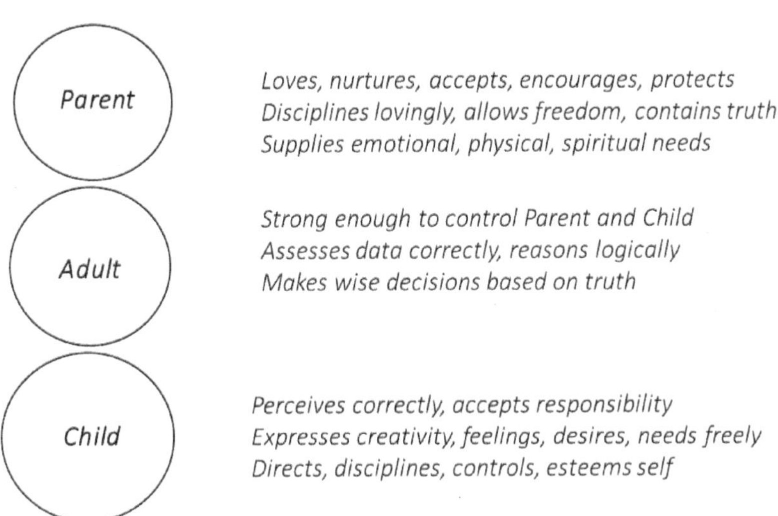

Figure 8. BALANCED EGO STATES (healthy personality)

Thus, his Adult will be strong and effective because it will not always be occupied with checking the Parent data against reality for truth or calming the conflict between the Parent and Child. So, we see that the strong Adult of the emotionally healthy young person has control over the Parent and the Child which enables him to make wise choices. We all know that the ability to make wise decisions is of supreme importance because many of us have broken hearts and ruined lives due to our destructive choices.

We should keep in mind, however, that the Biblical method of parenting described is an ideal which is rarely achieved. As we have seen, because of our sinful nature, the negative styles of parenting are much more prevalent in our society. Consequently, the

Adaptive Child, through its emotions of fear, anger and guilt is, more often than not, controlled by the undesirable programming of the Parent. The Adaptive Child then controls the Adult by forcing it to think and act according to inner vows which were made in childhood. These negative vows ensure that the Adult will be weak and ineffective, consistently making destructive decisions.

7. BIRTH ORDER EFFECT ON EGO STATES.

The birth order position which a child occupies in his family usually plays a significant part in how his parents interact with him. Every time a child is born, the entire family environment changes. Therefore, parents may adopt a different method of parenting with each child as he or she enters the family circle. As we have learned, the parenting pattern predominantly employed with a child profoundly affects the attitudes and behavior which he will develop. The fact that parents are prone to employ a different style of parenting with the second or youngest child than they did with the oldest explains why children in the same family often have markedly dissimilar personality traits. Dr. Kevin Leman has written a very entertaining book, *The Birth Order Book*, which describes the personality characteristics usually found in the eldest, the second and the youngest, as well as, the only child.

a. FIRST-BORN CHILD. Leman describes the first-born child as being perfectionistic, reliable, conscientious, well-organized, critical, serious, scholarly, conservative, legalistic, loyal, self-sacrificing, and self-reliant. First-borns are high achievers who are driven to success in their given fields. Researchers have shown that a much greater percentage of first-borns end up in professions which require great mental discipline, precision and structure, such as law, medicine or science. First-borns thrive on having things organized and under control—"a place for everything and everything in its place."

It is not difficult to understand why first-borns develop these particular personality characteristics. Since they are the first children born in a family, they receive the most attention, pressure and discipline. They are expected to do the most work and assume the most responsibility. They often hear, "You know better than that! You are the oldest and I expect more from you!" First-borns strive so hard to be perfect that they often become frustrated and guilt-ridden when they fail to "meet the marks."

As adults, when they can no longer hack it with all of the expectations and demands put on them by their internals, they often seek help from a counselor. Consequently, the majority of people whom a counselor sees are first-borns. This fact has made my chosen profession much easier since I am the "perfect" example of a first-born. My attempts to deal with my own feelings of inadequacy led me to choose the profession of counseling as previously noted. In fact, I am convinced of that frustration in counseling. Since I have never felt that I was able to measure up either, I am able to identify completely and empathize deeply with all of the emotions of the oldest child.

Although Leman admits that it is "a bit rash to saddle any birth order with a blanket label," he believes first-borns have one—"perfectionist." I have no argument with this label since this is definitely my "scarlet letter." I give most of the "credit," however, to my mother, also a hard-driving first-born, because she trained me so well. For example, I was not only required to clean the sink after doing the dishes, but also to wipe it dry and shine the faucets!

My mother made a "career" out of ironing. She ironed everything—sheets, dish towels, pajamas, underwear, even diapers! She dipped the pillowcases, shirts, etc., in heavy starch which had been boiled. She would then hang them on the clothesline where they would dry stiff as boards! They would then be "sprinkled down," rolled up tight, placed in a basket, and covered with a damp cloth. Here they would "rest" all night in anticipation of morning when I would have the pleasure of ironing them. I never minded though, because I really enjoyed ironing—probably because it was something which I could do "perfectly" and thus, please my mother.

I am sure that most of you will have trouble relating to all of this "procedure," but this is the way it was done in the "good old days." My mother, about whom I could tell many such stories, relates that even after she was married, she would clean her mother's home because my grandmother did not clean well enough to suit her. However, in all fairness to my mother, a precious, beautiful lady whom I love deeply, I must say that she has "mellowed" greatly over the years. Her "character has truly been proven" as she has courageously braved the storms of many trials.

My mother contracted tuberculosis when she was pregnant with my youngest brother. She was only allowed to look at him through a window until she was released from the sanatorium a year after he was born. She has suffered with many physical problems since, in addition to almost losing her home several times when my father's business ventures failed, leaving them penniless. Her fortitude, faith and strength have been a great inspiration to me as she truly does know, as she is fond of saying, "how to abase and abound just like Paul." What I admire most about my mother is her remarkably positive attitude. She is one of the few Christians who truly practice the principle of praising God for everything—good and bad! But I will save her story for another book.

Although my daughter recently "complimented" me by remarking that I was not nearly as "bad" as I used to be, I will probably forever be stuck with the label of "perfectionist." I do believe Leman's first-born sister has topped me a perfectionism, however. Leman describes her as a person who would iron the "Welcome" mat, if possible. He tells about the time she wore a negligee on one of the Leman family camping trips and about the clear vinyl runner which leads to every room in her home. Now I most definitely would never wear a negligee on a camping trip! Although I will admit that I have considered covering the carpet in the traffic areas of *my* home with vinyl, I would never really do it—probably only because I hate plastic, though!

Leman explains that there are two basic types of first-borns: compliant and anxious to please or strong-willed and aggressive. The compliant first-born is the reliable, obedient, conscientious "model child" who has a strong need for approval, and thus, strives to please everyone. The aggressive first-born is extremely performance-oriented and strives hard to be the "top dog." While the "people-pleasing" first-born tends to become a caregiver and servant of people, the power-driven first-born often becomes a top executive and a "workaholic."

Most first-borns would say that their parents employed one of the overcontrolling patterns of parenting, most likely the authoritarian or the perfectionism pattern since these two parenting methods require the most performance from a child. Therefore, according to Millon, the personality type of the compliant first-born would be passive ambivalent, while that of the aggressive first-born would be active independent. Which of the two personality types a first-born child becomes, especially when raised by an authoritarian parent, depends largely on his temperament.

b. ONLY CHILD. Only children often have the most difficult lot in life since all of their parents' energy and attention is focused on them. Also, they are often very lonely, especially if they have few playmates. The struggle to survive in an "adult" world often makes it difficult for them to relate to their peers. As adults, they usually get along far better with people who are much older or much younger than themselves. So much is expected of them that they grow up resenting always having to behave like "little Adults."

Leman states that to describe the only child, simply add the word "super" to all the characteristics applied to the first-born. Only children, especially those who are the products of a very structured, disciplined upbringing, are super-reliable and super-conscientious. These children have never felt able to live up to their parent's expectations and demands, so they are always striving to prove themselves. They are often very conforming and confident on the outside, but inside they are seething with anger and rebellion. Although they appear to be on top of everything, along with the repressed anger and resentment, they usually feel very inadequate, inferior and "never quite good enough." The only child, like the eldest, will most often become either the active independent or the passive ambivalent personality type.

Some couples wanted more children but, for certain reasons, had to be satisfied with only one. Leman calls these "only children"—usually born when their parents were older—"special jewels." Their personalities are often a blending of the characteristics of the first-born and the last-born. Like last-borns, they are often pampered and spoiled, making them very self-centered and attention-seeking. Special jewels tend to feel that the world should revolve around them. Since they have been overindulged by their parents, they tend to have some of the traits of the passive independent personality type.

Thus, special jewels are often terrifying blends of both the active and the passive independent personality types, especially if they have been raised by very authoritarian, yet overindulgent, parents. These "only children" are often very critical, demanding, self-centered, and intolerant of others, expecting them to perform perfectly while also catering to their every whim. We can surmise that the secretary of a top executive who is a special jewel is in for a very rough time!

c. MIDDLE-BORN CHILD. The experts agree that the characteristics of the middle-born child are the most difficult to define because this child is influenced, to a large extent, by his perception of the sibling directly above him. Thus, the second-born is most influenced by the first-born, the third-born is most influenced by the second-born and so on. For example, if the second-born senses that he may be able to compete with the first-born, he may try to do so. But if the older sibling is smarter, stronger, more talented, etc., the second-born will probably go the opposite direction. Therefore, the second-born child may become either a "pleaser" or an "antagonizer." According to Leman, any number of lifestyles can appear in the middle-born, but they all play off of the child directly above him.

Although our daughter turned out to be the last-born child in our family, she certainly proved this theory to be correct by going the opposite direction of her brother. Our son, the first-born of two first-borns, acquired all of the personality traits of the eldest child. He is very reliable, conservative, serious, disciplined, and succeeds at everything he tries. Our daughter, who is three years younger than her brother, sized up her competition early and decided that she would not even attempt to compete. She did manage to find the "chink in her brother's armor," however, and went for that. Our son is very shy and reserved and has difficulty relating socially. So, his sister, realizing early on that she had a charismatic, bubbly personality, became the "life of the party." As a "social butterfly," she could really outshine her brother! I came to expect her teachers to say, "Your daughter has great potential, but she doesn't apply herself. She spends most of her time talking in class." As we shall soon see, her personality is characteristic of the youngest Child in the family.

While the characteristics of middle-borns are not easy to predict, their feelings are. Leman points out that they always feel the "squeeze" from above and below. They do not feel special or unique growing up. Both the first-borns and the "babies" have their own special spots, but the middle children feel left out, bypassed and upstaged by both the oldest and youngest siblings. Feeling like he is the "fifth wheel" in his family draws the middle-born child to his peer group. Here he is just the right age—not too young to get the privileges and respect given to the oldest child, nor too old to receive the pampering and attention lavished on the youngest child. Thus, friends become very important to the middle Child.

Leman states that many middle children decide to meet their needs for recognition and approval by becoming good mediators. Being in the middle forces them to become skilled at negotiating and compromising. As adults, middle-borns can often cope with problems better, especially those concerning relationships, because they learned how to "give-and-take" while growing up. Leman believes that the best description of middle children is "balanced." Thus, the middle-born child may turn out to be the most well-adjusted adult in the family, provided he is not harboring a lot of repressed anger and resentment due to the hurts inflicted upon him because of his birth order position.

d. LAST-BORN CHILD. Leman describes the last-born child as an outgoing charmer, personable manipulator and a "people person." He is affectionate, carefree, vivacious, precocious, engaging, impetuous, and brash. The youngest child is most likely to be the "family clown" or entertainer. Leman, the youngest of three siblings, declares that all he ever wanted was attention. He would do whatever it took to get people to laugh, point or comment. He attributes his desire to achieve "stardom" to a brother, five years older than he, whom he rated a 9.75 in everything and a sister, eight years older, whom he rated a perfect 10.00. He scored himself somewhere around 1.8 in comparison to their abilities and achievements.

No wonder Leman swiftly accepted his big sister's request to become her high school's mascot when he was only eight years old. He quickly earned the nickname, "Demon Leman," by yanking off the tail of another school's "tiger" mascot during halftime!

Leman comments that he lived up to his nickname throughout his school years, his antics even driving one of his teachers to quit teaching! He relates how he "livened up" his first-born perfectionist sister's wedding rehearsal dinner held at a swank hotel. Her gift to him for being in her wedding was a bright plaid pair of Bermuda shorts. He immediately did a quiet change in the rest room and reappeared attired in a suit coat, tie and the shorts! His sister's face turned bright red as her perfect evening dissolved before her eyes.

Often parents are too exhausted to give the last child much instruction or firm, but loving, discipline, so they tend to let him shift for himself. They often fall into using one of the under-controlling patterns of parenting—over-submission or overindulgence—on their youngest child. This results in the last-born becoming either the active dependent or the passive independent personality type.

Since his parents are usually too pooped to train him, the youngest child usually receives a lot of "parenting" from his older siblings. This means that last-borns may be cuddled and spoiled one minute and put down and made fun of the next. In self-defense, last-borns often develop a cocky attitude that covers up their self-doubt and confusion. They frequently say, "They wrote me off when I was little; they wouldn't let me play—I'll show them!" Thus, the babies of the family are often charming and lovable one minute, and rebellious and difficult to handle the next.

In conclusion, it should be kept in mind that not every child will automatically develop the personality traits most representative of youngsters in his birth order position. But whether a child is born first, last or in the middle of his family plays a significant enough part in determining the parenting method adopted with him to be taken into account. As counselors, *we* can help our counselees gain insight into the development of their souls by explaining the effect which *their* birth order position had on the way in which they were parented, and consequently, on the attitudes and behavior patterns which they developed.

B. CONSEQUENCES OF PARENTAL PROGRAMMING.

1. DEFENSE MECHANISMS.

Now that we realize the great extent to which the Adaptive Child is controlled by the generally undesirable programming of the Parent, resulting in repressed inner turmoil, we may wonder how we are able to function as adults as well as we are. We can imagine how unbearable life would be if we were constantly aware of the unresolved Parent-Child conflicts going on within us and our resulting negative emotions. We would not be able to pursue any positive goals or experience any enjoyment in life. Consequently, we all learn ways to shut the painful conflicts occurring within our souls out of our minds so that we are not consciously bothered by them. We all use many of these learned devices, called defense mechanisms, which protect us from having to deal with painful reality.

On the one hand, these defenses are destructive because they hide the true nature of the condition of our hearts from us and the relief which they give is illusory because the problems still reside in our hearts. On the other hand, defense mechanisms are necessary for our emotional survival because they help preserve what little security and self-esteem we might have. When a person's defense system totally breaks down, his Adult is excluded; the conflict between his Parent and Adaptive Child takes over and he becomes psychotic.

Repression is the primary defense mechanism underlying all of the others. As we have seen, during childhood each of us buries our wounds and the resultant bitter root judgments and negative emotions from past rejections in his or her Child (heart). "... the intent of man's heart is evil from his youth" (Gen. 8:21). Then throughout adulthood, we repress and push back down into the subconscious any unacceptable and irrational thoughts (hatred, judgments, aggressive fantasies) and feelings (anger, unforgiveness, bitterness) which might attempt to enter our consciousness. In this way, we are able to deny the painful, undesired truth about ourselves. "The heart is deceitful above all things and desperately wicked; Who can know it?" (Jer. 17:9 NKJV). "He who hates disguises it with his lips, but he lays up deceit in his heart" (Prov. 26:24).

Our ego (soul) then develops secondary defense mechanisms, listed in **Table 5**, which help us cope with life in a supposedly rational and socially acceptable way. Since our defense mechanisms operate subconsciously and automatically, we are not aware of their daily functioning in our lives.

2. SYMPTOMS.

Since defense mechanisms hide the true nature of our problems from our awareness, they are expressed in disguised forms as symptoms. Symptoms are problems and pains that we can easily identify, but their root causes lie unrecognized in the hurts, judgments and negative emotions buried in our hearts. Symptoms have been multiplying at a speed faster than light in recent years as more and more people are consistently turning their backs on God and allowing Satan to ravage their lives. Thus, the list of symptoms is endless, as indicated by the partial list given in **Table 2**. We have already discussed some of these, but it would be helpful to take a look at others that are very common.

a. PUNISHING OTHERS. Symptoms may be divided, as we have noted from **Table 2**, into two categories–those which we use to "punish" others and those by which we "punish" ourselves. As we have seen, some individuals who have been rejected and abused make judgments as children that all people are cruel and deserve to be punished. Instead of repressing their anger, they decide to express it directly; therefore, they make inner vows that they will punish other people.

There are active and passive ways which we use to punish others. We are all familiar with the easily recognized verbal and physical displays of anger. The media is filled with accounts of rape, serial killers, gang warfare, child abuse, and molestation–even "white slavery" rings selling children to be used for prostitution, "kiddie porn," and rituals involving Satanic worship! It seems as though legions of voracious demons have been turned loose to prey mercilessly on victims as the "sins of the forefathers are being visited upon the sons!" The alarming increase in the number of sociopaths, especially in our inner cities, verifies this fact. The Los Angeles Police Department recently put a thousand extra policemen on duty one weekend in an effort to stem the rising tide of gang warfare and drug dealing.

(1.) Antisocial Personality Disorder. The terms "antisocial personality," "sociopath" and "psychopath," which are used interchangeably, refer to an individual whose behavior is predominantly amoral or antisocial. As noted in the section "Exclusion of Parent," his irresponsible and impulsive actions satisfy his own immediate needs and interests without concern for obvious social consequences. More than likely, as a child, his parents actively rejected him, treating him brutally or harshly depriving him of all emotional and physical needs. Thus, he displaced his anger against his own people in general, all of whom then became his deadly enemies. Since he believes everyone is against him anyway, he has no hope beyond survival and enjoyment of immediate gratification.

Occasionally, a sociopath may be the product of parents. Since this person was never disciplined as a child and always got his own way, as an adult, he still expects to be treated in the same manner. Thus, he is narcissistic and demanding, exploiting people and doing whatever he wishes.

Since his Internal Parent is either extremely weak and ineffective or completely blocked-out, the sociopath feels no guilt, remorse, shame, or anxiety over his delinquent behavior. He displays superficial charm which he uses to manipulate people, but he is incapable of true affection. He is often a pathological liar, swindler and thief, who is aggressive and often violent. He may be addicted to alcohol or drugs as another sign of rebellion.

Most persistent criminals are sociopaths. Many are in prisons, but some live in the community as unscrupulous business or professional men. In his book, *The Mask of Sanity*, Hervey M. Cleckley, M. D., gives a detailed and interesting account of a sociopathic psychiatrist who exploited his patients financially and sexually.

The third chapter of second Timothy describes how vile men will be in the last days: "...lovers of self, lovers of money, boastful, arrogant, revilers, disobedient to parents, ungrateful, unholy, unloving, irreconcilable, malicious gossips, without self-control, brutal, haters of good, treacherous, reckless, conceited, lovers of pleasure rather than lovers of God." Although this is an excellent description of sociopaths, we must remember that these victimizers are also victims of abusive, deprived childhoods. Thus, their evil deeds are symptoms which have their roots in the unrecognized, unresolved pain buried in their scarred and ravished hearts.

*(2.) **Manipulation.*** The more subtle, passive ways of hurting others are not as easily recognized as the direct ones. Many consist of "games" involving emotional manipulation and control that occur in the marriage relationship, such as a spouse who withdraws and refuses to communicate every time his or her mate wants to discuss a problem in their relationship. Other examples of manipulative games include a spouse who is always bringing up past hurts and making "Parent" statements, such as, "You will never change," "a mate who is always late," "one who continually forgets things," and "one who will do anything for friends, but neglects his own family."

A wife may make tearful, passive insinuations which infuriate her mate and then wonder why he verbally abuses her. Or she may play the game of exiting dramatically, slamming the door and locking herself in the bedroom. A spouse or parent may sabotage plans by agreeing to go somewhere and then cancelling due to the "unfortunate" fact that "something came up at the last minute." A parent may play "martyr" by constantly reminding her child how unappreciative he is when he makes a decision on his own. A person may gossip, make sarcastic remarks or "joke" in a way that belittles others.

A seductive woman may "lead a man on" and then "attack" him when he "falls" for her advances, or a man may convince a woman that he loves her and then disappear when she tells him that she is pregnant. An individual who is jealous, self-centered and covets power, money, recognition, etc., finds many ways of manipulating to get what he wants from another person. Berne has written a very insightful, informative book called *Games People Play*, which describes the ingenious methods people use to control others.

As stated before, we must keep in mind that all of the indirect, manipulative ways which people use to hurt others are just symptoms pointing to the need for healing of the wounds and pain buried in their bruised and broken hearts. Both the direct and indirect means of punishing others will be "put to death on the cross" when soul healing takes place, and the counselee forgives and learns how to face his emotions honestly and deal with them, becoming a victor in Jesus instead of a victimizer.

b. PUNISHING OURSELVES. We have also noted previously that many rejected and abused individuals, although they decide as children that all people are mean, just as victimizers do, also make judgments that people are bigger, stronger and smarter; therefore, it is not safe to disagree with them. So, they decide that the wisest course to follow would be to agree that they, being children, are at fault and deserve to be punished. Thus, they repress their anger toward others, and directing it inward toward themselves, vow that they will punish themselves. Fear of being rejected, self-condemnation and guilt that they have done something wrong are the feelings which result from their inverted anger.

As adept as we are at finding methods to hurt others, we are even more ingenious when it comes to discovering ways to punish ourselves. Of course, we must keep in mind that Satan and his legions of demons are always there "helping" us subconsciously devise methods to victimize others or ourselves! Although symptoms are not caused by demons, they do "open the door" for evil spirits, giving them permission to "add fuel to the fire" and, thus, intensify the particular symptoms suffered by an individual. Let us take a look at some of the numerous symptoms which are destructive to ourselves.

Self-pity and depression are common consequences of inverted anger. People suffering from these symptoms are continually preoccupied with negative thoughts of how inferior they are, how things never go right, how nobody cares, why bother trying, and so on. Anger turned inward combined with self-pity invariably leads to depression. Severe depression will be discussed later under neurotic and affective disorders.

Accident proneness is a symptom in which a person is always accidentally breaking things, hurting himself physically or making the wrong decisions in his purchases. Procrastination comes from the Internal Child being programmed to resist because of all the admonitions a person received as a child. This negative programming undermines his ability to do what is expected of him in the present. As a result, he is unmotivated and undisciplined and usually fails at everything which he tries to accomplish.

Bulimia-anorexia nervosa is a disorder—prevalent among women, in which a person eats voraciously and then forces herself to vomit. Subconsciously, she is angry because her parents always expect too much of her, so she "gets back at them" through this form of relatively "acceptable" self-destructive behavior. Suicide is an attempt to get the love, attention and acceptance longed for through self-destructive behavior. A masochistic person continually "sets himself up" to be used, abused and rejected. An example would be a woman who always attracts and marries victimizers.

(1.) Psychosomatic Disorders. Due to the relentless stress of the present age, psychosomatic disorders are very common. Since soul and body work together, experiences that affect our psyche (soul) also affect our soma (body). Thus, in psychosomatic disorders, our repressed hurts and the consequent anger affect the chemistry in our blood and the electrical impulses in our nervous system. Usually a single organ system which is controlled by the autonomic nervous system is involved. While the physiological changes involved are those that normally accompany specific emotional states, the changes are more intense and more sustained. The individual may or may not be consciously aware of his emotional state.

Because we all have different biological makeups, each of us is more vulnerable to certain physical problems than others. A few of the more prevalent psychosomatic disorders are migraine headaches, hypertension, asthma, hyperventilation, peptic ulcer, colitis, dysmenorrhea (painful menstruation), amenorrhea (failure to menstruate for several months), impotence, frigidity, muscle and joint pain, and arthritis.

(2.) Indulgences. Indulgences include a wide variety of behaviors through which we indulge our fleshly desires in an attempt to satisfy our unrequited need for love, attention and acceptance. When we are frustrated in relationships or accomplishments, we can escape from reality and gain instant pleasure by gratifying our carnal appetites. But the enjoyment is only temporary, and the aftermath brings feelings of guilt and self-condemnation which convince us that we deserve even more punishment. Thus, a vicious cycle is set up which Satan uses to drag us more deeply into self-destructive indulgences. Any fleshly indulgence on which we have become dependent as a substitute for God's love has become an idol before God in our lives. "...promising them freedom while they themselves are slaves of corruption; for by what a man is overcome, by this he is enslaved" (2 Pet. 2:19).

We are entertaining our carnal passions more today than ever before in this country because we have bought Satan's lie that sin does not exist. Since sin is nonexistent, there are no consequences for sin, so we should "grab all the gusto" we can! After all, we only "go around once." Some examples of the many ways in which we attempt to satisfy our emotional needs are food, drug and alcohol indulgences, gambling, compulsive spending, and accumulating material goods.

We have also become addicted to all forms of entertainment—television, videos, music, movies, sports events, etc.—which give us vicarious pleasure and an escape from reality. As we are all aware, watching television and video programs has become the number one national pastime! Teenagers are addicted to rock music videos, men to television sports events and women to "soap operas" and "talk shows."

There has also been a recent rise in "thrill seeking" as people attempt to fulfill emotional needs through various types of death-defying feats, such as: hang gliding, rock and mountain climbing, motorcycle "jumping," ski "hot-dogging," and skydiving. Some "daredevils" are even putting their lives in total jeopardy by skydiving off of sheer cliffs with the full realization that drafts can throw them against the rock walls at any time!

In recent years, we have also become extremely narcissistic in our preoccupation with our bodies and our efforts to maintain a youthful appearance. Indulgence in cosmetic surgery and compulsive exercise have been the result. Some individuals relate that they feel irresistibly compelled to run a certain number of miles or engage in body building exercises for a certain length of time every day. This compulsion is probably due to the fact that they have become addicted to the "high" that comes from the endorphins (chemical substances) that are released during strenuous exercise.

The number of people involved in the cults and occult has grown dramatically as evidenced by the recent interest in programs like Shirley MacLaine's and in occult activity, such as: "channeling," "crystals," "meditation," "astrology," "levitation," etc. Community colleges now offer a plethora of courses in parapsychology and police forces regularly contact spiritualists for "help" in solving criminal cases. Who can forget the "Jim Jones incident," where scores of people in his cult followed him to Guyana and ended up drinking poison at his command! It is also terrifying to conjecture how many people now participate in Satanic worship rituals, as evidenced by a news report that thirty cats had been found "surgically disemboweled" in one month in one county alone!

The "sexual revolution" has propagated the devil's lies that in the past we have been "too inhibited" sexually and that there is nothing wrong with sexual promiscuity and hedonism. As a result, it is the rule now, rather than the exception, to substitute lust for love and to indulge, guilt-free, in fornication and adultery! On a recent program, a young man bemoaned the fact that although he desired to be monogamous, he felt forcibly compelled to engage in promiscuous sex. One metropolitan area was forced to post "No Parking" signs all along a major boulevard because the area was being inundated by prostitutes who had heard that they would not be arrested for plying their trade because the jails were full!

In a recent study, it was found that twelve and thirteen-year-old black girls were ridiculed by their peers if they were not sexually active. They were also being encouraged by their classmates to have a baby "so they would have something to love" and because "they had nothing else to look forward to anyway." The youngest grandmother discovered by the study was only twenty-five years old! As we have seen, promiscuous individuals are desperately searching for the attention and love which they did not receive from their parents.

We can deduce from the foregoing discussion that although we hurt ourselves, for the most part when we indulge our flesh, others—especially loved ones, also suffer because of our actions. "Now the deeds of the flesh are evident, which are: immorality, impurity, sensuality, idolatry, sorcery, enmities, strife, jealousy, outbursts of anger, disputes, dissensions, factions, envying, drunkenness, carousing, and things like these, of which I forewarn you, just as I have forewarned you that those who practice such things shall not inherit the kingdom of God" (Gal. 5: 19-21). "Do not love the world, nor the things in the world. If anyone loves the world, the love of the Father is not in him. For all that is in the world—the lust of the flesh and the lust of the eyes, and the boastful pride of life—is not from the Father but is from the world" (1 John 2:15,16).

(3.) Sexual Deviations. Although sexual promiscuity is sinful, it is not considered to be a sexual deviation because it is heterosexual and genital. A sexual deviation is best understood as a failure of psychosexual development due to the Internal Parent-Child conflict. Thus, the sexually deviant individual, in most cases male, fails to progress from infantile to mature sexuality. He usually has a pervasive fear, often unconscious, of sexual contact with adult females. A sexual deviation, then, may be defined as a persistent preference for any form of sexual behavior that is a substitute for genital coitus with an adult of the opposite sex.

Although not considered a sexual deviation, pornography, which is widespread in all forms of media today, including television, videos, movies, magazines, and "strip shows," is used by Satan to seduce males to engage in all modes of sexual behavior, including deviant. In a video made before Ted Bundy was executed, he testified how his insatiable appetite for sadomasochistic pornography finally lead him to many violent acts of rape and murder. As counselors, we should be familiar with the definitions of the more prevalent sexual aberrations, even though we may find a discussion of them distasteful.

Masturbation may be defined as sexual pleasure obtained by manual stimulation of the genitals. The technical terms for ore-genital activity are cunnilingus; the apposition of the mouth to the female genitals and fellatio, the apposition of the mouth to the male genitals. Sodomy is the term for intercourse per annum. Any of these acts may occur heterosexually or homosexually. Homosexuality may be defined as oral-genital or anogenital (sodomy) activity between two males. Homosexual behavior in females is known as lesbianism. Bisexuality involves sexual activity with both males and females.

In the deviation of fetishism, part of the body or an inanimate object produces sexual excitement or gratification. The person may over respond to the legs, breasts, hair, etc., or he may make fetishes of female underwear, stockings, shoes or some other piece of clothing. Voyeurism consists of obtaining sexual gratification through observation of the genitals or the sexual behavior of others, while exhibitionism may be defined as exposure in public of the male genitals before a woman or child. Obtaining sexual satisfaction by wearing clothes appropriate to the opposite sex is termed transvestism.

The attainment of sexual gratification through the infliction of bodily or mental pain on others by physical or verbal means is termed sadism. In a broader sense, sadism refers to any type of cruelty or extreme aggression. The term is derived from the Marquis de Sade (1740-1814), a French nobleman, revolutionary politician, philosopher, and writer who recorded a wide variety of perversions in a novel entitled *The Curse of Virtue and the Blessing of Vice*. Unbelievably, a demonically inspired rock star recently promoted sexual sadism, including murder and violation of the corpse (necrophilia), in one of his albums.

Sexual gratification obtained through suffering bodily or mental pain is called masochism, although the term is also applied in a wider sense to any type of acceptance of pain. The term is derived from Leopold von Sacher-Masoch (1836-1895), an Austrian nobleman, writer and journalist, who desired women to treat him like a slave. However, women more often than men exhibit masochistic behavior. In the eighteenth century, a number of Englishwomen became addicted to flagellation; that is, whipping as a sexual excitant, perhaps as a continuation of treatment which they had received from parents and teachers. Dr. Magnus Hirschfeld (1868-1935), a German physician and sexologist describes a "flagellation club" whose members met once a week to whip each other! Similar masochistic and sadistic practices were formerly widespread in monasteries, convents and boarding schools.

Sexual activity of any type with a prepubertal child is called pedophilia, while sexual activity by an adult with an adolescent up to the age of sixteen is called hebephilia. Incest is sexual activity between persons whose blood relationship is closer than is sanctioned by the culture. Zoophilia or bestiality involves sexual relations with an animal. To avoid reader confusion, it should be noted here that sadism and the various forms of child molestation, being sexual deviations, have been included in this section, even though they are means of inflicting suffering on others rather than on ourselves.

An individual who persistently engages in some type of sexual aberration is unlikely to approximate normality in any area of his life, nonsexual as well as sexual. The further his sexual preference is from adult genital heterosexuality, the more pathological his personality is likely to be. The majority of sexual deviates tend to be shy, reserved, uncommunicative, and uncomfortable in relationships with adults. They are usually extremely ignorant and misinformed about sexual functioning. In severe forms of deviation, marked signs of anxiety and depression or apathy and indifference are common.

Studies have found that mothers of homosexuals tend to be dominating, smothering and seductive, while the fathers were either absent from the home or weak, ineffective and rejecting. Besides suffering abuse and rejection from emotionally disturbed parents, it was discovered that virtually all sexual deviants had also experienced abusive or perverse sexual episodes as children which had contributed greatly to the arrestment of their psychosexual development.

All of the promiscuous and homosexual individuals which I have counseled had either been molested or had participated heavily in sexual experimentation with their peers when they were children. One homosexual even related that one day during his childhood, as he was contemplating engaging in sexual activity with another young boy, a brilliant light shone through the window in the hayloft and an audible voice said, "Do not do what you are about to do as you will always regret it!"

The first chapter of Romans describes the fate of the unrighteous and ungodly. God will give them over in the lusts of their hearts to impurity, degrading passions and depraved minds. "...men abandoned the natural function of the woman and burned in their desire toward one another, men with men committing indecent acts and receiving in their own persons the due penalty of their error" (Rom. 1:18-32). We can surmise that AIDS (acquired immune deficiency syndrome), along with numerous venereal diseases, are some of the penalties received for sexual sins which are abominations in the sight of God!" ...Do not be deceived; neither fornicators, nor idolaters, nor adulterers, nor effeminate, nor homosexuals, nor thieves, nor the covetous, nor drunkards, nor revilers, nor swindlers, shall inherit the kingdom of God (1 Cor. 6:9,10).

"Beloved, I urge you as aliens and strangers to abstain from fleshly lusts which war against the soul" (1 Pet. 2:11). The problem is that there is a war going on within our souls which causes us to give in to our fleshly lusts. Many pastors instruct individuals whom they counsel to stand against the irresistible, demonic forces that drive them to succumb to their lusts. Those who do attempt to conquer their addictions through sheer will power or by standing against demonic powers usually fail miserably because the root of their problems has not been dealt with yet. Thus, Satan still has a right to tempt them to engage in the particular passions that control their lives.

Often these brothers and sisters shift their fleshly desires from a socially and spiritually unacceptable indulgence, such as alcohol, to an "acceptable" one, such as food. Because eating is a necessity, we often feel that it is one of the few pleasures which we do not have to give up when we become Christians. As a consequence, "gluttony" is a term that is rarely heard mentioned in Christian circles.

Again, we recognize that a counselee can get rid of symptoms which hurt himself and others only by allowing Jesus to reveal and heal the pain of the traumatic events that occurred in his childhood which allowed certain lusts to gain a foothold in his life. As Jesus resolves the Internal Parent-Child conflict through soul healing and replaces the love and acceptance which the counselee never had, he will be delivered from his symptoms since they will no longer be needed. He will remain free of them if he continues to develop an intimate love relationship with his heavenly Father, expecting Him to fulfill all of his emotional needs.

(4.) Psychoneurotic Disorders. Before discussing psychoneurotic disorders, a distinction between these and a neurotic personality should be made. Each of the neurotic disorders is characterized by identifiable symptoms, while the term "neurotic personality" refers to a constellation of personality traits. A neurotic disorder may or may not evolve from a neurotic personality. In other words, the individual who tends to be compulsive—orderly, perfectionistic, etc.—may at some time develop clinically identifiable compulsions or simply continue to have compulsive traits.

The personality of the individual who attempts to fulfill all of his emotional needs through overperformance in his occupation has previously been described. The characteristics of the "workaholic's" personality, typify what may be termed "the neurotic personality." The "typical" neurotic tends to have a rigid, controlling Internal Parent full of "shoulds" and "should nots" and an extremely weak or excluded Natural Child. Despite his inner turmoil, he is perceived by others as moral, reliable, responsible, truthful, and conforming. He is overly inhibited, but due to his repressed anger, he may be passively stubborn or display aggression indirectly. Feelings of fear and guilt enforce his hypersensitivity to the opinions and criticisms of others. Being a perfectionist, he perceives himself as falling far short of his ideals and ambitions, and fears that others will perceive his failure. He has an unstable self-concept and is unsure of whether he is an unusually good and sensitive person or whether he is really bad, inconsiderate and weak.

If we are astute, we can certainly perceive that, as Christians, many of us, including pastors and leaders, have or tend to have neurotic personalities. When the dominating Parent controls the Adaptive Child, our attitudes and actions reflect a law-based mentality which may be defined as legalism. Even though we may believe that we are not under law, but under grace (Gal. 2:16), we think and live as though we were under law. Thus, we attempt to control our lives and the lives of others and make every effort to succeed in conforming to the demands of the rigid, Internal Parent.

These demands most often consist of conforming to external requirements, such as doing and saying the "right" things. Since the legalist is strongly convinced that his thinking, attitudes and behavior are correct, he is unaware of his true condition—one of emotional and spiritual poverty, as well as pride and self-righteousness. He finds no peace or contentment in his legalistic, self-righteous attitudes, however, because he continually lives under an oppressive cloud of guilt and fear of failure and rejection due to the fact that he can never live up to the expectations of his demanding Internal Parent.

The legalistic Christian, strongly repressing his anger and keeping his fear and guilt firmly under control, is very resistant to insight because he is so sure that he is totally dedicated to serving God. He may attend church faithfully, be devoted to prayer, witnessing and church activities—he may even move in the gifts of the Spirit—but the only fruit that he will ever bear is "dead works" if he does not "know" Christ. "Not everyone who says to Me, 'Lord, Lord,' will enter the kingdom of heaven, but he who does the will of My Father who is in heaven will enter. Many will say to Me on that day, 'Lord, Lord, did we not prophesy in Your name, and in Your name cast out demons, and in Your name perform many miracles?' And then I will declare to them, 'I never knew you; depart from Me, you who practice iniquity'" (Matt. 7:21-23).

There has been much speculation on the meaning of these sobering words of our Savior. Perhaps they indicate that if we, as Christians, practice either license (engaging in the destructive desires of the flesh) or legalism (controlling our life and the lives of others by enforcing conformity to the Internal Parent), we may fall into the ominous category of not doing the will of the Father. However, those individuals practicing license are usually always aware of their inequities, while those performing legalistic activities, such as the Pharisees, are blind to their sinfulness. Whether the conformist is conscious of his condition or not, however, because his dedication and service are not built upon a love relationship with God, but upon fear of failure and guilt, his soul (Parent) is in command of his spiritual life. Therefore, the Holy Spirit is not able to provide the insight, correction, discipline, and direction needed for his emotional and spiritual growth and vitality.

In the event that the legalist is no longer able to keep his fear and guilt tightly controlled, even though he is still able to repress his anger, he becomes a potential candidate for one or more of the neurotic disorders. A dramatic failure, personal tragedy or crisis may lead to the onset of one or more identifiable symptoms of a neurotic disorder. Although his emotional breakdown may appear tragic, God will work it for his good in that he may, for the first time, begin to get "honest" with God and allow the Spirit to reveal the true nature of his heart.

Let us now take a look at some of the symptoms which people with neurotic disorders may experience. Generally, they suffer intense anxiety and feelings of being overwhelmed and powerless to cope with the daily responsibilities of life. Although they are able to relate to reality, unlike individuals suffering with psychotic disorders, a sense of helplessness and hopelessness pervades their lives. Ephraim Rosen, Ronald E. Fox and Ian Gregory, in their book, *Abnormal Psychology*, list five major neurotic disorders: *anxiety, hysteria, phobic, obsessive-compulsive, and depressive.* Although an in-depth study is not possible, it would be helpful to discuss each disorder briefly in order to become familiar with its characteristics.

An individual afflicted with an ***anxiety neurosis*** complains of feelings of extreme fear or dread without any apparent cause. Although his fear is irrational, he views the world as threatening and is uncertain of his ability to handle even the mildest stress. His chronic state of anxious apprehension is periodically punctuated by intense anxiety attacks during which he is flooded by terror and panic. His heart pounds furiously; he cannot breathe; he shakes, becomes dizzy, feels that he is losing his mind, and that his heart or head might burst. An attack may be brought on by some behavior that is unacceptable to the person or it may precede a situation in which he must make a good impression, such as a social gathering. Thus, this condition might be described as one in which the person's Inner Child is intensely "hooked" by his Inner Parent.

There are two types of ***hysterical neurosis***: *conversion* type and *dissociative* type. Conversion hysteria, which has been declining in frequency may be defined as a neurotic reaction in which anxiety is converted into a loss or alteration of a sensory or motor function of the body. Three symptom subtypes may be recognized: sensory symptoms, motor paralyses and disordered movements. Sensory symptoms consist of a loss of sensation in any of the senses, such as temporary blindness, deafness, etc. In motor paralyses, the person's ability to perform voluntary movements is diminished, such as temporary paralysis of a leg or an arm, or his voice may be affected so that he is unable to speak.

Symptoms of conversion hysteria often appear suddenly in emotionally charged situations; they may disappear just as suddenly. Often, they can be modified by suggestion alone. The symbolic meaning of a conversion symptom depends on the individual's past history. Cases of "hysterical pregnancy," in which menstruation ceased and the patients' abdomen swelled, have been documented.

Dissociative hysteria is a neurotic reaction in which anxiety is converted into a disordering or loss of the state of consciousness. The major symptoms of dissociative reactions are amnesia, fugues, somnambulism, and multiple personality. These symptoms usually appear abruptly as a reaction to obvious stress and often disappear fairly quickly. Amnesia may be partial, e.g., the patient may forget only his name or address, or it may be complete, e.g., he may forget all the events of a particular period. A fugue is a combination of amnesia and physical flight. The person usually flees to a place where he has fewer responsibilities as he is really trying to escape his fears.

Somnambulism consists of behavior—walking, talking and eating—in a sleeplike state for which the individual is afterward amnesic. This behavior, especially sleepwalking, may occur in childhood and then be outgrown. This symptom has been attributed to a clash between dependence on the family and a drive to be independent and flee the family environment.

A person with Multiple Personality Disorder (MPD)manifests different, relatively complete systems of emotional and cognitive reactions at different times. These reaction systems, or alternate personalities, are usually very unlike each other because each contains elements repressed by the other. In recent years, Satanic Ritual Abuse (SRA) has emerged as the most common factor responsible for MPD. The unbelievably horrendous abuse suffered by children subjected to SRA has led them to use dissociation to cope with the resulting trauma. In order to survive the horrors of SRA, these children develop alternate personalities which may or may not be aware of each other's existence.

Dr. James G. Friesen's very enlightening book, *Uncovering the Mystery of MPD*, describes in detail the origins, characteristics and treatment of MPD as related to SRA. To our dismay, we are discovering that MPD and SRA are much more prevalent than we could have ever imagined!

Although schizophrenia literally means "split-minded," it should not be confused with multiple personality disorder. The alternate personalities of the neurotic with this disorder are relatively integrated, intact and able to relate well to reality, while the schizophrenic's personality is disintegrated and fragmented, rendering him unable to relate to reality; that is, psychotic. Thus, his mind is "split" among various psychological processes; for example, his affect (mood or emotional state) may be incongruous with his thinking—he laughs while telling a sad story.

Phobias are characterized by intense fear of an object or situation—fear which the patient may recognize as unrealistic. Phobic individuals go to great lengths to regulate and restrict their activities in order to avoid what they fear. A traumatically frightening experience may become the basis for a strong conditioned fear reaction, such as a fear of dogs resulting from being attacked by a dog in childhood. However, a more important source of phobias consists of the repression of an impulse, emotion or need, often hostility, and a displacement of the resulting fear to an external object or situation. For example, a child's anger toward his parents may be repressed, and the consequent fear displaced, resulting in a phobic reaction to dogs—or cars, germs or anything.

As in hysteria, the symbolic meaning of a phobia depends on the person's past history. For example, acrophobia (fear of heights) may, in one case, represent fear of abandonment and, in another, a suicidal urge. In both cases, however, the fear comes from repressing anger resulting from painful wounds. Agoraphobia (fear of open spaces) is prevalent in many women who have repressed hostility because they feel "trapped" in the home. The fear and guilt which they feel due to their repressed anger renders them literally unable to leave their homes.

Since ***neurotic obsessions and compulsions*** are motivated by unconscious conflicts, they are more intense and persistent than the "normal" obsessions—a tune running through one's mind—or compulsions—straightening pictures or arranging things "just so" on tabletops that we all experience. Obsession refers to the persistent intrusion into thoughts of an unwanted idea or impulse;

for example, obsessive fantasies of aggression. Compulsion may be described as an overwhelming urge to perform an irrational act or ritual, such as dusting the furniture many times a day.

As in hysterical and phobic reactions, an impulse, need or emotion may be repressed and displaced onto a thought or behavior which then becomes obsessive or compulsive. Kleptomania, for example, may be a displacement of a repressed need for love and affection, the objects stolen substituting for love. Pyromania is thought to be a displacement of repressed sexual impulses because the tension build-up and release which pyromaniacs describe seems similar to that experienced during the sex act.

The oppressive Parent of a person may also force his Child into obsessive or compulsive reaction-formations. In other words, an obsession or compulsion may result from a reaction- formation against an unacceptable impulse or emotion and express an attempt to expiate guilt. Examples are compulsive hand washing or house cleaning or an obsessive struggle to think only pure thoughts, all arising out of guilt.

In my own case, I reacted to my mother's excessive control by cluttering every square inch of my huge, upstairs bedroom during the week. Then every Saturday, I would compulsively clean every square inch—even pulling out both twin beds to vacuum underneath them. I now realize that I was angrily rebelling against my mother's control and perfectionism during the week by cluttering my room. I would then express the reaction-formation of compliance by compulsively cleaning my room every Saturday in an attempt to expiate my guilt at having rebelled.

A special type of obsession or compulsion is excessive doubting; that is, when a decision is necessary, the person cannot make up his mind in thought or action. For example, he may spend hours ruminating whether to read a book or write a letter. An extreme case is evident in a patient who parked his car and left it because he was unable to decide whether to turn right or left in order to circle the block and arrive at his home!

The majority of obsessive-compulsives have very striking personalities. They tend to be neat, methodical, rigid, perfectionistic, obstinate, and stingy. Relatively cool intellectualizers, they avoid affect by isolating it from ideas. Overcontrolled and unable to react spontaneously to other people, they try to love by rules and regulations. Obsessive-compulsive patients are thought to have had perfectionistic parents who were meticulous and intolerant of noise and disorder. While generally true, I have also found, in my experience, that many obsessive-compulsive women have been molested. Thus, they may be attempting to rid themselves of feelings of guilt, shame, and defilement by compulsive washing and house cleaning and obsessive struggling with impure thoughts.

Depressive neurosis differs from the discouragement and gloom which we all feel at certain times in that it is much more intense and of longer duration. The depressive patient feels listless, dejected, despondent, and lonely. He is continually oppressed by feelings of fear, guilt, unworthiness, self-condemnation, and self-pity. He tends to be helpless, weeps at the slightest provocation and may have appetite disturbances. As we have seen, depression may be defined as a turning of anger and hostility inward against the self. Thus, the cardinal feature of this disorder is the tendency to blame and hate the self rather than to express anger and aggression openly against others. Depression is the most common of all the neurotic disorders with twice as many women as men suffering from it.

Minor neuroses include hypochondriasis, neurasthenia and depersonalization. Hypochondriacs have an exaggerated concern about their health and are often convinced that they are afflicted with numerous maladies which are terminal. They resemble obsessive patients in that they ruminate excessively over a substitute for the emotional problems which they wish to avoid.

In depersonalization, the patient does not feel real or feels that the situation in which he finds himself is not real. The predominant feeling state is one of unreality or estrangement from the self or from the environment.

The neurasthenic person is tired both mentally and physically, unable to concentrate, irritable and prone to headaches. His fatigue stems from the general bodily tension that accompanies his worries and other emotional stresses. Excitement is likely to snap him out of his fatigue, but it recurs when routine activities are resumed. It has often been called the "housewives" neurosis, since it occurs frequently in housewives who are bored and feel neglected by their husbands. Many depressives also report symptoms of one or more of these neuroses.

*(5.) **Affective Disorders.*** The most conspicuous feature of affective disorders is a marked deviation in mood from the normal which is manifested as either depression or euphoria. *Manic-depressive* is the major affective disorder; any combination of mania and depression may occur. Individuals with this disorder are often considered psychotic because euphoria or depression, when sufficiently intense, usually includes a break with reality.

Three degrees of increasing severity of depression have been observed: simple depression, acute depression and depressive stupor. The person with simple depression is only somewhat anxious and discouraged. He is much more likely to fight simple depression, whereas in the more severe degrees, he gives up the struggle. In an acute depression, the individual feels despondent, dejected and desperate. He feels tired, listless, talks in a monotone, has decreased mental alertness, a morbid outlook and a despairing mood. He is extremely intropunitive and feels worthless, hopeless and remorseful. Depressive stupor, occurring only in a few cases, consists of a state in which the patient is unresponsive and motionless for long periods of time, usually requiring tube feeding.

Manic behavior may also be subdivided into three degrees: *hypomania, acute mania and delirious mania. **Hypomania*** is relatively mild. The patient feels zestful, self-confident and energetic. He is full of ideas, monopolizes conversations and may behave foolishly or impulsively. A trivial frustration may plunge him into depression. ***Acute manic behavior*** is marred by elation, exaltation, accelerated thought, and speech and motor excitement. He is gay and animated, has delusions of grandeur, is insensitive to pain, and heedless of the consequences of his behavior. He may become sarcastic, vulgar, aggressive, and insist on having his own way. ***Delirious mania,*** which is very rare, is marked by a furious excitement, constant shouting and laughing, delusions of both grandeur and persecution and vivid hallucinations. The patient tears his clothes, upsets furniture and may try to hurt himself or others.

Depressive or manic episodes sometimes occur during pregnancy or immediately after childbirth. One of my counselees experienced an acute manic episode a few days after childbirth which

I will never forget! Her frantic husband called and implored me to come over immediately. I rushed over and got the baby, which she insisted she was going to nurse, away from her. While her husband went to buy bottles and formula, I had to endeavor to care for a crying newborn and keep a "mad" woman under control!

First, she grabbed the matches and attempted to light the stove. After I wrestled these away from her, she ran outside. After swinging furiously on the swing set for the apartments, she accosted the mailman! Extremely embarrassed, I mumbled something to the effect that she was "sick" and managed to coax her to go back in the house. She was short, stocky and very strong, so there was no hope of controlling her physically. New in the Spirit, I was binding demons right and left!

Finally, her husband returned and took her to the hospital. I was totally exhausted when he came back and related how she had literally tried to jump out of the car on the way! I will never forget that day as long as I live! By the way, this precious lady has been healed by the Lord, is writing a book and recently received her degree as an LVN! "...With man, it is impossible, but with God all things are possible!" (Matt. 19:6 ESV).

(6.) Schizophrenia. Among psychiatric disorders, *schizophrenia* is one of the most baffling. Although there have been many hypotheses, the nature and cause of the disorder still remain matters of dispute. As we noted previously, the schizophrenic's distorted and disintegrated personality renders him unable to relate to reality. We also noted that schizophrenia literally means "splitting of the mind." According to the experts, the splitting which takes place in the schizophrenic's mind occurs among the various psychological processes within the personality. As we shall discover later, the "expert's split" is only the result of the "real split" which takes place within the schizophrenic's personality. First however, let us look at some of the symptoms which the individual suffering from this disorder experiences.

Swiss psychiatrist and eugenicist, Dr. Paul Eugen Bleuler (1857-1939) believed that the split among the psychological processes within the schizophrenic's personality was manifested in four primary symptoms: *loosening of thought associations, autistic withdrawal, ambivalence, and inappropriateness of affect.* **Loosening of thought as-**

sociations refers to the patient's tendency to combine irrelevant ideas, dart from one idea to another in a fragmented and disconnected manner or repeat a few simple ideas over and over. Consequently, his thinking seems bizarre, illogical and unpredictable. In general, his thinking tends to be concrete; he has trouble with abstract concepts. An example is cited in which a patient was asked, "Is something weighing heavily on your mind?" He replied, "Yes. Iron is very heavy."

The looseness, fragmentation, distorted logic, and concreteness of schizophrenic thinking were labeled "primary process" by Sigmund Freud (1856-1939), the father of psychoanalysis. Primary process refers to the immediate discharge of impulses without regard to logic or the demands of the environment. (In contrast, "secondary process" refers to thinking controlled by logic, environmental demands and anticipated future consequences.) Primary process is uninhibited and uncontrolled.

Autistic withdrawal may be defined as the symptom in which the severely disturbed schizophrenic breaks completely with reality and withdraws into a world of his own. He is completely preoccupied with his own inner world in which his fears, ideas and fantasies are predominant. His thinking, speech and behavior are dominated by his inner life. Consequently, he misinterprets and distorts reality. For example, a smile may be interpreted as a sneer.

Ambivalence refers to the conflicting feelings that exist simultaneously within a schizophrenic's soul. He is ambivalent toward himself and others. For example, the severely troubled schizophrenic may strip off his clothes in front of people while berating himself for his immodesty or he may alternate rapidly between laughing and crying. An emotional response free of contradiction is difficult for him.

Inappropriateness of affect means that the schizophrenic's affect may be out of keeping with reality or his own thoughts. For example, disturbing news may be greeted with laughter. His affect may not be regulated by social standards; e.g., he may use very obscene language or masturbate openly with no shame. He may sit expressionless for hours or overreact, jumping from mood to mood.

Secondary symptoms of schizophrenia include hallucinations and delusions. Hallucinations may involve any one of the senses, but they are usually auditory. The patient hears "voices" which keep up a running commentary on his behavior or thoughts, or they converse with each other. They may threaten, curse, criticize, warn, or command him. The patient may also see visions, smell foul odors, perceive peculiar tastes in his food, feel unwarranted pain, cold, heat, electric currents, or delicate touches. Sexual hallucinations are fairly common; e.g., a patient may feel peculiar sensations in his genitals which he interprets as interference by some external agent. He may exhibit a "sixth sense" in which he feels the presence of a force or person not actually present or reports that "others can feel his feelings." As Christian counselors, we would definitely attribute hallucinatory experiences to demonic activity!

Delusions are false beliefs which are gross distortions of reality. A schizophrenic's delusions are expressions of his needs and fears and may be based on his hallucinatory experiences. He may have delusions of grandeur; e.g., he may believe that he is a king before whom people should bow down. Delusions of persecution are very common; e.g., he may believe that all of his misfortunes are due to an individual or a nameless group. In a delusion of reference, the patient may believe that the content of books or magazines or the words and actions of other people refer to him. For example, a college student believed that the major purpose of the college was to conduct an elaborate experiment in which she was the sole subject. In somatic delusions, the patient may believe that all his strength has been drained out of him by a secret process, that his bones are water, or that only his head is alive. Again, delusions would certainly appear to be caused by the activity of evil spirits!

Distortions of memory, as well as speech and motor disturbances often occur in schizophrenia. The patient may be mute, excessively talkative, abnormally loud, or repeat words monotonously. He may manifest a muscle rigidity or fixity of posture or repeatedly perform mechanical gestures. He may be stuporous or overactive. He suffers from anxiety, an impaired capacity to experience pleasure and strongly craves protection and dependency.

The schizophrenic's symptoms are regressive, i.e., indicative of a lower level of functioning that is characteristic of a mature adult. However, his behavior is different from that of a normal child, indicating rather, a distortion of infantile modes of behavior. He often behaves like an extremely anxious child who attacks the very people whose attention he desperately desires.

Although there are a number of types of schizophrenia, approximately half the people suffering from this disorder are classified as ***paranoid schizophrenics***. This type of schizophrenic manifests delusions of reference, grandeur and persecution accompanied by vivid auditory hallucinations. Although less disturbed in appearance and behavior than other types, his life is controlled by his delusions and hallucinations which tend to be fairly straightforward projections of his drives and anxieties early in the course of his disorder. Later on, however, as they become more all-inclusive, they also become more disorganized. Consistent with his delusions, he is likely to be suspicious, serious, intense, and often hostile, argumentative and assaultive. He tends to become quiet, withdrawn, and apathetic as his personality deteriorates over time.

Disorganized schizophrenia is characterized by incoherent babbling, strange gestures, grimaces, giggling, quick and impulsive actions which are sometimes assaultive, and bizarre appearance. A person suffering from this disorder may experience bizarre, unsystematized delusions and vivid hallucinations. He may regress to very infantile behavior.

Catatonic schizophrenia is characterized by motor disturbances expressed in either inhibition (stupor, mutism, rigidity) or excessive activity and excitement. The catatonic patient may swing dramatically from one extreme to another, or he may remain fixed in an unusual posture for hours. He may imitate another person's movements or repeat words said to him. In the excited state, he becomes extremely agitated and destructive. He may destroy things and hurt himself or others. He experiences vivid hallucinations and delusions.

There has been much debate and speculation concerning whether a genetic predisposition to schizophrenia exists in the individuals who develop this disorder or whether environmental determinants are the sole cause. In their book, *Pigs in the Parlor*, Frank and Ida Mae Hammond relate that they were working intensely in deliverance with a person who was not improving. The Lord eventually revealed that the problem was schizophrenia, which He defined as a "disturbance, distortion or disintegration of the development of the personality."

The Lord instructed Mrs. Hammond to fold her hands, interlacing her fingers tightly together. He then explained that each hand represented one of the competing, dual natures existing within the schizophrenic's personality, one being "rejection" and the other, "rebellion." He then presented to her a "hands" chart explaining that the words listed on the hands represented the various demons that had entered and formed a nest in this person's soul when she was very, very young.

The Lord stated that the "hurricane" on the illustration symbolized the "storms" which the schizophrenic continually creates around himself as the symptoms which were previously described are manifesting in his life and affecting others. The "arrows" represent people who are trying to relate to the troubled individual. Notice that some of the arrows are combined with hurricanes, meaning that these persons are unstable. Consequently, they bring their own storms into the situation. Other arrows depict stable individuals who can engage in the schizophrenic's storm without being caught up in the turmoil. As counselors, of course, we must be "straight arrows without hurricanes!"

The etiology of the development of the soul of a schizophrenic was discussed previously under "Exclusion of Adult." Taking into account this discussion, we might surmise that this woman was a victim of exceedingly dysfunctional parents from whose unpredictable behavior she received many contradictory messages. These double-bind messages then created such an intense conflict within her soul, that during childhood, her confused, undeveloped Adult gave up and quit trying to make sense out of things. Unable to decide whether to punish herself (rejection) or others (rebellion), her personality disintegrated before it had a chance to develop. This disintegration undoubtedly "opened the door" for evil spirits to enter her soul and take on the characteristics of her internal conflict (rejection versus rebellion).

Thus, as an adult, locked in her inner world which is controlled by demonic forces through hallucinations and delusions, she alternates between punishing herself and punishing others, exhibiting all the symptoms of psychotic behavior. "A double-minded man is unstable in all his ways" (James 1:8 KJV). Double-minded, translated as being of "two minds," comes from a compound Greek word literally meaning "two souls."

As Mrs. Hammond explains, helping the schizophrenic fall out of agreement with the demons that have usurped his identity is a long, slow process requiring a tremendous amount of love, effort and patience. "How can two walk together unless they be agreed?" (Amos 3:3 TMB). Since the schizophrenic does not know who he really is, she states that deliverance must work in balance with the development of his "real self." I believe it is important to realize that deliverance is only one component of the soul healing process. This process, including deliverance, will be discussed in detail in the next section.

As the Lord revealed to Mrs. Hammond, schizophrenia (like all other symptoms and disorders caused predominantly by parental programming) always starts with rejection. As we have seen, rejection often occurs first in the womb. UCLA researchers have even reported that paranoid schizophrenia seems to have its roots in the womb. Examination of brain tissue from ten deceased schizophrenics revealed a disorganization among cells within the hippocampus, a portion of the brain believed to be associated with the expression of emotion. This report raises some very interesting questions which lead to some fascinating speculations. Could it be possible that rejection in the womb or some type of prenatal trauma caused well-ordered brain cells to be thrown into disarray in these individuals? We must continually "...ask, seek and knock," requesting the Spirit to '...reveal the treasures of darkness and the hidden wealth of secret places'" to us (Isa. 45:3).

(7.) Paranoia. The essential feature of ***paranoia*** is the development of systematized, closely interrelated and permanent delusions. In paranoid individuals, intellectual functioning is better preserved, and emotional and social responses are more appropriate than in paranoid schizophrenics. Paranoids usually have a history of occupational and marital failures. Their strong, repressed feelings of inferiority are masked by delusions of grandeur or rationalized by persecutory delusions. They may also have delusions of jealousy and influence or erotic delusions in which they fear sexual attack.

Paranoids tend to be egocentric, narcissistic, introverted, mistrustful, jealous, sensitive, and suspicious. Their conversations are likely to revolve almost exclusively around their delusions. For example, one man was convinced that he was the rightful owner of a baseball stadium. Over a twenty-year period, he spent all the money he could spare in litigation against the legal owners of "his" ballpark and "his" team. Thus, the paranoid often behaves in a manner that elicits the rejection which confirms his expectations.

(8.) Brain Syndromes. Organic brain syndromes are disturbances of behavior due to pathological disturbances in the brain. Although brain syndromes appear to fall within the domain of physicians, we must, as counselors, be familiar with them so that we will be able to recognize when a counselee's symptoms are caused by an organic disorder.

A brain syndrome may be classified as acute, meaning that the changes in brain functioning are reversible or chronic, meaning that the changes in brain functioning are irreversible. The patient with an acute syndrome may be in a state of stupor in which he is lethargic and immobile, or he may be in a coma in which he is unconscious. Most often, however, these patients become delirious, manifesting symptoms, such as: incoherence, perceptual confusion, clouded consciousness, tremors, disorientation, hallucinations, and transient delusions. Chronic syndrome patients exhibit progressive intellectual deterioration defined as dementia.

An important fact to remember is that brain damage may cause any of the symptoms which have been described under the various psychological dysfunctions: neurotic, schizophrenic, affective, and paranoid disorders; sexual deviations or psychopathic behavior. An identical type and degree of brain damage in any two persons may result in totally different symptoms depending on the personality traits of each individual.

Acute brain syndromes are often associated with biochemical brain changes which may result from a tremendous variety of causes. Among them are diseases accompanied by high fever, such as: malaria, pneumonia and typhoid fever; infections within the skull caused by encephalitis, syphilis or meningitis; excessive use of alcohol or drugs; toxic metals, such as lead; carbon monoxide; head injury; seizures in epilepsy; brain tumors; illnesses, such as pernicious anemia, hypothyroidism, Huntington's Chorea, Alzheimer's disease, and injection of excessive insulin.

Although it is recognized that endocrine, metabolic and nutritional disorders, as well as poison and drug intoxication, can cause brain syndromes, it is not well known or accepted that food and chemical allergies can cause biochemical brain changes which produce acute brain syndromes. Our excessive consumption of refined carbohydrates, "junk food," alcohol, tobacco, caffeine, and prescription drugs has created alarming nutritional deficiencies in our population. We persist in poisoning our food, water and air with tremendous amounts of pollutants, such as insecticides, preservatives and additives which poison our foods, chlorine and other chemicals which contaminate our water supply, and carbon monoxide and other gases which pollute our air. It is surprising to me that more people in our nation do not experience chronic physical and emotional symptoms due to contaminants! The statistics are rising every year, however. Approximately half of America's population currently suffers from some form of degenerative disease.

Each individual's ability to handle toxins, pollens, foods, and chemicals absorbed from the environment differs considerably according to his unique physiological makeup. The more defective his ability—by inheritance, nutritional deficiencies, etc.—the more likely a person is to develop maladaptive symptoms when exposed to food and environmental contacts.

There is extremely convincing evidence that both neurotic and psychotic, in addition to physical, symptoms may result when certain individuals are exposed to various foods, chemicals or inhalants. William H. Philpot, M.D., and a psychiatrist, states in his book, *Brain Allergies: The Psychonutrient Connection*, that 92 percent of 250 patients classified as schizophrenic developed psychotic symptoms when exposed to foods and chemicals; 64 percent manifested psychotic symptoms when they ate food containing wheat; 51 percent when they were given corn products; and 51 percent when they drank milk. Approximately 75 percent reacted psychotically to tobacco and 30 percent to items made from petroleum products. The emotional symptoms evoked ranged from mild neurotic symptoms, such as anxiety and depression, to gross psychotic symptoms, such as ***catatonia, dissociation, paranoid delusions, and visual and auditory hallucinations.***

One of Philpott's cases involved a seventeen-year-old boy, diagnosed a paranoid schizophrenic, who had not been helped by tranquilizers, psychotherapy or electric shock treatments. Believing that people were out to kill him, he had to be put in restraints because of his attacks on people. The psychiatrist placed him on a fast during which he was given only spring water. On the fourth day of the fast, all of his symptoms left him, and he was released from the restraints. On the fifth day, he was fed a meal of wheat only. Within an hour, all of the psychotic symptoms returned! Further testing revealed that all his symptoms disappeared when wheat was withheld, and they consistently returned when he was given foods containing wheat.

Philpott describes another case in which he "turned off" the delusion of a paranoid schizophrenic by arranging for him to avoid all petroleum products in addition to fasting for four days. On the fifth day, he exposed the patient to exhaust fume extract which induced the symptoms in minutes. The doctor was able to turn off the delusion again by having him inhale oxygen and carbon dioxide. This man's history revealed that he had been overcome by fumes while driving a propane-fueled fork truck in an apple warehouse cooler. After this incident, he developed psychotic attacks which always coincided with his driving the fork truck in the apple cooler. Another significant factor is that when he waxed his crew-cut on one occasion, he literally went crazy!

One-third of Philpott's patients reacted to various chemicals such as insecticides, preservatives, additives, and chlorine. One paranoid schizophrenic had been well until he began smoking. After becoming symptom-free on the fourth day of his fast, he was given a cigarette. While smoking it, he became delusional and four men were required to subdue him and place him in a seclusion room! Philpott estimates that about 80 percent of the population is allergic to certain foods and chemicals, 75 percent being allergic to tobacco.

Unfortunately, drugs, such as tranquilizers and antidepressants, have become the major therapy used in treating emotionally disturbed individuals. Drugs, of course, do not remedy the cause of an emotional problem; at best, they offer some relief from symptoms. Tragically, they also produce lethargic, nonproductive, dependent people who are at great risk of developing a chronic degenerative disease due to the slow poisoning of their bodies.

Philpott relates the tragic example of a schizophrenic who developed Parkinson's disease after being on the tranquilizer Thorazine for five years. Although he is now off Thorazine, the psychiatrist states that he is like a shaking zombie with tremors in both his arms and legs. Another pitiful case concerned a young girl who developed tardive dyskinesia after taking the tranquilizer Haldol for three years. Her symptoms (head jerking from side to side and tongue moving in mouth constantly) continue even though the tranquilizer has been discontinued.

The medical profession is finally becoming alarmed at the incidence and chronicity of physician-induced illnesses. The United States Health Department is now warning doctors to be prepared to justify their continued use of drugs in patients who have negative reactions to them. Abram Hoffer, Ph.D., MD, states that he has seen many hyperactive young children who were placed on the drug Ritalin, which brings the hyperactive symptoms immediately under control, later degenerate into adult schizophrenics because the underlying metabolic problems remained untreated. Philpott was personally alarmed by a patient who died a silent coronary death. An autopsy revealed that her heart's conduction system had deteriorated in a manner that has been associated with continued tranquilizer use. In the appendix of his book, Philpott presents a detailed discussion of the nature and specific causes of drug-induced illnesses, including methods by which some have been successfully treated.

Thus, a few doctors, including psychiatrists, are finally beginning to "see the light" and recognize that a healthy body is based on healthy cells. Therefore, they are choosing to build up the cells through the use of nutrients rather than tear them down with drugs. As counselors for the Lord, our goal should also be to inspire our counselees to build healthy bodies as well as souls. To start with, we need to encourage them to discontinue the use of the three "deadly white powders"—sugar, salt and white flour—and to cut down their consumption of fats, including red meats and dairy products. We should inspire them to increase their intake of raw and steamed vegetables, whole grains, beans, fish, and chicken, and to develop a vigorous, well-rounded exercise program.

"Do you not know that you are a temple of God, and that the Spirit of God dwells in you? If any man destroys the temple of God, God will destroy him, for the temple of God is holy, and that is what you are" (1 Cor. 3:16,17). As we know, each of our temples is composed of body, soul and spirit, which God is commanding us not to destroy. Since, as God's counselors, we ought to "practice what we preach," we should make every effort to become healthy physically, emotionally and spiritually ourselves, while stimulating our counselees to do likewise!

From our study of symptoms, we have discovered that the variety of ways in which we punish others and especially ourselves is staggering! We have also discovered that although most emotional symptoms are probably caused by wounds and scars resulting from faulty parental programming, some may be the consequence of allergic reactions to particular foods and chemicals. This may be especially true in the case of chronic psychotic symptoms occurring later in life or after suffering some physiological trauma. Thus, as counselors, we realize the importance of relying on and completely trusting in the Holy Spirit to reveal the source of a counselee's problems and then to direct us in the healing process of this individual as Jesus accomplishes the work. To aid in remembering and categorizing the extensive list of symptoms of pathological behavior, an outline is given in **Table 6**.

C. THE PERSONAL SPIRIT.

Having studied at length the psychological and even some of the physiological effects of the environment on the development of the soul, the question arises as to what role, if any, the spirit of man plays in soul development. Secular behaviorists have long been interested in studying the psyche of man, a Greek word meaning "soul." But few of them even mention the spirit of man, let alone understand the personal spirit well enough to discuss its purpose in man's life. As "instruments" of the Holy Spirit, the truth concerning the purpose and functions of the personal spirit has been revealed to us. "I thank you, Father, that you have hid these things from the wise and intelligent and have revealed them to babes" (Luke 10:21).

According to Genesis 2:7, the personal spirit is the breath of God's life within man; without it, the body and soul would not be alive. "Then the Lord God" '...breathed into his nostrils the breath of life; and man became a living thing.'" Thus, the spirit of man might be thought of as the "energizing force" which gives life to the soul and the body, comparable to the battery which turns on a flashlight or the electricity which lights up a light bulb.

1. FUNCTIONS OF PERSONAL SPIRIT.

Sandford, in his book, *Healing the Wounded Spirit*, lists what he believes to be nine of the many functions of the personal spirit, the ***first*** being to enable us to worship, that is, to feel the anointing of the Lord in a worship service and to enter into His presence. "God is spirit, and those who worship Him must worship in spirit and in truth" (John 4:24).

The personal spirit's ***second*** function is to make it possible for us to commune with God in an intimate way, to bask in His love and to comprehend His Word. "The unspiritual man does not receive the gifts of the Spirit of God, for they are folly to him, and he is not able to understand them because they are spiritually discerned" (1 Cor. 2:14 RSV).

The personal spirit's ***third*** task is to enable us to hear and receive guidance from God through the small, inner voice and other revelations of the Holy Spirit, such as visions, dreams, etc., while the ***fourth*** is to give us the ability to receive inspiration so that we can think creatively and come up with original ideas. The ***fifth*** function of the spirit is to make it possible for us to transcend time, i.e., to remember and relive happy memories of the past and to dream about the wonderful plans God has for us in the future.

Enabling us to communicate with others by empathizing, i.e., identifying with them and feeling what they feel, is the ***sixth*** responsibility of the personal spirit. The ***seventh*** is to create the glory of marital sexual union, bringing a couple into an intimate and precious "knowing" of one another, as their spirits flow out to each other. The ***eighth*** duty of the spirit is to help us sustain and overcome illness. "The spirit of a man can endure his sickness, But as for a broken spirit who can bear it?" (Prov. 18:14). "A joyful heart is good medicine, but a broken spirit dries up the bones" (Prov. 17:22). Proving the validity of this scripture, a secular book describes how a man laughed his way back to health by watching old slapstick movies!

I have had much experience with this spiritual function as I have endured much physical suffering. The most graphic experience that I can recall occurred one evening when I was lying on my bed in pain, and my spirit, having completely separated from my body, soared above me, rejoicing and praising God! I know that when I feel my spirit waning, it is a warning that I will sink into self-pity and depression if I do not immediately ask Jesus to strengthen and breathe His life into my spirit so that it will remain light and buoyant!

2. DISORDERS OF PERSONAL SPIRIT.

The ***ninth*** responsibility of the personal spirit is to provide us with a conscience which works before the event to keep us out of trouble, not just afterwards to make us aware of sin. After counseling many people who, even though they were born again and filled with the Spirit, did not seem to be able to walk righteously in the Lord, the Sandfords asked God, "Why don't these people have a working conscience?" The Lord answered that they did not have an alert, functioning personal spirit; their personal spirit was "slumbering."

He revealed that if a baby does not receive enough warm, loving, human touch, his spirit will "fall asleep" because it has not been drawn forth to function. As will be discussed later, studies have shown that babies even die from lack of touch, probably because their spirits have been "starved." Rocking, cuddling, fondling, and nuzzling all nurture, awaken, and draw forth an infant's spirit to fullness of life.

Thus, we can understand why the parental pattern of passive rejection is the most damaging to a Child's soul. The lack of touch and interaction with the youngster ensure that the needs of his spirit are not being met. So, instead of drawing his child's spirit forth to life which would energize his soul, the passively rejecting parent, by withholding the touching and affection that is vital for a spirit's healthy development, causes it to wither, "putting it to sleep."

As counselors, we should suspect that counselees have a slumbering spirit if they are unable to feel the anointing and presence of God, if reading the Word is mechanical and unexciting to them and if they never have any revelations or "rhema" words from the Lord. A few meaningful questions will tell us whether a person thinks creatively, is able to empathize with another individual, and if his conscience warns him before he acts or if he just feels remorse afterwards. Of course, we must keep in mind that none of our spirits are fully awake; they are all slumbering to some extent, more in some areas than in others.

Sandford also describes the condition of "spiritual imprisonment" which the Lord revealed often occurs when a person experiences overwhelming trauma in the womb. As a result, his Inner Child may rebel and turn away from life, not wanting to risk leaving the security of the womb, causing this person to remain "spiritually imprisoned in the womb." The Lord also revealed that, in like manner, an individual experiences dyslexia when his Inner Child rebels in the womb and forces his Adult to make the decision not to be born emotionally. As a result, the spirit of this person has "turned around and is now residing in his body backwards!"

One other strange revelation given to Sandford concerning homosexuals seems to belong in this section on the personal spirit since one of the functions of the spirit concerns sexual relations. God explained to Sandford that He created each of us to possess both a male and female pole. Men develop mainly in the male sphere but also have a female nature which their mates help develop. Women, likewise, have a male nature which their husbands fulfill when they "become one flesh." The Lord said that He revealed this in Gen. 1:27 which states, "...male and female He created them" instead of "...male ***or*** female He created them."

In the case of homosexuals, our Creator disclosed that, due to prenatal trauma or a sinful experience, these poles have become reversed. Studies have shown that most homosexuals were molested or involved in some sexual encounter early in childhood. Thus, it is highly probable that the male and female poles became reversed at this time. After his male and female poles have become reversed, a person struggles with strong sexual desires toward individuals of the same sex.

Although these revelations may seem strange and peculiar to us, and we may not fully comprehend what they really mean, we must remember that "...God's ways are not our ways" (Isa. 55:8). If we, as counselors, realize this and remain completely open-minded and teachable, the Holy Spirit will impart to us "...the treasures of darkness and the hidden wealth of secret places" (Isa.45:3) because "...He will guide us into all truth" (John 16:13).

Thus, a counselee's spirit may be slumbering, imprisoned, wounded and bruised, or his sexual poles may be reversed due to the rejection, abuse, neglect, and trauma which his soul suffered in utero or during his formative years. The exciting news is that the Lord Jesus, through the process of soul healing, can repair all of the damage which a person's soul has sustained, freeing his spirit to perform with fullness of life in each of its duties!

3. CONDITION OF PERSONAL SPIRIT.

Our first and foremost concern as counselors should be the eternal condition of the spirits of our counselees. Without question, the eternal state of their spirits is, of course, significantly more important than the state of their souls or bodies. As we all know, they can enter heaven with crippled and scarred souls and bodies and with slumbering and imprisoned spirits, but not with spirits that have not been cleansed by the blood of Jesus from all the stains of sin. "I have decided to deliver such a one to Satan for the destruction of the flesh (soul and body) that his spirit may be saved in the day of the Lord Jesus" (1 Cor. 5:5).

a. SALVATION. Therefore, before beginning the process of soul healing, a counselor must make sure that his counselee has received Jesus Christ as his personal Savior and Lord. In rare cases, the Spirit may lead the counselor to ask Jesus to do some healing first so that the counselee might experience God's unconditional love. Generally, though, the counselor can begin by explaining that because the first couple God created disobeyed Him, the intimate relationship they had shared with Him was broken. Consequently, all men are now born into this state which we call spiritual death. "For as through the one man's disobedience the many were made sinners, even so through the obedience of the One the many will be made righteous" (Rom. 5:19).

The "One" referred to is, of course, God's Own Son, Jesus Christ, Who, as the "spotless Lamb," was nailed to the cross where He shed His precious blood so that the sins of all mankind might be forgiven! Hallelujah! "...all things are cleansed with blood, and without shedding of blood there is no forgiveness" (Heb. 9:22). "And there is salvation in no one else; for there is no other name (than Jesus) under heaven that has been given among men by which we must be saved" (Acts 4:12).

Thus, the Son of God Himself bridged the gap between sinful man and holy God, restoring to man the possibility of having the intimate relationship with God that Adam's sin had broken. The counselor may then explain that the counselee may have this intimate relationship with God himself, in addition to the free gift of eternal life with Him, simply by asking Jesus to forgive his sins, come into his heart and take complete control of his life. "For as in Adam all die, so also in Christ all shall be made alive" (1 Cor. 15:22 NSA 1977). "God so loved the world, that He gave His only begotten Son, that whoever believes in Him should not perish, but have eternal life" (John 3:16).

After explaining that he must choose of his own free will whether he wishes to accept God's gift or not, the counselor may then ask him for his decision. If he agrees to receive Jesus as his own personal Savior, the counselor may lead him in a prayer similar to the following one:

"Dear Lord, forgive me for all of my sins.
I thank you for dying for me and shedding your
priceless blood upon the cross. I invite you
to come into my heart and be my personal Lord
and Savior. I surrender my life to You and ask
You to help me follow You. Make me into the
kind of person You want me to be. In Jesus'
name, I thank You."

The counselor should then reassure the counselee that if he has sincerely asked Jesus to save him and take control of his life, He has done just that. "If you confess with your mouth Jesus as Lord and believe in your heart that God raised Him from the dead, you shall be saved" (Rom. 10:9). He should, however, be warned that Satan may try to burden him with guilt over his past sins and tell him that he is not worthy to receive salvation. He may be instructed to bind the evil one's lies if this occurs and to inform him that Jesus "...did not come to call the righteous, but sinners" (Matt. 9:13).

Many of us, especially those who have been raised by legalistic and judgmental parents, have great difficulty comprehending God's unconditional love and forgiveness because our parents' love felt so conditional. We felt approved and loved by our parents when our behavior was perfect. So, it is hard for us to believe that our heavenly Father does not wait for us to change, but He forgives us while we are yet sinning.

Lawrence E. Nielsen, Ph.D., in his book, *The Liberation of the Soul: An Introduction to Biblical Psychology*, relates that he had been a teacher in a Bible college for 15 years before the real meaning of God's unconditional forgiveness dawned on him. He lived under a cloud of guilt that he was not doing enough for the Lord and finally began to despair of serving Him at all. But one afternoon when he was feeling depressed, "heaven broke loose on his soul," and he finally understood that he was loved, accepted and forgiven just as he was, even if he never did another thing for the Lord! It is so hard to grasp the true significance of God's unconditional love and forgiveness!

A counselee may well ask, "If I have been saved and born again, do I still need soul healing?" To answer this correctly, we need to understand that salvation has two dimensions: ***eternal*** and ***temporal***. From an eternal perspective he is saved—body, soul and spirit, as his "old nature" was crucified with Christ on the cross almost 2000 years ago! From a time-perspective, he is saved only in his spirit. His soul must go through a "death and resurrection" process before he will be able to experience the "salvation" of his soul in the temporal dimension. Thus, during the process of sanctification, "...our inner man is being renewed day by day" (2 Cor. 4:16). "That I may know Him and the power of His resurrection and the fellowship of His sufferings, being conformed to His death" (Phil. 3:10).

Jesus won back for us on the cross everything that Satan stole from all mankind through Adam. Thus, from an eternal perspective, the Holy Spirit's work of sanctifying our souls is already accomplished, and it is as though we were already in heaven. Although this is hard for us to comprehend, God is continually urging us to see our souls by faith from an eternal perspective. "While we look not at the things which are seen, but at the things which are not seen; for the things which are seen are temporal, but the things which are not seen are eternal" (2 Cor. 4:18). This concept will be discussed further when we study the blood covenant.

Thus, the counselee may be told that as he totally surrenders his soul to the Lord, allowing Him to bring it to death and resurrection through the soul healing process, his soul will be healed, purged, set free, and "made alive" in Christ ("saved") in the here and now! Therefore, what was accomplished from an eternal perspective through the shed blood of Christ will finally become a reality for him in the temporal dimension. "Work out your salvation with fear and trembling; for it is God who is at work in you, both to will and to work for His good pleasure" (Phil. 2:12,13).

b. BAPTISM OF HOLY SPIRIT. Baptism in water may be explained to the new convert as the outward sign that he believes his body, soul and spirit have been "crucified and resurrected in Christ" and, thus, saved for all eternity. "Therefore, we have been buried with him through baptism into death, in order that as Christ was raised from the dead through the glory of the Father, so we, too, might walk in newness of life. For if we have become united with Him in the likeness of His death, certainly we shall be also in the likeness of His resurrection" (Rom. 6:4,5). He should be encouraged to receive water baptism and also the baptism in the Holy Spirit through which he will receive power to grow spiritually and to daily walk with Jesus.

The counselor may explain to the new believer that the first chapter of Acts tells that Jesus commanded his followers not to leave Jerusalem, but to wait for what the Father had promised. He said that they would be baptized with the Holy Spirit at which time they would receive power to be His witnesses in Israel and to the remotest part of the earth. On the day of Pentecost, they were indeed filled with the Holy Spirit as a violent, rushing wind filled the house and a "tongue of fire" rested on each one! They spoke with other "tongues" as the Spirit gave them utterance, and Peter, who had denied knowing Christ three times, stood up and spoke boldly about Jesus the Nazarene to thousands! Quoting from Joel 2, he said, "And it shall come about in the last days, God says, that I will pour forth of My Spirit upon all mankind, and your sons and your daughters shall prophesy, and your young men shall see visions, and your old men shall dream dreams." (Acts 2:17).

The counselee may be assured that this same power will be his if he simply asks Jesus to baptize him in the Holy Spirit. He may receive it by faith the same way he received salvation. The counselor may lead him in a prayer similar to the following:

> *"Dear Jesus, I do believe that You are the baptizer in the Holy Spirit and that You wish to give this gift to me. I ask You to cleanse me from all unrighteousness and to baptize me in the Holy Spirit right now. Thank You for filling me with Your Spirit and giving me the gift of tongues."*

The counselee may be encouraged to open his mouth by faith and speak out whatever new words or sounds come to him even though it may seem foolish. "For God has chosen the foolish things of the world to shame the wise" (1 Cor. 1: 27). So, speaking in tongues begins with our choosing to humble ourselves and speak, trusting that God will give the utterance, "Open your mouth wide and I will fill it" (Ps. 81:10).

If the counselee does not receive his "prayer language" immediately, he should be assured that he has still received the baptism of the Spirit. "How much more shall your heavenly Father give the Holy Spirit to those who ask Him?" (Luke 11:13). He may be encouraged to relax and just praise and worship God, trusting that as he immerses himself in glorifying the Lord, the gift of tongues will be released within him. People sometimes do not acquire this gift because they are too anxious, trying too hard and not trusting the Lord.

When he obtains his spiritual language, he should be urged to use it often because it is the Spirit in him praying directly to God, bypassing his mind, building him up spiritually, and praying beyond his understanding and ability. "For one who speaks in a tongue does not speak to men, but to God." '...One who speaks in a tongue edifies himself'" (1 Cor. 14:2,4). "The Spirit also helps our weaknesses; for we do not know how to pray as we should, but the Spirit Himself intercedes for us with groanings too deep for words" (Rom. 8:26).

The counselee may be informed that the gifts of the Spirit can now operate in and through his life. The gifts, which the Spirit distributes to each person as He wishes, are "...the word of wisdom, word of knowledge, faith, healing, effecting of miracles, prophesy, discerning of spirits, various kinds of tongues and interpretation of tongues" (1 Cor. 12:1-11). The gifts operate for the benefit of the body of Christ and should be exercised in love according to First Corinthians, Chapter 13.

Although he should earnestly seek the gifts, the counselee may be told that the main purpose of the Spirit is to change him into the image of Christ and to manifest the fruit of the Spirit in him. "The fruit of the Spirit is love, joy, peace, patience, kindness, goodness, faithfulness, gentleness, self-control;" '...If we live by the Spirit, let us also walk by the Spirit'" (Gal. 5:22-26). He must be told that, again, it is his decision to allow the Spirit to accomplish His work of sanctification in him, bringing him to the death of himself. He must relinquish all control, self-sufficiency and pride and become as a little child—totally dependent upon the Spirit.

"Except you become as little children, you cannot enter the kingdom of heaven" (Matt. 18:3). Even though the Adult of an individual may make this decision readily, we have discovered that his Child is really in control and it usually has other ideas—hence, the necessity for soul healing!

The counselee may be informed that it is also the Holy Spirit's function to "...guide us into all truth" (John 16:13) and to "...teach us all things" (John 14:26). Paul states in the second chapter of 1st Corinthians that the Spirit "...searches the depths of God, knows His thoughts, and teaches us the things freely given to us by God." But he goes on to say that the natural man cannot understand the things of the Spirit because they are spiritually appraised. He rebukes the Christian men of Corinth, saying that they are still babes in Christ to whom he cannot give solid food because they are still fleshly and, therefore, would not be able to receive it.

We sometimes wonder why so many Christians cannot perceive God's truth or hear His voice clearly. Paul is saying that until we allow God to burn out our flesh, we cannot hear the still, small voice of the Spirit with any clarity. Thus, the counselee may be told that as long as the Inner Child of an individual is still controlled by parental programming, that person will be unable to perceive things correctly (truth). We might say that his "telephone and power line" to the Spirit is clogged with garbage. As we have noted, the more this person allows the Lord to heal his soul and purge his heart, the more he will be released from the programming of his Internal Parent. This liberation from the Parent will flush the garbage out of his "direct line" to the Spirit so that his Adult will be able to perceive and understand the truth which the Spirit is attempting to reveal to him.

Therefore, the counselee should be encouraged to open his heart to the healing of the Lord so that the "eyes of his heart might be enlightened," freeing him from the destructive blindness that resides therein. He must be warned, however, that the Spirit is very sensitive—He will not go anywhere He is not invited. The Word of God tells us "...not to quench the Spirit" (1 Thess. 5:19). He is quenched when we do not give him our souls and allow Him to heal, liberate, guide, and enlighten us. The counselee should be urged to depend upon the Holy Spirit, rather than man, for understanding and enlightenment, for He will give him far more that is relevant to his life than he can ever receive from man. Counselees who desire to learn more about the Spirit and His gifts can be referred to the excellent book, *Holy Spirit, My Senior Partner,* written by David Yonggi Cho.

c. LIBERATION FROM OCCULT. People get involved in the occult because they are searching for the love which they never received, for the reason for their existence or for a source of power to provide them with guidance, healing and quick solutions to their problems. As we know, God and Satan are the only two sources of power, hidden knowledge, guidance, and healing. Desperate for answers and power, many people who get involved in occult practices do not know that the real source of their guidance and power is Satan.

For example, my husband and I got involved in "Transcendental Meditation" about twenty-two years ago while we were still just "traditional" Christians. We bought the lie that it was just a "scientific" method to help people relieve stress and renew their energy. Since I had been suffering from extreme fatigue due to physical problems, Satan easily snared me with the "promise" of increased strength. Before we could receive the promised "gift," we were required to go through a short ceremony "honoring" the Maharishi, during which I felt extremely uncomfortable. I refused to bow before his picture, thinking that I could just get the "scientific" method without getting involved in whatever else was going on.

Although my husband was never able to actually "meditate," I will have to admit that "meditating" was an enjoyable and uplifting experience. I believe that God protected us from all of the demonic effects of our actions because He knew that we were ignorant of the facts and that we loved, honored and worshipped Him as the one true God. About a year later, we received the baptism of the Holy Spirit and God began revealing the truth about Transcendental Meditation to us. Sadly, many traditional churches are so dead spiritually and so ignorant about Satan's schemes that it is easy for their members to fall into the evil one's traps.

An interesting footnote to this story is that many times when I feel "totaled," as I lay my head back, I just seem to drop off into another "dimension." The Spirit (or more probably, an angel) puts me into a sort of "trance-like state" in which I am completely "gone," although I am able to hear things going on around me. I would describe this condition as similar to being in a coma, although I am sure I could come out of it if I had to. After about an hour, I "awake" from this "comatose state," feeling absolutely refreshed and energized. I believe this "fill-up" is a blessing which the Lord gives me because this type of ministry is very draining, so He gives me the "lift" I need to keep going. It is exciting to know that God always has something better to give us in exchange for every counterfeit "gift" with which Satan tries to trap us!

Since occult activities are so widespread in our day, every counselee should always be asked if he has ever been involved with the occult in any way. Following is a list of occult media through which Satan and his demons give supernatural revelation, guidance and power:

Astrology	Fortune-telling	Levitation
Witchcraft	Satan Worship	Colorology
Séances	Ouija Boards	Sorcery
E.S.P.	Palmistry	Divination
Telepathy	Phrenology	Astral Projection
Clairvoyance	Tea Leaves	Dungeons & Dragons
Tarot Cards	Talismans	Yoga Meditation
Parapsychology	Numerology	Transcendental Meditation
Crystals	Automatic Writing	Channeling
Pendulum Healing	Devil's Pentagram	Black Arts
I Ching	Reincarnation	Rosicrucianism
	Scientology & (all other cults)	

NOTE: *This list is, by no means, exhaustive as there are so many occult practices today.*

The counselee should be informed that God's Word forbids men to participate in any occult practices, called "abominations" by God (Deut. 18: 9-12). Demonic oppression, subjection and possession are the penalties which those who dabble in the realm of the occult will inevitably suffer. The necessity of confessing the specific sins of his occult involvement and asking the forgiveness of his merciful Father must be emphasized. Confession exposes the strategy by which Satan held him in bondage so that the evil one can no longer continue his work of oppression and confusion. "He who conceals his transgressions will not prosper, but he who confesses and forsakes them will find compassion" (Prov. 28:13).

Since he opened the door and granted the devil access to his life through occult involvement, the counselee must now renounce Satan, command him to depart and break any pact he might have made with him, knowingly or unknowingly. The counselor may lead him in a direct command to Satan similar to the following:

> "Satan, I renounce all involvement which I
> have had with you in the past, and I command you
> to depart from my life in the name of Jesus. By
> the blood of Jesus, I break any pact or agreement
> that I made with you, and I claim back any
> part of my soul which I may have given to you.
> I bind all of your activities and cancel all of
> your assignments against me in the powerful name
> of Jesus Christ! I plead the blood of Jesus
> over me to protect me."

The counselor should break any curse which may have come upon the counselee in the following manner: *"I put the sin of witchcraft (state the occult activities in which the person participated) upon the cross of Jesus. I place the cross between John and Satan and break any curse that may have come upon him from his involvement in this sin. Forgive John and cleanse him from all of the effects of his sin with Your precious blood, Jesus."* If other generations of his family were also involved in the occult, generation curses (described under the next topic) will have to be broken also.

The need to close all doors through which Satan might have gained access must be emphasized. Therefore, the counselee should be directed to destroy all occult objects, charms and literature which he might still possess. "Many also of those who had believed kept coming, confessing, and disclosing their practices, and many of those who practiced magic brought their books together and began burning them in the sight of all" (Acts

19:18,19). To keep the doors closed, the necessity of growing spiritually and walking in the will of God according to His Word cannot be overemphasized.

4. HERITAGE OF PERSONAL SPIRIT.

Our discussion on the spirit of man and the part it plays in the development of the soul would not be complete if we did not include a section on the spiritual heritage which is a part of every person who is born into the world. Just as each of us inherits certain physical and emotional characteristics, so we also inherit certain spiritual blessings or curses.

a. GENERATION CURSES. As we have seen, there are innumerable ways by which we bring curses upon ourselves. The most common way is, of course, through our sins. "For the one who sows to his own flesh shall from the flesh reap corruption" (Gal. 6:8). We have also discovered that even as small children, when we judge our parents, we receive curses "...in that our lives will not go well for us and we will die young" (Deut. 5:16). Also, the "...standard of measure by which we judged will be measured back to us" (Matt. 7:1,2). We have seen that many of our parents pronounced judgments or word curses against us which we accepted and believed and continued to pronounce against ourselves.

Unfortunately, when we die, our sins do not die with us. In Gen. 22:18, God said that He would bless all the nations of the earth through the seed of Abraham because of his obedience. Just as our seed is blessed by our obedience, it is cursed by our disobedience. "I, the Lord, your God, am a jealous God visiting the iniquity of the fathers on the children, and on the third and fourth generations of those that hate Me" (Deut. 5:9).

Thus, whatever sins we do not repent of, our descendants must keep on reaping generation after generation. So, however unfair it may seem, we are born into this world with, for the most part, either blessings or curses as part of our spiritual heritage. Since our world is so infested with sin, most of us inherit more curses than blessings at our births. Lest we be too quick to judge this as unfair of God, we should remember that we have also inherited, without any merit on our part, many blessings from our forefathers as a whole. The list is endless—electricity, cars, television, art, music, etc. Shall we say then that it is unfair of God to let us reap the curses of our ancestors' sins, but not their blessings? God is more than fair in that He allowed His precious Son to suffer the agonizing death due to us because of our sins. He has made every provision for us through Jesus' cross and spotless blood—a fact of which most Christians are ignorant. "My people are destroyed for lack of knowledge" (Hosea 4:6).

So, we see how important it is for a counselor to diligently seek to discover, not only the curses under which a counselee is laboring due to his parental upbringing, but also those which are part of his spiritual heritage. Asking specific questions about family members—parents, grandparents, aunts, uncles—regarding divorces, addictions, occult involvement, etc., will help disclose the particular curses which a counselee has inherited.

As the counselee describes his family history, destructive patterns will begin to emerge which appear to be descending through the generations. Some examples of these descending patterns are: addiction to alcohol; drugs; food; divorce; suicide; illness; accidents; financial problems; physical and emotional abuse; molestation; sexual perversion; lust for power, money, sex, fame; closed wombs; habitual lying; stealing; phobias; occult involvement; insanity—to name just a few of the obvious ones. If any of these tragedies occur in succeeding generations, a curse upon the family should be suspected.

In *my* own family, my dad's father left his productive farm in Nebraska because he was "convinced" that he would strike it rich in New York. Instead, he lost everything. Continuing this harmful pattern, my father was forced to file bankruptcy and is now penniless due to his "conviction" (delusion) that he could "get rich quick" by investing in oil. My youngest brother joined my father in his oil business and came close to having to declare bankruptcy also. My other brother, subconsciously following the destructive pattern of the family, became a broker in the high-risk commodities market.

Since my husband and I broke this curse over my family, this brother is no longer a broker and is looking for an even more secure job than the one which he acquired after quitting the commodities market. The Lord has also provided my youngest brother with a secure job so that he no longer has to depend solely upon the oil business for financial survival. So, we have seen the power of the authority which we have in Jesus to break family curses even when the recipients were not aware of what was taking place!

Whether or not anyone in his family has ever been involved in the occult should routinely be asked of every counselee. God says, "...I will set My face against that person and will cut him off from among his people" (Lev. 20:6). Without delay, the law begins to operate and succeeding generations reap many ways of being cut off, perhaps through tragic deaths among the males or no males being born. Whatever shape it takes–whether deaths, divorces, financial disaster, etc.,–even the spiritually uninformed seem to recognize that there is a curse on these families!

b. LIBERATION FROM GENERATION CURSES. During soul healing prayer, God will reveal any generation curses which a counselee's family are under that were not discovered through questioning. As counselors, we must break these generation curses and put destructive family patterns to death on the cross of Christ. A counselor can accomplish this task by stating that he is placing the cross between a counselee and his parents with the authority Jesus has given him. He then declares that he is putting certain sins of these parents on the cross and asking God to forgive and cleanse them of these sins.

He states that he is placing the cross between the counselee's father and his parents, between them and their parents and so on, back through the generations repeating the same procedure for his mother's family. He then breaks the curses resulting from these sins and asks Jesus to cleanse the bloodlines of both sides of the counselee's family from these curses and all of their effects with His precious blood. "Behold, I have given you authority '... over all the power of the enemy, and nothing shall injure you'" (Luke 10:19).

For example, if alcoholism has destroyed many members on the father's side of a counselee's family, a counselor can pray, *"With the authority Jesus has given me according to Luke 10:19, I place His cross between John and his father. I put the sin of alcoholism upon the cross and ask You, Father, to forgive and cleanse John's father and ances-*

tors of this sin. I put the cross between John's father and his parents, between them and their parents, and so on back through the generations. I break the curse of alcoholism from this family so that it may not be passed on to John or his descendants, and I ask You, Lord, to cleanse the family bloodlines of this curse and all of its effects with Jesus' spotless blood." The counselor may then bind the demon of alcoholism and break any hold which it has on any member of John's family. He may ask his heavenly Father to send angels to bring each one out of darkness into His light.

The Sandfords claim that they have received countless testimonies from people who have seen all of the members of their family set free after breaking generation curses. Thus, they believe this is one of the most important keys which God has revealed since it gives us the power and authority to set families free in Jesus' name!

Part II.

DEATH *of the* SOUL

Our study of soul development has shown us that many, if not most, of our souls have been bruised and scarred as a result of our negative developmental histories. Thus, we recognize the great need for soul healing among the many wounded soldiers in Christ's army.

You may ask, "Why do we need this soul healing stuff? Can't God just heal us instantly?" Of course–He can and often does heal us instantly of some emotional hurts; otherwise, many of us would be in mental hospitals! But He does not usually choose, although He can, of course, to heal us of all the wounds of our past instantly. If He did, we would be "spoiled" and would probably not retain our healing since we would take it for granted.

As parents, we do not give our children everything they want instantly because our overindulgence would prevent them from maturing. So, our Father, in His infinite wisdom, deals with our hearts gently one layer at a time, like peeling the layers of an onion. He alone knows which hurts a person's Child is ready to give up and at what time. The Holy Spirit is a "gentleman," and just as He does not force salvation or the baptism of the Spirit on us, neither does He force emotional healing on us.

Since soul healing is usually a slow, gradual, step-by-step process, the enormity of the task should not be underestimated. The counselee must be set free from the unforgiveness, judgments, vows, and curses which make up the script which his Child is still acting out in response to the control of his Parent. Only after this death of his soul (self), will his Adult be uncontaminated enough and strong enough to allow God to "rewrite his script" with His love and truth, causing his soul to be resurrected in Christ.

Since the counselee's Child is controlled by much fear, anger, hatred, guilt, etc., and has built many walls (defenses) to protect the counselee from further pain, we can see that the task of the counselor is magnanimous! But, although our job as counselors is often painstakingly slow, requiring endless patience, our comfort lies in the fact that we are only vessels and that the real work is accomplished by the Holy Spirit. We are only required to be obedient and trust that the Spirit will work through us in whatever way He chooses!

As God's vessels of healing and deliverance, I believe our mandate from Him is stated in Isaiah 61:1-3:

> "The Spirit of the Lord God is upon me,
> Because the Lord has anointed me
> To bring good news to the afflicted:
> He has sent me to bind up the brokenhearted,
> To proclaim liberty to captives,
> And freedom to prisoners;
> To proclaim the favorable year of the Lord,
> And the day of vengeance of our God;
> To comfort all who mourn,
> To grant those who mourn in Zion,
> Giving them a garland instead of ashes,
> The oil of gladness instead of mourning,
> The mantle of praise instead of a spirit of fainting.
> So, they will be called oaks of righteousness,
> The planting of the Lord, that He may be glorified."

A. SUBSTITUTE PARENT.

In order to be used by God as the instrument through whom He "binds up the brokenhearted and proclaims liberty to the captive," a counselor must first develop a relationship of trust based on love with his counselee. He accomplishes this by becoming the vessel which God uses to provide the love and unconditional acceptance which the counselee's parents could or would not provide. In this role of "substitute parent," a counselor seeks, in a small way, to become the encouraging, loving, supportive, nurturing, dependable, and understanding parent which the counselee never had.

1. DEATH TO SELF.

Since, as a substitute parent, a counselor becomes the "bridge" which takes the counselee to his heavenly Father, he must ask himself, "How well can my counselee see Jesus in me?" To become a sturdy, strong bridge, a counselor must develop his own intimate love relationship with God and walk in His righteousness and truth. He must have an awareness and understanding of himself, allowing the Holy Spirit to continually heal, cleanse, purge, deliver, sanctify, and transform him into the image of Jesus (1 Pet. 5:10).

Since the goal of soul healing is crucifixion of the soul-man and resurrection in Jesus, a counselor cannot help a person reach this goal unless he himself has gone the "...way of the cross" (Matt. 16:26). If he tries to take a shortcut, his ministry will soon crumble because Satan has legal rights to attack him due to the "holes in his hedge."

If a counselor has not resolved his own childhood conflicts and his motives are not pure and his attitudes right, Satan will gain a foothold through what psychology calls "countertransference." The words and actions, or even just the presence, of a counselee may activate attitudes and feelings in the counselor's Inner Child that developed during his childhood interactions with his parents. Thus, his Child becomes hooked, and he will react to the counselee as if the counselee was his parent. Feeling the same hostility and rejection he once felt toward his parent, the counselor may transfer these feelings onto his counselee.

Also, any area of a counselor's heart which is still unrepentant will attract counselees with that same area of sin. For example, if a counselor has lust in his heart, even though it is repressed, Satan has permission to bring him counselees with similar lustful spirits. Because they have similar spirits, there will be constant transference of demons between them, and the counseling cannot progress. "Hedge-holes, which allow demons to "bounce back and forth," are probably the reason many deliverance ministries are short-lived.

Dying to his flesh will also ensure that a counselor will not fall into the deadly trap of self-idolatry. According to Sandford, the "kingdom of self" lies at the core of us all. In *Healing the Wounded Spirit*, he states:

> "At the core of us is something so evil it cannot be healed, only slain. There is a ruling center so devious as to allow us to role-play all the actions of surrender to God, or service and love to others, without ever allowing itself to be detected, much less put to death.
>
> We are jealous of Jesus Who was elevated to be Lord of all. We are full of striving, therefore, to establish the kingdom of self, none more so than those who have learned the secret of service to others. How better to play God?" (pgs. 364-365).

Self-idolatry produces no fruit—nothing but dead works—because all of our works for the Lord are filled with self-glorification, no matter how much we protest that we give Him all of the glory. The insidiousness of this sin is that we all truly believe we have been through this death of the self. But few of us have. There are many levels, many nailings of our flesh to the cross before the final crucifixion and the resurrection of our soul in Jesus is accomplished.

As counselors, we must humble ourselves and allow God to take us all the way to the cross—no matter how painful—and to help us "...deny ourselves and lose our lives for Christ's sake"

(Matt. 16:24-26). The end result—a circumcised heart—is worth the pain and sacrifice because it will bear much fruit. As counselors, we cannot lead our counselees along the "via dolorosa" unless we have first walked the path. As Kathryn Kuhlmann said in her dramatic way during one of her last appearances, "I can tell you the hour and the minute when Kathryn Kuhlmann died... it cost me *eeeverything*!!"

Since a dead person does not feel or desire anything, idealistically, true death to ourselves means that we will no longer feel any anger, hurt, jealousy, pride, etc. We will no longer be selfish or self-centered, nor will we insist on getting our own way, because we have laid all our rights, expectations, needs, and desires on the altar. If self is truly dead, we will not "be jealous, arrogant, brag, seek our own way, get provoked, or take into account a wrong suffered; that is, we will hardly notice when we are done wrong" (1 Cor. 13:4-8).

We will "be of the same mind, maintaining the same love, united in spirit, intent on one purpose, doing nothing from selfishness or empty conceit, but with humility of mind, we will regard the other person as more important than ourselves, and we will look out not only for our own personal interests, but for the interests of others" (Phil. 2:2-4).

Thus, although a counselor should diligently seek the operation of the gifts of the Spirit in his ministry, the development of the fruit of the Spirit—love, joy, peace, patience, kindness, goodness, faithfulness, gentleness, self-control (Gal. 5:22-26) is vital because the "gifts profit us nothing if we have not love" (1 Cor. 13). A dedicated counselor fears God and desires and relentlessly seeks to become a pure vessel through whom the love and power of the Holy Spirit can flow to the counselee. The Spirit's perfect love then begins to melt his heart and heal the hurts in his Child, and the counselee begins to realize how special and precious he is to God.

2. COMMUNICATION SKILLS.

a. LISTENING AND EMPATHIZING. Thus, as a loving substitute parent, a counselor realizes that his first task is to focus his full attention on actively and attentively listening to his counselee.

Often, it is the first time anyone has ever cared enough about him to actually listen to him with sensitivity and understanding. The counselee will see the compassion of Jesus in the eyes of his counselor as he empathizes with his pain.

A well-trained counselor will empathize, not sympathize, with his counselee. He will "experience," "get into," and "feel" the pain of his counselee, but he will not feel sorry for him. Sympathy does not bring healing because it reinforces self-pity and excuses the counselee from working on the root causes of his behavior. Also, empathy allows the counselor to "experience" the pain while remaining objective, while sympathy pulls him into emotional involvement, which endangers his ability to remain unbiased.

b. DRAWING OUT FEELINGS. As he shares in his counselee's pain, a counselor will help him uncover and identify deep feelings which he may have repressed and denied due to their threatening nature. Helping a counselee express their feelings is often difficult because most of us were raised by parents who did not know how to recognize and communicate feelings; nor did they allow us to express any emotions. They certainly were not aware of the necessity of dealing with feelings, rather than repressing and denying them. Instead of drawing out our feelings when we became angry, they usually sent us to our rooms with the saying, "Children should be seen and not heard," ringing in our ears!

Thus, as counselors, just as we must receive healing of our own childhood conflicts and scars before we can assist others with theirs, so we must also learn how to identify and communicate our own feelings before we can help others recognize and share theirs. Learning how to express our *feelings*, rather than our judgments and opinions, takes a tremendous amount of effort and dedication.

Even before we received the baptism in the Spirit, my husband and I learned how to discover and express our feelings on a deep, intimate level by using the Marriage Encounter technique called "dialogue." Every day for eight months, we answered a specific question pertinent to our lives by describing our feelings in the form of a love letter to each other. In the evenings, we exchanged our love letters and worked on sharing our feelings until we could both deeply "experience" the other person's emotions. To describe a feeling, we used examples from nature, physical sensations, objects, or past experiences to which the other person could relate.

For instance, using an example from nature, my husband described how insecure he felt after receiving the baptism in the Spirit. He shared that he felt like a young sparrow about to leave the nest. He felt secure, protected, confident, and enthusiastic in the nest (our fellowship) because he was surrounded by the love and acceptance of his brothers and sisters. But when he tried to leave the familiar environment of the nest, he felt scared, vulnerable, unprepared, and unstable. He felt like he was flying aimlessly in unfamiliar territory without any sense of direction. He felt rudderless—like he had nothing to guide or govern his course and like he was groping for something to stabilize him.

Counselors who wish to gain experience getting in touch with and expressing feelings can also practice communicating their emotions in the form of love letters written to their mates or to God. They can ask the Spirit to uncover, bring to the surface and help them describe their deepest feelings by using experiences from their past, everyday objects or examples from nature. As counselors, this exercise prepares us to be able to draw out the feelings of our counselees more effectively.

Dr. Gary Smalley and John Trent, Ph.D., have written a captivating book, called *The Language of Love*, in which they describe "word pictures" as communication tools which activate both the intellect and the emotions of a person, helping him to "experience" another person's words, not just hear them. They relate that our response to a word picture is like driving into a fog. When we encounter thick fog, we become instantly alert, straining to see what lies ahead. In like manner, an emotional word picture forces us to strain mentally to see what lies behind the images it portrays. The "fog lifts" when we "break out" into a clear understanding of what emotions or concepts are being communicated. Smalley and Trent give many poignant illustrations of word pictures in their book, including one hundred and one examples which they have gathered over the years.

One example concerned a woman who felt unappreciated and neglected by her husband after many years of marriage. Using an object, she compared herself to a beautiful, leather-bound, gold-trimmed book which was presented to her husband at their wedding as a gift from God. At first, she was cherished, shared with others and handled with care. But as time passed, she was put on the shelf to gather dust. How she wished that her husband would take her off the shelf, dust her off and open her up again!

Using an example from nature, another person shared that he felt like a hamster in a maze of hills and dark holes, weary from wrong turns and dead ends. He was scared that he might never make it out of the maze. He felt like people were watching him; some would encourage him, while others would make fun of his plight. He often did tricks to try and amuse these people, but he never felt like he was one of them.

Thus, word pictures are effective tools which can help counselees get in touch with their emotions. As counselors, we can help draw out the feelings of our counselees most effectively by describing objects or situations to which they can relate. For instance, a counselor may know that his counselee, feeling deeply hurt and rejected by her husband, is now lavishing her unrequited love on her beautiful German Shepherd. He might ask her to picture with him her dog waiting anxiously all day by the door, just savoring the moment when she would walk through that door, feed him, give him a treat and shower him with all kinds of love and attention.

He might then ask her to imagine how hurt, abused and rejected this faithful, loving dog would feel if his mistress yelled at him, hit him with a stick and kicked him outside with no food or water, instead of loving and nurturing him. The counselor would then ask his counselee if she also feels wounded and abandoned, just as her dog would if she treated him as cruelly as her husband had treated her!

A counselee who is receiving no affection or nurturing from her husband might be asked by her counselor if she feels like a beautiful rose that is wilting, shriveling up and dying from lack of tender loving care. A counselor might ask a young, exhausted, single mother who is trying to meet all of her children's needs if she feels like she is shooting the rapids alone in a canoe, paddling desperately in an attempt to avoid the rocks, first on one side, then on the other. Sometimes her canoe turns completely around, and, occasionally, it even turns upside down and then rights itself again. He might ask her if she feels panicked and scared that she might not make it through to calmer waters!

As counselors, we can ask the Spirit to give us word pictures which will really unlock and accurately depict the emotions which our counselees are experiencing. We know that we have "hit the nail on the head" when they exclaim, "Yes, that's exactly how I feel! How did you know?" We can also encourage our counselees to begin writing love letters to God through which the Spirit will unveil and help them communicate their most intimate feelings in the form of word pictures. They can also be instructed to ask and expect the Lord to write love letters back to them. The prophecy was "birthed" in several of my counselees in this manner.

c. COMMUNICATING CONCEPTS. Not surprisingly, researchers have shown that people remember concepts far longer and much more vividly when a visual aid or a word picture is used. In fact, the more unusual the object or story, the longer the idea is remembered. Thus, using word pictures is a very effective method of locking concepts into a counselee's memory.

Smalley and Trent relate that Corrie ten Boom, a survivor of the Holocaust, always used an object or story to illustrate any point which she wanted her audience to remember. When she spoke before a group, she often held up the back side of a large sample of tapestry. Threads hung every which way, and no clear design could be discerned. "Our lives often look this way," she would say. "When I was in the concentration camp, there was nothing but ugliness, turmoil and disorder. But then I looked to God to make sense out of my world." She would then turn the tapestry piece around, revealing to her listeners an exquisitely woven crown. "He made it clear to me why He added a certain thread or color, no matter how painful the stitching might be!"

When I am facing a difficult situation, the Spirit always reminds me of another story which Corrie told. She had asked her father how they would survive if they were ever taken to a concentration camp because they were helping the Jewish people. He reminded her that when she was a little girl and was going to travel somewhere on the train, he would not give her the ticket until she got on board. He then explained that when the time came for them to go to the concentration camp, her heavenly Father would be right there with her ticket!

We should not be surprised to learn that God invented word pictures and that the Bible contains more examples of them than any other book ever written. For instance, just a few of the word pictures used to describe our Savior are: the Bread of Life, the Light of the World, the Good Shepherd, the Rock of Ages, the Door of the Sheep, the Lamb of God, the Vine, a Grain of Wheat, the Chief Corner Stone, the Lily of the Valley, the Rose of Sharon, the Root of Jesse, a Crown of Beauty, and a Royal Diadem.

Isaiah 40 is replete with word pictures, such as, "Behold the nations are like a drop from a bucket and are regarded as a speck of dust on the scales..." '...It is He who sits above the vault of the earth, and its inhabitants are like grasshoppers, Who stretches out the heavens like a curtain and spreads them out like a tent to dwell in.'" Psalm 91 declares, "He will cover you with His pinions, and under His wings you may seek refuge; His faithfulness is a shield and a bulwark." Psalm 92 states, "They (righteous men) will still yield fruit in old age; they shall be full of sap and very green."

Jesus, of course, understood and took full advantage of the fact that word pictures quickly grasp people's full attention and then cement concepts into their memories forever. His teachings, often called parables, are filled with illustrations taken from everyday tasks with which the Jewish people were familiar, such as, planting, harvesting, fishing, making bread, etc. The word "parable" comes from the Greek word "parabole," which means "a placing beside"—hence, a comparison.

In nine of his parables given in Matthew, Jesus employed word pictures which compared the kingdom of God to the following: a mustard seed, yeast, a pearl of great price, a treasure hidden in a field, a net which caught all kinds of fish, a land owner who hired men to work in a vineyard, ten virgins, a man who gave talents to his servants, and a man who sowed good seed, but weeds came up. We certainly cannot say that our Messiah did not try to explain to us what the kingdom of God was like! Thus, the primary method which Christ used to teach spiritual concepts was through the use of word pictures drawn from objects and tasks common to His brethren. How marvelous if we could be as skillful at using word pictures in our counseling as Jesus was!

d. COMMUNICATING CORRECTION. As counselors, not only can we help our counselees express feelings and remember concepts, but also lovingly correct them by using word pictures. For example, the Bible recounts the emotional word picture with which God instructed Nathan to confront King David concerning his "affair" with Bathsheba and his "arrangement" to have her husband killed in battle. Nathan related to David that there was a rich man and a poor man in a certain city. The rich man had many flocks, but the poor man had only one little lamb. He and his children raised it as a pet, letting it eat their bread, drink out of their cups and sleep on them. A traveler asked the rich man for one of his flock, but he would not part with any of his lambs. Rather he took the poor man's pet lamb and prepared it for the traveler's dinner.

David's anger burned against the rich man as he proclaimed that he deserved to die because he had done this terrible thing and had no compassion. Nathan then stunned David by saying, "You are the man! ..." '...You have struck down Uriah the Hittite with the sword (and) have taken his wife to be your wife'" (2 Sam. 12:7,9). This story convicted King David so mightily that his heart was pierced and he instantly repented! Thus, this graphic word picture forced David to face his sin and also feel some of the emotional pain and trauma that he had caused others.

When I was counseling the parents of rebellious young people at Teen Challenge, my "challenge" was to discover how to lovingly explain to them that God wanted them to quit trying to control their children's behavior and put them in His capable hands. One of the most difficult concepts to explain to counselees is how to take 100 percent of their hands off of people and situations and turn them over to God. All of the parents wanted to "shape up and knock some sense" into their teenagers themselves. The only reason they had come to me was because their methods were not working! I struggled to find ways to tell them, first, that they must love and accept their children unconditionally, and second, that they must "let go and let God."

To help these parents accomplish this task, the Lord advised me to share with them the word picture which He used in the story of the prodigal son. According to this story, the prodigal son's father used great wisdom when his son asked for his share of the estate. I can just imagine the reaction most of us would have if our sons came to us and asked for their inheritances and permission to "go see the country." "Are you kidding?" we would shout! "There's no way I'm going to give you that much money and let you go squander it bumming around the country! Are you crazy? And what makes you think you're old enough to leave home, anyway? Forget it! Hell will freeze over before I will let you leave home with all of that money! And that's my final word!"

The prodigal son's father was wiser than most of us, however. He knows that this particular son would never settle down and do something profitable with his life until he had satisfied his fleshly desires. He also knew that after he had squandered his fortune, he would realize his mistake, repent and come back home. Apparently, this father felt it was worth the price to have a repentant, broken, humbled son. Sounds like he had been asking the Lord for wisdom and guidance instead of trying to handle his son his own way!

I then explained to the parents that, instead of trying to control his son's behavior, this wise father allowed him to make his own choices. He then turned him over to God and trusted that the Almighty would have His way with him. He accepted this son just as he was, although he realized that he would waste all of his money. We know that this father did indeed accept his son unconditionally because, if he had not, he would have been furious when he discovered that he had no money left. Instead, this humble father was overjoyed when his son returned home, penniless, but broken! Most fathers would be too proud to sit around and do nothing while their sons squandered all of their hard-earned money because it would make them look foolish. But this father swallowed his pride and, as a result, God gave him much grace, returning his son to him completely changed!

Using Abraham's story as a word picture, the Spirit then told me to remind these distraught parents that Abraham had also obeyed God when he placed Isaac, the seed of Israel, on the altar. We know that Abraham trusted God completely with Isaac's life since he would have plunged his knife into his son if God had not stopped him. We know the outcome of the story, but Abraham did not. He just had total faith that God would take care of his son if he obeyed Him.

In this same way, God requires all parents to "lay their children's lives on the altar," that is, to let go of their behavior completely and turn them over to Him, trusting Him to bring them to repentance. Parents must learn to take authority in the spiritual realm over demonic forces, rather than in the physical realm over their children by attempting to control their rebellious behavior. They must not try to change, manipulate or dominate their teenagers' behavior because this will literally "tie God's hands," rendering Him unable to fully work in their lives.

Another word picture designed for correction which the Lord gave me to share with these troubled parents is the concept of what occurs when we hold a pile of sand in our hands. If we clench the sand tightly in our fists, it spills out between our fingers, and we will lose most of it. But if we allow the sand to rest lightly on our open palms, most of it will remain. Applied to our teen's behavior, if we "hold onto them tightly," that is, if we control every move they make, they will rebel, and we will lose them. But if we "hold them loosely," that is, if we give them freedom to make their own decisions, we will not lose them.

A word picture depicting this same concept concerns a rider who tries to keep control of his horse by holding his reins too tightly. The pressure of the bit against his mouth will cause the horse to buck and throw off his master. Whereas, this same horse will obey the commands of his master if he holds his reins loosely and gently guides him.

Thus, parents can learn from these word pictures that they are allowed to give their teenagers wisdom, guidance and counsel from the Lord, but they must allow them to make their own decisions. As adults, our heavenly Father gives us wisdom and direction when we ask, but then He allows us to make our own choices. He never forces His will upon us; He allows us to freely choose whether to follow His guidance or not. As parents, He expects us to give our teenagers the same consideration.

The Lord revealed to me a truth concerning the age at which a child should be held responsible for his own behavior. Although the law of our land considers this age to be eighteen, Jewish law declares that a boy who has celebrated the ceremony of "bar mitzvah," occurring immediately after his thirteenth birthday, is now responsible before God for obeying His commands. It is interesting to note that at his son's bar mitzvah, a Jewish father declares, "Blessed be He who frees me from the responsibility of this boy!" Thus, God considers thirteen, the first year of the teens, to be the age at which a child should be allowed to make his own decisions and assume responsibility for them. Most parents will balk at this, but it is truth, nonetheless!

When God allowed my son-in-law to be put in jail on a false charge in order to get his attention, He gave me a corrective word picture to share with him which used an experience from his past. When riding his brother's high-spirited stallion named Buck, Neal would try to dominate him and run him too hard. But this stubborn, strong-willed horse was not named "Buck" without good reason! After he had gotten his fill of Neal's controlling spirit, he would stop short in the path, lower his head and buck his rider off! On one occasion, Buck even plunged down a sharp ravine, throwing Neal forward until he was hanging onto the stallion's neck for dear life, beating his head and screaming at him to stop!

I explained to Neal that he was just like that headstrong horse! God had to break his will and show him who was boss. Like Buck, until his strong will was broken, God could not make him into the "kind of horse" He wanted him to be, for example, a riding, race or work horse. Like Buck, he had to quit "doing his own thing" and start obeying his master's commands. Only then would God be able to develop his full potential in Jesus. Although Neal understood what God was saying to him through this word picture, it took quite a while before he finally gave up trying to "get his Rider off his back!"

Thus, we see that corrective word pictures do not always immediately bring about the results desired. Nevertheless, a counselor should attempt to connect a correction with his counselee's past experiences because this gives him a direct path to this person's emotions. By linking his message with his counselee's past feelings, the counselor's correction is conveyed with much more impact, clarity and vividness. Also, when a counselor uses word pictures to convey corrections, the Inner Child of a counselee does not feel threatened since his counselor is speaking to him in the Adult ego state, rather than the Parent. Since this does not hook his Child, making him feel angry, guilty or defensive, he is able to really listen, get into the story and discover how it applies to him.

Counselees should be encouraged to ask the Spirit to give them word pictures which will appropriately communicate their feelings and thoughts to their mates, children and others. As we shall discover, the Spirit not only imparts suitable word pictures to counselees, but also places actual pictures in their minds during soul healing prayer. These "visions" are used by God not only to help counselees uncover and express their most intimate feelings, but also to reveal truth and heal and cleanse their hearts, thereby setting them free.

One example concerns a counselee who was distressed because she no longer had any passionate feelings for her husband. During soul healing prayer, the Spirit revealed that she was feeling guilt and condemnation concerning a long-past indiscretion. The Spirit then gave her a vision of her heart with a padlock on it. She saw Jesus give her a key and ask her to unlock her heart. When she did so, she saw a vision in which the word "SHAME" had little wings on it and flew away. This meant, of course, that Jesus was healing her of the shame she had carried around for so many years. She immediately felt the burden of guilt and condemnation lift and a deep peace envelop her! Praise God for His marvelous healing touch!

The Spirit then proceeded to give this counselee a picture of herself burning in a fire while her husband kept turning up the flame! The Lord was revealing to her just how she felt about her husband! After she was able to release her hurts to Jesus, she was able to see her husband as a little boy, begging her to let him take her out of the fire and heal her wounds. Indeed, she admitted that her husband had tried many times to do just that, but she had not allowed him to get close to her. Rather, she had turned off her feelings for him and erected many stone walls around her heart. After much healing by the Master, she was finally able to see a picture of her husband's "little boy" lifting her "little girl" out of the flames. She then saw him tending to her wounds while soothing, comforting and nurturing her, thereby healing her deep scars.

e. ORGANIZING INFORMATION. The counselee in the preceding example had received enough healing from Jesus previously to be able to allow the Spirit to reveal her innermost feelings during prayer. However, she did say that she really had to "fight with her little girl," as she put it, to get her to face her hurts and surrender them to her Healer. She was severely tempted to dash out the door, but her desire to get healed and have an intimate relationship with her husband overcame her need to repress "unsafe" experiences and feelings.

Before many counselees get to the place of being able to completely "unlock their hearts," they need assistance not only in discovering and expressing feelings, but also in processing information. While talking about his concerns, the counselee will often avoid information which his Inner Child may have distorted or denied due to its threatening nature. Repression or denial is, as we have seen, not only the most prevalent, but also the most difficult defense to break through.

As he approaches experiences that stir up feelings that threaten his Child, the counselee often becomes anxious, confused or defensive (his Inner Child is hooked by his Internal Parent). Desiring to avoid these unpleasant emotions, he often passes over this unsafe material and quickly goes on to information that is "safe." The discerning counselor, however, recognizes this maneuver, called "resistance" or "blocking," and, in a subtle and gentle manner, helps the counselee bring this unsafe data into awareness.

For example, a shy student might be seeking counseling because of her concern about her recent arguments with her roommate. She might be focusing her attention on discussing her close relationship with her roommate and her admiration for this girl's boyfriend, while vaguely alluding to feelings of envy. Since envy is not an emotion that she can readily accept, the counselor, in a sensitive and delicate way, must help her become aware that her feelings of jealousy toward her roommate may be the source of their arguments.

However, as counselors, we must always be totally tuned in to the Spirit in order to know whether the counselee is "ready" for certain threatening material to be brought into awareness. The more bruised and damaged a counselee is, the more carefully he must be handled. One of my counselors-in-training describes a counselee who is unable to receive truth concerning information that is the slightest bit threatening as "fragile." Just like a fragile vase, care must be taken not to "break" him, so that he will not put up more defenses and remain forever deceived by the distorted perceptions of his Inner Child. Thus, we can see how important it is for the fruit of the Spirit to be "ripened" in a counselor if he is to gently and carefully help his counselee receive the healing and truth that will set him free.

A counselor not only helps bring unsafe material into awareness for his counselee, but he also helps him organize and integrate information in a concise manner. He sorts out, clarifies and interprets data for the counselee and then feeds his insight back to him, often in the form of a question. He induces the counselee to function in the Adult ego state by asking him if he agrees with his conclusions or to choose which of several, he thinks might be correct.

For instance, a young man might be seeking the reason he does not like his job. After organizing and interpreting the information given to him, the counselor might ask, "Do you think the reason you don't like your job might be because your father wanted you to take it? Or perhaps you might be afraid that you can't do it well enough?" If the counselor has interpreted the data given to him accurately, he knows which of these conclusions is correct. But he wants his counselee to come to his own conclusions through processing and interpreting all of the facts in the Adult ego state.

Another example of helpful organization and insightful interpretation of data occurred with a fifty-year-old woman who was feeling upset with her husband. She was trying to understand his reasoning that it would be better to remodel their house after they had saved the money rather than cash in one of their bonds. She also could not understand why she felt depressed even though their business was finally a success after many years of hard work. She still was not happy, even though they had money. She just felt "torn and confused." When the counselor asked her, "Do you think you might feel frustrated and angry because your husband is still saying that someday the two of you are really going to live, even though you finally have enough money to do it now?" She broke down and cried, "Yes, that's it! I feel hopeless—like I will never get to do anything!"

Individuals who received many "double-bind" messages from their parents in childhood have the most difficulty processing information as adults. In double-bind communication, a child receives two messages which are contradictory. He does not know how to respond to these conflicting messages because he "loses" no matter what he does. There is just no way to please his parents!

For example, a mother may say to her daughter, "Please eat some cake. I baked it especially for you." Immediately after she eats it, the mother may say, "You really are overweight." Thus, if she eats the cake, her mother won't like her because she is fat, but if she doesn't eat it, she will hurt her mother's feelings!

While in the Army, a son might send his paycheck to his mother with the understanding that she would use part of it for her living expenses and save the rest so that he could attend college after discharge. When he asks for his share, she might tell him that she spent it all, adding, "A good boy wouldn't ask for it." This puts him in the impossible position of either giving up what is due him or being a "bad boy!"

Much time must be spent processing information with counselees who have received numerous double-bind messages. They often feel very anxious and confused, especially when they have to make choices. No matter what decisions they make, they feel guilty and afraid. The more healing the Inner Child of one of these counselees receives, the more ability he will have to perceive information correctly with his Adult. As his Parent "loosens its grip" on his Child, distorted material will no longer be threatening, allowing it to be exposed to the light of the truth.

f. UNDERSTANDING COMMUNICATION. Understanding what is taking place during the process of communication will also help a counselee perceive data correctly. We learned that the language of Transactional Analysis can help us analyze and understand the transactions that take place when we communicate. To review, each transaction consists of a stimulus by one person and a response by another. The response of the second person becomes a new stimulus to which the first person responds. Using Berne's language, we are able to discover which ego state–Parent, Adult or Child–is generating the stimulus and response of each person.

It would be helpful at this point to review the clues listed on **Table 6** which help us identify whether a stimulus or response is in the Parent, Adult or Child ego state. These clues include not only the words used, but also the tone of voice, facial expressions and body gestures. Assisted by these clues, a counselor can help his counselee begin to identify the Parent, Adult and Child in transactions involving himself and others. It would be helpful to give the counselee some examples of different types of transactions which occur in ordinary communication.

(1.) Complementary Transactions. According to Berne, one rule of communication is that when the stimulus and response make parallel lines on the transactional diagram, the transaction is complementary and can go on forever (see **Figures 9, 10 & 11**).

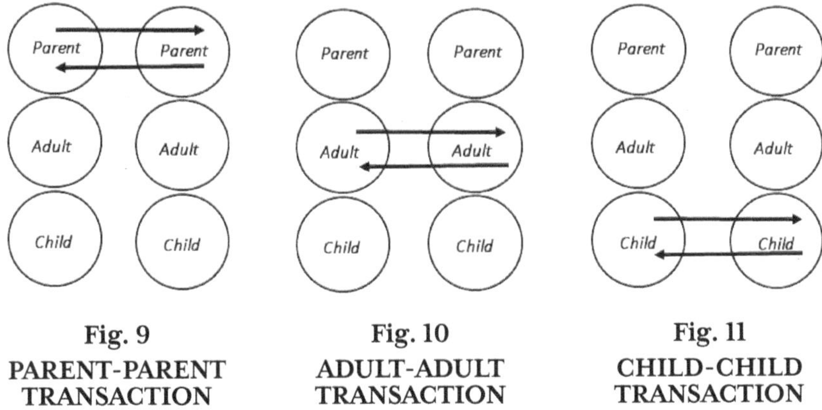

Fig. 9
PARENT-PARENT TRANSACTION

Fig. 10
ADULT-ADULT TRANSACTION

Fig. 11
CHILD-CHILD TRANSACTION

Following are some examples of complementary transactions:

PARENT-PARENT TRANSACTIONS

STIMULUS: "Can you believe the show these televangelists put on? They really get worked up!"

RESPONSE: "They are really something, aren't they! I bet most of those so-called healers use 'plants' in the audience that just say they were healed."

STIMULUS: "Yeah, I'm sure most of the people claiming to be healed weren't really sick at all. Most of these guys are in it for the money, you know."

RESPONSE "For sure! Can you believe all the hypocrites that are claiming to be Christians now?"

These transactions are called Parent-Parent because they are the same type of judgmental exchange these individuals, as children, overheard from their parents. They can continue on forever with no data input from reality. Unfortunately, people—Christians included—enjoy the good feeling that comes from finding fault. According to Berne, this is because when we blame and find fault, we replay the early blaming and fault-finding which is recorded in the Parent. This makes us feel Ok because the Parent is OK, and we are "coming on" Parent. Sad to say many Christians, like these two "saints," thoroughly enjoy playing a good game of "Ain't It Awful!"

CHILD-CHILD TRANSACTIONS

STIMULUS: "Pastor John didn't even say, "Hello" to me today. I don't think he likes me."

RESPONSE: "Well, he asked Joan to lead the Women's Bible Study. I really thought he was going to ask me, but he probably likes her better. Everyone likes her. I sure wish I could find a church where the leaders really practice Christian love!"

STIMULUS: "Well, I hear that the people at Agape Fellowship are really loving. Maybe we should try that church next Sunday."

These two ladies are engaged in the satisfying "Child-stroking" game of "Poor Little Me." Since the Child loves to get, rather than give strokes, there are very few game-free complementary Child-Child transactions. Unfortunately, since many of our youth today did not receive the nurturing they needed as children, their main goal is to get strokes. They accomplish this by engaging in gathering material goods, continual sexual activity, drug-taking, gang warfare, etc. Thus, there are many Child-Child transactions going on today as people live on a self-seeking basis and use each other for sensory stimulation. But relationships of this type do not last very long because Child-Child transactions cannot exist without the permission and supervision of the Adult.

For example, my husband and I experience exhilarating, joy-filled Child-Child transactions when we spend Saturdays riding our tandem bicycle and eating in fancy restaurants. Yet the Adult makes the arrangements for these fun-filled experiences. The Adult made the money to buy the bicycle and eat in nice restaurants. The Adult in each of us also made possible our joy of togetherness by working on our relationship for thirty-three years. When the Adult is not involved, the Child gets tangled up in crossed transactions, which will be discussed later.

ADULT-ADULT TRANSACTIONS

STIMULUS: "I really learned a lot from the seminar on finances Saturday. It was so informative."

RESPONSE: "I learned a lot, too. I found out how important it is to tithe. Would you like to go to the one on marriage?"

STIMULUS: "Sure! When is it?"

Transactions which process data or solve problems are Adult-Adult transactions. They can go on forever as long as they deal with reality data. Other types of complementary transactions are Parent-Child, Child-Parent, Adult-Parent, and Child-Parent (see **Figures 12 & 13**).

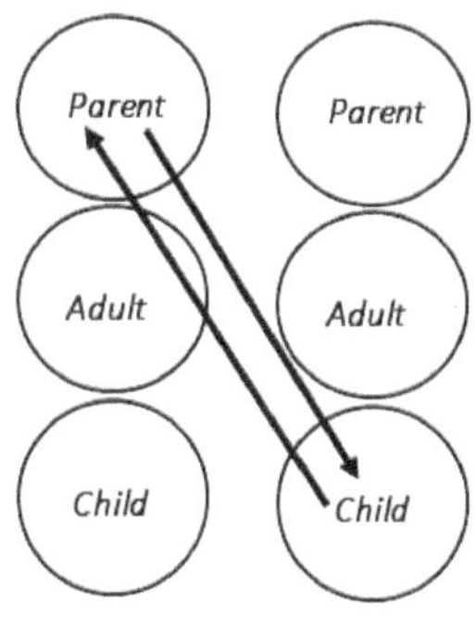

Fig. 12
PARENT-CHILD TRANSACTION

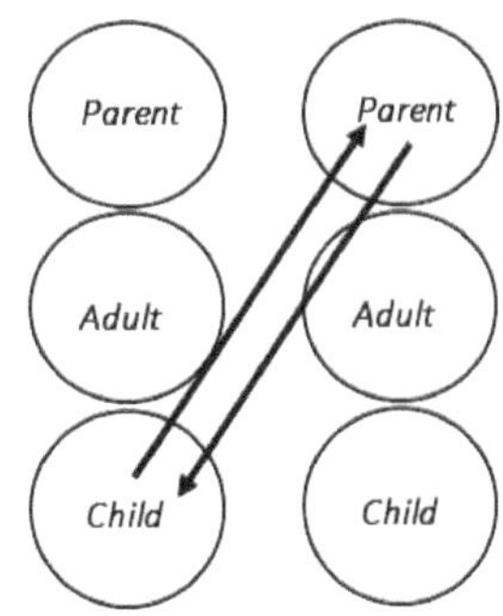

Fig. 13
CHILD-PARENT TRANSACTION

PARENT-CHILD TRANSACTIONS

STIMULUS (P) "You have to take that dress back. You know you can't afford it. Why don't you ever use your head?"

RESPONSE (C): "I don't want to! Don't be so mean! You know I really need this dress for the party Saturday."

STIMULUS (P) "You don't need any more clothes and you know it! You also know the Bible says, 'Submit to your husband!'"

CHILD-PARENT TRANSACTIONS

STIMULUS (P): "I feel horrible! What a hangover! Please, honey, be a good sport and call work. Tell 'em I can't make it in today. Make up some excuse or something."

RESPONSE (C): "Oh, you just never seem to know when to quit drinking! You've really got to try and stop!"

STIMULUS (P): "I promise I'll try, sweetie, but please call – just one more time. I promise it won't happen again."

RESPONSE (C): "Oh, all right, I'll call, but just one more time."

In these marriages, one mate has assumed the parental role, while the other has adopted the part of the child. Many marriages are based on Parent-Child relationships in which one mate is willing to take responsibility for everything and look after the other one. This type of relationship, which is popularly labeled "codependent," is the subject of many books and talk shows today. This can be a satisfying relationship as long as neither spouse wishes to change roles. But if one or the other tires of the arrangement, the codependent relationship is disrupted, and problems begin. Spouses playing the role of the Child often cannot exist without being involved in a relationship. Thus, they might be called "relationship addicts."

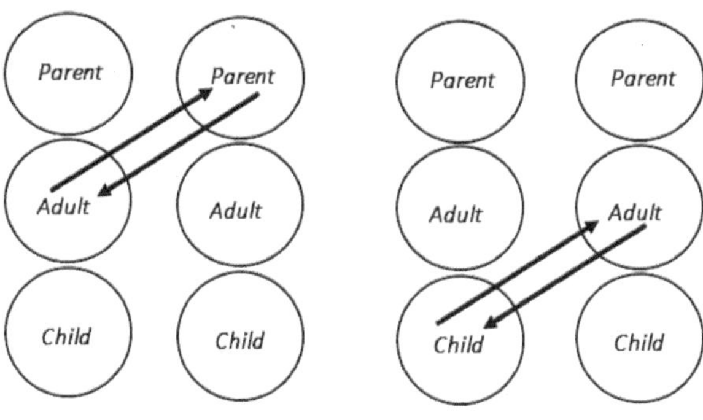

Fig. 14
ADULT-PARENT TRANSACTION

Fig. 15
CHILD-ADULT TRANSACTION

ADULT-PARENT TRANSACTIONS

Adult-Parent Transactions are shown in **Figures 14 & 15**.

STIMULUS (A): "I really want to stop smoking. Will you help me by really letting me have it if I light up? Maybe you could also get rid of any cigarettes you find around."

RESPONSE (C) "That sounds great to me! I'll start by crushing this pack of cigarettes right here!"

Adult-Parent transactions obviously have great game possibilities. As soon as this husband turns over the responsibility to stop smoking to his wife's Parent, he could become a "naughty boy" and play "If It Weren't For You, I Could" or "Try And Catch Me."

CHILD-ADULT TRANSACTIONS

STIMULUS (C): "I don't feel like I can close the deal on this sale today. It's just too big for me to handle!"

RESPONSE (A): "I know you can handle this sale, honey. It isn't any bigger than that huge sale you landed last month."

This husband's frightened Child is asking his wife's Adult to recount the reasons why he can make his big sale. Her response was Adult because she gave him some reality data. It might have been reassuring Parent with no reality data: "You always make your sales, honey, so there's nothing for you to worry about." Or she could have given him a harsh Parent response which denied his child's feelings: "Of course you'll make this sale—don't be stupid!" In this case, it would have been called a crossed transaction which always means trouble because it stirs up memories of cruel parental treatment.

*(2.) **Crossed Transactions:*** Another rule of communication, according to Berne, is that when stimulus and response cross on the P-A-C transactional diagram, communication stops (see **Figures 16 & 17**).

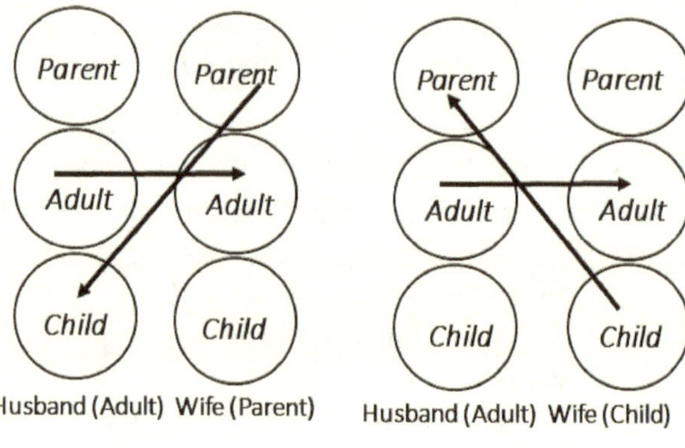

Fig. 16
CROSSED TRANSACTION

Fig. 17
CROSSED TRANSACTION

Fig. 16.

STIMULUS (A) "Honey, where are my keys?"

RESPONSE (P): "How should I know! Probably right where you left them!"

Fig. 17.

STIMULUS (A): "Honey, where are my keys?"

RESPONSE (C): "Why do you always yell at me? I'm doing the best I can."

A complementary response to this husband's request might have been, "I think I saw them on the dresser," or "I don't know, but I'll help you find them." But if this wife has a wounded, Inner Child, his Adult request will hook her Child. In this case, she will respond either in the Parent or Child, making this a crossed transaction. Either reply would have stopped communication by hooking the husband's Parent or Child. Since the Adult is no longer in control, a series of angry exchanges between Parent and Child will probably ensue. Crossed transactions can lead to many games, such as "It's All You," "Uproar" and "Now I've Got You!"

Harris states that the origin of the non-Adult responses is in the "not-OK" position of the Adaptive Child. A person dominated by his hurting Inner Child "reads into" comments things which are not there. Examples might be:

STIMULUS (A): "Where did you get the steaks?"
RESPONSE (C): "What's wrong with them?"
STIMULUS (A): "I love your new dress!"
RESPONSE (C): "You never did like the color red on me."
STIMULUS (A): "Pass the potatoes, dear."
RESPONSE (P): "And you call me fat!"

As one of Harris' patients declared, "My husband says I could read something into a cookbook!" Thus, people who take whatever is said wrong are rarely in the Adult ego state. Berne states that the person who always comes on Child is really saying, "Look at me, I'm not OK." The person who is always coming on Parent is saying, "Look at you, you're not OK and that makes me feel better about myself."

Some transactions can involve all three ego states. Harris gives the example of a very creative man who came home and wrote "I love you" in the dust on the coffee table. In this case, realizing that being loving was important to his marriage, he chose to stay in the Adult. But even though his Adult was in charge, both his Parent and Child were involved. His Parent was saying, "Why don't you ever clean this house?" His Child was saying, "Please don't get mad at me if I criticize you." This can turn into a complementary transaction if the wife is "OK enough" to take a little constructive criticism. If not, her Parent might respond, "When was the last time you cleaned the garage?" or her Child might send her out to the nearest mall to run up their credit cards.

Since the Parent and Child occupy primary circuits in communication, they tend to come on automatically in response to stimuli. Thus, even though a person may understand that replying in the Parent or the Child to an Adult statement cuts off communication, he is often powerless to reply in the Adult. The only way to help an individual stop this destructive cycle of crossed transactions is to strengthen his Adult by taking him through the soul healing process. His hurting Child must be healed with God's love, and his dominating Parent must be reprogrammed with God's truth. Only when his Child is no longer controlled by his Parent will his Adult be strong enough to perceive data correctly.

Thus, the stronger a counselee's Adult is, the easier it will be for him to process information correctly instead of taking what people say wrong because of his past hurts. A person with a strong Adult is also able to recognize when his Child is hooked and to express his feelings in the Adult in the correct way. An individual whose Adult is in charge is able to keep communication flowing smoothly since he is rarely the cause of crossed transactions, and he knows how to handle them when they do occur.

Therefore, as part of the soul healing process, a counselor should help his counselee determine which ego states are coming on during transactions. This is particularly important during marriage counseling where crossed transactions are commonplace. Due to past hurts and built-up anger, the Child in each spouse is easily hooked, resulting in either the Parent or the Child coming on as they attempt to communicate. The counselor has his work cut out for him as he struggles to get each spouse to stay in the Adult and describe what his Child is feeling. But until each mate's Adult has been sufficiently strengthened through the healing process, they will find it difficult to determine which ego states are coming on during transactions, enabling them to communicate more effectively.

g. REFLECTION. Occasionally, a counselor will come in contact with a counselee who is very shy and withdrawn. However, in fifteen years of counseling, I have only had several people who were reticent to talk. By far, the majority of my counselees have had the opposite problem! They often block the real issues by talking "nonstop" about nonconsequential things. In these cases, by sorting out and interpreting pertinent information, I gently and subtly draw them back to work on the real issues. I much prefer loquacious counselees, however, as there is a certain amount of emotional release which occurs through talking, enabling them to become receptive to healing more quickly. Also, I find counseling much easier when I do not have to "drag" information out of people!

The most effective technique to use with the occasional uncommunicative person is called "reflection." The counselor simply reflects back whatever the counselee says. For instance, a counselee might say, "I went to see my oldest daughter yesterday." The counselor would just repeat what she said, "Oh, yesterday you saw your oldest daughter. How is she?" Reflecting back what she says reassures the counselee that what she is saying is being accepted which encourages her to open up and share more.

I realize now that the Lord led me to begin using this technique with my son when he was small. Although he was rather shy and had trouble communicating, he would always open up when I gave him my full attention and repeated what he had just said. Recognizing that his conversation was being favorably received, he felt that it was "safe" to disclose more of himself. It may be that many people have difficulty communicating simply because no one has ever taken the time to listen attentively, while patiently and lovingly encouraging them to open up and share their innermost thoughts and feelings.

h. TRANSFERENCE. Sometime during the process of soul healing, a concept called "transference" may occur. This concept refers to the counselee's tendency to transfer to his counselor feelings that were experienced toward his parents during his childhood. For instance, at some point he may feel the same anger, hatred and resentment which he once felt toward his parents. Employing the defense mechanism of displacement, the counselee may then displace these emotions onto his counselor. He may also idealize his counselor or become jealous of the other counselees and desire to be the counselor's favorite. He may feel guilt and self-condemnation if he thinks he has disappointed his counselor in any way. These internalized Parent-Child conflicts which are being relived must be resolved in the present relationship between the counselor and counselee.

Personally, I have experienced very little transference in my years of counseling. The fact that I do not, of course, consider myself in any way to be the "savior" or "source of healing" of any counselee probably accounts for this. First and foremost, I continually emphasize that Jesus is the Healer and Deliverer; I am just His vessel. I try always to point every counselee to Jesus, striving to make him solely dependent upon his Redeemer to heal his soul and meet all of his needs.

Another reason that I have not experienced much transference may be due to the fact that soul healing concentrates on healing a person's wounds and bringing him to forgiveness, whereas, secular psychotherapy does not generally recognize the importance of forgiveness. Secular psychotherapists believe that anger is the root cause of symptomatic behavior; therefore, they tend to dwell on helping the patient "get all of his anger out." Patients are encouraged to scream, shout, pound pillows, and even throw darts at pictures of parents or others with whom they are angry. God has revealed to me that, ironically, instead of releasing anger, these techniques actually build more anger!

Naturally, as the patient focuses on his anger and his desire to get revenge, demonic spirits of anger, hatred, bitterness, rage, etc. will be drawn irresistibly to him. "His last state will be worse than his first." On the contrary, during soul healing, when Jesus touches and heals a counselee's hurts and scars, he is able to forgive those who have hurt him, resulting in the Savior's love melting away all of his anger and hatred.

Therefore, I do not believe transference should be of concern to the Spirit-filled, anointed counselor. As he continually accepts even the most unacceptable thoughts and feelings of his counselee, the ability of the counselee's Inner Child to trust him as a loving substitute parent grows. As the counselee allows more and more denied and distorted data to be exposed to the light, his defenses dissolve, and he gradually begins to gain insight into the root causes of his destructive, life-controlling behavior and attitudes. Understanding the reasons for his behavior is not healing in itself, but it is the light that leads the way to the healing Balm of Gilead.

During the process of counseling and soul healing, I cannot emphasize enough how important it is for us, as counselors, to walk softly, in reverence and awe of the Lord and to be extremely sensitive to the leading of the Holy Spirit. We must "delight in the fear of the Lord" as Jesus did. (Isa. 11:3) Since every person is unique in the creativity, talents and gifts with which God has blessed him, each of us will be used somewhat differently by the Lord. Since every counselee is also a unique creation of God, we may be led to minister somewhat differently to each one.

Thus, just as our Messiah laid down His priceless life for each of us individually, so must we lay down our lives in a unique way for each of our counselees. The Lord impressed me with this truth recently while viewing a television program which showed one of the most precious things I have ever seen anyone do for another. A tiny Japanese brother and sister were walking down a sidewalk, holding hands. He was about six years old and she was about five. Coming to a rather broad, deep break in the sidewalk, the little boy jumped over it. He then tried to help his sister, but there was no way she could get over to the other side. Contemplating for a moment, he then "stretched" his small body over the opening, somehow hanging on with his fingers and toes, and forming a "bridge" over which his little sister walked! He then hopped up and they continued strolling down the sidewalk, holding hands.

Just like this little one, each of us must lay down his life for his counselees, becoming the "bridge" over which, they may walk to get to their heavenly Father. As "bridges," we help protect our counselees from the raging, tempestuous "waters" of demonic forces which lash out at them, attempting to prevent them from getting across to the safety of their Daddy's waiting arms. We absorb the fury of the tumultuous, crashing waves as Satan and his hordes try to "collapse us" so they can dash our counselees against the rocks below!

Sadly, not everyone for whom we lay down our lives will make it safely across their bridges. Satan knows exactly which "waves" to send lashing up at our counselees. Some of these waves of demonic forces will be so strong that they will snatch them from their bridge and throw them into the turbulent waters below! Denial is the primary "soul snatcher." For example, one woman was able to receive some soul healing from the abuse which she had suffered as a child but refuses to recognize that she had also inflicted abuse upon her own children.

During soul healing prayer with another woman, the Spirit revealed the shocking truth that her aunt–her mother's sister, had given birth to her! Surprisingly, she was comfortable with this truth and was actually relieved to hear it as it answered a lot of questions and explained certain feelings which she had. She probably did not experience much trauma concerning this revelation because, even though she was the result of an affair between her aunt and her own father, her "mother" had lovingly raised her as her own "daughter."

When confronted with the truth, the counselee's aunt readily admitted that she was her birth mother. Her "mother," however, became hysterical, emphatically denied this fact and told her "daughter" that she would have her committed if she continued to spread this preposterous lie! This poor woman was living in a state of denial and actually believed that she had given birth to this counselee. Rather than risk her mother's rejection by exposing the family "skeleton" and revealing the truth to her family, this counselee allowed herself to be snatched from her bridge by the demon of denial!

Thus, although the majority of our counselees will make it safely to the other side, we must face the tragic truth that some will not. Although we continue to pray and grieve for them, it is their choice whether or not to give up their stubborn wills and go all the way with Jesus. The Lord can go only as far in soul healing as a counselee will let Him.

Therefore, we can see that healing the souls of our counselees is a long, slow, often heart-breaking process, requiring much patience, compassion and understanding from us. Unfortunately, some saints have attempted to bypass this arduous process by performing deliverances on people, assuring them that this would forever take care of all of their emotional, attitudinal and behavioral problems.

B. WHAT ABOUT DELIVERANCE?

1. PITFALLS OF DELIVERANCE.

You may have been asking, "Just how does deliverance fit into the concept of soul healing? Obviously, exorcism of demons is part of the soul healing process, but it is only *part* of, not the *whole*, process. Since we live in a world of quick and instant gratification of needs, in the early days of the Charismatic movement, we tended to view deliverance like a "magic wand" which could instantly cure all of our ills! We became overenthusiastic about exorcism, viewing it as an overweight person sees a diet pill. He believes that this pill will melt away his fat without his having to change his lifestyle and become disciplined in his eating habits.

Thus, in our spoiled and pampered society, we are always trying to treat the *effects* of our problems, whether they be physical, emotional or spiritual, without working on the *cause*! The cost of treating the cause is too high for us because we would be required to change our thinking and our behavior from our ways to God's ways. If we chose, in every instance, to repent, that is, to turn, from our natural way of looking at and doing things and go God's way, our lives would totally change. Therefore, deliverance could be described, not as a one-time event, but as a "process of being delivered from thinking and going our own way" so that we would be free to choose to walk in God's truth and light.

Another pitfall of deliverance is that Charismatic Christians have tended to glorify it, thus encouraging deliverance ministers to unknowingly give Satan permission to put on a show at the expense of the person being exorcised. Many deliverance ministers are controlled by pride and ambition, so they are constantly finding demons in people and jumping in to deliver them because every spirit exorcised is another "notch in their guns!" Also, some of those ministering deliverance are attempting to cast out the same demons which control their own souls, so transference of spirits takes place more often than not!

Thus, we can see that there has been much zeal without wisdom, sometimes resulting in people ending up in a worse condition than they were in before deliverance! A demon does not take his eviction lightly—"...after he passes through waterless places and finds no rest, he decides to return to his house" (Luke 11:24). If he finds that nothing has changed, "...he takes along seven other spirits more evil than himself, and they go in and live there, and the last state of the man becomes worse than the first" (Luke 10:25,26).

American televangelist James Robison relates his experience just after being baptized in the Spirit. He was consumed with lust, so he took a plane to a place where Christian brothers delivered him from a spirit of lust. They gave him scriptures to claim, etc., but when he returned home, he did nothing further to ward off the demonic attack which was guaranteed to occur. Consequently, he became possessed with many more spirits which were eviller than the first, and "burned in a horrible fire of lust" from which it took him years to get free. Thus, we see that exorcism is very serious business which should not be undertaken lightly without guidance from the Holy Spirit! Follow-up consisting of soul healing and discipling is absolutely essential!

2. ROOT CUTTING OF CHARACTER TREE.

Demons can enter a person's soul only if they have been given permission to do so through sin or generation curses or, in rare cases, through physical trauma. In their book, *Pigs in the Parlor*, the Hammonds stated that, without question, the majority of demons encountered during their ministry entered people during childhood. The Hammonds cited bitterness as probably the most common opening for demons, stating that spirits of unforgiveness and bitterness keep alive every detail of a person's hurts by reviewing them continuously in the person's mind.

It makes sense then, to close the doors through which these spirits entered by asking Jesus to heal the wounds which caused the unforgiveness and bitterness. To substantiate this theory, the Lord gave me a vision of a tree which represents the character structure which each of us has developed since childhood. A seed which symbolizes the little spirit of a child is planted in contaminated soil which represents the rejection, abuse and deprivation which this child received from authority figures, especially his parents.

The wounds which his spirit suffers lead him to make the judgment that his parents and others are cruel and deserve to be punished, as depicted in **Table 2**. His anger leads him to reject, condemn, hate, and refuse to forgive his parents and other authority figures, including God. As noted in the discussion of the law of judgment, he then becomes bitter which leads him to rebel and retaliate by making an inner vow that he will punish these people. These sinful mental attitudes are symbolized by the roots of the tree. "See to it '...that no root of bitterness springing up causes trouble, and by it many be defiled (Heb. 12:15).

Just as the roots of a tree are buried underground where they remain unseen, so these attitudes are buried in the subconscious or heart (Child). "Out of hearts of men proceed evil thoughts, adulteries, fornications, murders, thefts, covetousness, wickedness, deceit, lasciviousness, an evil eye, blasphemy, pride, foolishness; all these evil things come from within and defile the man" (Mark 7:21-23 KJV).

Thus, this child's character is formed out of the attitudes in his heart and he becomes a victimizer whose character structure is portrayed by the tree on the left side in **Illustration 1**. "As a man thinks in his heart, so is he" (Prov. 23:7). Each branch of his tree represents a sinful mental attitude or behavior pattern which is a symptom of the attitudes buried in his heart.

On the other hand, as discussed before, if a child whose spirit is wounded decides that it is not safe to rebel and retaliate against his parents and others because they are stronger, out of fear he will decide to "agree" with them that he deserves to be punished. Thus, he will repress the anger, rejection, condemnation, hatred, unforgiveness, and bitterness which he feels toward them and turn it toward himself. Instead of rebelling and retaliating against them, he punishes himself by becoming a victim whose character structure is portrayed by the tree on the right.

Since the attitudes and behavior patterns symbolized by the roots and branches of the trees are sinful, demons (portrayed by bats) have permission to come in and sit on them. I believe that the "root" demons are the "strong men" or ruling spirits over the other lesser demons. These "root" demons "fertilize and water" the tree by keeping alive every detail of a person's hurts and wounds. During deliverance, the bats (demons) are plucked out of branches, possibly even out of the roots, but since the tree is still there, they can easily return. But if the person is receptive to a soul healing process which is anointed and thorough, the Lord's ax will be laid to the roots of the tree (character structure) and it will fall, leaving no branches or roots (sinful attitudes or behaviors) on which the bats (demons) may again rest. "And the ax is already laid at the root of the trees; every tree therefore that does not bear good fruit is cut down and thrown into the fire" (Matt. 3:10,11 NAS 1977).

Cutting out the roots of our sinful characters is effective, powerful and long-lasting since we are dealing with the cause, not the effects of our sins. To illustrate, after Jesus heals the many hurts buried in his Child (heart), the counselee is able to see his parents, God and others, including himself, through the light and love of Jesus. He is then able to repent of his anger, hatred and bitterness, forgive everyone, and break the judgments and inner vows which he made as a child, healing his wounded spirit.

This deep repentance from the heart then cuts the strongest roots of all his sinful attitudes: anger, rejection, condemnation, unforgiveness, hatred, and bitterness. This, in turn, destroys the strongholds of rebellion and retaliation in the victimizer; since his hatred and bitterness are gone, he no longer has a reason to rebel against his parents, God or others. The sinful attitudes (branches) of selfishness, abuse, pride, control, etc., are demolished (toppled with the tree) as he allows Jesus to melt his stony heart and fill him with His compassion and agape love for others.

When Jesus heals the wounds of the victim, he is able to see his parents, God and others as Jesus sees them. Since Jesus has removed all threats to him, the victim no longer has any reason to be afraid of authority figures; thus, the stronghold of fear has been destroyed. "For the weapons of our warfare are not carnal, but mighty through God to the pulling down of strongholds" (2 Cor. 10:4 KJV).

The victim is now able to recognize and repent of the anger, rejection, condemnation, unforgiveness, hatred, and bitterness which he had repressed and turned against himself. He is then able to forgive everyone, including himself, and break the judgments and inner vows repressed in his Inner Child (heart). As Jesus heals his broken heart and shows him who he is in Christ, the "branches" of insecurity, unworthiness, guilt, self-condemnation, etc., "come crashing down with the tree."

Since the counselee's Child is no longer under any delusions concerning his Parent data, his Adult is now free to repent of and change his sinful attitudes and behavior. Since the counselee has fallen out of agreement with the demons corresponding to his sinful attitudes, they have no choice but to leave! "Starving out" the demons is the most effective way to expel them because we have more assurance that they cannot gain entrance to our souls or bodies again.

During the process of soul healing, deliverance often occurs without any forceful dislodging of the demon. As an example, a prostitute whom I counseled knew that she had a demon of lust. She renounced, repented of and nailed all lust to the cross, and asked Jesus to cleanse her with His precious blood. When I asked the Spirit to show us the door through which this demon had entered, He revealed that she had been molested as a small girl.

As Jesus healed her scars and cleansed her of all defilement, making her spotless with His omnipotent blood, a spirit of lust came screaming out! With Jesus' love, she was able to forgive her abuser and break her judgments and vows against men—"I hate men; I will never trust a man again, etc." If this woman now fills her house with the Lord, puts on her full armor and determines to walk in righteousness, this demon of lust will find the door shut and bolted when it tries to return!

Thus, as the Sandfords point out, discernment of the presence of a demon is not a mandate to exorcise it at that moment. They state in *The Transformation of the Inner Man* that they seldom have to speak directly to demons to defeat them, that if a person's inner house of character is transformed in Jesus, the demons must flee, having no house in which to dwell. Many of my counselees have indicated the peaceful departure of demons with statements like: "Something just broke free and left me;" "I feel peace now, like a thousand pounds just left my body;" "As Jesus cut the chains, it felt like something lifted right out of my body!"

But sometimes a counselee will not be able to respond to healing because the control of the demons is too strong. This is usually the case if the person has been involved in the occult, witchcraft or false religions. Many adults who suffered Satanic ritual abuse as children have been thoroughly programmed to believe that they belong to Satan, especially if they were forced to participate in heinous rituals, such as being "married" to Satan, signing "the book" in their own blood on their fourth birthday or participating in human sacrifice. Some adult survivors from families involved in the occult relate that they were called to a deathbed when they were children where evil spirits from a dying relative were imparted to them. These are known as "family" or "familiar" spirits and are passed down as part of a child's heritage.

Thus, the Internal Parent of an individual from an occult family is so intensely programmed to believe that he is spiritually united with Satan that his Inner Child is completely controlled by this belief. The belief that he belongs to Satan combined with demonic strength creates a powerful, almost impenetrable, demonic stronghold which grants Satan spiritual "rights" to control this person's life.

More complications arise when a victim of SRA also suffers from multiple personality disorder. Much harm has been done by deliverance ministers who have mistaken alternate personalities for demons and attempted to cast them out. Also, demons may be attached only to certain alters, leading to disagreement among the various personalities concerning exorcism. More will be discussed regarding these complications and how to deal with them later.

Thus, in most cases, following the leading of the Holy Spirit, it is sufficient to bind a demon, break its stronghold over a person's life and command it to go in Jesus' name. But in cases where Satan has gained a strong foothold and has established definite rights over a person's life, a more proscribed mode of exorcism is often required to "set the captive free."

Wisdom has led the Sandfords to discern whether a person has sufficient resolve by which to discipline himself to walk in a new and righteous way, and I would add, to withstand future evil spirits by employing spiritual warfare on his own. They see indications on the counselee's part of sincere attacks; only if repentance and genuine hatred of the sins which the demons have been perpetrating through him, will they choose to exorcise. They always follow up deliverance with working on the root causes of the demonization, thereby demolishing the residence of the demons.

Therefore, guidance from the Holy Spirit is the key in discerning who should be exorcised, also in deciding how and when deliverance should take place. The Spirit may lead the counselor to gather a group together to help minister, to have them fast and pray for a certain length of time, etc. As we know, any believer has the authority to cast out demons in Jesus' name. "And these signs will accompany those who have believed: in My name they will cast out demons" (Mark 16:17).

But everyone involved in administering deliverance must be completely convinced of his authority in Jesus because demons know whether any unbelief or fear is present. "And the evil spirit said, 'I recognize Jesus, and I know about Paul, but who are you?'" (Acts 19:15). Demons also know if there is any sin present in those ministering. Sin enhances their power and allows transference of spirits to take place, as mentioned earlier. So those administering exorcism must know their authority in Jesus and be walking righteously in His ways, having crucified their flesh, or Satan will gain control of the proceedings.

3. ADMINISTERING DELIVERANCE.

The candidate for exorcism should be asked to confess, repent of and renounce his sins before God and those present. He is to confess specific sins of any involvement in the occult and renounce them, knowing that renunciation is the act of turning away from sin and forsaking all evil. Again, deliverance is not to be used merely to gain relief from distress, but to gain freedom from demonic control in order to begin obeying God and walking in His ways. An excellent prayer which may be read by the person seeking liberation is one written by Bible teacher Derek Prince, reproduced in **Table 7**.

Satan has assigned his evil forces in a chain of command over nations, cities, churches, homes, and individuals. The one in charge of the exorcism begins by taking authority over all the higher powers that have control over the demons indwelling the person being delivered. He then binds the "strong man" or ruling spirit which is over the lesser demons possessing the person. "Or else how can one enter into a strong man's house and spoil his goods, except he first binds the strong man? And then he will spoil his house" (Matt. 12:29 KJV). A comprehensive list, derived by the Hammonds, of common demon groupings with their respective rulers is given in **Table 8**.

The deliverance minister then commands all indwelling spirits to unlink themselves from one another and forbids them from lending any help to one another. As the Holy Spirit leads, he commands the specific spirits to go in the name of Jesus, while the others in the group are praying, praising, singing, or reading scripture. For example, he might say, "Demon of false religion, you have no right to stay in this person. He is a child of God, bought by the blood of Jesus. His body is the temple of the Holy Spirit and you must go! I bind you, break your hold over John and command you to go in the mighty name of Jesus Christ of Nazareth! According to Holy scripture, I have authority over all the power of the enemy!"

The demon may respond by declaring emphatically, "I don't have to go! I have every right to stay in this person!" He may seek to instill fear in those ministering by making threats, such as, "I'll get you! I'll come into you if you cast me out! I'll ruin your life, your finances, your marriage, your health, etc.!" Everyone conducting the exorcism must know beyond a shadow of a doubt that all evil spirits must go and that they cannot harm any believer because they have already been defeated by the death and resurrection of Jesus Christ!

The question always arises, however, as to whether we should converse with demons or not. Their extensive experience has led the Hammonds to conclude that we should not converse with demons unless the Holy Spirit indicates some specific purpose to do so. The Spirit may direct the deliverance minister to ask a demon to name itself, to reveal how it gained entry into a person or, in some cases, to reveal the names of other indwelling spirits. The key, once again, is to adhere strictly to the guidance of the omniscient, omnipotent, all-knowing Holy Ghost!

The Hammonds warn against conversing with demons for the purpose of acquiring knowledge. The Holy Spirit is our source of knowledge, wisdom and guidance, so we do not have to rely on the lying mouths of evil minions for information. The Hammonds state that the novice is prone to want to hear demons talk but will soon learn that this is not necessary because they all say the same things, mixing in a little truth with their lies. Demons cleverly use conversation as a delaying tactic so they will not have to leave. They also enjoy distracting the workers by putting on a "show" intended to get them to admire and laugh at their antics. What the evil fiends really hate to hear are the words, "Shut up, and come out!"

Sometimes a demon will manifest violently when called out, often throwing the person being delivered to the floor, requiring those ministering to restrain him. We have all heard stories about five men not being able to hold down a person of small stature, due to the supernatural strength of demons. The Spirit informed the Hammonds that violent displays are, not surprisingly, often caused by a spirit of violence. Thus, casting out a spirit of violence usually causes violent manifestations to subside completely. The Hammonds relate a fascinating case in which evil spirits reacted violently every time a woman was touched. When anyone touched her, they would cry out, "Don't touch me!" When they commanded this "Touch-Me-Not" demon to come out, there was no further display of violence! Evil spirits can also be bound in Jesus' name and commanded not to manifest in any way.

The person being freed should be encouraged to enter into the warfare by commanding the spirits to go, letting them know in no uncertain terms that they must leave as he wants no further part with them! Involving him in the battle will help him understand that, although he is receiving help with his initial deliverance, the responsibility to remain free rests solely with him. He must know his authority in Jesus if he is to remain free of evil spirits. "Behold, I give unto you power to tread on serpents and scorpions, and over all the power of the enemy, and nothing shall by any means hurt you" (Luke 10:19 KJV).

A point to remember is that it is not the volume of our voice that causes demons to tremble and obey; rather it is the amount of confidence we have in our authority in Jesus. Demons seem to sense any lack of confidence in a deliverance minister. We can better understand our authority if we learn about the tremendous power which the blood of Jesus has. The blood cleanses, redeems, sanctifies, and justifies the believer. Therefore, songs, scriptures and references to the blood of Jesus are filled with power. According to the Hammonds, it is not effective to just repeat the word "blood" or the phrase, "I plead the blood" over and over. What is effective, though, is giving testimony of what the blood does for the believer.

Demons cannot stand to hear about everything the blood does for us who are bought with its price. "Much more then, having been justified by His blood, we shall be saved from the wrath of God through Him" (Rom. 5:9). "We have confidence to enter the holy place by the blood of Jesus (Heb. 10:19). "How much more will the blood of Christ "...cleanse your conscience from dead works to serve the living God?" (Heb. 9:14). "All things are cleansed with blood, and without shedding of blood there is no forgiveness" (Heb. 9:22). "...and through Him to reconcile all things to Himself, having made peace through the blood of His cross" (Col. 1:20).

The Hammonds say that when they asked a demon why he could not stand to hear about the blood of Jesus, he said, "Because it is so red, because it is so warm, because it is alive and it covers everything." Since the blood of Jesus is alive, it is as powerful today as it was when Jesus died! It is atoning blood. Atone means "to cover." Evil spirits have already been defeated by the priceless blood of Jesus which covers each and every believer! No wonder demons hate to hear about the power in the blood of Jesus! More will be discussed about this power in the precious blood of Jesus later.

The individual being delivered will know, in most instances, when a demon departs. Often, he will cough, yawn or even become nauseous and vomit phlegm, a slimy substance. This type of dramatic demonstration of expulsion is not mandatory, however. The person may feel a yoke break off his neck, a band break around his head, or see Jesus drive the demon out, or a whirlwind take it away. The principal evidence indicating that the evil spirit has left will be the great sense of relief and peace the person feels, plus the assurance of the Holy Spirit.

If no demons have been expelled after about ten or fifteen minutes of testifying about the power of Jesus' blood, the Holy Spirit should be asked to reveal what the hindrance is. The Spirit may reveal that the individual being liberated has some kind of "occult object" on his person, or he may not have repented of some sin or fallen out of agreement with the demons, all of which give the evil fiends "legal" rights to stay. The Holy Spirit may direct the deliverance minister to bind off the demons' actions and fast and pray before proceeding. "But this kind does not go out except by fasting and prayer" (Matt. 17:21).

Dr. Lester F. Sumrall states in his book, *Demons—The Answer Book*, that in the Bible it never took a long time to set anyone free. He emphatically declares that if a person is not delivered within a short period of time, the one ministering had better stop and talk to God. He also bluntly points out that screaming and yelling and rolling on the floor is not what sets a person free. Faith alone sets people free!

Again, I want to carve this point in stone—deliverance of demons is just the beginning; it is not an end in itself! All that has been accomplished is that the person who was delivered is no longer totally controlled by Satan. But Satan can control us through oppression so mightily that we will once again open the doors to possession. So, a counselor must never, never, never declare the job finished after exorcism! The victory has not been won; the real work has just begun!

We might compare deliverance to the experience of being baptized in the Spirit which is not an end in itself either; it is also just a beginning. When we receive the baptism in the Spirit, we are opening the door to the Holy Spirit, allowing Him to take over more and more in our lives, to purge us, refine us, and change us into the image of Jesus. In like manner, being delivered just means that we are closing the door on Satan, taking the control of our lives, which he stole, back from him. "The thief comes only to steal and kill and destroy; I came that they might have life and might have it abundantly" (John 10:10).

Therefore, neither the baptism in the Spirit, nor deliverance, is a one-time experience. Just as we are being baptized in the Spirit daily as He reveals God's ways to us so that we can walk in them, so are we being delivered daily from our ways of thinking and acting. The work of the Spirit is to bring us to complete repentance from going our own way (death of our soul [self]), so that we can decide to go God's way (resurrection of our soul in Christ).

Thus, much work is left to be done after deliverance. The Holy Spirit must be allowed to bring up, work on and heal the root causes of how the evil spirits gained entrance into the delivered person's life in the first place. Only then will these entrances be shut and bolted permanently (death of his soul). This individual must then be shown how to open the door to the Spirit, allowing Him to "fill his house" (soul) with Jesus (resurrection of his soul).

To be filled with Jesus is to be filled with purity and power. Purity comes when we are sanctified and able to abide in Christ, resulting in the fruit of the Spirit being operative in our lives. Power comes through receiving the baptism of the Holy Spirit, resulting in the gifts of the Spirit being operative in our lives. Our souls must be healed and set free before we can be filled with the purity and power of Jesus, allowing the fruit and gifts of the Holy Spirit to flow freely through us.

4. LEADING OF HOLY SPIRIT.

The end result of soul healing, in my opinion, is really "sanctification." The method employed by the counselor, correctly applied under the direction of the Spirit, could rightfully be called disciplining. As stated before, the secret of effective counseling (disciplining) is to be totally attuned to the leading of the Spirit every moment. I have learned from my experience that God is unbelievably patient and that He usually moves very slowly. We, being the impatient ones, are often way ahead of Him.

Ironically, insensitivity to God's timing seems to be particularly evident among Christian counselors and pastors, especially those who are untrained. Secular counselors realize that people will only receive what they are ready to receive, whether it be guidance, healing, deliverance, etc. So, it is the counselee, not the counselor, not even God, who controls how fast soul healing progresses!

As was pointed out previously, the reason soul healing progresses so slowly is that we all employ many defenses to protect us from having to deal with reality because it is so painful. As we learned, defense mechanisms are necessary for our survival, so we can understand how crucial it is for a counselor to be extremely careful not to tear down a counselee's defenses.

Thus, the importance of being attuned to the direction of the Spirit is apparent, since only He knows how and when a counselor will be able to get through a counselee's defenses so that he will be able to receive the insight or healing that is being offered. The difficulty does not usually lie in getting the counselee's mind (Adult) to comprehend an insight, but in assisting the process of discovery so that the Spirit can cause the heart (Child) to understand. "The eyes of the heart must be enlightened" (Eph. 1:18).

Jesus knew exactly how to "enlighten the eyes of the heart" and heal the Inner Child in every instance. He knew when to ask a question, relate a parable, confront a person, etc. By studying the different ways in which He related to people, we see that He treated each person as a unique individual.

For example, when Simon, a Pharisee, said to himself that if Jesus were a prophet, He would not allow a sinful woman to touch Him. Jesus humbled him by confronting him with a parable. He praised the woman by pointing out that she showed much love by washing His feet with her tears, kissing them and anointing them with perfume, while the Pharisee had neglected the expected amenities. Jesus exaltation of the woman cleansed and healed any scars remaining from her past sinful life and washed away any guilt, self-condemnation or unworthiness which she still felt (Luke 7:36-50).

Jesus healed Peter's wounds and washed away the guilt and self-condemnation which he surely felt after denying Him by asking him three times if he loved Him. Each time that he assured his Lord that he loved Him canceled out and healed the scar from one of Peter's denials. The fact that Jesus instructed him three times to tend His sheep reassured Peter that his Master still considered him worthy and capable of caring for His people, cleansing away any self-doubts or unworthiness which he felt (John 21:15-17).

Our Savior related to people so successfully because He did nothing of Himself. "Truly, truly, I say to you, the Son can do nothing of Himself, unless it is something He sees the Father doing" (John 5:19). Thus, we, as counselors, can aspire to be so completely empty of ourselves that we will be open vessels through which the Spirit can flow freely. The Spirit will then be able to lead us to share an experience, ask a question, etc., as only He knows what will touch and enlighten a counselee's heart.

Our tendency, as counselors, is to try and hurry the soul healing process. We may push, pull or prod a counselee too much to try to change his attitudes and behavior. But relating to him as controlling "parent" will only incite the counselee's Child to rebel.

Thus, one of the greatest attributes of an effective counselor is tremendous patience and long-suffering so that he will be able to wait on the Lord and not strive to do His job for Him. For only Jesus can bring us to die to our flesh and only He can bring us to resurrection life. Only our Lord can "...bring to the point of birth and not fail to bring forth" (Isa. 66:9-11). As counselors, He does not need our help, only our cooperation!

A discerning counselor will allow his counselees to set their own pace. He will follow Paul's lead and "...become all things to all men" (1 Cor. 9:19-22). He will set his tempo and even his manner of speaking to match that of his counselees. Eventually the patient, loving acceptance of the counselor will enable the counselee to trust him enough to let down his defenses and come to the realization that hurts, judgments and vows that need to be dealt with are repressed in his Child.

C. FORGIVING WITH THE ADULT.

As the Spirit convicts the counselee of the need to forgive his parents and others, the counselor can lead him to choose to forgive with his Adult. If he believes that he has a right to be angry and refuses to forgive, the counselor can explain to him, gently and lovingly, that, as a Christian, he is "bought with a price and is not his own" (1 Cor. 6:30). Thus, he has forfeited his rights. We become angry at a person because we have judged that he is violating some right or not fulfilling some expectation of ours.

An exercise the Lord gave me which helps a counselee to forgive is to have him write down all of the rights and expectations which he is holding onto. These are then wrapped as a gift and placed "on the altar" as a sacrifice to God. In a vision, God revealed that this supreme sacrifice is much more precious than silver and gold to Him because we can give Him no greater treasure than our decision to give up our rights to judge and hold onto unforgiveness and bitterness!

An example illustrating this principle might concern a mother who discovers a messy house when she arrives home. She gets angry at her children because she has judged them as violating her right to have a neat house and her expectation that they will help her keep it neat. If she is able to give up her right and expectation and place them on God's altar, her anger will melt away and forgiveness will come easily.

In some instances, it may also be necessary for the counselor to bring the counselee to the realization that he feels God has failed him in some way. In these cases, he assures him that it is all right to be angry with God. He helps him admit his anger and discover what right he believes God has violated or what expectation he feels He did not fulfill. He then helps him release this right or expectation to God and place it on His altar so he can forgive Him with his Adult.

D. HEALING OF MEMORIES.

Many times, we hear people say, "I have forgiven that person, but I still feel angry and hurt." The goal of healing of memories, the main component of the soul healing process, is for Jesus to heal the hurts in the counselee's Inner Child so that all pain and anger is removed, and his Child is able to forgive. This forgiveness from the heart is much deeper and more liberating than forgiveness from the mind. The decision by his Adult to forgive opens the door to give God permission to accomplish this deep healing.

But even though the counselee's Adult may give permission for healing, it is really his Inner Child's permission that is needed since this is where the hurts are recorded. Whether the Inner Child grants his permission or not can only be discovered during the actual process of healing of memories. Any resistance concerning healing of memories coming from the counselee's Adult can be dealt with by informing him of the truth, while barriers put up by his Child have to be eliminated by prayer and spiritual warfare.

To help alleviate any fears or doubts the counselee's Adult might have concerning the process of healing of memories, the counselor may inform him that he is just an instrument of the Holy Spirit and that the Spirit is in control and will reveal only the memories which He desires to heal. Thus, the Spirit will not bring back any experiences for which the counselee is not ready to receive healing.

The counselor should reassure him that healing of memories enjoyable and fun because Jesus is so gentle, loving, comforting, and even humorous when He heals. When he feels that the counselee 's trust in Jesus' love is stronger than the pain of his memories, at least as far as his Adult is concerned, the counselor can proceed with the healing of his memories. What the counselee's Child feels is always a mystery which must be unraveled during the soul healing process.

1. SPIRITUAL WARFARE.

Before this process can begin, however, there is a battle to be waged in the spirit world. I always begin my counseling days covering everything with detailed prayer. Also, my husband is a great prayer warrior and an excellent covering who prays with me and for me continually. We bind the activity of all demonic spirits—spirits of unbelief, doubt, confusion, deception, mind-control, rebellion, rejection, anger, hatred, bitterness, unforgiveness, pride, fear, suspicion, distraction, self-hatred, unworthiness, guilt, self-pity, double-mindedness—to name a few.

My husband and I render these spirits deaf, dumb and inoperative in Jesus' name and inform them that they may not interfere or create resistance of any kind. We cancel Satan's assignments against me, any other counselors and the counselees, plead the blood of Jesus over us all, and ask God to station warring angels around the counseling sessions to keep out all demonic forces.

Spirits of the occult must also be bound because, since faith visualization is the tool given by God to be used in healing of memories, Satan, of course, has a counterfeit. Some cults—Terry Cole-Whitaker's, for example, are doing counterfeit healing of memories, especially rebirthing, on large groups of people.

Dave Hunt, an American Christian apologist, in his book, *Seduction of Christianity*, failed to present truth to the body of Christ because he did not distinguish between the legitimate gift of the Spirit and Satan's counterfeit. Indeed, his judgments should have been leveled against the cults counterfeiting the gift instead of the anointed ministers who have legitimate ministries. But all of this criticism just reinforces my strong belief that healing of memories is a very powerful gift of the Spirit which Satan intensely hates and is trying to destroy!

When the Lord led me to begin ministering in healing of memories sixteen years ago, I did not know there was any such thing as a counterfeit spirit. But even though I never bound any demon of Spiritism, I have never had any problems. When I asked the Lord how I had been covered, He said that I had simply trusted Jesus and believed what He said in Luke 11:9-13. So, if we are in God's will, trusting Him and He has anointed us for this ministry, Satan cannot touch us!

But because of all the bad publicity, some counselees may have doubts about "faith visualization." There is one sure way to test it. During the visualization, the counselee can ask "Jesus" if He is the Son of God, come in the flesh, who died for our sins and was resurrected. If it is a demon impersonating Jesus, he will disappear!

Hunt did not mention testing the spirits because he does not believe that God gives us visions. He believes it is wrong to picture Jesus in our minds at all.

After binding the demons, my husband and I invite the Holy Spirit to anoint and use the counselors as His instruments, giving us wisdom, speaking truth and manifesting His gifts through us. We ask Him to open the minds of the counselees so they can receive truth and to melt their hearts so they can receive healing.

We ask the Spirit to baptize the counselors with love and to show forth and minister the fruit of the Spirit through us to the counselees. Because, although the gifts are important, it is vital that the counselees leave the counseling sessions with love, joy and peace in their hearts. A sure sign that a session has been successful is if the counselee feels the fruit so strongly that he does not want to leave! He just wants to bask in the Lord's presence! Thus, every counselor should wage spiritual warfare before attempting healing of memories.

2. PERMISSION OF INNER CHILD.

I believe that healing of memories is accomplished most effectively when both the counselor and counselee close their eyes, relax in the Lord's love, enter His presence with praise, and allow the Spirit to take over. I begin by worshiping and praising the Lord, thanking Him for His overwhelming love for the counselee, that "He bore him in his mother's womb, is intimately acquainted with all his ways," etc., praying Psalm 139 over the counselee.

As I ask the Holy Spirit to bring to mind the particular memory He wants to heal, the counselee will usually recall a certain experience. Satan may try to distract him by throwing weird images into his imagination. In this case, I bind the demons of fantasy, delusion, mind-control, confusion, doubt, unbelief and render them deaf, dumb and inoperative. If no memory comes to mind, it usually means that the counselee's Inner Child has not granted the Spirit permission to go back into his past.

Many, if not most, people can relate to God with their Adult but have failed to form a deep, intimate, love relationship with Him because their Inner Child does not trust Him. More often than not, a person's Internal Child sees God in the same way that he sees his parents. So, if his parents were controlling, abusive, irrational, unreliable, condemning, etc., his Inner Child will believe that God is also that way. This individual may believe in his mind (Adult) that "every good and perfect gift comes from God" (James 1:17), but in his heart (Child) he is not convinced. And "as a man thinketh in his heart, so he is" (Prov. 23:7).

We can imagine the concept the Inner Child of a woman who has been molested by her father has of God! Most likely, her Internal Child despises and is afraid of men and has vowed not to trust any man ever! This includes God since, supposedly, He is a "man." Any inner vow made as a child is so powerful that it controls a person's life even as an adult. Even God cannot go against an inner vow because He would be violating a person's free will if He did.

A counselee's Child withholds his permission for healing his past wounds because of one of two reasons. Either he is afraid to trust God with his painful repressed memories, or he believes his anger is justified and rebels against letting go of his hurts. Thus, we can understand why it is so important for a counselor to become a loving, caring, accepting, trustworthy "substitute parent" to the counselee. As his trust in his counselor grows, so does his trust in God as his loving Father. For the counselee whose emotions are severely damaged, this trust takes time to develop.

To obtain his Inner Child's permission to heal his past wounds, the counselee's Adult is instructed to break the vow that he will never trust anyone or allow anyone to "get inside his soul," as one counselee put it. His Adult then instructs his Child to grant the Spirit permission to take him back into his past. The counselee may be instructed to bind any demonic forces—rebellion, anger, fear, doubt, deception, suspicion, etc.—that might try to interfere with his healing and to render them deaf, dumb and inoperative.

The counselor then binds any resistance from Satan and cancels his plans. He asks Jesus to dissolve any walls, blocks or barriers and to mend the counselee's broken heart with his precious love because "perfect love casts out fear" (1 John 4:18). The counselee can then be asked to picture himself as a child walking up to Jesus, taking His hand, and giving Him permission to take him back into his past.

How the counselee's Inner Child feels will be made evident at this time by his response as a small child. One of my counselees saw herself as a fearful little girl cowering in a corner begging Jesus not to make her go back! Another saw herself stamp her little foot and turn her back on Jesus, while another saw her small self put her head on Jesus' shoulder and go to sleep! One who had been so severely abused that she had very little recall of her childhood saw herself as a child crumpled up into a tiny ball.

As I prayed, asking Jesus to flood her with his love and heal her wounds and scars, she was able to get up and walk, but she kept getting knocked down while she was trying to get to Jesus. She was able to see herself run into His arms and let Him hold her, but it took almost an hour of Spirit-led, "creative" prayer before she could walk up, take His hand and give Him permission to take her back to her childhood!

Thus, the Spirit was showing this counselee that, although her Inner Child was able to receive comfort and love from Jesus, she had difficulty trusting Him enough to allow Him to take her on the journey back to her past. By far, the most effective way to dissolve fear in the counselee's Child is to patiently, persistently pray that Jesus will make up for all the love that she had not received and heal her scars with His healing balm. Since perfect love casts out fear, immersing the counselee's Child in Jesus' love never fails to work!

When the counselee's Inner Child has granted his permission, Jesus will take him back to a memory. The counselee is instructed to let Jesus give him a picture of himself reliving the experience, feeling the same emotions that he felt at the time. This is possible as we learned from Penfield's experiments, because recorded experiences and their associated feelings are available for replay in the present in as vivid a form as when they happened. Since Jesus is not bound by any "time element," He can translate a memory into the present and heal it as if it were actually happening now.

Sometimes the counselee is able to visualize the event but feels no emotions. Again, this means that his Inner Child is not ready to release his hurts to the Lord. One counselee cried profusely when Jesus healed her of the pain, guilt and shame she felt when she "spanked" her six-month old baby fifteen years ago. But when the

Spirit brought back the memory of her parents dropping her off at an orphanage with her little red suitcase at the age of five, telling her that she would have to stay there until she could behave properly, she felt no emotions—just "dead inside."

She had repressed and denied all of her feelings concerning this experience because her parents had "killed" her emotionally. In this case, I asked Jesus to heal her little, crushed heart, breathe His life into her wounded soul and spirit and revive her emotionally so that her Inner Child could release her repressed emotions. Thus, it is important for the counselee not only to visualize a memory, but also to experience the feelings which he felt during the event. Only then will the counselor truly know that the hurts in his Inner Child have been released and healed and that he has forgiven his parents from the depths of his heart.

3. MIRACLES OF SOUL HEALING.

As the counselee visualizes Jesus entering the memory being healed, he will see Him doing the very thing that would have helped the most at the time of the original incident. For example, one counselee saw herself as a little girl struggling to hold her mother's head over the toilet as she was vomiting. Jesus entered the door, told her He would take care of her mother and that she was to go out and play. As she ran out, feeling free and happy, He closed the door behind her. Thus, Jesus healed her by lifting the tremendous burden of having to be responsible for the care of her sickly mother from her small shoulders!

As the counselee relives the memory with Jesus present, the counselor prays that Jesus' love and healing power will flow through him, cleansing and healing his wounds and scars with His healing oil. The more the counselor immerses himself in the experience, visualizing it and feeling what the counselee is feeling, the more inspired and creative his prayer will be. Many times, counselees have told me that right before I prayed something specific, they would already be seeing the very thing I prayed taking place!

The counselor can be so led by the Spirit in restorative prayer that he is not aware of what took place until it is over. An example of this concerns a session in which I was called in to help one of my counselors. Thinking we were still doing healing in the womb,

I began praying that Jesus' love would flow into the counselee as a "fetus." After a time, the counselee began gasping for breath, so I prayed repeatedly that Jesus would breathe His breath of life into her as a baby and call her little spirit forth to life.

Finally, the counselee began breathing easily again, so I continued praying, asking Jesus to cleanse her blood as a baby and exchange her blood for His. She felt a prick in her arm, then numbness and tingling in her arms and legs. Transfusion came to my mind, so I prayed and visualized Jesus' blood flowing through her veins as a baby until the tingling was gone even in her fingertips and toes. It is important to keep asking the counselee what she is feeling and patiently praying through until Jesus is finished.

I then felt peace flowing into the counselee as a baby as she fell asleep. Indeed, all three of us in the room fell asleep for a moment! The counselee then related that she had been an RH negative premature baby which explained the traumatic experience Jesus had just healed! She had been taken from the womb by Caesarean and had fought to live as her body was drained of its blood and transfused with new blood! I praise God for this very unusual healing of a memory!

Another example of Jesus healing a painful memory concerns a woman who made an inner vow as a child that she would save her parents' marriage no matter what. So, when her parents announced that they were getting a divorce and then both just nonchalantly went out for the evening, she was left all alone, feeling devastated, betrayed and abandoned! Jesus healed this memory by giving her a vision of her coming back, talking about the divorce and helping her express her feelings. They explained carefully that they both loved her very much and that she did not in any way cause their divorce, nor was she responsible for saving their marriage. That they would care enough to do this touched her deeply, and she cried profusely!

I then asked Jesus to cleanse her with His blood from the "false" guilt she felt from "failing" to keep her family together. She broke her inner vow that she had to save her parents' marriage and visualized herself giving Jesus this task. Since she was continuing to carry out her vow by trying desperately to save her own marriage, breaking her vow allowed her Inner Child to release this job to her

Savior also. She had not been able to release her marriage to God before, even though she had made an Adult decision to do so, because her Child was not in agreement.

Some memories are so traumatic that they have been totally denied and repressed. One counselee related in a frightened, small child's voice, as she was gasping for breath, that she saw blue all around her. The counselor surmised that she must have been drowning. As she asked the Spirit to reveal this memory, she saw the little girl's stepfather trying to drown her by holding her head under water! We cannot even begin to imagine how devastating such an experience would be to a helpless child! Only Jesus can heal such a terrible trauma! Even if a therapist could uncover this memory, he would not be able to heal the horrible wounds and scars suffered by this child.

Sometimes the Lord heals and delivers a person very quickly. Such was the case when I counseled a woman who had been a prostitute. She stated emphatically that she was "all prayed up," had been fasting, and wanted to receive inner healing and deliverance from a spirit of lust which she knew she had. As I asked the Holy Spirit to show us how this evil spirit had gained entrance, He revealed that she had been molested as a small child. As she was healed and cleansed of this experience, the demon of lust came screaming out!

After this the Spirit led me to take her through healing in the womb, during which she felt severe rejection which Jesus healed. He continued healing many childhood memories, one of which was the time when she was abandoned by her parents. She sobbed and sobbed but wanted to continue. We broke soul ties, curses and inner vows and dealt with her whole life in one exhausting session! She stated confidently that "it was finished," and she would not need to return.

Oh, that all soul healing would be that easy and accomplished that fast! The key to her quick soul healing seemed to be that she was strong in the Lord, had prayed and fasted and was ready to release everything to Him. So, we can see from this example that the rate at which a person receives soul healing depends on how willing he is to release his hurts to Jesus and receive healing from Him.

How personal the Lord is and how intimately He knows us is also revealed while experiencing healing of memories. In one case, a counselee had been traumatized when she read *Black Beauty* because she had identified with the beautiful horse who was shot, sent to the glue factory and dismembered—all described in vivid detail in the book. Jesus healed her by giving her a vision of a canary being released from a cage. This brought to her remembrance a dream about a canary she had had as a child which was so real that she had looked all over for the canary when she awoke.

Thus, Jesus healed her subconscious identification with the worthless, unwanted horse by showing her that He had transformed her into a beautiful canary whom He was setting free! Only our Maker can heal us so personally! The Spirit then revealed that from this experience the counselee had acquired a subconscious fear that whatever she read might be traumatic. This fear had caused her to suffer from extremely poor reading skills all her life. After the Lord healed her fear, her reading skills improved dramatically! I give God all the praise and glory for such beautiful emotional healings!

a. HEALING OF ABORTION MEMORIES. I could relate many examples of Jesus healing the scars and shame of women who have received abortions. Even though many of them had asked God to forgive them, they still felt a lot of quilt and pain. Some had denied and repressed their abortions because they could not live with what they had done. One woman came in for counseling because she was "clinging to her six-year-old son, feeling compelled to ask him over and over if he loved her.

When I asked the Spirit to reveal the healing that she needed, He immediately brought back the memory of an abortion she had experienced. Thus, she was displacing the loss of her aborted baby on her son, overprotecting and treating him like a baby. Her displaced guilt compelled her to demand constant reassurance of his love, but she was never reassured because she was really asking her aborted baby if he could forgive her and love her. With this counselee the Lord revealed to me how He heals the emotional trauma which results from an abortion.

In visualization, the Spirit brought back the memory of the counselee sitting in the clinic after she had received the abortion. She felt the agony, loneliness, hurt, guilt, shame—all the feelings she had experienced during that time. When I asked Jesus to heal the scars of this memory, we both saw Him holding a baby boy out to her, as he told her that this was her son. He then asked this counselee to give her baby a name, hold him and love him.

Jesus revealed to me that He could heal the trauma the baby went through physically, but the mother must heal the shock of the emotional rejection he felt by bonding him to her with love. Accepting her baby and bonding him to her removes the mother's guilt and shame. The counselee was sobbing as she held her baby, rocked him, told him how much she loved him, and asked him to forgive her. After a while Jesus gently took the baby back and told her that her son was waiting for her in heaven. It was a beautiful experience, and we both felt the Spirit very strongly! The counselee was in ecstasy with Jesus and felt His peace and love flowing through her!

As we know, Satan fills people with fear concerning inner healing because it is dangerous to his kingdom. Thus, he has tried to deceive some people into thinking that when Jesus heals an abortion memory, He is bringing the baby "back from the dead," which the Bible strictly forbids. However, this is not the case since Jesus is going back into the time when the abortion occurred and doing what He would have done had it been possible for him to enter the experience supernaturally at that time. Since our Lord is omnipresent, there is no time element for Him.

Whenever people try to contact the dead, it is for the purpose of gaining information, as in Saul's case (1 Sam. 28), which is why God forbids this practice. However, it is interesting to note that God Himself brought people back from the dead on several occasions. Moses and Elijah appeared with Jesus on the Mount of transfiguration and Moses, as we are aware, had died (Matt. 17:3, Deut. 34:5). Also, "...many bodies of the saints who had fallen asleep were raised and came out of their tombs and appeared to many" (Matt. 27:52, 53).

Also pertaining to this problem, if a parent or someone has died and memories need to be healed involving this person, Jesus is going back into the time when these memories occurred. So, the counselor is not bringing this person back from the dead as Satan has tried to deceive some people into thinking. This problem had never occurred to me because over the nineteen years I have been used in healing of memories, Jesus has healed the pain of many memories which involved people who had died.

b. HEALING OF MOLESTATION MEMORIES. I could relate many examples of our Master healing the wounded spirits of counselees who have been abused or molested. As they relived these experiences with their associated feelings, they saw Jesus come in and heal their wounds and scars. In the case of molestation or rape, it is not necessary for the woman to relive the memory, but her Inner Child should feel the emotions—terror, anger, shame, etc.—which she felt at the time.

In most cases, children are molested by relatives or close family friends. So, the Inner Child of a counselee feels guilty and ashamed because she did desire attention and love from these people, so somehow, she must have done something to cause this terrible thing to happen to her. The Inner Child of a counselee who was involved in incest has extremely confused feelings—feeling intense hatred and love for her father simultaneously—which she generally displaces on other men. Since the only understanding she has of love is connected with sex, she will attempt to satisfy her need for love through sex. Thus, many women who have been molested become promiscuous because they are still working out their Internal Parent-Child conflict while seeking a loving father relationship.

A married woman who has been molested may be very seductive, strongly desire sex and make herself very desirable to her husband. But she will usually sabotage their lovemaking by not being able to climax or enter into it emotionally or by rejecting her mate after leading him on. Her ambivalent behavior indicates that even though she desires her husband's love, her Inner Child despises him for "using her as an object" just like her father did. Naturally, this love-hate relationship is extremely frustrating to her husband and may eventually drive him to become a victimizer. In addition, she may suffer from any one or more of the numerous symptoms previously described.

Therefore, we can see how crucial it is for a counselee to receive emotional healing for the trauma of molestation. First, the counselor asks the Holy Spirit to bring back the memory of the counselee being molested and all of the feelings she felt at the time. Fear, anger, hatred, shame, guilt, betrayal, defilement, and degradation will, most likely, be the emotions she will experience. As the counselor asks Jesus to come in and heal the trauma of this hideous memory, the little girl will see Jesus rescuing her from her violator. One counselee saw her father turn into a snake and slither away as her Savior banished him from the scene!

The victim may feel intense anger and hatred, especially if the molester is her father, which she must be allowed to express. In this case, the counselor asks her to tell her dad exactly how she feels about his appalling behavior. With Jesus protecting her, she may tell him how much she hates him, that he ruined her life, made her promiscuous, destroyed her ability to have a good relationship with a man, laden her with a burden of guilt and shame, and caused her to suffer with anxiety, panic attacks, depression, addictions, or other symptoms. She should be allowed to say or do whatever she desires to express her anger so she will finally be able to release her hurts to her Lord and Redeemer.

One counselee timidly expressed her feelings to her father while hiding behind Jesus. Another brave little girl struck her dad many times, while another even saw herself plunge a knife into her father's heart! My first reaction to this shocking vision was, of course, that this was going too far! But the Lord reassured me that she was just releasing the anger and hatred which she had bottled up for many years. Then she saw her Master come in and lovingly "heal" her dad; she was finally able to give her excruciating pain to Jesus.

In this case, I worked with this victim for seven years before she was able to allow the Spirit to bring back the buried memory of the many years her father had tortured her with incest. This is the same lady who, when asked about her parents, declared emphatically, "I have no parents!" Because she had received absolutely no love from either of her parents and had suffered severe abuse and neglect from both of them, her hatred and bitterness were, understandably, quite intense and deeply rooted!

The counselee will usually want to know why her father or whoever molested her did such horrible things to her. Jesus will always reveal some very intimate, heart-rending details about how her perpetrator was abused and often molested when he was young. Her Redeemer will help her to see this man's deeply wounded Inner Child through His unclouded eyes and feel his pain and anguish with His loving heart. If she was courageous enough to tell her mother about her victimization, she may also ask Jesus why she did not listen to her or protect her. In most cases, it is more difficult for a victim to forgive her mother than it is her molester because she was supposed to take care of her.

As the counselor asks her how she feels about her mother's denial of her problem, the counselee will probably say that she feels not only totally betrayed and abandoned by her, but also extremely confused, disappointed and frustrated by her lack of acknowledgment and protection. Most of these mothers do not have the emotional capability or strength to even look at, let alone acknowledge and rescue their children from their husbands' despicable behavior. Thus, much to their children's chagrin, they live out their lives entirely in denial!

Jesus will again "enlighten the eyes of the little girl's heart" and reveal how abused her mom was as a child and often that she was also molested. He will show her how terrified she was of her husband and how petrified she was of leaving him and trying to support her children on her own. It continually amazes and excites me that Jesus not only reveals why a person was abusive, but also lets the victim actually feel the pain and agony suffered during childhood by his abuser! Many times, I have seen counselees sob in agony as they felt the pain and torment their parents or mates suffered as children. Only the Master can touch and melt our hearts with the pain of those who have wounded us so that we can not only truly forgive, but also truly love them! Praise God for His awesome love and power!

Another question that is invariably asked by a victim of molestation, especially of incest, is why God allowed these unspeakable things to happen to her. Although the counselor can explain to her that because God gave men free will, He cannot interfere with their actions even when they are despicably vile, she needs a more personal answer. Therefore, I always have the counselee ask Jesus this question directly. One woman was amazed and thrilled when her Savior told her that He had allowed these terrible things to happen to her because He knew He could trust her to be strong enough in character to eventually be able to forgive and love her father. She was very moved that Jesus said He trusted her even though He knew she did not trust Him!

Our Messiah lovingly shows these wounded lambs that every pain, anguish and degradation which they have suffered is exceedingly more precious to Him than the most costly treasure. He then gently asks them if they would be willing to place all of their suffering upon His altar and offer it up to their heavenly Father as a sacrifice of love. The Lord has shown me that the only gift we really have to give Him is our pain and suffering. This priceless gift costs us dearly because it requires us to give up our rights to hold onto and nurture our hurts.

As one counselee saw herself as a little girl place her tiny crushed heart on the Lord's altar, the Spirit gave me a vision of God "reeling back and forth on His throne" as He inhaled the sweet fragrance of her sacrifice! Our Father told me that nothing thrilled or delighted Him more than this little one's sacrifice! Indeed, He was in great awe that she was willing to present Him with her most cherished treasure! Thus, only their heavenly Daddy knows how much each precious gift of pain has cost the giver whose little soul and spirit have been so cruelly violated!

When the little child of the counselee is willing to release her hurts to her Comforter, she will be able to picture Him holding her close as she snuggles into His bosom. As the counselor asks Jesus to heal her deep wounds and scars with His healing balm, the counselee will feel His sweet, gentle love flowing through her, filling her with warmth and tenderness. The counselor then asks the Lord to cleanse away all of the shame, guilt, defilement, and degradation which she feels with His beloved blood. Jesus will give the counselee a picture of Him washing her as a little girl, cleansing away the feeling that she is "dirty" and unworthy and then clothing her in a beautiful white dress—His white robe of righteousness!

In one session, the Spirit brought back a repressed memory of a counselee being molested as a baby by her father as she was lying on her changing table. Her tiny pink dress was all soiled and wrinkled. After her healing, she saw Jesus putting the same pink dress on her, but now it was sparkling clean and beautiful! He even put pretty shoes on her and little socks with lace edges. Again, I find it remarkable that although the King of Kings possesses all of the power, honor and glory in the universe, He is so sensitive and perceptive that during soul healing He meets each little Inner Parent's unique needs down to the last detail! What an awesome King we have!

Next, the counselor breaks all ungodly soul ties between the counselee and her violator and asks the Father to send out angels to bring any parts of the counselee's soul that went out to her molester back to her and take any parts of his soul that went out to her back to him. He places the cross between the victim and her abuser, puts his sin of molestation upon the cross and asks God to forgive him and cleanse him with the blood of Christ. He then puts any curses of lust, promiscuity, masturbation, pornography, sexual perversion, etc., on the cross and breaks them. He asks the Lord to deliver the counselee from any hold these sins may have on her and to cleanse her from any effects from them. If the victimizer is her father, the counselor places the cross between her father and his parents and back through the generations and asks Jesus to cleanse the family bloodlines of any curses of incest, sexual perversion, lust, etc.

The counselor can then help the counselee's little girl forgive her abuser by having her picture him standing before the Master. Under the anointing, no one can stand before the Lord of Lords during visualization without seeing themselves as they really are. "No creature is hidden from His sight, but all things are open and laid bare before the eyes of Him with whom we have to do" (Heb. 4:13). The counselor asks the Redeemer to penetrate the molester's heart with His convicting love and bring him to repentance for the horrible things that he did to his victim. He also prays that Jesus' love will melt the victim's heart and flow through her out to her abuser. She will then be able to forgive him for violating her and wounding her so deeply. With her Savior's agape love, the counselee will finally be able to truly forgive her victimizer from her heart. Thanks be to God! It will now be easy for her to break her bitter root judgments of him and allow the Lord to melt away all of her hatred, anger and bitterness.

I continue praying, working and feeling with the counselee until she is able to visualize and experience deep healing. Although tears are not necessary for healing to take place, there is usually much sobbing as the counselee releases her pain to Jesus. This type of therapy is very draining because I "feel" the intense conflict going on in the little child as she struggles to let go of her pain. I enter into and "help" her gain the victory in this fervent battle with her flesh and the devil.

Often the counselee will feel various physical sensations, such as "choking," "suffocating," "tightness around the head or chest," "pains in the stomach or other parts of the body, etc." The counselor need not be alarmed by this, but he should reassure the counselee that her physical discomfort is due to her struggle to release her painful emotions. He should bind and cancel any demonic activities and keep asking Jesus to melt the walls of distrust around her broken heart with His precious love.

When she is at last able to let go of her hurts, I feel the struggle cease, the bondage break and blessed peace flow forth! Often, I will feel an "electric charge" of the Spirit's power flow through me when a person releases their hurts and deep healing takes place. I cannot tell you what a marvelous experience this is! Often the counselee will also receive a vision uniquely suited to her needs. After her healing, one incest victim saw herself as a little girl joyfully pulling on Jesus' beard and jumping off His shoulder into His lap! The Lord was showing her that it was safe to have fun with him like a Daddy which was something she had always desired.

How long it will take for a victim of molestation to let go of her hurts, pain and scars depends on how deeply she has been hurt and how much she has nurtured her feelings. It will also depend on whether she has just repressed her feelings or subconsciously denied the experience of being molested. If the experience was traumatic enough for the victim's Inner Child to deny that it even happened, it makes sense that she will do everything in her power to keep it from being disclosed. So, even if the Spirit reveals that it did happen by bringing the memory back in a vision, the counselee may still deny it. In this case, which is rare, the counselor can do nothing because the healing of a memory is based upon the recipient's accepting that it did happen and then allowing Jesus to heal the trauma associated with the experience.

Going through the visualization of a memory does not automatically bring healing either. If the counselee's Inner Child does not let go of her hurts, the Lord cannot heal them. I worked with one woman for over a year during which she and I both received many beautiful visions of Jesus healing her. But she refused to let go of her hurts, although she had received only slight rejection from her parents and others compared to other counselees. Every session she just cried and wallowed in self-pity until I finally lost patience and told her, lovingly, of course, that I did not feel that we were getting anywhere. Fortunately, although I have had several very difficult counselees, she is the only one I have ever had to give up on!

Thus, since God will not take anything from us that is not freely given to Him, soul healing is often a very long, slow process. It can proceed only as fast as the counselee can release her wounds and hurts, relax in the Lord, and receive healing from Him. Some people will receive only enough emotional healing to allow them to cope, but later, hopefully, they will be ready for more. Therefore, I would again emphasize how important it is for a counselor to let a counselee go at his own pace, rather than attempt to force the subconscious to release material before the person is ready. A counselor must always keep in mind that he is only God's instrument to be used however He wishes to accomplish whatever He desires. He must allow the Holy Spirit to be in charge at all times and to disclose only the issues and memories which He wants to resolve and heal because only He has perfect timing!

c. HEALING OF SATANIC RITUAL ABUSE MEMORIES. The horrors of Satanic Ritual Abuse (SRA) have only been revealed recently because the accounts of the survivors have been too hideous to be believed by the general public. However, to those of us who are Spirit-filled, the vile acts which Satan penetrated on these victims during childhood will come as no great surprise! Neither will we be surprised to hear that their numbers are multiplying and that the need for help is staggering!

Since secular therapists tend to separate psychological issues from spiritual ones, they are finding themselves virtually helpless to meet the specialized needs of these particular clients. Therefore, God is calling us, His chosen ones specifically trained in soul healing, to answer the cries of this special group of "wounded lambs." My fervent, daily prayer is that God will raise up many people who are willing to get involved in and/or pray for this crucial, end-time ministry.

To further complicate matters, survivors of SRA are often plagued with the symptom of Multiple-Personality Disorder (MPD). This is understandable since during childhood they were subjected to despicable acts of extreme abuse and torture by family members, who were, in most cases, involved in some form of the occult. Thus, they learned to use dissociation, a God-given coping mechanism, to help them deal with the intense pain and to protect them from the effects of the severe trauma accompanying SRA. In his fascinating book, *More Than Survivors*, Friesen states, "Dissociation is the instant, complete forgetting of a trauma. It effectively disconnects the person from the event. The traumatic memories are stored in alternate personalities, sometimes called 'alters,' where the events remain hidden from the other personalities" (pgs. 13,14).

Not only does dissociation allow the person to live without awareness of pain, but "switching" from one alter to another can also help him cope with the different tasks of his life. You may ask, "Well, if this individual can cope so well, why ask the Spirit to bring back his horrible, repressed memories?" Problems arise because the alters of a person suffering from MPD usually live entirely different, sometimes opposing lifestyles.

For example, one alter may go on exorbitant shopping sprees, resulting in the main (host) personality finding his house full of unwanted goodies when he "switches back in." Alters have been known to commit crimes, function as prostitutes, worship false gods, and perform numerous other activities which totally disrupt the lives of those suffering with MPD. Precious time is lost, and relationships are damaged as each alter vies to carry on his or her particular lifestyle.

Therefore, an individual with multiple personalities usually desires to have them "integrated" or merged into one whole, emotionally healthy personality. As we know, only God can perform such a miracle! I must admit that I found the subject of MPD and how to deal with it complicated, overwhelming and exhausting at first, especially Friesen's method of mapping hundreds of personalities and his clinical diagnosis of mountain and mesa patterns! My reaction was, "Forget it, I'm too tired for all this!" As usual, the Lord came through loud and clear! I was reminded of the saying, "Keep it simple, stupid!" God has such a marvelous sense of humor!

The Lord explained to me that the method of treatment for persons with MPD was exactly the same as that for people suffering from other symptoms—healing the pain and trauma inflicted on them in childhood, breaking generation curses, soul ties, inner vows, etc. Thus, my job was simply to take them through the soul healing process as the Holy Spirit directs, and Jesus would integrate the alternate personalities when the time was right. However, the soul healing process is more complex in MPD simply because the counselor is working with more than one personality. Also, the counselor must be able to discern the difference between an alter and a demon.

Unfortunately, many Spirit-filled believers, uneducated about MPD, have wrongly assumed that alters were demons—an understandable mistake. Nonetheless, much damage has been done by Christians who have tried to cast out alters or have barred saints from working in their churches because they were possessed with many "demons." Thus, although a person with MPD may also have demons, the alternate personalities are not demons. I repeat, alters are not demons!

When an alter emerges, especially an angry, demanding, arrogant one, the tendency is to speak harshly to it, tell it to "go back," and generally treat it like a "non-person." Instead, the counselor should treat every alter with respect, understanding and kindness, responding to him as he would any other person. He should tell each alter that Jesus loves him so much that He died for his sins, asking each one, as the Spirit leads, if he would like to give his life to the Lord. As the alters begin to realize how very much their Father loves them, they will be able to trust Him enough to make a joint decision to allow Him to heal their past hurts and do whatever is needed to unite them into one emotionally healthy personality. Thus, the counselor's goal is to help each alter experience His Daddy's love so fully that he will have no problem totally releasing his will to Him!

However, it is not always easy to differentiate an alternate personality from a demon! If the counselor is not sure whether he is speaking to an alter or a demon, he should just keep treating the entity as if it were an alter. As the Lord explained to me, if it is a demon, this despicable fiend will soon show its hand! This is important because the counselor should do everything possible to gain the trust of all the alters so they will all work together with him. This trust is quickly destroyed if one of them is treated with disrespect as if he were a demon! For those inexperienced with demons, they usually speak with raspy, low male voices, saying things like, "He's mine! You can't have him!"

More Than Survivors: Conversations With Multiple Personality Clients by Friesen recounts an extremely enlightening dialogue between a pastoral counselor and the alters and demons residing in his counselee. The counselor eventually discovered that his counselee had both an alternate personality and a demon named Philip residing in Him! After discovering the real name of this demon (Theta), this wise counselor did not immediately try to exorcise it. Instead, he kept commanding it to step aside" while he worked to get each of the alters to individually renounce this demon. Eventually, they all did, and Theta had to leave because the whole personality system had agreed that he must go, undermining his stronghold. Of course, the counselor should then ask the Spirit to reveal how this demon gained entrance so that any open door through which he might reenter could be forever closed.

Since I have only recently begun working with SRA survivors suffering from MPD, my experience in this area is limited. The exciting thing is, however, that I do not have to be concerned about this because I fully trust the Spirit to give me the wisdom, discernment and guidance and Jesus to perform the soul healing, deliverance and integration required to free His beloved lambs. Thank God that He does the work, while we are only called to be His instruments!

Unbelievable as it seems, most survivors of SRA have been forced to endure hellacious experiences of both sexual abuse and human sacrifice, completely destroying the precious innocence of their youth. One of the counselees with whom I am working has been sodomized by her father, molested by her mother and brutally beaten by both of them. Her grandfather, a kingpin in the Mafia, owned a house of prostitution where, as a young girl, she was sexually abused by many men. She was "affectionately" known as "the Mafia princess."

This counselee's wealthy grandfather built a cathedral where he was involved in satanic rituals with one of the priests. Around the age of thirteen, she was dressed as a "bride" and forced to "marry" Satan in a ritualistic ceremony performed by this priest. During soul healing she saw Jesus come in and heal the horrendous trauma of this experience. As I asked her Savior to sever each and every soul tie between Satan and her, she saw Him cutting all the chains off her and releasing her from all satanic bondage.

She renounced any ties with Satan as I prayed that angels would bring back to her any part of her soul that went out to the devil and destroy anything Satanic that had attached itself to her. This precious child of God saw her Bridegroom cleanse her from all defilement, dress her in a beautiful white gown, and put a gold ring on her finger! She was filled with joy as she was now married to the King of Kings! He told her that she was and always would be His "Little Princess!"

In another session, the Spirit brought back the memory of this dear lady being raped by the priest in a satanic ritual also at the age of thirteen. Jesus came into this memory, healed her of all the hideous scars resulting from this trauma and cleansed her of all degradation and depravity with His priceless blood. She then recalled being taken out of school and hidden away in a convent due to the pregnancy resulting from this rape.

This baby was, of course, considered to be Satan's child. I shall never forget this precious victim's screams of terror as she relived the unspeakable memory of being forced to sacrifice her cherished baby in a satanic ceremony! She held her hand high in the air, poised as if struggling to stop herself from plunging a knife into her helpless child. "No, no, don't let the baby stop crying! Please don't stop crying! I can't make the baby stop crying! Please don't make me! The baby has to keep crying!" she screamed in horror!

Words cannot describe how heart-rending her sobs were! For the first time, I was unable to shake my feelings after a session. I felt "haunted" that evening by her pitiful, helpless sobs. I was deeply grateful that I did not have to handle anything this traumatic in the early days of my ministry!

Mercifully, this dear saint saw Jesus come into this memory and gently take the knife from her hand. He miraculously healed this horrendous memory by bringing her "golden-haired baby boy," as she fondly described him, back to life and tenderly placing him in her arms. She sobbed with joy as she clutched her baby tightly to her bosom and gently rocked him. Eventually she handed him back to her Lord as He lovingly reassured her that He would take good care of her baby in heaven until she arrived. She wept tears of gratitude and joy as Jesus told her that He had "replaced" her loss by giving her a golden-haired boy as her second child. Understandably, this counselee had suffered for years from nightmares of babies crying helplessly.

Many heinous acts of abuse occur during the rituals held on the major holidays and feast days recognized by Satanism. Thus, many survivors of SRA often experience various emotional and physical symptoms on or around these dates. This particular counselee always suffered severe symptoms during the week before Easter. Thus, one Friday before Good Friday, the Spirit brought back a memory of her being sexually violated as a young girl while tied to a cross during a satanic ritual. Her hysterical sobbing was unbelievably gut-wrenching!

By this time the Lord had, to my delight, raised up the group He had promised me, naming it **Wounded Lamb Ministries**! Several women from the group were weeping uncontrollably on the floor, obviously experiencing her unbearable pain. Another was anointing her feet and praying that Jesus would heal them while she was having a vision of Him untying them. After what seemed to be an interminably long time, this counselee saw Jesus come and lift her ever so gently off of the cross. She saw Him cuddle her close to His bosom, heal the traumatic effects of this vile experience and cleanse her of all defilement with His priceless blood. Her Bridegroom then clothed her in a beautiful, white gown while one of the ladies saw Him hand her a beautiful gold crown with many jewels in it! Another had a vision of her flooded with brilliant light while we all felt the awesome presence of angels surrounding us! Praise be to God!!!

I am *sooo* grateful that God's timing is always right! He was faithful to bring help when I needed it most! I was so drained and exhausted after this dramatic session that I had to be prayed up off the floor! Thus, due to the enormity of the ordeals endured by SRA victims, I believe it is important to have groups of at least four or five people working with them. The burden of praying, "feeling the pain," breaking the curses and otherwise assisting the counselee is eased when shared by a group of anointed people. Also, it is so much more exciting and fun when the gifts of the Spirit are flowing through many saints, one receiving a vision, another a word of knowledge for the counselee, while another is breaking demonic forces and curses off of her!

What unity and intimacy are formed when saints allow the Spirit to have full control! Unfortunately, not many believers are healed and free enough to "be of one mind, united in spirit, intent on one purpose, and doing nothing from selfishness and empty conceit." I continually pray Phil. 2:2-8 over **Wounded Lamb Ministries.** I believe that many problems dividing the body of Christ would be resolved if each of us would, above all else, truly consider "the other as more important than ourselves!"

Ironically, the victims of SRA with whom I have worked have been the ones most eager to reach out and help others after they have received healing. Considering what they have suffered, their love, tenderness and patience is beyond belief! They are proof personified that the more pain a person has endured and placed on His altar, the more compassion, understanding, and empathy Jesus gives them for others.

As one SRA victim explained in the book, *More Than Survivors*, she now realizes that God was not standing in a corner with His hands tied behind His back, watching people do despicable things to her. He was on the altar and the cross with her. He was beaten and bloodied and horribly abused, and He knew each feeling and pain she suffered. She now knows a God who is well acquainted with grief—the "man of sorrows" the Bible talks about. She now sees herself as one who had the opportunity to identify a little bit more with what Christ went through, and, therefore, she has come closer to Him. She goes so far as to say that she does not believe she could have known the depths of His love if the suffering had not happened! Amazing!

Truly, God can and does cause all things to work together for good when we choose to put them on His altar as a sacrifice of love and praise! However, this admirable survivor of ritual abuse did not come to this realization overnight! It took her five long, often agonizing years of therapy before she could trust God and believe that He really did love her.

It is almost impossible for SRA victims to trust God, not only because of the torturous maltreatment they have suffered, but also because their Internal Parent has been so strongly programmed by Satan's followers. Due to such potent brainwashing, they have great trouble believing that God even has the power, let alone loves them enough to heal their emotional scars!

Mind control is the key element used to subjugate and silence SRA victims. They are subjected to a rigorously applied system of programming, brainwashing and indoctrination through the use of hypnosis, mind-altering drugs, hunger, thirst, pain, sleep deprivation, isolation, etc. The purpose of this mind control is to compel them to keep their abuse secret and to become functioning members of Satanism who carry out the directives of their leaders without being detected by society. Some of the judgments and inner vows relentlessly drilled into the Internal Parent of SRA victims are listed in **Table 9**. This information was compiled by Monarch Resources, a group dedicated to "Helping End Abuse and Ritual Torture (H.E.A.R.T.)."

One of the many ways to program victims is to force them to chant certain phrases repetitiously. Lauren Stratford was commanded to repeat the phrases "Satan is my father" and "I obey Satan" over and over for thirty minutes at a time, three times a day. She relates that she was saved from these chants becoming truths in her mind because as she said them out loud, in her heart she silently repeated, "Jesus is my Father" and "I obey Jesus only." Even so, she says she sometimes felt that Satan was becoming her father. Having discovered how immensely powerful judgments and vows made in childhood are, we can readily understand this!

The counselor should ask the Holy Spirit to reveal any judgments or vows the counselee may have been forced to make and/or chant as a Child. He should instruct the counselee to break these judgments and vows and to ask Jesus to cleanse his soul of all the effects of them. The counselee can then be encouraged to re-program his Internal Parent with new judgments and vows based on God's Word which will be discussed later.

Knowing how strong the Internal Parent's control is over the Inner Child, we realize that his counselor and others will have to expend a great amount of time, effort and love on an SRA victim before he will even begin to trust God to help him. The survivor of SRA whose story I have been relating came to me originally for help with her eight-year-old twin sons. Although I was able to do some soul healing with her, she would completely come "unglued" if I even so much as mentioned the word "demons!" She was terrified of even the thought of them! I worked with her for several years, loving her and becoming involved personally with her family. She is the counselee whose acute manic episode I described previously. After she moved away, I was no longer able to see her, but I kept in touch with her through writing.

About twelve years later, I felt led by the Lord to send this precious lady some material and ask if she would like to resume seeing me as she lived closer now. She was thrilled because she was praying for help and asking God to open the door if there was any way we could get together again. Because she was now a much stronger Christian and a foundation of love had been laid, she was finally able to trust God and me enough to allow the Spirit to bring back and heal the trauma of her hideous memories of ritual abuse.

Needless to say, I was amazed and appalled when these memories began surfacing in someone I had known for so long! But her excessive fear of demons, manic-depressive episodes and periodic emotional breakdowns now began to make sense. Due to the fact that I had laid a firm foundation of love and trust, she was able to receive healing from the Lord quickly and easily. Thank you, Jesus!

At first the memories were so shocking that it was difficult for her to believe that they had really happened. After a session of intensive prayer requesting the Spirit to bring these memories completely out of the subconscious into the conscious realm, along with commanding Satan to lose them, she was able to believe such heinous things really did happen to her. She is now much stronger emotionally, having received soul healing and a new identity in Christ. As a result, this dear friend has an intense desire to help bring healing to others, especially those wounded lambs who have been violated by satanic ritual abuse. She "knows that she knows that she knows" that only Jesus can set them free!

Another very special lady with whom our **Wounded Lamb Ministries** group is currently working has also been through SRA. As a result, she suffers from MPD as well as many physical problems. A foundation of love and trust was laid for her by faithful, compassionate friends in her church and a loving Christian doctor. One dedicated saint became her "mother figure," ministering to her in the hospital and helping her with all the problems unique to those laboring with MPD.

Thus, enough groundwork had been done to enable this child of God to trust our group to begin doing memory work. Interestingly, before we had a chance to ask the Spirit to bring back the memory that He wanted to heal, the alter who carries a lot of the core personality's anger emerged. She furiously declared, "What good is all this, anyway? This is all a big waste of time! She (the host personality) should just go home!"

I respectfully explained to this alternate personality that Jesus was very powerful and that He could heal the emotional hurts and scars from the counselee's past. I said that she wanted to give it a try and see if it might work. I told the alter that Jesus loved her also and wanted to heal her pain as well. I humbly appealed to the alter to allow the host personality to come back and see if She left peacefully and allowed the core personality to return.

The Holy Spirit then brought back a traumatic memory of molestation which Jesus tenderly healed. An interesting point concerning this counselee is that one of her "child" alters would always emerge to relive and receive healing of the pain this particular alter still carried from the memory she actually experienced.

One of these shocking memories revealed that her parents had always made her throw away the toys she received on Christmas morning before the day was even over! She was actually required to go out in the snow, throw them into a dumpster, light a match and set fire to them! All because she had, supposedly, "done something wrong"—something absurd like fold her doll clothes incorrectly! Unbelievable! You can be sure that all of our "little girls" felt her horrible anguish at having to burn up all of her new Christmas toys! It would seem less traumatic for a child not to receive any toys at all than to have to burn them up!

Amazingly, her child alter was able to see Jesus come into and heal this devastating memory! She was actually thrilled that He was helping her light the matches and throw her toys in the trash, while comforting her and reassuring her that He would give her much more beautiful gifts than she could ever imagine! She was excited that it actually felt warm even though she was standing out in the snow without a coat! She was filled with joy and literally bouncing up and down because Jesus was *sooo marvelous*! It is a treat to work with this sweet saint since she, through her child alter, literally obtains emotional healing as a "little girl"—certainly the ideal way to get it!

Another exciting fact she disclosed is that she (the adult core personality) is always present when Jesus is healing her child alter! Coexistence of the core personality with the Child alter during healing of a memory is important since it means that the counselee has now made that memory part of her, integrating it into her whole personality. Therefore, it seems reasonable to assume that the more memories carried by the different alters are healed and integrated into the host personality, the easier it will be for the alters to allow Jesus to merge them into one whole, emotionally healthy personality. How remarkable our precious Savior is!

Now that I think back, it thrills me to recognize how the Lord directed **Wounded Lamb Ministries** in our work with this special saint! After she had received healing of several memories during our weekly group meetings, He "arranged" to have only four ladies whom she trusted work with her on a day when there just "happened" to be no family members in the home in which we met. The reason for this is now crystal clear. Some extremely powerful demonic activity was encountered during that session. How awesome to serve a God who has our lives planned down to the last detail!

The Spirit first brought back the horrifying memory of this sweet lady being forced to sacrifice her baby as a young girl. This was not a buried memory, and one of her child alters received healing from the trauma of it quite easily. She saw Jesus come in and "put the heart back into her baby boy," whom the Lord had given the name David. He cleaned up all of the blood from the scene and then cleansed her of all defilement, guilt and shame. She saw her loving Savior rocking and cuddling tiny David before He took him to heaven to wait for her there. At this point, the core personality reappeared. She was thrilled that the pain and ugliness were finally gone from this memory–healed and cleansed by the omnipotent Blood of Jesus! What a marvelous miracle!

Next, the Spirit brought back the unspeakably appalling memory of this counselee being violated as a young girl by her uncle and a large black man in her uncle's butcher shop. They had draped her over a stool, placing her stomach on the seat and tying her arms to her legs underneath it. Unbelievable as it seems, one was sodomizing her while the other was forcing her to perform oral sex on him! They would then actually exchange positions and continue performing these dreadful, lecherous acts on her! Only Jesus knows the terrifying pain and suffering she endured during this hideous ordeal!

The child alter who was reliving this experience was quite resistant to allowing Jesus to come into this situation. First, she said that she didn't want Him to come in because "He would get dirty and He had to stay clean." We finally convinced this little one that Christ had been the "dirtiest" person of all because He had taken everyone's sins on His back and actually become sin for us when He died on the cross.

Next, she claimed that Jesus could not see her because she was behind the big freezers. When we assured her that He could see everything because nothing was hidden from his sight, she insisted that He could not come in the door because the "laws" were up by the door. This lady's father was from a Jewish family. We assured her that Jesus would have no problem crossing the threshold because He had fulfilled the Jewish law and He was Lord of Lords and King of Kings over the law and all things. Just when her child alter finally let Jesus approach her, a demon took over this counselee's body and she rose up ominously out of her chair!

This evil spirit adamantly announced that this person was his, and we could not have her because he had rights! He began growling menacingly and cavorting around the room as we attempted to restrain his movements. Although this woman is six feet tall and large and we were in a beautiful home with many lovely, breakable things, I felt complete peace as the Spirit quietly reassured me that no one would get hurt and nothing would be broken. I knew then that God was surely with us because this would really take a miracle! If five men had not been able to restrain a small woman, as related earlier, we did not have a prayer without much assistance! We are all exceedingly grateful for the many angels who undoubtedly helped us that day!

Although the demon attempted to kick, bite, scratch, and grab us, especially our hair, two or three of us were able to hold him down relatively easily. At one point, he broke loose; growling vehemently and spitting and endeavored to leave the house. At another point, he was prancing around in circles on the couch, shrewdly trying to distract us by putting on a show. This was clearly a very intelligent demon as he made many clever remarks in an effort to divert us from our mission. We would try to shut him up by placing a hand over the counselee's mouth, which he would then strive to bite.

This ingenuous adversary also tried to deceive us by "pretending to be asleep." The counselee's eyes would close, and her body would go completely limp, lifeless like dead weight. We would then endeavor to "wake him up" by shaking her head and slapping her cheek gently, telling him he could not "hide" and commanding him to come back, etc. The situation was very frustrating because I found that I had amazing strength to control the demon's actions, yet I did not want to hurt the counselee in any way.

The whole scene was quite wild as none of us were experienced in dealing with such a powerful, lively, stubborn demon. Although my three partners had not even taken part in a deliverance before, they exhibited remarkable faith, maturity and stamina! This affirms the fact that when God is directing the action, everything is under His control and proceeds according to

His plan. When asked, the evil entity informed us that he was the demon of Baal and that his point of entry was "up her a**!" This explained why he manifested right when Jesus came in to heal the memory of this dear saint being sodomized. He also told us that we had gained ground and lessened his stronghold on her due to the memory that had just been healed. He confidently added, however, that she was still his and we would never have her! I must admit it was gratifying to hear such a mighty demon confirm that healing of memories was the way to undermine demonic strongholds!

We all, quite vociferously and vigorously, bound this evil force, broke its power and commanded it to quit manifesting and come out in Jesus' name numerous times. We claimed all the rights the blood of Jesus had purchased for this child of God as His heir and fellow heir of Jesus Christ. We sang, claimed scripture, anointed her with oil, and even sponged her with "Holy Water!" This diabolical devil spat at us and brashly mocked the blood of Jesus, insisting that it had absolutely no power over him!

Knowing that his foothold was too firmly entrenched, after a while I commanded him to allow the core personality to return. Although this precious lady is a very devoted Christian, one of her alternate personalities was known to worship Baal. Understandably, the fact that her alters were not in agreement that this demon had to go gave him undeniable rights to stay.

Also, the host personality is a classic passive dependent whose Internal Parent has been rigidly programmed by Satanists with many of the beliefs listed in **Table 9**. The principal parental judgment controlling her Inner Child is that she must always obey. The life-controlling inner vow made by her Child is that she will avoid conflict at all costs by always being perfectly obedient. As we shall see, her child alters are firmly controlled by this vow. Therefore, since this counselee has multiple personalities that are not in agreement, in addition to a rigid script controlling her Inner Child, demons have been able to gain strong footholds in her soul which are not easily broken.

The host personality returned, totally oblivious to what had just taken place. She was very apologetic and worried that she might have offended or hurt one of us. We assured her that she had not and that we all still loved her. We did not think it wise to share too much of the proceedings with her—only a few funny incidents, as we did not wish to embarrass her.

After a refreshing rest and a delicious lunch served by our gracious hostess, we decided to partake of communion. Although we felt the Lord's love and anointing, we all watched, guardedly, as our dear sister raised the communion cup to her lips. Instantly, grape juice spewed all over and the cup flew from her hands, announcing "you know who's" return! Round two did not last long, however, as we had all had enough. After some grappling with the demon, one of the women, a nurse, held the counselee's nose while she poured the contents of another communion cup down her throat! The core personality returned immediately, and I knew our battle with the enemy was over for today!

Lying on the couch exhausted, this brave survivor now had no trouble seeing Jesus come into her memory of sexual abuse. Her child alter saw Him gently untie her hands and feet and lift her into His strong, loving arms. Holding her close to His bosom, He rocked and soothed her, healing all her deep scars and pain. After cleansing away all of the trauma, horror and depravity with His glorious blood, her sweet Lord placed a beautiful white dress and pretty little shoes and ruffled socks on His precious child. Feeling a great sense of relief that this ordeal was over, she fell into a deep, peaceful sleep. Overcome by a feeling of awe and reverence, I knew that we had been privileged to take part with the angels in bringing about a wondrous miracle that day!

We all hoped that we had seen the last of the demon of Baal, but I felt sure that he would be back. Sadly, this counselee is also afflicted with many severe physical problems. But even though the next day she ached all over, especially her arms from being restrained, in a few weeks, she agreed to another session. This time the Spirit brought back the dreadful memory of "the table," from which she pleaded to be spared. "No, no, not the table! Please don't make me go down to the table! Please don't make me get on it! I can't do it—it hurts too much!" her child alter cried out! Needless to say, our hearts were breaking for her, and we were more than willing to quit right then and there! But, of course, we knew this was not what God wanted, so I gently assured her that all of our "little girls" would go down and get up on the table with her and help her get through this ordeal.

Apparently, this appalling satanic ritual had taken place in a church because she had to walk down the aisle to a table placed, most likely, at the altar. After much persuasion, she saw herself, tightly gripping our hands, walking hesitantly down to the dreaded table. People dressed in robes with hoods on their heads, including her mother, were standing around the table. After placing this precious child on the table, they tied her arms and legs to it, with her head, somehow hanging over the top of it. Then, as inconceivable as it seems, one man after another got on the table and forced her to perform oral sex on him!

The child alter was writhing and crying pitifully, "No, please don't! No, I don't want to! Please stop; it hurts!" But then, amazingly, she would say devotedly, "Yes mommy, I will do it. Yes, mommy, I will obey you." She would swallow, gagging pathetically, and then repeat this ghastly "duty" again and again! It was heart-wrenching to see how desperately she desired to please her mother and gain her approval!

Watching her groan and writhe in pain as she relived this horrifying memory was more than we could bear! We tried frantically to bring Jesus into this gruesome scene, but this sweet child presented every reason why He could not help her. She protested that she had to obey her mother, that Jesus wouldn't come to this bad place, that He shouldn't come as he would get "dirty," and that maybe He couldn't come because He wasn't able to! Incredibly, in the midst of this horrendous abuse, she kept complaining that a bright light coming through a high window was shining in her eyes. After what seemed like an eternity, she finally saw Jesus coming in the distance. Hallelujah!

But just when victory appeared imminent, the vile spirit once again reared his ugly head! Growling and hissing ferociously, he declared that she still was and always would be his! No doubt he was furious because we were dealing with the atrocious events that took place on that horrid table. So, he manifested even more violently this time, but we just kept binding him and commanding him to let the child alter return. It should be noted here that, as before, one of the groups called our pastor, my husband and other prayer warriors to do spiritual warfare for us.

Terrified when she came back, this little one implored us pathetically not to make her go back. Irresistible as her cries were, we lovingly beseeched her to return so that Jesus could heal her pain and set her free from the horror of this memory forever. Reluctantly she went back, but we did not make much progress before the demon returned, kicking, clawing and seething viciously! I lost count of how many times this powerful evil entity reappeared—probably five or six.

At one point when the child alter returned, she noticed some blood on her arm. Shocked and confused, she was sure that we had been hurting her! Turning to her trusted mother figure, she begged her to let her stop now and go to sleep. Fearing for her health, this dear lady seriously questioned whether we should continue. Knowing that we must see this ordeal through even though this little one was also tearing at my heart strings, I gently reassured them both that it would not take much longer, and that Jesus had the victory. About this, I had no doubt!

Hoping to break the demon's main stronghold, I asked the young alter to repeat after me, "Jesus is stronger than Satan and all the demons of hell!" The instant she repeated this, the demon of Baal, raging fiercely, burst forth with a vengeance! After struggling with this depraved spirit for a while, another child alter appeared, insisting that her friend wanted to play now and that she had to come and color with her. Promising that Jesus would take good care of her friend, he convinced her that His will must be done.

Reappearing, the child alter calmly informed us that Jesus wanted her "big person" (adult core personality) to come down the aisle and get up on the table with her. The counselee saw herself doing this as Jesus came closer to the gruesome scene. She then felt like she wanted to get rid of all the "icky stuff" she had swallowed. But as she attempted to bring it up, the sordid spirit made one last endeavor to stop the proceedings. He was not out long before the host personality returned, horrified and panic-stricken!

Shaking and running around the room, she looked at me with terror in her eyes, pleading desperately, "Get it off of me! Please hurry! Get it off! It's like a huge, horrible, scratchy, brown coat all over me! It's killing me, smothering me! I can't stand it! Please, help me!" Having no idea what this "thing" might be, but knowing it had to be demonic, we all frantically began breaking the evil forces off of her and commanding them to go.

Finding no relief, this tormented soul ran to the kitchen, put her head in the sink, and implored us to douse it with the dish sprayer! Still in indescribable agony, she then ran to the bathroom, crying that she had to wash it all off! Having some slight concept of the torture she was suffering, I urged her to jump in the shower, clothes and all. Turning the shower on full force, she drenched herself. When I finally reached in the shower to turn it off, I found her crumpled in a ball in the corner.

Her child alter was quietly saying in an exhausted, but sublimely peaceful, voice, "He's here. Jesus is untying my arms and legs and lifting me off the table. He's holding me tight in His big, strong arms. Oh, it's *sooo* warm and safe here! I want to stay in His arms forever! He's going to take me away now." Concern and anxiety suddenly filled her tiny voice. "Oh PLEASE, Jesus, I want mommy to come, too. Please, please bring her, too! Oh, her face is really ugly in her hood. Jesus says mommy has to stay. She's not ready to leave yet. I have to trust Him. Okay, Jesus."

Lost in the incredible vision, she continued calmly, "Oh, all the awful people are gone now, and a beautiful light is filling the whole room! Jesus is taking one out of the room now and closing the door behind us. He is putting two big angels with swords at the door. It's all over now. I can rest." Her voice was so serene and full of awe and there seemed to be an ethereal essence about her. "Thank you, Jesus," I sighed with relief and immense gratitude. I told her what a remarkable job she had done and that Jesus and all of us were sooo proud of her! Dry and comfortable, she immediately fell into a deep, contented sleep.

Even though her arms ached the next day and her thumb had somehow been dislocated, this dear sister was very glad she had gone through the difficult process to gain her hard-won victory. Even as Jesus, she endured the cross for the joy set before her! Elated, she exclaimed that now every time she thought about the room where the atrocities took place, it was empty, All the terrible people were gone, the dreaded table was bare, and a brilliant light filled the room! Her voice was filled with reverence and disbelief that the Lord had actually erased the scars and trauma of this particularly painful memory. We give You all the glory and praise, Jesus!

Since we have not had another session with this courageous survivor yet, I cannot say for certain that the demon of Baal has finally departed. What I *can* say for certain is that our Redeemer won the victory over him at the cross. Therefore, as she continues to submit to His healing and deliverance, all evil forces must flee because this precious child of God is 100% sold out to God!

In fact, I have been astounded by how deeply devoted both of these very special saints are to the Lord, considering all of the barbarities they have suffered. They are, without a doubt, the most compassionate, sensitive, self-sacrificing women I know! So eager to help others and serve their Master, they do not even so much as hesitate to count the cost! No doubt this is because they have already paid a price most of us cannot even begin to comprehend! Well acquainted with grief, they are much closer to the Man of Sorrows than the rest of us.

Having been up on the cross with Jesus, no emotional pain is too agonizing for them to look at, understand and get into. Even more amazing to me is how deeply sensitive they are to the slightest pain of another person; hurts which seem so insignificant compared to what they have endured. They would insist, however, that I give all the honor and glory for their astounding sensitivity to the King of Kings!

God, of course, has mighty plans for these two brave survivors. As an example, an acquaintance recently called one of them and said that the Lord had told her to ask her to come and stay at her home. Although feeling apprehensive and reticent, she agreed to go. When told that Jesus could heal the pain of her memories, her hostess was eager to receive whatever God had for her. Impressed by how happy and peaceful she was after receiving soul healing, her husband, who works with Vietnam veterans suffering from Post-Traumatic Stress Disorder (PTSD), was also interested in hearing about it.

Sometime later, the eighty-year-old lady who lived across the street came over. She said that God had told her to "humble herself and go ask the blonde nurse visiting across the street what God had for her." Even though she had long nurtured her anger and bitterness, this lady easily received deep healing of her emotional scars and wounds. The "blonde nurse" was so excited and thrilled that she was not even fazed when she broke her leg the next week! A few days later, she slipped while reaching for her crutches, fell and injured her back. Satan was obviously not too happy about her good deeds!

In spite of these calamities, she was ecstatic that God had used her and that she had been able to "accept love" from the grateful ladies whom she had blessed! This daughter of Zion had never dared hope that the God of the universe could or would use her in such a mighty way! She shared that her hostess remarked that she looked like a "little scared rabbit" when she came to her home to minister! By the way, her injuries have not stopped her ministry.

Praise God for fulfilling the scripture He gave me years ago that "He would assemble the lame and gather the outcasts and make the lame a remnant and the outcasts a strong nation and the Lord God would reign over them in Mount Zion" (Micah 4:6-8). We in **Wounded Lamb Ministries** truly epitomize the gathering of the lame and the outcast! We praise our Father that we are able to richly bless others only because of God's mighty anointing of love and power in both the gifts and fruit of the Spirit! A beautiful, heart-rending poem written by one of the "outcasts," describing her struggle to surrender her pain to Jesus is portrayed in **Table 10**.

I chose to describe in detail our sessions with the SRA victims for several reasons. SRA resulting in individuals, especially women, suffering from MPD, is becoming much more prevalent in our society. Since the church as a whole is not meeting the needs of people effectively or doing spiritual warfare against satanic forces, more individuals are being lured into the occult than ever before. Therefore, it is imperative that believers learn how to work with and meet the specialized needs of SRA survivors, particularly those suffering from MPD. Much harm has already been done to these disparaged individuals by well-meaning, albeit unknowledgeable Christians, adding insult to injury. This, fellow saints, is an unforgivable travesty!

As was noted before, the burden for treatment should fall on Christians because we are, or should be, capable of dealing effectively with the spiritual, as well as the psychological, issues which these particular people face. Accomplishing this goal will require training pastors and laymen, not only in how to heal the ravaged souls and spirits of SRA victims struggling with MPD, but also in how to help them develop healthy living routines.

When a church is providing support and a sense of community for one of these survivors, she feels loved and wanted. As believers reach out to her with compassion and accept her unconditionally, any non-Christian alters which are part of her personality system will be drawn closer to Jesus. Understandably, not much healing and integration can take place until most of her alternate personalities are loyal to Jesus. As our Lord said, "A man cannot serve two masters."

Because they were controlled and programmed so strongly, alters who have been converted to Christ from the occult often feel abandoned, lonely and vulnerable. Thus, they may need an inordinate amount of attention and nurturing from God's people. I believe our Father is calling us to provide a healthy, safe, nurturing extended family for these hurting alters, as well as all abused adults and children. If the Christian community fails in this task God is calling us to, magnanimous though it is, more and more desperate, hurting people will be enticed by Satan into cults, the occult, homosexuality, drugs, etc. Demonic forces operating through the poor souls who have already been taken captive by them, are more than willing to meet the needs of every lonely, wounded victim!

The members of a church attended by a person diagnosed with MPD should be trained not to react with shock or disapproval when different alters appear, including the angry, difficult ones, but to accept and love them just as they are. This will help establish a foundation of trust so this individual will be willing to submit to soul healing conducted by a trained, Spirit-led group of laymen (counselors) in the church. Hopefully, sharing our group's experiences will help prepare these Spirit-led counselors to accept and deal with whatever gruesome, gory acts may have been perpetrated on victims of SRA. There is no deed so vile that they have not experienced it! Even so, the glorious fact is that neither is any deed so heinous that the King of Kings cannot heal the devastating effects of it!

Hopefully, our experiences will also point out the powerful stronghold a demon may have on an SRA victim due to the rights which he gained through ritual abuse. Our sessions also reveal that this demonic foothold, in all probability, can be broken only by allowing Jesus to heal the trauma of this ritual abuse. Thus, our work with SRA survivors confirms what I believe the Lord revealed to me—soul healing closes the doors through which demons gained the right to enter a person's soul. Their rights to inhabit a soul having been abolished, demons have no choice but to leave and never return!

Last, but not least, I have discussed our work with SRA survivors in detail because of the latest tactic Satan is employing to plant doubt in people's minds concerning the validity of SRA—the False Memory Syndrome (FMS). The ever-popular talk shows have been thoroughly indoctrinating people with the notion that most of the repressed memories which come back, especially those involving incest and SRA, are simply not true. Since Humanism has convinced our society that man is basically good, the idea that he could perform such despicable, horrendous deeds on women and children is just too repulsive and unbelievable to accept!

Some women have, indeed, recanted on these shows and declared that they had "lied," that they were not really subjected to the despicable acts of incest and SRA. They claim that these wretched memories were implanted in them by unscrupulous therapists for the purpose of getting insurance money. Most of these so-called therapists employ regressive hypnosis (RH), which claims to bring back memories from past lives, reinforcing the belief of reincarnation. Having watched tapes of people supposedly reliving memories from former lives, I have to admit they are absolutely convincing. These persons display all of the intense emotions and behavior which we see when an individual is reliving a memory revealed by the Holy Spirit! Amazing!

Even though practiced by some Christian therapists, I do not believe in using hypnosis to bring back memories because it can open up our souls and spirits, making them vulnerable to demonic activity. However, I do believe that memories revealed under hypnosis can be valid. Some examples of "womb memories" returning during hypnosis which have been verified by the subjects' parents are related in the next section.

Nonetheless, regressive hypnosis is obviously demonic because it assumes that we all lived previous lives before being born as the people we are today. It is astounding how many people are falling for this lie from the pit of hell! Apparently, being deceived by this lie opens up a person's soul so that Satan and his cohorts can somehow replay the memories, possibly, of individuals who lived in former times. Thus, most likely, it is not the therapists, but evil spirits, who are implanting false memories. I have no idea how they are able to do this or why God has allowed Satan to have so much power except that I believe that we are definitely living in the last days!

Sincere people have even stated on talk shows that repressed memories of "encounters with aliens" surfaced while they were under regressive hypnosis. They described these "aliens" as ugly, grey, three-foot tall creatures with almond-shaped eyes and angry mouths who screech like mice! Others declared that they had actually seen beings of this exact description in person. One desperate lady alleged that one had been visiting her at night every few weeks. He would lie on top of her and try to get her to relive her past sexual experiences. She was not sure if he had "raped" her, but she had suffered excruciating pain in the vaginal area. These devastating encounters had even destroyed her marriage!

Everyone was completely convinced that these creatures were aliens because some people had also seen UFOs. The sincerity in their eyes and voices, plus the fact that they all gave exactly the same description of these beings, made it impossible for me to question the veracity of their stories. It appears that Satan has a plot going to make mankind believe that demons are really aliens resembling E.T.! Are we in desperate need of a rival or what?!

The FMS is, of course, Satan's clever tactic to convince people that SRA does not exist and that the poor unfortunates claiming to have been subjected to it are simply lying. I was shocked and appalled to hear believers on a Christian radio show emphatically declaring that Stratford's revealing book, *Satan's Underground*, was nothing but lies, written for her profit! Jesus, save us from ourselves!

As the Word says, in the end-times, even the elect will be led astray. We most certainly must be gentle as doves and wise as serpents to sort out the truth from the lies and be able to help all of the deceived, tortured souls God will be sending to us. Because the church as a whole is apathetic, weak, divided, and uninformed, it appears that only a small army of saints will be ready to meet the challenge!

d. HEALING OF WOMB MEMORIES.

(1.) Experiences In The Womb. Even though I have discussed at length how to work with and bring about healing of the devastating memories of SRA victims, we should keep in mind that they represent only a small portion of all the hurting, abused souls in our communities. Many, if not most, of these victims of abuse have suffered severe rejection in the womb. Therefore, sometime during the process of soul healing, the Holy Spirit will bring back the memory of the traumas which a counselee experienced in the womb.

In his fascinating book, *The Secret Life of the Unborn Child*, Dr. Verny states that since his experience in the womb is a child's first taste of the world, it establishes his expectations. He goes so far as to say, that how he experiences the womb actually creates certain character predispositions. If it is hostile and rejecting, he will anticipate that his new world will be equally uninviting. Thus, he will be predisposed toward distrust, suspicion, fear, and introversion.

A study done by Dr. Gerhard Rottmann of the University of Salzburg, Austria, as cited in Dr. Verny's book, on 141 women, found that mothers who wanted their babies both consciously and unconsciously (shown by psychological testing) had the easiest pregnancies, most trouble-free births and the healthiest offspring—physically and emotionally. The mothers who did not want their babies had the most devastating medical problems during pregnancy, and bore the highest rate of premature, low weight and emotionally disturbed infants.

On the basis of a study done on 1300 children and their families, also cited in Dr. Verny's book, Dr. Dennis Stott estimated that a woman locked in a stormy marriage runs a 237 percent greater risk of bearing a psychologically or physically damaged child than a woman in a secure, nurturing relationship. He found that unhappy marriages produced children who, as babies, were five times more fearful, jumpy and emotionally dependent than the offspring of happy relationships.

Many studies found that a trauma occurring during a pregnancy produced hormones in the woman which flood her baby with anxiety. In one case, a woman's husband had threatened to kill her and in another, the husband had died in an accident. In both cases, the violent kicking of the fetus was tenfold what had been recorded before the traumas occurred. Studies also reveal that the child in utero reacts with violent kicking to rock music and to the music of Brahms and Beethoven, while reacting favorably to the music of Mozart and Vivaldi.

Dr. Michael Lieberman, as cited in Dr. Verny's book, showed that an unborn child grows emotionally agitated (as measured by the quickening of his heartbeat) each time his mother even thinks of having a cigarette! Smoking causes a drop in his oxygen supply since it lowers the oxygen content of the maternal blood passing the placenta. This thrusts him into a chronic state of uncertainty and fear since he never knows how long this oxygen drop will last or how painful it will be. This situation predisposes him to have severe anxiety and fear after birth.

Some fascinating cases show that it is possible to begin teaching an unborn baby. A gifted musician stated that he was able to play certain pieces sight unseen. His mother solved this mystery by relating that all the scores he knew sight unseen were ones she had played while pregnant with him. In another case a two-year-old was chanting to herself, "breathe in, breathe out" over and over. The mother, who had lived in Toronto during her pregnancy, realized that her daughter could not have picked this phrase up from television because it was only used in Canada. Thus, she must have memorized the words while still in her womb!

Another case concerned a small French child who neither spoke nor appeared to hear when spoken to. Under treatment, the doctor noticed that she improved markedly when he spoke English instead of French. The mystery was solved when her mother casually mentioned that during her pregnancy she had worked in an import-export firm where only English was spoken!

Even the Bible refers to the prenatal influences upon a child. In Luke 1:44, Elizabeth exclaims, "For behold, when the sound of your greeting reached my ears, the baby leaped in my womb for joy!"

Some studies seem to indicate that paranoid schizophrenia, or "schizophrenia with paranoia," as doctors now call it, has its roots in the womb. Examination of the brain tissue from 10 deceased schizophrenics revealed a disorganization among cells within the hippocampus, a portion of the brain believed to be associated with the expression of emotion. Researchers speculated that normally well-ordered cells within the brain of an unborn child could be thrown into disarray due to maternal distress.

Thus, we can see from these studies and cases that a person's experiences begin in the womb and affect him the rest of his life. Every adopted child has experienced rejection in the womb. He has absorbed his mother's fear, anxiety, guilt, shame, confusion, anger, and pain. He is confused about his identity and his right to live which, in turn, affects his will to live. Even in the womb, judgments may be made, such as, "No one wants me, so something must be wrong with me." "I'm a burden, a mistake." Inner vows may also be made, such as, "Since no one wants me, I refuse to be born." Of course, he will be born physically, but his decision not to be born may result in his not being born emotionally. How this takes place will be explained later.

Thus, a child may react with anger and resentment and rebel against life or withdraw in fear while still in the womb. His first bitter root judgments and inner vows are made while yet in the womb, setting him up to become either a victim or a victimizer. "The wicked are estranged from the womb; These who speak lies go astray from birth" (Ps. 58:3).

Dr. Verny illustrates this in a case concerning a baby who kept refusing her mother's breast although she would devour a bottle of milk. He experimented to see if the baby would take milk from another mother. She grasped her breast and began sucking lustily. When he questioned the mother about her baby's baffling behavior, she replied casually that she had wanted an abortion, and the only reason she had the baby was because her husband wanted it. We can assume then that the baby made a judgment and a vow such as, "Since my mother refused to bond with me before birth, I will refuse to bond with her after birth."

(2.) Experiences at Birth. The Sandfords' list of the attitudes and behavior most commonly observed after birth for each condition suffered by a child in utero is reproduced in **Table 11**. Then, as if this were not enough trauma for a little one, Dr. Verny makes the following bold statements: "How a child is born—whether it is painful or easy, smooth or violent—largely determines who he becomes and how he will view the world around him. Birth is the first prolonged emotional and physical shock a child undergoes which he never quite forgets. He experiences moments of incredible pleasure which alternate with others of great pain and fear.

One moment he is floating blissfully in a pool of warm amniotic fluid, the next he is suddenly thrust into the birth canal and the beginning of a trying experience that may last for hours. For most of that time, maternal contractions will push and pull at him, then his still-fragile skull may suddenly be seized by two steel forceps and his six, seven or eight-pound body pulled forward at a force equal to forty pounds of tension on his neck.

He will then find himself in a cold, noisy, harshly lit room, surrounded by a group of strangers who clutch, probe and pull at him. Meanwhile his mind is recording every feeling, gesture and movement. Even the most minute details leave indelible memory tracks, although most of us cannot recall these memories later" (pgs. 97-99).

Apparently, oxytocin (the hormone which induces uterine contractions produces an amnesiac effect on the baby as it is secreted by the mother during labor and birth.

Dr. Cheek, an obstetrician, as cited in Dr. Verny's book above, demonstrated that birth memories do exist in an experiment which he did on four young men and women whom he had delivered. He put them under hypnosis[2] and asked each to describe how his or her head and shoulders were positioned at birth. In every case what the person told Dr. Cheek was confirmed by what he had recorded in his files. They also accurately described the way in which they had been delivered.

---

2 Although I do not condone hypnosis because it opens the mind, giving Satan access to it, I believe the memories it reveals can be accurate.

Dr. Verny formulated five categories of birth-related psychological hazards. The lowest risk category is, of course, simple uncomplicated vaginal births. The second category is Caesarean deliveries of which one long-term effect is an intense craving for all kinds of physical contact. Dr. Verny believes this is because the baby delivered by Caesarean is deprived of the sensual moments a vaginally delivered baby has during birth. The third category is breech births and the fourth is minor umbilical cord difficulties which cause throat-related problems.

The fifth category is premature births which would, of course, vary in severity. A few days' prematurity would be of little consequence, while a few months can be both physically and emotionally devastating to the child. In one study of 20 schizophrenics, Dr. Samoff A. Mednick, Director of the Psykologisk Institute in Copenhagen, as cited in Dr. Verny's book above, found that 70 percent had suffered complications at birth or during their mothers' pregnancies. In another interesting study on 16 men who had committed violent crimes, he found that 15 had had extraordinarily difficult births. (The 16th had an epileptic mother.) Dr. Verny describes a case in which a six-year-old boy was tormented by frightening nightmares. He would thrash about, curse, yell, scream, talk about an odd light and speak in a foreign language. After listening to a broadcast about how dreams can express unconscious birth memories, his mother suddenly realized that her son's nightmares grew out of his own birth memory. After an extremely difficult labor, he had been born prematurely, almost dead. The exhausted doctors had yelled and cursed, and a priest had given him the last rites in Latin!

How the mother feels at the moment of birth has an enormous influence on how she delivers, according to Dr. Verny. If she is relaxed, confident and looking forward to her child's birth, chances are very good that her delivery will be simple and trouble-free. If she is racked with doubts and worries and is in conflict about the prospect of becoming a mother, the risk of complications rises. In a study done on 50 women, half of whom were rated as seriously troubled and half as normal, all of the troubled women had at least one complication during delivery. Not one of the "normal" women had any complications delivering.

Dr. Verny states that the child is acutely aware of his mother's feelings during delivery. He gives an example of a woman whose birth memory suddenly surfaced during therapy. She was talking about something totally unrelated when suddenly her facial expression changed, and she began describing how frightened her mother had been during her birth. She believed that fear had made her mother withdraw into a protective ball. "I knew she wasn't going to help me be born," the women said, "and I was scared because I'd have to do it all by myself." Another patient, delivered by Caesarean said, "I could feel my mother's terror as the knife began cutting across her stomach."

Anxiety also causes a laboring woman to tighten her pelvic muscles, which in turn, leads to the excessive use of forceps. Dr. Cheek cites tension and migraine headaches as problems often traceable back to forceps delivery. He gives the example of a man who had a history of headaches in the forehead just above his right eye. Under hypnosis, he recalled his birth experience which apparently was a harrowing one. He remembered his mother's cries and then felt his head explode with pain.

His forehead above the right eye hurt the most, but he also felt something sharp at the back of his neck toward the base of his skull. To Dr. Cheek, this sounded like an attempt at a high-forceps delivery that had backfired. The pain should have been located at the sides of the infant's head, behind the ears. The patient's mother later corroborated his story, which seemed to explain his headaches, in every detail.

Dr. Verny also describes the trauma a baby goes through as the result of induced labor. Mothers who have experienced induced labor report that they feel like their contractions are being imposed on them from the outside. As a result, they lose control of their bodies and it is more difficult for them to push in rhythm with their contractions. The baby, who is not ready to be born, is thrust out of the uterus by its contractions, but gets very little help from the mother who is not in harmony with her body or with him. The contractions may stop altogether, and the baby is often eventually pulled out by forceps.

Dr. Verny believes that since even the best births involve pain, it is inevitable that all of us are left with a subconscious residue of primal anger. This is normal, but an infant who experiences the hurts of rejection in the womb, plus the trauma of a painful birth, probably makes many bitter root judgments, resulting in a large residue of unexpressed anger. Lacking an outlet for this anger, he may turn it inward against himself.

This was exemplified by Dr. Verny in a case concerning a man who was a severe chronic depressive. Under hypnosis, he said that he felt as if he was being pushed up and down in an elevator which made him feel first angry and then depressed. The doctor concluded that the rhythmic movement of the elevator symbolized sexual intercourse. The patient felt that something in the elevator symbology connected with his mother with whom he had never gotten along.

On a hunch, this person called and asked his mother if she had had sexual intercourse with his father while she was carrying him. She said that his father had come home drunk and forced himself on her sexually close to her due date. She went into labor three hours later. Thus, the doctor concluded that the patient had internalized his anger at his mother for not "protecting" him, which accounted for his deep and prolonged depression.

Allowing the mother to bond with her baby immediately after birth is also extremely beneficial to both. Many studies have shown that mothers who bond right after birth are much less anxious and their babies are healthier, more stable emotionally and intellectually more acute than infants taken from their mothers right after birth. These studies also show that women who bond early behave much differently toward their children. Up to three years later, bonding mothers are still acting more attentive, enthusiastic and supportive. Very few of them yelled or shouted at their children. Instead, they gently suggested that they pick up their toys, treating them with respect rather than issuing orders.

Thus, to thrive emotionally, intellectually and physically, an infant needs the special kind of loving contact that only bonding fully develops in his mother. Without it, an infant will literally wilt and die—a condition called marasmus which means "wasting away." According to Dr. Verny, during the nineteenth century, it killed more than half of the infants born and was responsible for nearly one hundred percent of the deaths in foundling homes.

Even a little stroking produces miracles as was shown in a study done on babies in a pediatric intensive care unit. The infants that were stroked for five minutes every hour for ten days gained weight and grew much faster than those that were not touched. Four years later, it was also shown that they scored fifteen points higher on IQ tests.

All of the preceding studies by secular doctors seem to support Dr. Verny's observation that hundreds of the people he has seen have been deeply scarred by destructive prenatal influences and that their afflictions can be explained only in terms of what happened to them in the womb at birth. But why do the events which occur during the first stages of life affect us so much more intensely than those which occur later? The answer to this question is that the unborn child and the newborn child have not developed any defenses or understanding yet. For this reason, they cannot soften or deflect the impact of experience. What affects them does so directly. That is why maternal emotions etch themselves so deeply on our psyches and why their tug remains so powerful later in life.

We can conclude from these observations that healing in the womb and at birth is of utmost importance. I believe the Lord has revealed to me that healing of the womb and birth experiences is the most effective healing He can perform because these memories form the deepest roots of our character structure. Thus, they have the greatest effect on our future lives because their impact is the strongest.

(3.) Rebirthing the Soul. The first step in healing womb experiences is to ask the Spirit to reveal the circumstances of the counselee's conception. In my cases—in more instances than not—the Spirit revealed that the child was conceived out of wedlock. This immediately brought a curse of illegitimacy down upon the child which gave Satan the right to bring some kind of destruction upon him.

To break the curse, the counselor places the cross of Jesus between the counselee and his parents. He puts the sin of fornication upon the cross and asks God to forgive the parents and cleanse them of their sin. He breaks the curse and calls for the blood of Jesus to cleanse the counselee's blood of this curse, thus, removing Satan's grounds to attack him through the curse of illegitimacy. In these cases, the counselee experiences extreme emotions—rejection, fear, confusion, shame, guilt, insecurity—coming from his parents, especially from his mother. Dr. Verny relates a story which he heard about a patient who suddenly began describing a scene in which he had been enjoying himself with people all around, when suddenly the mood in the room changed. People began crowding around him, pointing their fingers accusingly at him. He felt angry and frightened and did not know what to do. When he mentioned this scene to his mother, she related an incident which took place when she was pregnant with him. She was having fun at a party when several of her friends learned that she was illegitimately pregnant. Their criticism, although unspoken, was very frightening and humiliating and hurt her very deeply.

In these cases, the Spirit reveals the tremendous fear and guilt which the mother felt as she attempted to explain her plight to her parents and the extreme rejection which she usually received from them. In visualization, Jesus comes into this memory, heals her hurts and scars, and washes away her guilt with His precious blood as He forgives her. Touched by the love of Jesus, her parents, relatives and friends also forgive her, give the young couple their blessing and gather around as Jesus joins the couple in holy wedlock, removing the curse of illegitimacy.

The counselee sees Jesus telling his parents that He will be with them and help them raise their child. The counselor prays that the counselee, who has been experiencing all the negative emotions which he originally felt as a baby in the womb, will begin to feel love, acceptance, approval, and security coming from Jesus and his parents. If he feels insecure about his identity, the Spirit may lead the counselor to ask God to call the name of the counselee, according to Isaiah 49:1; "The Lord called me from the womb, from the body of my mother He named me."

Dr. Rita Bennett, LMFTA, Litt.D., in her book, *You Can Be Emotionally Free*, describes a case in which a woman's parents did not name her until she was six months old. As a baby, she felt unimportant and not worth the trouble to name. During prayer, she heard Jesus call her name which made her feel important and worthwhile because He knew what she was going to be called even before her parents knew.

Since the Spirit leads the prayer for healing in the womb, a counselor will pray somewhat differently for each counselee. Dr. Bennett presents in her book a beautifully detailed format describing the baby's development in the womb and giving a scripture and prayer for each month (pgs. 173-180). The counselor can use this as a general guideline to follow as he prays for healing of the counselee from conception to birth.

The following is an example which might be typical of his Spirit-led narrative prayer:

"Thank You and praise You, Father, for choosing John before the foundation of the world (Eph. 1:4), for calling him by name from his mother's womb (Isa. 49:1), for forming his inward parts and weaving him in his mother's womb (Ps. 139:13), and for loving and wanting him even if no one else did. Melt away any rejection, confusion or doubts that he felt about whether or not he was welcome in his mother's womb with Your perfect love and acceptance."

"Show John, precious Jesus, his tiny self snuggled in the palm of Your gentle, loving hand. 'Can a woman forget her nursing child, and have no compassion on the son of her womb? Even these may forget, but I will not forget you. Behold, I have inscribed you on the palms of My hands'" (Isa. 49:15,16). "Flood little John with Your perfect love, let him feel Your warmth, security and peace flowing through him and melting away all fear and insecurity" (1 John 4:18). "Can you see Jesus, John, and feel His love and warmth flowing though you or are you feeling some negative emotions?" The counselor should intermittently ask the counselee is he is able to see and feel what he is praying or if he is feeling other emotions.

"Thank You, Lord, that You are beginning to form little John's inward parts and systems during his first month in his mother's womb. Thank You that You are protecting him and forming all of his organs perfectly because You formed him from the womb (Isa. 44:2). We praise You, sweet Jesus, that You chose the sex that he should be in the second month. See Jesus holding you in His hand, smiling approvingly, happy and pleased that you are a boy. Thank You, Lord, that You are forming little John's legs, arms, hands, and feet perfectly during the third month. We praise and glorify You; for he is fearfully and wonderfully made; marvelous are Your works!" (Ps. 139:14).

"Reveal, precious Holy Spirit, any trauma which little John suffered during the first three months." The counselee may describe a scene in which his parents are arguing, and he feels fearful, insecure and lonely. The counselor prays, *"Heal the hurts and scars in little John with Your healing oil, Jesus. Heal the hurts and wounds in his parents and fill them with Your love. We see them forgiving each other, embracing in love again, and asking little John to forgive them for frightening him. He feels love, peace, security flowing from Jesus and his parents into him—enfolding him and filling every part of his tiny being. Can you feel this, John, and see your parents forgiving each other and happy again?" "Thank You, precious Savior, that Your hand is developing and protecting John's little brain and filling it with Your life and a knowledge of You during his fourth month. We praise You, Lord, that his mother is beginning to feel life within her womb. We see her with her husband, both of them happy and filled with joy and excitement that their child is alive, thanking Jesus as He blesses her womb. Thank You, Jesus, that You are breathing life into all of little John's cells; thank You that "...You give life to all things'" (1 Tim. 6:13). "We give You all the glory that all of his organs are fully developed during the fifth month. Jesus' love and peace are flowing through every cell in his body, healing any feelings of fear or insecurity coming from his mother."*

"Thank You, precious Savior, for covering tiny John from head to toe with Your protective natural ointment. Anoint him also spiritually in a special way and consecrate him to You, Lord. 'Before I formed you in the womb, I knew you and before you were born, I consecrated you'" (Jer. 1:5). "Thank You for anointing and consecrating him to You, great and mighty God. See Jesus anointing you with His oil of joy, laughing as you "leap for joy," even as John the Baptist did in the sixth month in his mother's womb when he sensed the presence of Jesus! (Luke 1:44). Your parents are also feeling the joy of Jesus and becoming excited about your birth!"

"Reveal, sweet Spirit, any trauma which may have frightened John during his fourth, fifth or sixth month in his mother's womb." The spirit may reveal an extremely traumatic event such as the counselee's father beating on his wife's abdomen or, as in one case, pushing her down the stairs! The counselee felt herself rolling over and over, doing somersaults and then sloshing from side to side as her mother was rushed in an ambulance to the hospital.

In these cases, the counselor would pray, *"Protect John. Jesus, cover him with Your presence; enclose him in the palm of Your hand; surround him with a bubble of Your peace and protection; cover him with Your blood in the womb. Heal the wounds and hurts and scars which he received from this trauma; cleanse them and heal them with your healing balm."* He would just keep praying and claiming the word over the counselee until his emotions subsided. He may even rock him in his arms if the Spirit leads him to do this.

He continues praying; *"Jesus, please come into this tragic memory and heal it. Show John's father what he is doing; open his mind so he can understand the pain he is inflicting on his wife and child—the precious gifts You have given him. No man can stand before You without seeing himself as he really is. Bring him to repentance for what he has done. Help John understand why he was doing this terrible thing."* Jesus may reveal the fear and panic his father felt at the thought of providing for another child or some other reason for his demonic behavior.

The counselor continues, *"Can you see your father crying and asking your mother and you to forgive him? See Jesus holding your mother and healing her wounds and scars. Melt her heart and little John's toward him, Lord; give them Your love and understanding for him; help them forgive him."* The counselor continues praying until John's Child is able to forgive his father and break any judgments or vows he made in connection with this tragic experience. Only Jesus can heal the bitterness rooted deep within the Child of a person who has experienced such a tragedy in the womb. The counselor will then continue his narrative prayer; *"Bless little John in his seventh month, Jesus, fill him with Your love and surround him with Your peace. We see love and joy flowing from You into his parents; flowing from them into tiny John. We thank You that all of the parts of his body are formed perfectly this month and that his senses are developed. We give You all the glory and honor that 'his frame was not hidden from Thee when he was made in secret and skillfully wrought in the depths of the earth' (Ps. 139:15). You are protecting him and watching over him.'"*

"Praise You, Lord, that little John is fully formed in the eighth month and very active and his mother is very much aware of his presence! Your parents are filled with joy and excitement as they are anticipating your birth. You feel their anticipation and are beginning to feel excited about being born! Jesus is beaming as He looks at you because you are so spe-

cial, so beautiful and so precious to Him! You are His original, unique creation; there is no one else just like you in the whole world!"

"Thine eyes have seen my unformed substance; and in Thy book they were all written, the days that were ordained for me, When as yet there was not one of them. How precious are Thy thoughts of me, O God! How vast is the sum of them! If I should count them, they would outnumber the sand. When I awake, I am still with Thee" (Ps. 139:16-18).

Again, the counselor asks the Spirit to reveal any trauma that occurred in John's seventh, eighth, or ninth month in the womb. Although this is rare, the counselee may cry out that he does not want to be born; that he wants to die. He may have felt so much rejection or fear in the womb that he vowed not to live. These feelings may have resulted from an overwhelming trauma that occurred in utero, such as the one just described, which caused the counselee's Child to rebel, turn back from life and choose not to be born, fearing what he might encounter. As previously discussed, this inner vow would cause him to remain "spiritually imprisoned in the womb."

At this time, the Holy Spirit might give the counselor a vision symbolizing the counselee's imprisoned personal spirit. Some of the visions received by the Sandfords included a man frozen in an iceberg, a woman in a birdcage and a man in a hole in the ground. The most vivid vision described by John Sandford was one in which he followed Jesus down a dark tunnel to a huge ancient door, rusted and locked. It opened before the Lord, and they entered a "dungeon of hell." There, in a corner, huddled in a fetal position, chained by her wrists and ankles to a wall, was his counselee! She appeared ghostly white, emaciated and starved. With His beautiful, nail-scarred hands, Jesus broke her shackles off, cradled her in His arms and carried her out. Her skin turned from deathly pale to pink and she grew from a tiny, emaciated girl to a healthy woman, then beamed with pride as she frolicked in a lovely meadow.

Although I have not experienced quite this dramatic a scene, I have visualized the Lord cutting chains from counselees and had visions of butterflies bursting forth from cocoons and flower buds bursting forth into full blossoms as I asked Jesus to fill them with His light and love and breathe His life into them. I did not realize it at the time, but I was probably praying that slumbering spirits be awakened and imprisoned spirits be set free to function fully!

As pointed out before, researchers have speculated that maternal distress causing violent trauma to take place in the womb may also cause the cells of an unborn child to be thrown into disarray, resulting in paranoid schizophrenia. To correct this condition, the counselor may, while praying, visualize Jesus unscrambling the brain cells, organizing them and putting them in their proper place.

Not being aware of these things, as I prayed that her Savior would fill every cell of her brain with His healing love, light and life; one counselee, diagnosed as a mild paranoid schizophrenic, related that she felt Jesus lift off the top of her head, reach in and rearrange things! Thus, as counselors, we can see how vital it is to be open vessels through which the Spirit can flow freely, even though we may not realize what is really taking place!

As we saw previously, children suffering from dyslexia also vowed not to be born, resulting in their spirits turning around. In these cases, the counselor may visualize Jesus reaching in and turning his counselee's backward spirit around to face forward, asking Him of his soul to integrate and coordinate it with every other part and body. I have prayed in a similar manner with several counselees, one of whom felt herself spinning around and another who felt the Lord reach in and turn her spirit around!

The parents may have cursed their baby or wished that it would die, resulting in the Inner Child of the little one vowing not to be born; in which case, the curse of death must be broken. Thus, the Spirit may lead the counselor to pray concerning one or all of the above conditions before the soul can be rebirthed.

The counselor continues praying, *"I place the cross between John and his parents and put their sin of not wanting him to live upon it. Forgive them, Father, and cleanse them of this sin with Jesus' blood. I place the cross between John's parents and their parents' death and on back through the generations and break the curse. Let Your blood flow through little John, cleansing him of the effects of this death curse with Your precious blood."*

"See Jesus with your parents, reassuring them that He will always be with them, helping them to care for their child if they will only trust Him.

He brings them to repentance for not wanting their baby, and they ask their little one to forgive them. Can you see them repentant and asking you to forgive them, John? Heal little John's broken heart with Your love, Jesus, and fill him with Your love for his parents. Can you feel forgiveness for them, John?"

"Breathe the breath of life into tiny John's spirit, Lord God, and call him forth to life even as You breathed the breath of life into Adam (Gen. 2:7). Woo him with Your love; call his spirit forth to life, Father. Help him break his vow not to live; forgive him for not wanting to be born; fill him with the desire to live and to fulfill the plan which You have for him. If backwards, turn his tiny spirit around and fill it with strength to face life. Reach into little John's brain, unscramble the cells, organize and arrange them in correct order, put them in their proper places, sweet Lord."

"Let tiny John feel how special and precious he is to You, Father. 'You have set him apart even from his mother's womb; You called him through Your grace'" (Gal. 1:15). The counselor prays until John's Child feels a desire and great anticipation to be born, thus breaking his vow not to live. "Thank You, precious Savior, that John is feeling great joy at the thought of being born. He has accepted his family as the one which You chose for him. Give him Your special love for them and reveal to him that You will 'never leave him or forsake him.' (Heb. 13:5). See Jesus reassuring your mother that He will be with her during delivery and that she has nothing to fear. He is comforting and filling her with His peace.'"

"You suddenly feel pressure as the contractions are pushing and pulling at you. You feel Jesus' hand enclosing you as you are propelled into the birth canal. Fill little John with peace, Lord, protect him and melt away all fear as he goes down the dark, narrow birth canal. There is great pressure at your head and then it pops out; then your shoulders pop out and the rest of your body. Jesus is there to receive you and He holds you close to Him. You feel His love and strength flowing into you; you feel so secure and warm in His arms. He looks into your eyes and you feel how proud and pleased He is with you—His special, beautiful, unique creation!"

"Jesus smiles proudly at your mother as He places you on her tummy. She is beaming with pride and wonder as she looks into your eyes and bonds you to her. You feel her warmth, love, and joy flowing into you as you snuggle into her skin. Thank You, sweet Master, for bonding John to his mother; let him feel her love and warmth; make up for any love or bonding which he did not receive at birth."

"See Jesus cutting your cord, washing and wrapping you and lovingly handing you to your father. He smiles proudly and lovingly at you as he holds you close, stroking you, bonding you to him. You feel strength, security and assurance of your identity flowing from him into you as you snuggle close to him. Bond John to his father, Lord, and make up for any love or bonding that John did not receive from him. Awaken his spirit and call it forth to function with fullness of life, joy and vivacity through his father's touch!"

"Heal any hurts or scars and melt away any fear John received during his birth, Lord, whether from the bright lights; cold, noisy room; harsh treatment of the doctors spanking him, using forceps, etc. Reveal anything traumatic involving his birth which needs special prayer. The Spirit may reveal any one of the birth complications discussed earlier, in which case, the counselor asks Jesus to come in and heal any effects from the specific problem."

The Spirit may lead the counselor to pray a detailed rebirthing process for some counselees while for others he may lead him to pray a simpler one. The rebirthing does not have to be prayed through all in one session. The Spirit may even lead the counselor to go back to the womb for more healing at a later time. The counselor asks Jesus to seal the womb and cover it with His blood in the Spirit if the rebirthing is not completed in one session so that no demonic spirits may enter.

(4.) Reliving Childhood. The counselor may continue narrating and praying for healing throughout the rest of his life, such as, *"Jesus has His arms around your parents as they are taking you home. He is reassuring them that He will always be with them to help them care for you. You are nursing at your mother's breast, snuggling deep into her skin as she gently rocks you. Thank you, Jesus, for replacing all the love baby John did not receive from his mother. Let him feel her warmth and acceptance flowing into him. Call his spirit forth to life as she lovingly caresses him."*

As he did during the rebirthing, the counselor intermittently asks the counselee if he can feel love or if he is experiencing other emotions. He may feel anxiety and insecurity coming from his mother concerning whether or not she can be a good mother to him. In this case, the counselor prays, *"See Jesus reassuring your mother that He will always be with her, teaching her how to nurture and discipline her son and filling her with the fruit of the Spirit for him. Jesus is filling her with strength, courage and confidence that 'she can do all things through Christ who strengthens her'" (Phil. 4:13 NKJV).*

"Your father is holding you close, nurturing you, cooing at you, playing with you. Make up all the love John did not receive from his father Jesus. We see your love and acceptance flowing into John's father, then flowing into John. You feel so happy and peaceful with your parents. They are so proud and excited as you take your first step! See your parents caressing and cuddling you, singing and reading stories to you about Jesus as you snuggle in their laps."

"Thank you, sweet Jesus, for replacing all the love and nurturing that John did not receive during his first year. Awaken and call John's tiny spirit forth to function fully with fervent life through his parents' touch. Reveal any hurts, scars or traumas that little John suffered during his first year, precious Spirit."

The counselor continues his narrative prayer through the first five years. These are the formative years when the deepest emotional wounds are cut, leaving scars, and the root system of the counselee's character structure is being laid down. He may ask the Spirit to reveal the times when John felt abandoned and afraid, e.g., when he was lost in a store, chased by a big dog, left in the hospital, etc.

Many fearful memories may be repressed and forgotten as in the case of one counselee for whom the Spirit recalled many of them. She remembered being terribly frightened when she was lost in a store, left with relatives while her mother went to the hospital to give birth, and often, at bedtime, since her parents never prayed with her or tucked her in bed. These experiences may seem insignificant, but their impact is great when we are young. They are important because together they open many doors through which fear may enter. As the Lord "casts out the fear" in these memories with His perfect love, the counselee no longer suffers from fear and anxiety.

The counselor may ask John to picture himself doing the things which he had always wanted to do with his parents, things of which he had always felt deprived such as, camping, fishing, skating, having a birthday party, etc. He may ask him to visualize himself going with Jesus and his parents to the first day of school as he asks Jesus to take away any fear and heal any hurts received that day. He may ask the Spirit to reveal any wounds which John received from his classmates at school or from a teacher who may have embarrassed him in front of his class. All these events can be very traumatic for a small child.

In my own case, I thought the only problem on which I had to work was that my mother was possessive and critical. But the Spirit revealed that since my father was very passive and unable to show affection or communicate with me, I had been deprived of the nurturing, touching and character building which I needed from him. So, I pictured my mother releasing me and allowing me to make my own decisions, including mistakes, and my father holding and caressing me, communicating and doing things with me.

The missing father figure is the most common type of deprivation from which children suffer today. This lack of a loving, nurturing, accepting father can have extremely serious effects on children—driving girls into promiscuity and boys into homosexuality. This behavior simply means that they are continuing to search for their missing fathers. The increase in sexual perversion and in the number of stepfathers due to the breakdown of families, has led to a tremendous increase in child molestation which also opens the door to promiscuity and homosexuality.

Whether she was molested or deprived of a father, reliving her childhood with Jesus supplying the loving, understanding, nurturing father figure which she did not have is a crucial process in soul healing for the promiscuous girl. Equally important to the homosexual is reliving his childhood with Jesus replacing the loving and gentle, yet strong and masculine, father role model which he never had. This visualization is vital for children who have been molested because their perception of a father image is very distorted, and their concept of love is confused with sex. They cannot picture their fathers loving and caring for them without sexually abusing them.

In one case, the Lord gave the counselee a vision of herself as a small girl sitting on His lap completely naked. Jesus was holding, touching and caressing her as a normal father would without any sexual connotations. Replacing a missing father figure or restoring a distorted father image to a normal one is vital to the development of an intimate love relationship with God, since *we* have the same image of our heavenly Father that we have of our earthly fathers.

When working with a homosexual, in addition to asking Jesus to heal his memories and replace his father figure, the counselor breaks any generation curse of homosexuality, asking the Savior to cleanse his blood of any effects of this curse with His spotless blood. After calling upon the Spirit to disclose the childhood experience—there usually is one—that opened the door to sexual perversion, the counselor prays for the healing of this memory, requesting the counselee to break all judgments, vows, soul ties, etc.

The counselor then explains "the Lord's revelation to Sandford" that the male and female "poles" of a homosexual are reversed. While praying, he visualizes Jesus reaching in and disentangling the male and female poles and setting them in order. Although I have not had the opportunity to test this procedure, Sandford reports success in every case of homosexuality with which he has worked since God revealed this knowledge to him! He states that his counselees no longer had any sexual desire for individuals of their same sex! What a privilege to be vessels of the Spirit who gives us the "treasures of darkness and the hidden wealth of secret places!" (Isa. 45:3).

Discerning what pattern of parenting a counselee received will help the counselor know how to instruct the counselee to picture his Parent. If the dominant Parent was controlling and overprotective, the counselor might ask the counselee to visualize his Parent allowing him to be free and take risks, encouraging him to make his own decisions and plans, and then reassuring him that he still loves and accepts him even if he disagrees with his decisions. Women suffering from bulimia-anorexia, usually products of a perfectionist Parent, can visualize their parents allowing them to make mistakes while supporting them with unconditional love and acceptance and reassuring them that they do not have to earn their love by performing perfectly. Counselees whose parents were perfectionists, especially victims of bulimia-anorexia, carry heavy burdens of guilt since they believe that they are always failing even if they are achieving to the best of their ability.

To help a victim of guilt forgive herself, the counselor can ask Jesus to give her a picture of herself as an adult relating to herself as a child. He can entreat the Master to give the adult woman love and compassion for herself as a little girl, to help her see her little self as He sees her—feeling hurt and rejected. Jesus will give the victim a vision of herself as an adult asking her little girl to forgive her for expecting too much of her and not accepting her as she is. As her little child forgives her, she will see her adult self-embracing and cuddling her. Jesus' love and healing balm flowing through each of them will heal their relationship, enabling the victim of guilt to forgive herself.

As we have noted, counselees whose parents were authoritarian have often excluded the Natural Child, resulting in their not being able to have fun and enjoy life. They can be instructed to visualize their parents as happy, carefree and accepting, giving them permission to enjoy pleasures, express their creativity and act spontaneously. Extreme insecurity being his "nemesis," the over-coercive Parent can be pictured with a strong, mature Adult relaxed and secure in Jesus, able to Parent lovingly in a rational, consistent manner.

Although people raised by overcontrolling parents regularly seek counsel because they want to be free, individuals brought up by parents who are under-controlling rarely seek help since they are usually victimizers content with their script of controlling others. The one problem that may force a victimizer to search for assistance is the breakdown of his marriage, threatening him with the loss of his family. In the rare case that he does come in for counseling, he may be instructed to picture his over-submissive Parent not giving in to his manipulating behavior and letting him get his own way, but applying loving, yet strong, consistent discipline.

The counselee with an overindulgent parent may be asked to picture his parent not pampering, spoiling and indulging him, always allowing him to have his own way, but lovingly setting limits for him and exercising control over his self-centered desires. Needless to say, people used to getting their own way through manipulating are difficult to work with in counseling! As counselors, we must always keep in mind that "nothing is impossible with God!" (Luke 1:37).

The most difficult people with which to work, as discussed previously, are those who have been severely rejected by their parents. They have either withdrawn, having built impenetrable walls (often excluding the Adult which results in their being placed in mental institutions), or they have rebelled and become cruel victimizers (often excluding the Parent which results in their being put in prisons).

If the victim of an actively rejecting parent is able to release his hurts and receive enough love and healing from the Lord for his Inner Child to be able to forgive, he may be asked to picture his parent loving, nurturing and accepting him, while treating him with respect, gentleness, kindness, and patience. If he is not able to visualize his parent changed by faith with Christ's love, the counselor can help him relive his childhood with his Savior as his Father. Hopefully, after enough healing, he will eventually be able to see his parent transformed by Jesus' love.

The victim of a passively rejecting parent has usually received the deepest gashes and scars on his soul and spirit. Being deprived of love, touching and even attention to his physical needs leaves such a void in his life that he may totally lack an identity of his own. As we might expect, the counselor must invest a tremendous amount of love, time, patience, and energy as a substitute parent before the counselee will have received enough healing and nurturing to be able to forgive his parent. Reliving his childhood with Jesus replacing all of the love which he did not receive by meeting all of his neglected emotional, physical and spiritual needs will aid in accomplishing this. This counselee will generally suffer from an imprisoned spirit which the Deliverer must set free and a slumbering spirit which must be wooed to new life by picturing the Lord cuddling, caressing, nurturing, rocking, and stroking him.

If a counselee suffers from MPD, the counselor can lead each of his "alternate personalities (alters)" to a trusting acceptance of Jesus' love. The alters will then be able to allow Jesus to heal the emotional wounds incurred by this counselee, usually carried by the "child" alters. Healing his childhood scars will enable this person to forgive his abusers and break the curses, judgments, inner vows, and soul ties which bind him. Severing the roots of his "character tree" will require any inhabiting demons to depart. As the alters allow the Redeemer, "...in whom all things hold together" (Col.1:17), to take charge of integrating them at the appropriate time, He will eventually create the personality which is uniquely this individual's.

I can attest to the infinite patience required of the counselor, since I have worked with victims of incest, neglect and satanic ritual abuse. One young woman had been so extremely deprived that, although her parents had the finances, she was never bathed, fed or clothed properly during her childhood. She had never received any toys or experienced a Christmas or birthday celebration, nor was she allowed to have any friends. Although she was able to picture Jesus playing with her and some friends, giving her a birthday party, celebrating Christmas with her and her family, loving, cuddling and nurturing her, she was never able to visualize her father fulfilling any of her needs.

On the other hand, the victim of SRA about whom I previously spoke was able to visualize her father loving and nurturing her although he had sodomized her, violently beat her and offered her to be married to Satan and impregnated by a priest, resulting in her baby being sacrificed to Satan in a black mass! This SRA survivor's ability to see her father changed is, most likely, due to the fact that, in addition to the horrors she suffered as a child, she also learned about Jesus while the victim of neglect was raised by atheist parents.

Counselees may be instructed to work on visualizing their childhood needs being met during their prayer times, picturing themselves with their families, happily playing, singing and having fun together with Jesus. Through faith visualization, they can see Jesus mending their broken hearts, filling them with His love and fulfilling any needs and desires of which they felt deprived as children.

We may recall that the Biblical parent gives his child a balance of freedom, discipline and agape love. From this ideal parental pattern, we can see that counselees with overcontrolling parents need to picture parents allowing them to be free. Those with under-controlling parents need to see their parents disciplining them firmly, but lovingly, while those with rejecting parents should visualize their parents showering them with nurturing agape love. Reliving his childhood with the Lord healing his wounds and filling his emotional needs is still much easier, faster, and of course, infinitely more effective than employing the secular counterpart.

I recently viewed a television program describing the latest innovation in therapy, called "reliving your childhood." This procedure consisted of therapists attempting to replace all of the emotional deprivation of a counselee's childhood with their own natural love!

The therapists attempt to literally become substitute parents, while the counselees supposedly regress back to their birth. These therapists actually rock, cuddle, feed, some even breastfeed, their adult "babies!" To properly "relive" each month of the counselee's formative years takes approximately three two-hour sessions at $25 an hour! Unbelievable! The counselee demonstrating the method used stated that reliving her childhood had taken seven years!

As counselors, we are truly blessed that we are only required to be willing vessels through which our Father's supernatural love flows, healing damaged souls. I thank God that I have been privileged to witness numerous miracles of God's divine love healing many scarred souls. Even the thought of having to rely on my own feeble natural love to replace a counselee's childhood emotional needs for even one hour totally exhausts me!

E. HEART CIRCUMCISION.

Many people avoid, or even condemn, the soul healing process because they are afraid of what will be revealed in their own souls. The Child within each of us has spent its lifetime building walls around the heart, protecting it against further pain. As we have seen, the method used to parent a person combined with his temperament programs him to live out his life's script playing, for the most part, either the role of a victim or that of a victimizer.

Since the Child of the individual who has chosen the victim's role is afraid of his controlling Parent, and his Parent enjoys its dominating position, neither will give the Adult of this person permission to take charge of his soul. Likewise, since the Child of the victimizer has rebelled, turned off his Parent and is now in charge, he is not about to allow this person's Adult to get control of his soul. Thus, even though the personal spirit of both the victim and the victimizer cry out for healing and freedom for the whole person, in both cases they are not able to empower the Adult to stand against the protests of the Parent and the Child.

But when a person receives the infilling of the Holy Spirit, his personal spirit finally gains sufficient strength to empower his Adult. Whether this individual realizes it or not, he has given the Holy Spirit permission to begin working on the scars, judgments, vows, and sinful attitudes repressed in his heart, since the Holy Spirit's job is to transform him into the image of his Savior and Master. The Holy Spirit begins by bringing this person's sinful attitudes and behavior to his attention through His still, small voice, the conviction of the Word, the counsel of more mature Christians, etc. However, due to the effectiveness of their defense mechanisms—denial, repression and rationalization being the most powerful—many people are able to ignore these obvious warnings.

In these cases, the reinforcing power of the Holy Spirit enables the personal spirit of an individual to bring the troubled, sinful areas of his subconscious (heart) into the conscious realm. "For the Spirit searches all things, even the depths of God, for who among men knows the thoughts of a man except the spirit of a man which is in him?" (1 Cor. 2:10,11). Trying to get the person's attention, it sends out signals in the form of dreams, maybe even visions, which endeavor to point out destructive behavior patterns. If unheeded, these dreams may turn into nightmares and the behavior patterns into symptoms of emotional problems, such as outbursts of anger, depression or others listed in **Table 2**.

A graphic illustration of the personal spirit sending out a signal in the form of a dream concerns one which Jimmy Swaggart described a few months before his sin became known. Claiming that God had chosen him to get the sin out of the Assembly of God churches, he described a dream he had received in which the churches were hosting a stage show replete with large magazines containing obscene pictures in their centerfolds. He cried out in protest, weeping, but was ignored. After the people left, he began collecting the debris. When asked what he was doing, he replied in anguish, "I am trying to clean up the church! I am trying to clean up the church!"

Since any building, such as a house, church, hotel, etc., symbolizes the soul in dreams, his spirit was obviously sending a signal to try and get him to clean up his soul by dealing with his own sin of pornography! The behavior of pornography was a symptom indicating that there were repressed conditions in his heart that his spirit was pleading with him to recognize. Ignoring the warnings of his Christian brothers, his dreams and probably many other "red lights" from the Spirit, the Lord was finally forced to judge him.

Swaggart now states that God informed him that He had to "put his hip out of joint as He did Jacob's" (Gen. 32:24-32) because this was the only way He could get his attention. He laments that from now until Jesus returns, he will have to walk with a limp. What a lesson for the rest of us! Although God is infinitely merciful, sooner or later He will have His way with us. Job puts it this way: "But He is unique and who can turn Him? And what His soul desires, that He does. For He performs what is appointed for me and many such decrees are with Him" (Job 23:13,14). As the Psalmist laments:

> "Where can I go from Thy Spirit?
> Or where can I flee from Thy presence?
> If I ascend to heaven, Thou art there;

If I make my bed in Sheol, behold, Thou art there;
If I take the wings of dawn,
If I dwell in the remotest part of the sea,
Even there Thy hand will lead me,
And Thy right hand will lay hold of me" (Ps. 139:7-10).

Thus, there is no escaping from the omnipresent Spirit whose task is to search our hearts. "He who searches the heart knows what the mind of the Spirit is" (Rom. 8:27). "Would not God find this out? For He knows the secrets of the heart" (Ps. 44:21). "For the Word of God "...is able to judge the thoughts and intentions of the heart." "And there is no creature hidden from His sight, but all things are open and laid bare to the eyes of Him with whom we have to do" (Heb. 4:13). Therefore, we will save ourselves a lot of agony if we heed the first signals which He sends our way rather than waiting for His judgment to fall on us!

When my husband and I received the baptism of the Spirit during the height of the Catholic Charismatic Renewal, everyone was enthusiastically seeking to receive the power, anointing, and gifts of the Spirit. Very few spoke about, let alone sought to partake of, the main purpose of the Spirit—that of developing His fruit in us through sanctification, transformation, death of self, and resurrection in Jesus.

I am convinced that most of us have not allowed the Spirit to even scratch the surface of what is buried in our hearts. This has been confirmed recently by the exposure of the sins of some of the leaders of the body—obvious sins which had not been dealt with, among those which are buried deeply in their hearts.

Perhaps one of the reasons why God considered David to be a "man after His own heart" was because he did not try to hide anything from his heavenly Father. David acknowledged God's omniscience when he declared:

"O Lord, Thou hast searched me and known me.
Thou dost know when I sit down and when I rise up;
Thou dost understand my thought from afar.
Thou dost scrutinize my path and my lying down,
And art intimately acquainted with all my ways.

Even before there is a word on my tongue,
Behold, O Lord, Thou dost know it all" (Ps. 139:1-4).

David did not seem to employ many defense mechanisms. Instead, he was open and honest; he trusted God enough to allow Him to expose and bring to light everything which was buried in his heart. "But all things become visible when they are exposed by the light, for everything that becomes visible is light" (Eph. 5:13).

Above all, the desire of our Daddy's heart is to have the same intimate relationship with each of us which He had with David. Intimacy with God is not possible though, until we give the Holy Spirit permission to tear down the walls which we have erected around our hearts. In a vision which the Spirit gave me for a counselee, He disclosed how gently, slowly and lovingly He will remove these walls. In this vision, He was removing only one brick at a time from the counselee's wall because her heart, which the Spirit allowed me to see, was extremely bruised, tender and vulnerable.

Prophecies, dreams, and visions given recently by the Spirit to Joyner, Brandt and many others reveal that God is raising up an end-time army of chosen saints who will be willing to pay the price of dying completely to self, allowing God to heal, purge and purify their hearts. These chosen ones will be humble servants, not interested in reputation, position or accomplishment, because of their burning love for the One Who works through them. Nations will tremble at the mention of their names, but they will flee to the mountains when men try to exalt them in any way! Astonishing miracles and angelic appearances will be common to these saints while a visible glory of the Lord will appear upon some as God's power flows through them! They will be ministering with awesome faith in complete peace as earthquakes, pestilence, famine, plagues, wars, and other calamities create havoc around them!

Those chosen for this extremely high calling will undoubtedly have to undergo extensive "heart surgery" as they will be required to minister with a pure heart and unshakable faith in total obedience. Obviously, in order to operate continuously in God's perfect will, the Inner Child of each of these special servants cannot be crippled with anger, rebellion, fear, guilt, etc.

Anyone trapped in a victim's role will have to give the Spirit permission to "circumcise" the wall of fear surrounding his heart, transforming his fear into faith with His powerful healing touch. Any person playing out a victimizer's script will have to allow the Spirit to "circumcise" the wall of rebellion encasing his heart, transforming his rebellion into obedience. "But he is a Jew who is one inwardly; and circumcision is that which is of the heart, by the Spirit, not by the letter" (Rom. 2:29). Thus, only after their hearts have gone through circumcision and have been purified, will these children of God be able to walk in total obedience with complete trust in their heavenly Father. With pure hearts, they *will trust and obey, for there is no other way*!

Therefore, as counselors, our heart's desire should be to help our counselees become intimate with their heavenly Father so that they can become part of His great army, described in Joel 2:

> "They run like mighty men,
> They climb the wall like soldiers;
> And they each march in line,
> Nor do they deviate from their paths.
> They do not crowd each other,
> They march everyone in his path;
> When they burst through the defenses,
> They do not break ranks" (Joel 2:7,8).

Reading Joel 2 in its entirety, we get a true picture of just how awesome and powerful this army of saints will be! It seems obvious that the only people who will qualify for this end-time army are those who have allowed God to circumcise their hearts and burn out their flesh, i.e., to "kill" their souls and resurrect them in Christ.

Only then will they be able to "stay in their own path and not crowd one another" because they will each be following God instead of the scripts with which they have been programmed. Only when Christ's body becomes this unified will it be able to obey the orders of the Head. Only through total submission to the will of God will the Army of Christ finally become powerful and effective enough to impact the world!

Since we live in such an exciting, to say nothing of stressful time, we have all the more reason to urge our counselees to abandon their hearts to God along with us and cry out with the Psalmist:

> "Search me, O God, and know my heart;
> Try me and know my anxious thoughts;
> And see if there be any hurtful way in me,
> And lead me in the everlasting way" (Ps. 139:23,24).
> "Create in me a clean heart, O God,
> And renew a steadfast spirit within me.
> The sacrifices of God are a broken spirit;
> A broken and a contrite heart, O God,
> Thou wilt not despise" (Ps. 51:10,17).

Just how important God considers the condition of our hearts to be is revealed in **Table 12.** Just how great His desire is for us to lay our hearts bare before Him is revealed in the prophecy given in **Table 13**!

F. LIBERATION FROM JUDGMENTS, VOWS AND SOUL TIES.

If a counselee sincerely asks God to search the depths of his heart, the Holy Spirit will allow the spirit of that person to begin disclosing the wounds buried deeply within his heart. As the Inner Child of the counselee decides to release more and more of his emotional hurts to Jesus, trusting Him to heal them, the Master Builder will begin removing stones from the wall encasing his heart. During the soul healing process, the perfect, agape love of Jesus will melt each stone, one by one, until this wall is removed; that is, the heart is circumcised, exposing a vulnerable heart of flesh.

The hardened heart of the counselee has thus been softened by the gentle, patient love of Jesus so that his Inner Child is able to forgive his parents and all others who have hurt him. This deep repentance seems to "lift a veil from his heart," enabling the "eyes of his heart to be enlightened." "...a veil lies over their heart; but whenever a man turns to the Lord, the veil is taken away" (2 Cor. 3:15,16).

Since the barriers (defenses) erected by the Inner Child have crumbled, he is now able to trust God enough to allow Him to disclose the truth concerning his soul. Thus, no longer in bondage to the Internal Parent through fear or anger, the Inner Child of the counselee is now able to give the Adult permission to examine the data programmed in his Parent in the light of reality data (God's truth). As the Adult exposes many of the judgments and beliefs stored in his Parent tapes (belief system) as lies and myths, his Inner Child is no longer deceived.

Examining three of the most prevalent judgments, discussed previously, in the light of reality data, the Adult of a counselee, in all probability, will decide that his Internal Parent could not possibly always be right. Reasoning will lead this person to conclude that, although it may have been dangerous for him to disagree with his parents when he was small, his internalized Parent is no real threat to him now. In addition, now that this individual has grown up, his Adult will, most likely, conclude that the approval his Internal Parent is no longer important, let alone mandatory!

How exciting these revelations of the Adult are to the Inner Child of this person! Keep in mind that even though the counselee may realize intellectually that his judgments are false, he does not become truly cognizant of this fact until the "veil is lifted from his heart (Child)," enabling it to be "enlightened." As the "eyes of his heart (Child) become more and more enlightened," he awakens to the fact that he does not have to allow his Internal Parent to control him any longer! As he allows his Deliverer to lift more and more of the burden from his small shoulders, the Inner Child of a counselee becomes freer and freer! Many of my counselees have remarked how much lighter and more buoyant they felt after their souls had received some healing! Of course, this "heart enlightening" does not occur all at once but is a gradual process that takes place during the course of soul healing.

As the Adult exposes his three major judgments as lies and myths in the light of God's truth, the counselee's Inner Child is freed from self-deception, enabling him to allow his Adult to break these life-controlling judgments which keep him in bondage to his Parent tapes. The counselee may be instructed to break these judgments as follows: "I break the judgments that my parents are always right, it is dangerous to disagree with them and that their approval is necessary for me to feel accepted. In Jesus' name, I nail these judgments to the cross, putting them to death."

Many self-judgments, judgments against others and the resulting inner vows will be revealed as a counselee's Internal Child begins to fearlessly and even expectantly, let the Adult explore and analyze his Parent data. His Inner Child will then be able to allow the Adult to break the judgments and vows which the Spirit brings to light. Examples might be: "In Jesus' name, I break the self-judgments that I am stupid and the vow that I will always fail at everything;" "In Jesus' name, I break the judgment that all men are evil and will use me and the vow that I will never trust any man," and so on.

As he gains more and more freedom through the breaking of his judgments and vows, the Inner Child of a counselee will finally allow the ungodly ties binding his soul to the souls of his parents to be cut asunder! To accomplish this task, the counselor may pray as follows: *"In the name of Jesus, I break the ungodly soul tie between John and his father. I ask You, Father, to send angels to take back to John's father any part of his soul that went out to John in a way not sanctioned by You and to bring back to John any part of his soul that went out to his father in a manner not intended by You."*

The Spirit often gives the counselee a vision of Jesus cutting in two with a large pair of scissors or a sword an "umbilical cord" attaching the counselee to his Parent. As Jesus cuts the cord, there may be some bleeding, but it is healed when Jesus attaches the cord to Himself. The counselee might also see Jesus cutting him loose from chains that are wrapped all around him, binding him tightly, meaning that he is being freed from his parental programming.

All other soul ties must also be broken, especially those formed with partners during fornication or other illicit sexual behavior. Ungodly soul ties formed with substitutes for love (alcohol, drugs, food, sex, work, etc.) without which we subconsciously believe we cannot survive must also be broken. Whenever we become dependent upon someone or something as a substitute for God's love, making this person or thing an idol before God, we have formed an ungodly soul tie which must be severed.

Much as we would like it to be, the breaking of judgments, inner vows and soul ties is no "magic formula." Although they are broken in the spiritual realm, freedom from them must become a reality in the natural realm. But this, thank the Lord, is not our problem! Only the Spirit can liberate us from our past programming and transform us so that we might walk in victory in our daily lives. But He must have the full cooperation of the Child within each of us in order to transform us into "new creatures in Christ."

2 Corinthians 5:17 states, "If any man be in Christ, he is a new creature; "...behold, new things have come." The key to "the old things passed away/behold, new things have come" in this scripture is the phrase "in Christ." According to Webster's dictionary, the word "in" indicates "being within an encompassing material." So, to be "in Christ" we must be "within Him" as He encompasses or surrounds us. This is an intimacy which the Child within many of us will not allow until much healing has taken place.

Since God has given each of us a free will, He cannot force the Child within each of us to receive healing. Consequently, few of us truly become "new creatures in Christ." "Old things do not pass away" (death of the soul) and "new things come" (resurrection of the soul in Christ) because "as we think in our hearts (Child), so we are!"

Therefore, if we do not accept God's gift of soul healing which includes forgiving, breaking judgments, vows, and soul ties in the spiritual realm, the Spirit will not be able to bring our transformations into new creatures in Christ to fruition in the natural realm. Each individual's emotional healing and deliverance from bondage depends entirely upon how much the Child within him will release his will to the Spirit! If we do our part, the Spirit will have no problem doing His! Ways in which we can "help" the Spirit by surrendering our wills even further to God will be discussed in the third section, "Resurrection of The Soul."

G. REVELATION FROM DREAMS.

As stated previously, one method which the Spirit uses to draw our attention to the need for soul healing and deliverance from destructive attitudes and behavior patterns is through the use of dreams. The Holy Spirit enables the personal spirit within each of us to reveal the troubled, sinful areas—sometimes deeply buried in the subconscious (Child/heart)—of our lives by presenting them in dreams. Unfortunately, this exciting and fascinating method which God uses to reveal the inner self has been sadly neglected by His children.

Most of us have not seriously considered the messages being relayed to us through our dreams because they seemed to be delivered in a secret code which ordinary people could not decipher. Only psychologists or biblical "giants" like Joseph and Daniel seemed to hold the key to unlock their secrets. We seem to have forgotten that the same Holy Spirit that interpreted dreams for Joseph and Daniel resides in us. Since God is no "respecter of persons," He will interpret dreams for us just as surely as He did for the patriarchs of the Bible!

Although the Spirit will begin revealing what our dreams and those of our counselees are saying to us if we begin paying attention to them, God expects us to study to show ourselves approved. Herman H. Riffel, in his excellent book, *Your Dreams: God's Neglected Gift*, states that the church has, for the most part, ignored—even rejected, the study of dreams and visions, and has, therefore, lost the understanding of them. Thus, he and his wife asked God to help them find the truth concerning their interpretation wherever it was hidden and to give them the wisdom to use that knowledge for His glory.

After much confirmation from scripture, people, dreams, etc., they both concluded that God was leading them to study dream interpretation at the C. G. Jung Institute in Zurich, Switzerland, trusting the Spirit to give them discernment concerning the truth about this subject. The result of their study is a fascinating book in which rare and invaluable insight into understanding dreams and visions is given.

In his book, Riffel states that dreams are often hard to understand because their messages are given in a language of symbols that we must learn, just as we must learn a foreign language. Another reason we have difficulty understanding our dreams is because they reveal our blind spots, those things about ourselves which we do not see. The basic message of a dream, according to Riffel, is usually two-fold, showing the dreamer's present condition and what will happen if he continues going in the direction in which he is headed.

As an example, he relates a dream in which he was hiking up a steep mountain, leading his wife and three children. As he kept climbing up the treacherous trail, he suddenly realized that he had gone too far. Feeling the stones give way under his feet, he realized that he and his family were all going to slide down into a chasm below! Although he had previously written dreams off as coming from what he had eaten before retiring, he reluctantly concluded that God was trying to tell him that something needed to be changed in his life. For twenty years, he had kept his life and feelings under tight control as he rigidly pastored a small denominational church. But he had witnessed that the Spirit was beginning to "shake up" the denominational churches and thus, he received the dream's message that if he continued in "performance," he would end up in disaster!

In another dream which also revealed his "spiritual condition," he was driving his car, following a bus down a dirt road. The bus was stirring up so much dust that he could not see where he was going. Since a bus usually symbolizes a crowd of people in a dream, the interpretation was that he was "following the crowd" and therefore, did not realize the direction in which he was headed.

When Riffel began heeding his dreams and going in the direction in which the Lord wanted him to go, the Spirit began giving him dreams instructing him in how to stay on this "straight and narrow" path. In one dream, he was pushing a baby carriage with a little baby in it. When he came to the end of the street, he did not stop but pushed the carriage right up over his two-story house. Once during this dream, he lifted the carriage over his head and the baby fell out, but he was able to catch it.

The end of the street represented the "dead end" of his ministry as a pastor of the denominational church from which he had been dismissed when he became receptive to the new movement of the Holy Spirit. But the Spirit was instructing him not to stop but to carry the "baby" (new idea or concept) right up over the "traditional, religious" house in which his soul was then living. He would have to lift the baby (idea) over his head (get it past his mind) and the baby might fall out, but he would not lose it (the new idea).

In another dream, Riffel and a young girl were on a raft. Suddenly, she fell off and sank headfirst into the deep water. He dived in, grabbed her heel, and pulled her back on the raft. The Spirit was telling him in this dream that he had been neglecting the baby, grown older now, and she (the new truth) had almost been lost.

The Spirit may also encourage us in a dream by showing us that we are headed in the right direction. A counselee dreamt that she was in a small boxcar going straight up a steep mountain on a very narrow track. There was a huge, fat lady in front of her, mocking and laughing at her and trying to derail her small car. The counselee was worried about a very sharp turn at the top of the mountain, but she made it around the bend and arrived safely at the top!

This particular counselee had suffered with bulimia for fifteen years. Although delivered from this symptom, she still fought the compulsion to turn to food to meet her emotional needs. She had made a firm decision with her Adult however, had taken a strong stand against Satan and her Inner Child was turning more and more to the Lord to meet her emotional needs. The narrow track was her training ground and the fat lady was, of course, addicted to food, which had become her idol. The Lord was showing her that if she continued going in the direction in which she was going, not veering to the right or left, even though there would be some rough places (sharp turn), the stronghold which food had over her life would eventually be broken and she would finally be victorious!

1. DREAM SYMBOLS.

Although there is no single interpretation of a symbol that would hold true for every dream, it is necessary to have some basic knowledge of dream symbols in order to understand dreams. One of the most common symbols is the house which, as we have seen, represents the soul. In our dreams, we may relive painful experiences which occurred in the house of our childhood. These are, of course, telling us that the hurts and wounds buried in the Inner Child (childhood house) need to be healed.

A recurring dream which I have is that I am living in a huge house and giving a party for lots of people whom I am happily feeding and entertaining. This dream always completely baffled me because hospitality, especially involving cooking, is definitely not my forte! I wondered if the Lord was trying to tell me that I should give more parties. What a relief it was to discover that my dream simply meant that I am always feeding and caring for people's souls and spirits!

Recently, I have been having many dreams of larger and larger houses in which I am preparing many beds. In one dream I was preparing beds which were packed tightly together along both walls of a very long room. I was placing a huge alarm clock on a ledge behind each bed. Obviously, the Spirit is telling me to get ready, because He is about to bring in many more hurting people who need soul healing. The purpose of the alarm clocks was to remind them not to be like the "sleeping virgins," but to wake up and receive healing because the time is short!

Riffel relates that a woman dreamt that she was living in a beautiful house. One day, she began discovering doors leading to rooms which she did not know were there. One was filled with lovely furniture and one with objects of art. In the dream, the idea that there could be more rooms fascinated her, but it also frightened her. The beautiful home symbolized the fact that she was happy with herself. She was excited that there were things about her soul (rooms of the house) that she had not discovered, but also fearful that she would discover something about herself that she might not like.

People are also a common symbol in our dreams; yet, a common mistake in dream interpretation is to take them literally. According to Riffel, ninety percent of the time the people whom we dream about represent a part of ourselves. Such was the case when he dreamt of a boyhood friend who was very dogmatic. This dream brought to his remembrance the fact that he had recently been arguing very dogmatically with a friend. Thus, it would be helpful to always ask the Spirit to reveal what, if anything, people in our dreams represent to us and what they are doing in our dreams that we are doing in real life. We may dream of someone we know who is strong-willed, undisciplined, judgmental, rigid, etc. It is very probable that this individual may represent an area of our souls which we need to allow the Spirit to transform.

People in our dreams may also represent ideas or truths which the Lord wants us to accept, such as the baby and the young girl in Riffel's dreams. During a time when the "refining fire" under me was turned up high, I had a dream in which I was dancing cheek-to-cheek with a very repulsive, ugly person. I felt disgusted and was crying and saying, "Why do I always get things I don't want! I never get anything I want anymore!" The Spirit was telling me that I must embrace this time of refining and the trials that accompanied it, thanking God because they would work good things in me. "And we know that God causes all things to work together for good to those who love God, to those who are called according to His purpose" (Rom. 8:28).

God may also reveal the condition of the souls of others, especially loved ones in our dreams. One counselee dreamt that she was playing "Hangman's Noose" with her husband. In this game the person is "hung" if he does not guess all of the letters in a word. The word which she had given him was "gigantic." He had guessed all of the letters except the two g's when he threw up his hands in frustration, saying, "I give up! You might as well hang me because I can't get those last two letters." The two g's, of course, stood for God, and her husband was telling her that completely surrendering his heart and will to God was just too "gigantic" a task for him!

Automobiles in dreams represent means of transportation and are often linked to men as symbols of their egos. Riffel dreamt that he was driving a big, new car when he was stopped by a policeman who insisted on inspecting the car, even taking the motor apart. He felt confident that the car was good and would pass inspection. The big, new car represented the freedom which his Natural Child had recently found, while the policeman stood for the authority figure in him—the legalistic, controlling Parent.

Clothes are a common symbol in dreams which often reveal how we see ourselves or want others to see us—formal, casual, unkempt, or perhaps rigid, as in a policeman's uniform. We may be "dressed fit to kill," meaning that we want to destroy others by getting all the attention. If we are naked and desperately trying to cover ourselves, it usually means that we are fearful of having the innermost parts of our soul revealed.

Shortly after being told by a very ambitious, young pastor that I would no longer be allowed to counsel at the church because he did not believe that counseling and inner healing were necessary, I had the following dream. A young man came into my hotel room and insisted that I leave immediately. I found myself walking through the lobby without a skirt on, but I did not feel embarrassed as I felt sure that I would find one soon. God was telling me in this dream that, although I had been dismissed from my position (room) in the church (hotel), I should not feel ashamed. He was also assuring me that He would soon provide another church to be the covering (skirt) for my ministry.

Sexual dreams are often misunderstood, according to Riffel, because they are not speaking of the physical experience of sex at all. Since God intended sexual relations to be the most intimate union of man and woman, the sexual dream often describes the intimate union of the masculine and feminine parts of the personality. A dream depicting a sexual union between a male dreamer and an alluring woman might mean the uniting of his masculine part with that part of himself that is creative and feminine. Or a dream in which a woman is being wooed by a man might mean that the masculine or aggressive part of her is asking to be recognized and accepted.

Riffel relates a dream in which he spent the day with an intelligent, conservative woman who seemed to be a nurse. She and his wife got in the back seat of the car he was driving. Suddenly, he turned around and asked the nurse to marry him, to which she seemed to respond favorably. This was not a dream of infidelity but indicated that he was accepting the creative feminine part of himself which she represented. The fact that his wife observed his proposal to the nurse signified her approval.

Unfortunately, our society has become so preoccupied with sex that lustful thoughts dominate many people's imaginations. Their dreams are then so dominated by sexual fantasies that this channel for showing them an imbalance that needs correction is blocked. Only when they repent and receive healing of the root cause of this problem, will this creative channel be open to be used by the Spirit again.

Water is a frequent symbol used in dreams which, according to the Bible, may represent a source of life or a healing stream. Riffel relates a dream in which he was walking beside a very large, wide stream, carrying a white beach ball. Two young fellows wanted to take the ball from him, so he tossed it into the stream. He and the young men jumped in after it. The stream symbolized the living waters of the movement of the Holy Spirit. A circle signifies wholeness and the color white, purity or perfection, both depicted by the white beach ball. Just as a white ball is used to start a game of billiards, the white beach ball symbolized the key to action. The Spirit was, therefore, challenging Riffel to take action (throw the ball in) and jump into the Lord's life-giving stream.

In a dream, the vast waters of an ocean may refer to the deep unconscious part of ourselves. There may be a ship (representing life) on the ocean, which is being tossed to and fro, perhaps sinking. This dream, thus, contains a warning that our soul is in trouble (troubled waters)! We may find treasures in the ocean also, suggesting that valuable things can come out of what looks like tragedy.

Animals in dreams may represent different emotions—fear, anger, jealousy, lust, pride, etc.—which need to be recognized in ourselves and dealt with properly. Large animals, like the elephant, rhinoceros or bull, may charge us in our dreams, filling us with fear. If we face our fears by turning and facing these enormous animals, they will become friendly. When we awake, we can ask the Spirit to reveal what part of ourselves the animal in our dream represents. It may be the assertive part of us that wishes to be recognized. The fox and cat family may refer to that part of us which is cunning, sneaky or manipulative, while rats and vultures may signify sin in our lives. Birds may depict our thoughts or ideas, while the eagle may symbolize energy or wisdom, and fish, souls for God's kingdom.

Riffel dreamt that he was teaching a young bird, to which he had attached a string, to fly. Each time it flew, a cat would spring at the bird. The bird depicted the new spiritual part of him that he was trying to get airborne, while the cat referred to the legalistic, rigid, Internal Parent which was trying to destroy his newfound expression of life in the Spirit.

2. REVELATION OF FEARS.

Our fears and anxieties often come out in dreams. I could not begin to count how many times over the years I have dreamt that I could not make it to a college class or, if I did happen to get there, I discovered that I had not studied anything that was on an exam. These are common dreams depicting anxieties about college familiar to many of us. Mine were more intense, I believe, because I did miss quite a few classes and exams due to a recurring inner ear infection during my freshman year of college. I finally began facing that fear in my dreams and asking questions, such as, "Why am I still working on my bachelor's degree when I have two master's degrees?" The fear vanished immediately as I answered myself with, "Why, indeed! How stupid! "

Just as when we are awake, the only way to deal with fear in our dreams is to confront it. When we face it, instead of running from it, fear becomes powerless. To illustrate, a man had a dream in which an angry man was running toward his car. He cried out, "What shall I do, Lord?" The Lord answered, "Confront him." So, the man, shaking with fear, jumped out of his car, and positioned himself in front of this enraged person. The furious man looked shocked, and then he began to diminish in size from over six feet to two inches in height. When the man having the dream asked the Lord again what to do, He said, "Step on him," which he promptly did! Thus, when he confronted his own particular fear, which happened to be fear of speaking, it shriveled up and disappeared.

During a time when I felt frustrated and anxious because the growth of my ministry of soul healing was being hindered in numerous ways, I had many dreams in which I was struggling to climb up stairs or ladders which were filled with obstacles. The steps might also be moving or changing to many contorted positions, and I would sweat and strain trying to get up just a few of them! As I began to release my ministry to the Lord and trust Him with it, the steps became easier to climb and the frustration and anxiety diminished.

If a dream is continually ignored, it often becomes a nightmare. A teenager or even an adult, may have a dream in which he actually kills his parents. Although shocking and disturbing, this dream usually means that the Inner Child of this individual is trying to get free from his Internal Parent, which is still controlling his life. Feeling frustrated because he has not been able to accomplish this liberation from his Parental programming, he strikes out in a dream at the object of his anxiety.

One small boy dreamt that he was tied to a railroad track, and the train was roaring down the track. Keeping in mind that the meaning of the symbols in a dream always comes from the dreamer, the track in this dream represented the rigid discipline of his parents. The locomotive, the huge man-made machine, symbolized the powerful tradition in his home which he was trying to resist, but which he feared would demolish his identity.

A frequent nightmare, especially for children, is that of falling. A recurring nightmare which I had as a child was one in which I stepped into what I thought was an elevator. It turned out to be an empty shaft which I, feeling terrified, plummeted down. When I came to within an inch of hitting bottom, I awoke with a jolt! I did not consider this nightmare or my fear of heights to be unusual because I knew that many children suffered from the fear of falling. So, as an adult, I was surprised to discover that my fears had a basis in reality. One day my mother told me that because it had taken her five years to conceive a Child, she was a little frightened to care for me. Her doctor, not realizing the trauma he would be inflicting on a small baby's soul, raised me up high and dropped me! Apparently, he was trying to make the point that she did not have to worry about taking care of me because I would not break. I was probably sleeping and awoke with a shock when my mother caught me. At any rate, it was a traumatic experience which affected my life for years!

One mother related that she discusses her children's dreams with them at breakfast. By doing this, she is able to bring out and talk over with them any feelings or problems revealed by their dreams. If any hurts or fears are revealed, she can pray with them right away, asking Jesus to come into the dream and heal any wounds or "cast out any fears with His love." She has, therefore, established an excellent, non-threatening way to build an intimate love relationship between herself, her children and God, while also dealing immediately with any negative emotions encountered by her children before these feelings have a chance to scar their little souls.

Dreams may also point out the physical condition of the dreamer. At a time in my life when I had a heavy counseling schedule and was also supervising other counselors at a large church, I had this dream. Lots of people were enjoying themselves at a party which was going on in my huge house. Confident that everyone was being taken care of, I simply laid down on the couch and went to sleep! Shortly after I had this dream, the counseling department of my church was closed, and I, being on the brink of "burn-out," took a much-needed vacation from counseling.

3. REVELATION OF FUTURE.

God also uses dreams and, many times, visions to give us guidance and information concerning our future, just as He did Abraham, Jacob, Joseph, Moses, Daniel, Joseph (Jesus' father), Peter, Paul, and countless others down through the ages. During the time when I was still resting from counseling, the Lord was beginning to raise up a group of dedicated, sincere women to help in the ministry of soul healing. I had the following dream concerning the future of this group and our ministry with the Lord.

An Army recruiter was asking me if I would consent to serve in the Army. I replied that I was under the impression that nurses were needed, and I was not a nurse. Looking at my file, he said, "Oh, I see that you are a psychiatrist." Taken aback, I replied, "Well, uh, I guess so." Continuing, he said, "Great! We really need you because many soldiers get battle fatigue and have flashbacks of war scenes that need healing." I said, "Well, I am really tired, so I don't know. But, wait, maybe this is what the Lord has planned for this group He is raising up. But if we do it, I want you to know that we will do weird things which you might not understand." He replied, "Fine, you may do whatever you want to. You have a free rein as far as the Army is concerned!"

In another dream, the son of the owner of a large, prosperous company had fallen in love with me. He led me into a beautiful office, sat me at a desk with lots of phones and told me that he was promoting me to a higher position. Seated in front of the desk were many warm, smiling people to whom I felt instantly close. The owner, seated at my left, said that he approved of my promotion because he was also in love with me and that these people would be working for me. Although I felt wonderful and excited about the promotion, I was extremely concerned that these two men were in love with me because I loved my husband deeply! I woke up feeling totally confused and distressed because the dream had been so vivid that I felt it must mean something. The Spirit came to me immediately and assured me that the dream was from the Lord and that the owner of the company represented God, and His Son was, of course, Jesus! Well, as you might suspect, I was totally blessed! I could not believe the Lord would give me such a sweet, precious dream!

I had a third dream revealing the future of **Wounded Lamb Ministries**, the name God recently gave me for the soul healing team He is raising up. I was walking through the spacious lobby of the most beautiful, plush hotel I had ever seen. As I climbed the stairs to the second floor, I was startled to see a lavishly appointed foyer. Each time I climbed to a higher floor I was astonished to behold an even lovelier vista! When I finally reached the top, I saw a balcony on which a group of people were standing in a circle, holding hands. As I peered over the edge, I was amazed at how high up we were!

On the left side of the balcony there was an extensively broad expanse of stairs which streams of people were ascending. They all had on masks and were dressed as if they were going to a costume ball. The people holding hands all began to sing and circle faster and faster until I awoke, feeling extremely dizzy! The Lord revealed that this dream meant that He would take **Wounded Lamb Ministries** to "dizzying" heights! The soul healing group would help the people climbing the stairs remove their masks and costumes and find their true identities in Christ! Praise You, Jesus!

These dreams, of course, indicated that I would not be resting forever, but would soon be leading a ministry team that would bring emotional healing to the Army of Jesus Christ! The first dream also reassured me, at a time when opposition to soul healing was beginning to rise up, that we would be well-received.

At another time, when I was feeling anxious and concerned about all of the divorced women I was counseling who were carrying the heavy burden of financial, emotional, physical, and spiritual responsibility for their children, I had the following dream. I dreamt I was climbing the stairs to the room which had been mine as a Child. I could hardly get through because little girls were occupying every square inch of the stairs and of my spacious room! They were all standing very tall, each one holding a lighted candle up high. I felt tremendous strength and confidence emanating from one. Then they all sang a song which they had written just for me. Feeling so very touched and proud of them, I wept many tears of joy!

The Lord was, of course, reassuring me that the Inner Child in each of the women I counseled would make it, each one eventually becoming a strong, bright light for Jesus in His kingdom! I have had to hang onto this precious dream as I watched these women go through many trials, struggling under their enormous loads!

4. REVELATION OF DEATH OF THE SOUL.

Riffel relates a dream a man described in which he was attending the funeral of a friend. When he looked in the casket, he was shocked to discover that the body in it was his! Riffel assured this man that the dream probably did not mean that he was going to die. He interpreted the dream to mean that the body in the casket represented a part of this man's soul which had died, while the man attending the funeral was his conscious self. The part that died may have symbolized something bad in his personality with which he had long struggled or something good which he had ignored for so long that it had died. When a friend dies in a person's dream, it usually means that a part of the dreamer has died, but when the dreamer dies in his own dream it means, in most cases, that his soul has died.

Riffel dreamt that a nurse told him, gently but firmly, that he would die soon. Then he had another dream in which he was given one million dollars to distribute; each person was to receive one hundred dollars. Soon he was helping black women with babies get their portions. Then the scene changed to a monastery where a word was given that a man would soon die, a knife cleaving his heart! He realized that he was this man, but he knew that it was all right because he was a priest in this dream and dying was part of the ritual.

Riffel interpreted the dream to mean that he was soon to receive a great amount of energy; each part of him was to receive a little. The black women represented the unknown parts of him, while the babies symbolized new areas of growth. The second part meant that his soul would soon die, going through the ritual of death and resurrection, the knife being the instrument which separates the old from the new. Thus, the large amount of energy he was going to receive would be needed for his growth after his resurrection in Christ.

Several of the women whom I have counseled have had dreams or visions in which they saw themselves as little girls die and then be resurrected. In one case, a counselee had been hurt so deeply by her parents' extreme rejection and abuse that she even denied having any parents! After six years of working with her, the Lord melting the walls of stone around her heart with His precious love, her strong-willed Inner Child finally consented to trust Jesus and release to Him the horrible wounds inflicted upon her by her parents.

In one of the final sessions of her soul healing, the Spirit gave her a vision of herself as a small girl struggling on a bed. Legions of horrendous demons were all around her, sneering that she was theirs and that they would never release her! The Holy Spirit revealed many curses of the occult—witchcraft, Satan worship, fortune telling. He even revealed that she had been dedicated to Satan! When all of these generation curses were broken on the cross and the effects of them cleansed away by Jesus' blood, she saw the spirit of her little girl rise up and leave her body which remained motionless on the bed. Although she tried to get Jesus to come and help her little girl lying lifeless on the bed, He refused. She watched in amazement as this little girl became ugly, shriveled up and disappeared! Jesus then led this counselee out into the fresh air and sunlight, closing the door behind them.

Thus, her soul, which had been cursed, had died and been resurrected in Christ Jesus! "I have been crucified with Christ; and it is no longer I who live, but Christ lives in me; and the life which I now live in the flesh I live by faith in the Son of God, Who loved me and delivered Himself for me" (Gal. 2:20).

If we even had an inkling of what Jesus really won for us when He shed His blood on Calvary, we would be absolutely overcome by the awesomeness of His mighty deed!

> Surely our grief's He Himself bore,
> And our sorrows He carried;
> Yet we ourselves esteemed Him stricken,
> Smitten of God and afflicted.
> But He was pierced through for our transgressions,
> He was crushed for our iniquities;
> The chastening for our well-being fell upon Him,
> And by His scourging we are healed!

The Inner Child of another counselee was unable to trust Jesus to reveal and heal the pain of her past memories. Although she had always wanted to picture herself as a beautiful China doll, in a vision she saw herself as a tattered rag doll with no head or arms! The Lord then gave her a picture of the head of a China doll, but she knew it would not look right on her rag doll body. After much healing prayer, she saw her rag doll body nailed to the cross of Christ. But she was afraid to allow her Savior to resurrect her as a fragile China doll because China dolls always had to stay on the shelf since they broke so easily.

But Jesus solved this problem by giving her a vision of herself resurrected as an exquisite China doll which He then filled with glue which symbolized the Holy Spirit. She was then able to trust her Healer because she knew that a China doll filled with glue could never break! Thus, using imagery, Jesus was able to convince the Inner Child of this counselee that He was perfectly capable of bringing her soul to a final death and resurrection in Him!

Thus, we can see that dreams and sometimes visions, are invaluable tools which God uses to give us understanding and guidance for our lives. "I will bless the Lord who has counseled me; Indeed, my mind instructs me in the night" (Ps. 16:7). Like all of His other gifts, we must first decide that we want to receive God's help through our dreams, then ask Him to speak to us through them and finally seek His guidance to interpret them correctly. Practice in interpreting our own dreams will help us, as counselors, to interpret those of our counselees.

One guideline to remember when interpreting a dream is that the meaning of the dream must always be drawn from the dreamer. Seek to discover what the symbols of the dream represent to him and what he was emotionally involved in when he had the dream. Watch for the dreamer's recognition of the right interpretation. The dream interpretations presented by Daniel and Joseph to Nebuchadnezzar and Pharaoh both "clicked" with these powerful rulers as they recognized them to be correct. The Holy Spirit will give us the correct interpretations of our dreams and those of our counselees if we diligently seek His wisdom and guidance and make a determined effort to study "to show ourselves approved."

Part III. RESURRECTION *of the* SOUL

Even though a person receives from the Lord a dream or vision of his Inner Child "dying and being resurrected," this does not mean that the "death and resurrection of his soul" has immediately taken place in the temporal or natural realm. Would that it would be that easy! The dream or vision signifies that this individual's soul was crucified spiritually on the cross with Christ almost 2000 years ago and then resurrected with Him when He rose from the dead. "I have been crucified with Christ; and it is no longer I who live, but Christ lives in me" (Gal. 2:20). Thus, the Holy Spirit is revealing through the dream or vision that the work has been accomplished in the eternal or spiritual realm. But now, since this person's Inner Child has given Him permission, the Spirit is indicating that He will now be able to bring this work to fruition in the ***temporal*** or natural realm.

Thus, as we have seen, the death and resurrection of an individual's soul is a process which takes place over a period of time. How long it will take depends on how willing a person's Child is to trust the Lord and cooperate with the Spirit as He circumcises his heart with His "sword." Total death of self will not be accomplished, of course, until we are taken home to be with Jesus. However, this does not excuse us from cooperating fully with the Spirit whose task is to perfect us in Christ Jesus. "For I am confident of this very thing, that He who began a good work in you will perfect it until the day of Christ Jesus" (Phil. 1:6).

It must be possible for us to attain to some degree of perfection since Jesus Himself said, "Therefore you are to be perfect, as your heavenly Father is perfect" (Matt. 5:48). Paul said to the Romans, "Therefore I urge you, brethren, by the mercies of God, to present your bodies a living and holy sacrifice, acceptable to God, which is your spiritual service of worship" (Rom. 12:1). He also told the Corinthians that "...the temple of God is holy, and that is what you are" (1 Cor. 3:17b).

Are there any signs by which we might recognize that at least some "death and resurrection" has taken place in our lives? The greatest sign is, of course, the ability to feel love, compassion and forgiveness from the heart for our parents and others who have hurt us. "But I say to you, love your enemies and pray for those who persecute you" (Matt. 5:44). The only two commandments that Jesus gave us were to love God and our neighbor. Therefore, if love and all the fruit of the Spirit are becoming more noticeable in our lives, some death and resurrection has surely taken place.

The ability of a person's Internal Child to trust enough to relinquish his control to the Adult is another indicator that some death and resurrection has occurred. Because so many events in the present "trigger old tapes," replaying outdated Parent-Child conflicts, more often than not, our emotions (Child) have control over our reasoning processes (Adult). For example, a critical, demanding employer may remind an individual of his father, causing his father's cruel, condemning judgments to replay again in his head: "You are so stupid; you never do anything right; you might as well give up!" Although we have been taught that Satan places these negative thoughts in our minds, he is only able to replay the archaic tapes which comprise our past programming. As we have seen, these tapes of past events "hook" a person's Inner Child, causing him to feel hurt, angry, scared, rejected, unworthy, perhaps even immobilized, as his Internal Parent "beats on" his Inner Child once again.

The more soul healing an individual has received, the easier it is for him to recognize when his "Child has been hooked;" that is, when he is feeling strong emotions because his "Internal Parent is beating on his Inner Child." He now has the ability to choose to "get into the Adult" and examine his Parent data. His Adult will then remind his Inner Child that his Internal Parent is no longer a threat and that the old judgments and inner vows have been broken. Since these former judgments and vows are no longer valid, his feelings are no longer appropriate. How convinced the Inner Child is of the Adult's reasoning depends not only on how much an individual has been healed by God's love, but on how well his Internal Parent has been reprogrammed with God's truth.

A. REPROGRAMMING THE INTERNAL PARENT.

Exposing the misconceptions and myths contained in the Parent data as lies and breaking judgments and vows are not sufficient in themselves. Whenever something negative is taken away, it must be replaced with something positive. Therefore, a person's soul cannot be brought to resurrection in Christ until his Internal Parent is reprogrammed with new judgments composed of God's truth. If the Parent data of an individual does not contain truth, his Adult will not be capable of making intelligent decisions, even though his Inner Child has finally released its control of the Adult.

When a person's Internal Child finally relinquishes its control of his will and gives it back to his Adult, in whose charge it rightly belongs, it is an indication that the rebellious self-will of this individual has finally been broken. The Adult (will) of this person will now be permitted to fulfill its responsibility of making rational decisions after examining data from the Parent (mind), the Child (heart) and the outside world (reality).

1. POSITIVE JUDGMENTS.

In addition to examining and remaking the three most common judgments included in Parent data, which were discussed previously, the Adult's task is to examine all of the other judgments and beliefs contained in the Parent data to determine whether or not they are true. Much of this task will be accomplished during the soul healing process as Jesus reveals to the small child of the counselee why one or both of his parents pronounced such cruel judgments against him.

For example, during faith visualization, the counselee's little child may ask Jesus why his mother always called him "stupid" and told him that "he would never amount to anything" when, in fact, he was very intelligent. The Spirit may reveal that she projected her own poor self-image upon him because she was jealous of his intellect or that she rejected him because she had to drop out of school when she became pregnant with him which ruined her chances to have a career.

As the Inner Child of a counselee gains new understanding about why his Parent or parents judged him so harshly, it is able to allow the Adult to break the old judgments stored in the Parent data and replace them with new ones. Examples of new judgments concerning self might be: I am a child of God, a new creature in Christ, a joint-heir ruling with Him, and a priest to God; I am worthy and righteous in Christ; I am an acceptable, lovable, successful, valuable, intelligent person; I am a special, precious, beautiful, and unique individual made in the image of God; and I am a prized treasure, a costly jewel and a cherished blessing of God. Counselees can be encouraged to confirm who they are in Christ by stating the positive judgments from God's Word.

Cheryl Prewitt-Salem's effective booklet, *Abuse: Bruised but Not Broken,* lists positive judgments based on Proverbs 31 which women can also confess. Examples of new judgments concerning others might be: My parents and others are trustworthy, loving, caring, and compassionate; they accept and love me as I am; and they will support, encourage, affirm, and bless me.

When a person begins to declare such positive judgments about himself and others, he is "agreeing" with God that by faith, he and others are already sanctified and changed into Christ's image. "Now faith is the assurance of things hoped for, the conviction of things not seen" (Heb. 11:1). When a person begins to see others by faith as God sees them, God can make people to be a blessing to him. "When a man's ways are pleasing to the Lord, He makes even his enemies to be at peace with him" (Prov. 16:7).

2. POSITIVE IMAGES.

His new judgments will be reinforced as a counselee pictures himself reliving his childhood with Jesus and his parents who have been "transformed" by the love and power of his Lord and Savior. Referring to the previous example, the counselee might visualize his loving, encouraging father assuring him that God has given him a good mind and that he can accomplish anything which the Spirit leads him to do. One of the purposes of reprogramming the Parent tapes of a counselee is to create a nurturing, compassionate Internal Parent who will be able to supply the love and acceptance for which his Inner Child will never stop hoping and longing. Thus, the more time a counselee spends picturing his parents, who have been "recreated" by Jesus, loving, respecting and valuing him as a precious, unique creation of God, the more "positive data is fed into his Parent tapes," which accomplishes this goal.

A most effective way to build a nurturing, supporting Internal Parent is to instruct the counselee to picture himself as a little child sitting on Jesus' lap. He can imagine Jesus holding him, rejoicing him and filling him with His perfect love, peace and security. The Spirit advised me years ago to instruct my counselees to picture themselves cradled in Jesus' arms, then to visualize the love, confidence, worthiness, peace, security, joy, strength, power, faith, etc., of Jesus flowing from Him into them. Since our Lord is the source of every good and perfect gift, i.e., the Fountain of Life, we can draw from Him whatever good attribute or characteristic our souls might lack. "For it was the Father's good pleasure for all of the fullness to dwell in Him" (Col. 1:19); "...I am the Way, and the Truth, and the Life" (John 14:6); "...the water that I shall give him shall become in him a well of water springing up to eternal life" (John 4:14). So, counselees can be encouraged to imagine themselves "drinking" from Jesus the qualities they need and then to picture themselves, feeling confident, worthy, strong, etc., going out to face the world!

Just as the counselee can picture Jesus healing his hurts from the past and filling him with strength, peace, etc., in the present, he can also visualize Jesus providing his needs in the future. For example, if he is nervous about a job interview, he can picture Jesus sitting beside him during the interview, holding his hand while encouraging, strengthening and giving him the right words to say. He can visualize himself feeling totally peaceful, confident and secure as he trusts Jesus to take care of everything.

God gave us the gift of imagination so that we could develop creative ways to activate our faith. Unfortunately, most of us have let this precious gift lie dormant or we abuse it either by picturing ourselves negatively or by turning it over to Satan's demons of fantasy. "We are casting down imaginations, and every high thing that exalteth itself against the knowledge of God and bringing into captivity every thought to the obedience of Christ" (2 Cor. 10:5 KJV). "Finally, brethren, whatever is true, whatever is honorable, whatever is right, whatever is pure, whatever is lovely, whatever is of good repute, if there is any excellence and if anything worthy of praise, (let your mind) dwell on these things" (Phil. 4:8).

3. WORD OF GOD.

The best source of truth is, as we all know, the Word of God. Thus, as counselors, we must encourage our counselees in every way possible to continually feed God's word into their Parent tapes, reprogramming them with truth. As the Word of God is fed into their minds, the old programming will be washed away with the water of the Word. "And do not be conformed to this world (the result of past programming) but be transformed by the renewing of your mind (Parent)" (Rom. 12:2a). As we cleanse and renew our minds with the Word of God, new life begins to flow through our souls and spirits. "My son give attention to my words "...For they are life to those who find them" (Prov. 4:20,22). "You have been born again '...through the living and abiding word of God'" (1 Pet. 1:23 ESV). "...holding fast the word of life" (Phil. 2:16a).

a. DEVOURING THE WORD. Just as eating nutritious food nourishes our bodies, "eating" the Word of God nourishes our souls and spirits. Years ago, the Spirit revealed to me that when we read the Bible, it is analogous to taking a bite of food; when we meditate on the Word, it is like chewing this food; when we memorize Scripture, it is like swallowing the food. According to Webster's Dictionary, to "meditate" means to "contemplate," "dwell in thought," "ponder," "muse," "reflect upon," "cogitate" or "mull over." The Spirit revealed to me that meditating on the Word is analogous to a cow ruminating or chewing her cud which means that she brings up and chews more thoroughly food that has been chewed slightly and swallowed. Thus, to meditate on the Word means to ruminate or bring it to mind again and again. Memorizing the Word might be compared to a cow swallowing her cud the second time after the food has been thoroughly chewed.

"Thy words were found, and I ate them. And Thy words became for me a joy and the delight of my heart" (Jer. 15:16a KJ21). "Man does not live by bread alone, but by everything that proceeds out of the mouth of the Lord" (Deut. 8:3 RSV). "I have treasured the words of His mouth more than my necessary food" (Job 23:12).

Jesus said, "I am the living bread that came down out of heaven; if anyone eats of this bread, he shall live forever" (John 6:51). John stated that "the Word was with God in the beginning" and that "the Word became flesh and dwelt among us" (John 1:1,14). Thus, we are to feed on Jesus Who is the Living Bread, i.e., the Word of God. "And He is clothed with a robe dipped in blood; and His name is called the Word of God" (Rev. 19:13).

Counselees should be encouraged to ask God to give them a love and hunger for the Word as all-consuming as David's. In Psalm 119, David states that he would have perished without the Word in which he delighted. He treasured the Word which revived, strengthened and comforted him, taught him discernment and knowledge and gave him great peace and hope. Oh, that we would love God's Word as much as David does! Following are some excerpts from Psalm 119:

> "This is my comfort in my affliction,
> That Thy word has revived me" (Ps. 119:50 WBT);
>
> "I wait for Thy word.
> My eyes fail with longing for Thy word" (Ps. 119:81,82);
>
> "If Thy law had not been my delight,
> Then I would have perished in my affliction.
> I will never forget Thy precepts,
> For by them Thou hast revived me" (Ps. 119:92,93);
>
> "Oh, how I love Thy law!
> It is my meditation all the day" (Ps. 119:97 KJV);
>
> "I have more insight than all my teachers,
> For Thy testimonies are my meditation" (Ps. 119:99);
>
> "How sweet are Thy words to my taste!
> Yes, sweeter than honey to my mouth!
> From Thy precepts I get understanding;
> Therefore, I hate every false way" (Ps. 119:103,104 KJV);

"Thy word is a lamp to my feet,
And a light to my path" (Ps. 119:105 KJV);

"My eyes anticipate the night watches,
That I may meditate on Thy word" (Ps. 119:148);

"I have inherited Thy testimonies forever,
For they are the joy of my heart" (Ps. 119:111);

"...But my heart stands in awe of Thy words,
I rejoice at Thy word" (Ps. 119:161,162 KJV);

"Those who love Thy law have great peace,
And nothing causes them to stumble" (Ps. 119:165).

David's words assure us that as an individual feeds on God's precepts, false beliefs and outdated perceptions contained in his Parent data will be dispelled and replaced with truth. We can surmise from David's psalm that meditating on God's Word not only develops in a person an understanding, insightful, wise Internal Parent; it also builds a comforting, encouraging Parent who revives, directs and fills his Inner Child with peace and joy.

Solomon also strongly exhorts us in his proverbs to acquire wisdom and understanding through the Word of God:

"Acquire wisdom! Acquire understanding!
Do not forget, nor turn away from the words of my mouth.
"Do not forsake her, and she will guard you;
Love her, and she will watch over you.
"The beginning of wisdom is: Acquire wisdom;
And with all your acquiring, get understanding.
"Prize her, and she will exalt you;
She will honor you if you embrace her.
"She will place on your head a garland of grace;
She will present you with a crown of beauty" (Prov. 4:5-9).

I can testify from my own experience that David and Solomon's words are true. I was raised in a Christian home and a loving church in which Bible study was an integral part of my upbringing for which I will be eternally grateful. I always enjoyed reading the Bible, although I surely would have enjoyed it much more if I would have had one of the translations available today. The Old King James text is very difficult for a child to "digest!"

I especially loved hearing stories at Sunday School about the great leaders of the Bible. When I heard at a very young age how pleased God was with Solomon because he asked Him for wisdom instead of riches and honor, I also asked the Lord for wisdom because I wanted to please Him. I believe God has richly answered the prayer of my youth.

Because of my request for wisdom and the fact that, although my parents had their faults, their role models lined up fairly consistently with the Word of God, my Internal Parent was programmed with truth, wisdom and understanding. I received my share of hurts, of course, but God's Word always gave me understanding and insight about why people thought and acted in certain ways. Since I knew the Lord fairly well at a very young age, I was able to keep His characteristics separate from that of my parents. Thus, although I might have partially, I did not completely transfer the image which I had of my parents to God. As a result, I have been blessed that my Inner Child has not had to struggle with an intense fear and distrust of God.

When I received the baptism of the Spirit eighteen years ago, I was overjoyed because I had finally found the missing piece of the puzzle! As a child, I was always questioning why God did not perform today the incredible, instantaneous miracles which I read about in scripture. Having finally received the power of the Spirit—in addition to an easy-to-read translation of the Bible—I really began soaking up the Word of God!

After working hard at memorizing Scripture for several years, God revived a gift which He had given me as a child—the ability to memorize easily. Thus, even though I still work diligently at it, over the years, I have been able to memorize large portions of Scripture. God has rewarded me with a ravishing hunger for the

Word which is, as David relates, my joy, my delight and sweeter than honey to my mouth!

The more I meditate on the Scriptures which I have memorized, the more alive, awesome and powerful they become to me! "For the Word of God is living and active and sharper than any two-edged sword" (Heb. 4:12a). The more I repeat them, the stronger my belief that God always fulfills the mighty promises contained in His Word becomes! "You have seen well, for I am watching over My word to perform it" (Jer. 1:12 ESV). As I say the Scriptures which have become so special and precious to me, Jesus' life surges through me, and I am flooded with great excitement and joy! My relationship with my heavenly Father becomes deeper, sweeter and more intimate every time I dwell on His awe-inspiring Word, often in the "night watches." "When I remember Thee on my bed, I meditate on Thee in the night watches" (Ps. 63:6 KJV).

Of course, as counselors, we do not want to discourage our counselees by suggesting that they "swallow their food before they have even taken a bite!" Thus, we might start by stressing to them the importance of spending some time, even fifteen minutes, each day reading God's Word while asking the Spirit for wisdom and understanding. As a counselee devotes time to meditating on Scripture, the Spirit will give him special insight into the ways in which his daily reading pertains to him personally. Thus, stressing to counselees the importance of spending as much time as possible getting themselves into the Word of God and getting the Word of God into themselves cannot be overemphasized! They should be encouraged to continually give God's Word first place in their lives!

b. PRAYING THE WORD. A very effectual method of reinforcing the new judgments and beliefs with which a counselee has reprogrammed his Parent is often termed "praying the Word of God over himself." The counselee may be instructed to insert his name in any one of the promises or prayers contained in the Bible. For example, he might be asked to insert his name into the following scriptures which reveal how intimately God knows each of us:

> "Before I formed 'John' in the womb I knew him. And before 'John' was born, I consecrated him" (Jer. 1:5);

"For 'John's father and mother have forsaken 'John,' But the Lord will take 'John' up" (Ps. 27:10);

"Behold, I have inscribed 'John' on the palms of My hands" (Isa. 49:16);

"For Thou didst form 'John's' inward parts;
Thou didst weave 'John' in his mother's womb.
'John' will give thanks to Thee, for he is fearfully and wonderfully made;
Wonderful are Thy works,
And 'John's' soul knows it very well.
'John's' frame was not hidden from Thee,
When he was made in secret,
And skillfully wrought in the depths of the earth.
Thine eyes have seen 'John's unformed substance;
and in Thy Book, they were all written,
The days that were ordained for 'John,'
When, as yet, there was not one of them" (Ps. 139:13-16).

These remarkably personal Scriptures reassure a person that even though he may have felt rejected by his parents in the womb, God knew him before birth and consecrated and wove him in his mother's womb. Thus, if a counselee faithfully prays these Bible verses over himself, the affirmative judgments that God loved, knew and accepted him even before he was placed in his mother's womb will become deeply engrained in his Parent data.

A counselee's new judgments of himself and who he is in Christ will be reinforced as he prays the following Scriptures over himself:

"John' is My servant; I have chosen 'John' and not rejected him" (Isa. 41:9);

"Do not fear, for I have redeemed 'John;" I have called 'John' by name; 'John' is Mine!" (Isa. 43:1b);

"Therefore, if 'John' is in Christ, he is a new creature; the old things passed away; behold, new things have come" (2 Cor. 5:17);

"And if 'John' belongs to Christ, then he is Abraham's offspring, an heir according to promise" (Gal. 3:29 NAS 1977);

"To Him who loves 'John' and released 'John' from his sins by His blood, and He has made 'John' to be a kingdom, a priest to His God and Father" (Rev. 1:5,6);

"And because 'John' is a son, God has sent forth the Spirit of His Son into his heart, crying, "Abba! Father!" Therefore, "John" is no longer a slave, but a son; and if a son, then an heir through God" (Gal. 4:6,7 ESV).

Most Spirit-filled Christians know that as heirs of God they can pray over themselves and their loved ones any of the more than 2000 promises in the Bible. These promises of God grant us health, peace, strength, provision for our needs, comfort, protection, victory in Christ, guidance, wisdom, joy, and anything else that we children of God might need. Following are several examples of promises which the counselee might be given to claim for himself:

"He will cover 'John' with His pinions, and under His wings 'John' may seek refuge" (Protection) (Ps. 91:4a);

"I will also hold 'John' by the hand and watch over him" (Protection) (Ps. 91:4b);

"But 'John' who seeks the Lord shall not be in want of any good thing" (Provision) (Ps. 34:10b);

"The Lord is near to the brokenhearted, And saves 'John' who is crushed in spirit" (Comfort) (Ps. 34: 18);

> "The angel of the Lord encamps around 'John,' who fears Him and rescues him" (Help) (Ps. 34: 7).

The Bible contains many promises which counselees can be given to help them overcome fear, guilt and unworthiness and receive healing, finances, wisdom, and guidance. There are also approximately seven prayers presented in the New Testament which a counselee might be encouraged to pray over himself and others. Following is an example of one of these prayers:

> "May the Lord direct 'John's' heart into the love of God and into the patience and steadfastness of Christ in waiting for His return" (2 Thess. 3:5).

The more time a counselee devotes to praying the Word of God over himself, thus, claiming God's promises for himself, the more his heavenly Father's love and truth will be fed into his Parent data. The goal to reach for is, of course, that the Parent tapes of a person might finally be completely reprogrammed with the priceless and powerful Word of God!

4. THE NEW COVENANT.

A counselee might well ask what exactly gives him the right to claim the promises contained in Scripture for himself. In answering this question, basic truths concerning the New Covenant and the Blood of Jesus on which it was founded and based will be fed into his Parent data.[3] The counselor may explain to the counselee that a covenant involves a pact, or promise, between two parties in which each pledges to the other all his possessions, strength, even his life, and which is sealed with the shedding of blood.

The Old Covenant, which God established between Himself and Israel, of which Moses was the mediator, was based upon the Law which no man could fulfill because "all have sinned and fall short of the glory of God" (Rom. 3:23). Only Jesus, the Messiah, could fulfill all of the requirements of the Law which He did by of-

---

3 I have chosen to capitalize the word "blood" when it refers to the incorruptible Blood of Jesus in order to give honor to His priceless, precious Blood which conquered sin and death for all time.

fering up Himself as a sinless Sacrifice for sin. "But He, having offered one sacrifice for sins for all time, sat down at the right hand of God" (Heb. 10: 12).

Thus, Jesus, the Son of God, established the New Covenant by making the first one obsolete. "When He said, 'A New Covenant,' He has made the first obsolete" (Heb. 8:13). Therefore, our Savior is the "...mediator of a better covenant, which has been enacted on better promises" (Heb. 8: 6). As the counselor compares the Old Covenant with the New, the counselee will understand more fully why the promises of the New Covenant are so superior to those of the Old Covenant.

a. CLEANSED WITH BLOOD. Both the Old and New Covenants were sealed with the shedding of blood. A question the counselee might ask is, "Why does God place so much importance upon the shedding of blood?" The answer to this question is that God requires the shedding of blood for the cleansing of sin. "...All things are cleansed with blood, and without shedding of blood, there is no forgiveness" (Heb. 9:22).

The Lord explained to Moses that the life of all flesh is in its blood, and because it contains life, the blood is the factor by which atonement of sin is made. Thus, as David Alsobrook points out in his excellent book, *The Precious Blood*, it is the life (which is in the blood) and not the death (which is merely the method used to secure the blood) of the victim; that is, the means of atonement. "For the life of the flesh is in the blood, and I have given it to you on the altar to make atonement for your souls; for it is the blood by reason of the life that makes atonement" (Lev. 17:11).

Under the Old Covenant, God required the lamb, as well as other animals, to be offered as a sacrifice for the sins of man. "But if he brings a lamb as his offering for a sin offering, he shall bring it a female without defect" (Lev. 4:32). It could not have a blemish or defect on it anywhere. The Lamb offered as Jesus Christ was the only Man who never sinned; therefore, He was the only Person Who could take the place of the unblemished sacrificial lamb as our "Sin Offering." Our Redeemer was "...in all things tempted" and "...yet without sin" (Heb. 4:15 KJV). "Who (Christ) committed no sin, nor was any deceit found in His mouth" (1 Pet. 2:22).

Just as the guilt of the transgressor was passed from himself to the sacrificial lamb, so was the guilt of all mankind laid upon the Savior of the world. "But the Lord was pleased to crush Him, putting Him to grief; if He would render Himself as a guilt offering" (Isa. 53:10a). Jesus bore the sins of every person in His body on the cross. "But the Lord has caused the iniquity of us all to fall on Him" (Isa. 53:6b). Thus, God brought the judgment for our sins upon Jesus as the Sacrificial Lamb.

Just as the innocence of the Sacrificial Lamb was transferred to the transgressor, so the righteousness of Jesus is legally transferred to anyone who accepts Him as their Redeemer. "He made Him who knew no sin to be sin on our behalf, so that we might become the righteousness of God in Him" (2 Cor. 5:21). Thus, our Deliverer took our sins and through His Living Blood, gave us His righteousness in exchange! What an exchange!! How could anyone pass up such an incredible deal!!! Our Messiah literally became our sin and we became His righteousness!! Unbelievable!!! "Knowing that you were not redeemed with perishable things," "...but with precious blood, as of a lamb unblemished and spotless, *the blood* of Christ" (1 Pet. 1:18,19).

In order to atone for (expiate, remit, cover) the sins of Israel, according to the Old Covenant, the high priest was required by God to sprinkle the blood of the sacrificial animal upon the mercy seat (lid of the Ark of the Covenant) in the tabernacle (Lev. 16). Likewise, Jesus' living Blood was sprinkled on the mercy seat in heaven. "He entered through the greater and more perfect tabernacle, not made with hands, that is to say, not of this creation," "...and not through the blood of goats and calves, but through His own blood, He entered the holy place once for all, having obtained eternal redemption" (Heb. 9:11,12).

Although Jesus' Blood was shed for the sins of all mankind, His sacrifice must be appropriated by each person individually. As Alsobrook says, "Jesus shed His blood for us in order to give it to us" (pg. 27). Thus, each child of God must be sprinkled or covered by the precious blood of his Justifier. (To those) "...who are chosen according to the foreknowledge of God the Father, by the sanctifying work of the Spirit, that you may obey Jesus Christ and be sprinkled with His blood" (1 Pet. 1:2). The elect also cover themselves with robes that have been washed in the cleansing blood of the Lamb. "...they have washed their robes and made them white in the blood of the Lamb" (Rev. 7:14).

b. SEALED WITH BLOOD. The Old Covenant between God and Israel was sealed with blood. The writer of Hebrews relates what happened at that time as follows:

"Therefore, even the first covenant was not inaugurated without blood. For when every commandment had been spoken by Moses to all the people according to the Law, he took the blood of the calves and the goats, with water and scarlet wool and hyssop, and sprinkled both the book itself and all the people, saying, 'This is the blood of the Covenant which God commanded you'" (Heb. 9:18-20).

Moses sprinkled both the book and the people with the blood of sacrificial animals. Sprinkling the blood upon the book that contained God's Law, upon which the Old Covenant was based, bound God to His Word. Sprinkling all of the people with blood bound them to the covenant by the blood. God was joined to Israel by the blood that sealed the Old Covenant.

Just as Moses, mediator of the Old Covenant, said, "This is the blood of the covenant which God commanded you," so Christ, mediator of the New Covenant, said at His last Passover, '...This cup which is poured out for you is the New Covenant in My blood'" (Luke 22:20). In similar manner to the Old Covenant, the written record of the New Covenant, as well as the people who have been redeemed, are sprinkled with the sealing Blood of Jesus. Just as our Savior's blood binds God to His Word, so the redeemed are bound to God's Word by His priceless blood. Thus, God is bound to the redeemed by the blood of His Son which sealed the New Covenant.

Therefore, since the blood of Christ binds God to His New Covenant, God is held legally responsible for fulfilling the provisions laid down in His Word, the written record of His New Testament. What fantastic news! If only we could fully comprehend the meaning of this statement!! One day when I was claiming the promises in the Word for healing, the Lord said to me, "I have no choice but to honor the promises in My Word for you!" Those thrilling words gave me "Holy Ghost goose-bumps!"

But wait—there is a catch, of course. Since the elect are also bound to God's New Covenant by the blood, they are held legally responsible to fulfill the requirements which are laid down in God's Word. Although God never reneges on His part of the bargain, we, the elect, often fall far short of keeping our part!

c. REQUIREMENTS OF NEW COVENANT. What exactly are the requirements on our part and the provisions, on God's part, which are decreed under the New Covenant? As we know, God's first requirement for receiving His provisions is that we be justified and covered by the blood. "In Him we have redemption through His blood, the forgiveness of our trespasses, according to the riches of His grace, which He lavished upon us" (Eph.1:7,8).

The second requirement for eligibility is that we stay under the blood. God put a hedge of protection around Job because he offered blood sacrifices to Him continually. According to Job 1:5, Job continually rose up early and offered burnt offerings for all his children because they might have sinned and cursed God. Satan complained that God had "...made a hedge about him (Job) and his house and all that he had, on every side" (Job 1:10).

One of the provisions given in God's Word is the "blood covering" which consists of a hedge that protects us, as the children of God, on every side from Satanic attack. However, we can break our hedge and get out from under our blood covering by disobeying God's Word and not walking in His light. The Bible warns us that, "...whoso breaketh an hedge, a serpent shall bite him" (Eccl. 10:8 KJV). The apostle John states that "If we say we have fellowship with Him and yet walk in the darkness, we lie" (1John 1:6,7). "For if we go on sinning willfully after receiving the knowledge of the truth, there no longer remains a sacrifice for sins" (Heb. 10:26). Thus, the protection of our blood covering can be removed if we walk in darkness at all. This reveals why holiness is a must!

To stay under the blood, we must not only obey the commandments given in God's Word, we must also believe the promises set down in God's Word. "But My righteous one shall live by faith; and if he shrinks back, My soul has no pleasure in him" (Heb. 10:38). "And without faith it is impossible to please Him, for he who comes to God must believe that He is and that He is a rewarder of those who seek Him" (Heb. 11:6). "Therefore, I say to you, all things for which you pray and ask, believe that you have received them, and they shall be granted you" (Mark 11:24). Thus, the old song, "Trust and obey, for there is no other way," states very simply God's requirements for staying under the blood covering which makes us eligible to receive the benefits which God has for us under the New Covenant.

d. PROVISIONS OF NEW COVENANT. Perhaps the most astounding provision of the New Covenant is that unlimited and unrestricted access to God is now available to all who are covered by the Blood of the Master! Under the Old Covenant only the high priest, fearing for his life, could enter the Holy of Holies once a year. If he had committed any sin that had not been cleansed by blood, God might possibly strike him down. Since no one else could enter the Holy of Holies, a rope was tied around his leg so he could be pulled out in case God struck him dead).

Following the death of our Lord, the sixty-foot tall veil in front of the Holy of Holies was torn from top to bottom, signifying that the Lamb of God had fulfilled the Old Covenant. Under the New Covenant, which was put into effect at that time, any believer can now boldly approach God's throne at any time through the atoning Blood of the Lamb! How incredible!! How much better is the New Covenant than the Old because of the Living Blood of our Redeemer!!

Hebrews, chapter ten, describes the "new and living way which our Lord inaugurated:"

"Therefore, brethren, since we have confidence to enter the holy place by the blood of Jesus, by a new and living way which He inaugurated for us through the veil, that is, His flesh, and since we have a great priest over the house of God, let us draw near with a sincere heart in full assurance of faith, having our hearts sprinkled clean from an evil conscience and our body washed with pure water" (Heb. 10:19-22).

Notice that we are required to enter the holy place by the Blood of Jesus "in faith with clean hearts." These are the conditions which make us eligible to receive all of the benefits God has provided for us in His New Covenant.

Our Perfect Sacrifice is also our High Priest. Under the Old Covenant, the sacrifice of the high priest furnished only an annual covering which cleansed only the flesh but could not take away sins. In contrast, Jesus offered one sacrifice which cleansed away all sins for all time! Hallelujah!! "And every priest stands daily ministering and offering time after time the same sacrifices, which can never take away sins; but He, having offered one sacrifice for sins for all time, sat down at the right hand of God" (Heb. 10:11,12).

Although the high priests died and had to be replaced, Jesus lives forever to continually intercede for the believers—another incredible blessing which He has bestowed upon us under the New Covenant! Thus, our Advocate constantly stands before His Father, asking Him to have mercy on us and give us grace because we are His righteous (in "right-standing" with God), having been justified (just-as-if-we-had-never-sinned) by His Blood. Only as God looks at us through Jesus' ransoming Blood is He able to have mercy on us and shower us with abundant grace and bountiful blessings!

The writer of Hebrews details in chapter seven all the points that make the New Covenant a better covenant:

"So much the more also Jesus has become the guarantee of a better covenant, and the former priests, on the one hand, existed in greater numbers, because they were prevented by death from continuing, but Jesus, on the other hand, because He abides forever, holds His priesthood permanently. Hence, also, He is able to save forever those who draw near to God through Him, since He always lives to make intercession for them. For it was fitting that we should have such a high priest, holy, innocent, undefiled, separated from sinners and exalted above the heavens; who does not need daily, like those high priests, to offer up sacrifices, first for His own sins and then for the sins of the people, because this he did once for all when He offered up Himself. For the Law appoints men as high priests who are weak, but the word of the oath, which came after the Law, appoints a Son, made perfect forever!" (Heb. 7:22-28).

As our great High Priest, Jesus also understands how strong various temptations to sin are for us because he was tempted in all things, even though He did not fall. "For we do not have a high priest who cannot sympathize with our weaknesses, but One who has been tempted in all things as we are, yet without sin" (Heb.4:15).

Another wonderful advantage for us, the chosen, then, is that our Conqueror is able to help us resist and withstand temptation in the midst of trials because he was severely tempted in every one of the extreme tribulations that He was required to endure. "For since He Himself was tempted in that which He has suffered, He is able to come to the aid of those who are tempted" (Heb 2:18).

Thus, our sweet Savior is able to empathize with us, understand and relate to every temptation and trial that we encounter because He has already walked every path that we are required to. As our "...friend that sticketh closer than a brother" (Prov. 18:24 KJV), Jesus is by our side always, comforting us when we are hurting, encouraging us when we are discouraged, loving us when we are lonely, and protecting us when we are afraid. "For He Himself has said, 'I will never desert you, nor will I ever forsake you,' so that we confidently say, 'The Lord is my helper, I will not be afraid'" (Heb. 13:5,6).

Our gentle Shepherd suffers our pain right along with us as we walk through life's valleys. He gathers us "... as lambs in His arms and carries us in His bosom" (Isa. 40:11 ESV). "Even though I walk through the valley of the shadow of death, I will fear no evil; for Thou are with me; Thy rod and Thy staff, they comfort me" (Ps. 23:4 KJV). If one of us little lambs goes astray, our Good Shepherd will even leave the ninety-nine and go after the one (Matt. 18:12-14). Our beloved Shepherd Who "laid down His life for us sheep" (John 10:11) is the sweetest, most precious Gift we could ever receive!!

Another remarkable benefit of the New Covenant, as Alsobrook points out, is that the Passover Lamb's body was opened as a Fountain for sanctification in five areas—His back, His head, His feet, His hands, and His side. "In that day a fountain will be opened for the house of David and for the inhabitants of Jerusalem, for sin and for impurity" (Zech. 13:1). The Blood flowed from His back as a provision for our healing. The Blood flowed from His head, His feet, and His hands for the sanctification of our minds, our walk with God and our works in the kingdom. "Therefore, Jesus also, that He might sanctify the people through His own blood, suffered outside the gate" (Heb. 13:12). The Blood streamed from His side to represent our position at His side in the heavenlies.

Let us consider first the Blood that flowed from His back for our healing. Isaiah prophesied, "The chastening for our well-being fell upon Him, And by his scourging we are healed" (Isa. 53:5). Although this verse is generally used to claim the gift of physical healing, I believe that, even more important, it also makes provision for healing the wounds and scars of our souls and spirits. Peter seemed to know that the hurts which his soul and spirit suffered when he denied his Master three times were healed by his Redeemer's wounds. "...and He Himself bore our sins in His body on the cross, so that we might die to sin and live to righteousness; for by His wounds you were healed. For you were continually straying like sheep, but now you have returned to the Shepherd and Guardian of your souls" (1 Pet. 2:24,25). Keeping in mind that we often project our own behavior on others, Peter seems to indicate that after he appropriated the healing for his bruised soul and spirit from his Lord, he no longer strayed, but returned to his Shepherd.

Alsobrook gives a vivid description of the flagellum, the precision-made, skillfully applied Roman weapon, which was used to rip the flesh from Jesus' back. He states:

"The sharp bronze metal tips pierced at equally distant points into Jesus' back. The blows were placed high on the shoulder area and ripped the flesh in straight lines to the buttock area" (pg. 141).

In the Psalms, Christ's scourging was compared to the plowing of a field. "The plowers plowed upon my back; they lengthened their furrows'' (Ps. 129:3). The "plowers" were the Roman soldiers who scourged His back while the blood gushed from it. Thus, this Fountain of incorruptible Blood purchased healing not only for our bodies but, even more significantly, for our souls and spirits. All we must do to receive healing for ourselves—physically, spiritually and emotionally—is appropriate the Blood which coursed down our Savior's back.

The second area from which the Blood flowed as provision for the sanctifying of our minds was Christ's head. After weaving a crown of thorns which they placed on Jesus' head, the Roman soldiers began beating Him on the head with a reed (Matt. 27:29,30). This mock crown was platted from the common thorn bush whose thorns contain a stinging poison which was released into our Lord's scalp as His head was smitten with the reed. The tormenting itch and burning caused by the poison symbolized the poisonous thoughts with which the devil often assaults our minds.

Thus, our Substitute took all our evil thoughts and transferred His pure mind to us by the Blood which streamed from His head! What a wonderful blessing!! "But we have the mind of Christ" (1 Cor. 2:16). Thus, our minds have been sanctified, which simply means "set apart and made clean" by the purifying Blood of Jesus. The crown of thorns soaked with His Blood is our "helmet of salvation" (Eph. 6:17), which provides a protective hedge or a Blood covering for our minds. If we appropriate this Blood covering by keeping our helmets of salvation on at all times, we will not break our hedge protection; thus, the serpent cannot corrupt our minds (Eccl. 10:8). We can keep our thought life pure by keeping our minds stayed on Him and renewing them continually with the Word of God.

The third area from which the Blood flowed was Christ's feet, which furnished the sanctification for our walk on earth. The Passover Lamb is not only the Sin Offering for our initial redemption from sin, but is the Trespass Offering for our sanctification as well. Jesus' walk on earth was perfect with no blemish or stain of sin upon it. He was "holy, innocent, undefiled" (Heb. 7: 26). His feet were placed one over the other; then the sharp Roman spike was driven into His flesh. His feet were nailed to the cross so that by the innocent Blood that streamed from them, He might exchange our sinful walk for His perfect one! What an astounding exchange!!

The beautiful, nail-pierced feet of Christ soaked with Blood provide a protective hedge or a Blood covering for our walk. As discussed previously, we must stay under our Blood covering by "walking in the light" (1 John 1:6). We are to:

> "...walk by the Spirit, so that we will not carry out the desires of the flesh" (Gal. 5:16);
>
> "...walk in love" (Eph. 5:2);
>
> "...walk by faith" (2 Cor. 5:7);

> "...walk in the same manner as He walked" (1 John 2:6);
>
> "...walk in a manner worthy of the Lord, to please Him in all respects, bearing fruit in every good work and increasing in the knowledge of God" (Col. 1:10), and
>
> "...walk as children of light (for the fruit of the light consists in all goodness and righteousness and truth) trying to learn what is pleasing to the Lord" (Eph. 5: 8-10).

These Scriptures again point out the necessity of walking in obedience and faith so that there will not be any "holes in our hedges" through which Satan can enter to corrupt our walk. If our feet stay in step with God, we will stay under the Blood, allowing us to enter into intimate fellowship with our heavenly Father! This is our greatest joy! Oh, that we could walk as close to God as Enoch walked! "And Enoch walked with God, and he was not, for God took him" (Gen. 5:24). "By faith Enoch was taken up so that he should not see death, "...for he obtained the witness that before his being taken up he was pleasing to God" (Heb. 11:5).

Sanctification for our works is the fourth blessing which we receive from the Blood which gushed from Jesus' nail-pierced hands. In God's Word, the hand symbolizes one's works in the body of Christ. "...they shall lay hands on the sick, and they shall recover" (Mark 16:18). Sowing and reaping are accomplished with the use of hands in farming. Sowing the Word and reaping the harvest is the mission of all believers.

The work of Jesus' hands was holy and always blessed mankind—raising the dead, healing the sick, multiplying the loaves and fishes, etc. His loving hands did not deserve the spikes, but by the Blood that flowed from them, our hands are cleansed from filthy and dead works and set apart for the work of God! Hallelujah!! "For if the blood of goats and bulls and the ashes of a heifer sprinkling those who have been defiled sanctify for the cleansing of the flesh, how much more will the blood of Christ, who through the eternal Spirit offered Himself without blemish to God, cleanse your conscience from dead works to serve the living God?" (Heb. 9:13,14).

Every good work that we do as we minister in the body of Christ is acceptable to God as a pleasing sacrifice only through the Blood of Jesus. Therefore, our walk must be pure and holy if we want our works to be pleasing to God. If God blesses us with a mighty anointing and works many gifts of the Spirit through us, we must be extremely careful to remain humble and to give Him all the glory and praise. "I am the Lord; that is My name; I will not give My glory to another" (Isa. 42:8). "So then neither the one who plants nor the one who waters is anything, but God who causes the growth" (2 Cor. 3:7).

Also, we must be absolutely certain that the works we are doing in our ministries are in obedience to God's will. Many legalistic Christians are faithfully performing "church activities," totally convinced that they are serving God. Only after our souls have "died and been resurrected in Christ" will we be able to have an intimate relationship with God so that we can hear His direction for our lives and ministries. Too many Christians today are "doing their own thing," expecting God to bless it, rather than allowing Him to break them and "purge their consciences from dead works," so that they will be able to hear His voice!

The lovely, nail-pierced hands of our Messiah soaked with Blood provide a protective hedge or a Blood covering for our works. Thus, if we want our works to be anointed and bear much fruit, they must be covered with the sanctifying Blood of Christ. The Word of God instructs us concerning our works as follows:

> "Let your light shine before men in such a way that they may see your good works and glorify your Father who is in heaven" (Matt. 5:16);
>
> "We must work the works of Him who sent Me, as long as it is day; night is coming, when no man can work" (John 9:4);
>
> "Truly, truly, I say to you, he who believes in Me, the works that I do shall he do also; and greater works than these shall he do; because I go to the Father" (John 14:12);
>
> "Instruct them to do good, to be rich in good works, to be generous and ready to share" (1 Tim. 6:18);

> "Even so faith, if it has no works, is dead, being by itself "... show me your faith without the works, and I will show you my faith by my works," (James 2:17-18), and

> "Each man's work will become evident; for the day will show it, because it is to be revealed with fire, and the fire itself will test the quality of each man's work. If any man's work which he has built on it remains, he shall receive a reward" (1 Cor. 3:13,14).

As believers, many of us have not taken Paul's advice seriously to be careful about how we build upon our Foundation, Jesus Christ, with our works (see 1 Cor. 3). We haphazardly build with "wood, hay and straw" rather than "gold, silver and precious stones." Many of us just might be surprised when much of our works burn up in the fire on the judgment day of the saints! Let us, therefore, be cautious about how we build upon our Foundation by continually humbling ourselves and seeking God's will and direction in our ministries so that our works will not be pronounced "dead" when the King of Kings returns!

As we study the five areas from which Jesus' Blood flowed in the order in which they were opened up, it is amazing to note the progression:

(1.) The restoring Blood of the Balm of Gilead's back furnished the healing of our wounded souls and spirits (the healing of the Inner Child with love);

(2.) Next, the purifying Blood from the head of the Prince of Peace provided for the renewing of our minds (the reprogramming of the Internal Parent with truth);

(3.) The purging Blood from the Lion of Judah's feet sanctified our walk. Only after our scarred souls and spirits have been healed and our minds renewed will we be able to walk with God in love, holiness and truth;

(4.) The anointing Blood from our Good Shepherd's hands sanctified our works. Only if we walk purely with Him in His light and direction, will our ministry works be anointed and fruitful, and

(5.) Lastly, the conquering Blood from our Bridegroom's side symbolizes our position with Christ in eternity. I believe that we will receive our final position at the side of our King in the heavenlies after our works have been judged to see if we will receive any rewards or if only we ourselves will be saved, as through fire, our works having been burned up (See 1 Cor. 3:14,15).

Thus, we progress along the path of growth to maturity as Christians in the same order in which Jesus' flesh was opened as a Fountain of Blood for our healing, cleansing and sanctifying! What astonishing symbology!

The final, triumphant blessing which we, the elect, will receive then, is our exalted position at the side of our Messiah in the heavenly places. For we are the bride of Jesus Christ and we are eagerly waiting and longing for the grand and glorious day when we will be married to our beloved Bridegroom! Hallelujah!! "Let us rejoice and be glad and give the glory to Him, for the marriage of the Lamb has come, and His bride has made herself ready" (Rev. 19:7). "Then the sovereignty, the dominion and the greatness of all the kingdoms under the whole heaven will be given to the people of the saints of the Highest One; His kingdom *will* be an everlasting kingdom, and all the dominions will serve and obey Him" (Daniel 7:27). Glory to God!!!

5. AUTHORITY OF BELIEVERS.

Meanwhile, however, we are the army of Christ and there is a fierce spiritual battle to be fought and won! "Blessed be the Lord, my rock, who trains my hands for war, And my fingers for battle" (Ps. 144:1). Our Victor won the war for all eternity by shedding His costly Blood on the cross at Calvary. He regained the authority that Satan had stolen through Adam's disobedience in the garden. "...All authority has been given to Me in heaven and in earth" (Matt. 28:18). After recapturing that power and authority, He freely gave it to those who accept Him as their Savior.

Paul prayed that the believers at Ephesus would know "...the surpassing greatness of His power to us who believe" (Eph. 1:19). With this same supreme power "God raised Jesus from the dead and seated Him at His right hand in the heavenly places, far above all rule and authority and power and dominion, and every name that is named" (Eph. 1:19-21). Then God "put all things in subjection under His feet and gave Him as head over all things to the church, which is His body" (Eph. 1:22,23). Where are the feet? They are part of the body! Therefore, as believers, we are part of His body and are seated with Him in heavenly places, equipped with the same power, the same authority which He has!! Praise the Lord!! "God "...even when we were dead in our transgressions, made us alive together with Christ "...and raised us up with Him, and seated us with Him in the heavenly places in Christ Jesus" (Eph. 2:5,6).

Because our Messiah earned eternal redemption for us, we have been adopted as sons of God, and "...if we are sons, then we are heirs of God also and fellow-heirs of Christ" (see Rom. 8:15-17, Gal. 4:5-8). As heirs of God, we are now part of His kingdom. "For He delivered us from the domain of darkness and transferred us to the kingdom of His beloved Son" (Col. 1:13 ESV). "He has made us to be a kingdom, priests to His God and Father" (Rev. 1:6).

The child or the heir, of a king has the same rights as the king and consequently, has the same legal rights and privileges. As adopted sons of the Kings of Kings, we have been granted all the rights and privileges to which we are entitled as the "King's Kids!" Thus, as counselors, we must make sure that the Parent tapes of our counselees are reprogrammed with these truths concerning the authority which Jesus won for His followers with His Blood and gave to them under the New Covenant!

a. IN HIS NAME. As children of the King of all of the universe, one of the rights and privileges granted us is the use of His name, "...the name which is above every name, that at the name of Jesus every knee should bow, of those who are in heaven and on earth and under the earth" (Phil. 2:9,10). The name of Jesus Christ carries authority in every realm of the universe! Concerning His name, Jesus said the following:

"If you shall ask the Father for anything, He will give it to you in My name" (John 16:23);

"If you ask Me anything in My name, I will do it" (John 16:23);

"And these signs will accompany those who have believed; in My name they will cast out demons, they will speak with new tongues, they will pick up serpents, and if they drink any deadly poison, it shall not hurt them; they will lay hands on the sick, and they will recover" (Mark 16:17,18), and

The seventy disciples returned with joy, saying, "Lord, even the demons are subject to us in Your name!" (Luke 10:17).

Peter understood the full extent of the power and authority vested in the name of Jesus and he knew how to use it. When he was ministering to the lame man at the temple gate, he said, "In the name of Jesus Christ the Nazarene—walk!" He then "seized him by the right hand; he raised him up; and immediately his feet and his ankles were strengthened" (Acts 3:6,7). When they all marveled that the man was walking, Peter's answer was simply, "On the basis of faith in His name, it is the name of Jesus which has strengthened this man" (Acts 3:16). Oh, that we would all have the faith in that name that Peter had! After commanding the lame man to walk, Peter did not timidly wait to see if he was healed—Peter pulled him to his feet!

Brother Kenneth Copeland claims that the Holy Spirit revealed to him that "sickness," "drug addiction," "poverty," etc., are all just "names." Therefore, we can command each of these "names" to "bow the knee before the name of Jesus—the name which is above all other names!" Thus, the name of Jesus is the only name which can bring salvation, freedom, healing, prosperity, peace, joy, strength, love—anything which we may need or desire!

b. SPIRITUAL WARFARE. Now that we, the body of Christ, are convinced that we have the authority under the New Covenant to fulfill our commission to bring salvation, healing and deliverance to all mankind in His name, how are we to accomplish this calling? We must all go through a rigorous training program if eventually we are to become rulers over the governments of the world. "But the saints of the Highest One will receive the kingdom and possess the kingdom forever, for all ages to come" (Dan. 7:18).

Prince Charles of England was trained and disciplined according to an established program to prepare him for rulership as the King of England. God's method is also to put us, His elect, through an intensive training program to prepare us to administer His will over all of the earth. Like it or not, we are all in God's "boot camp" at this time! Thus, we are being prepared right now to reign with Him and to serve Him throughout eternity. It is hard to picture ourselves as rulers governing the kingdoms of the world, but nevertheless, this is our eternal commission as saints of Jesus Christ.

Therefore, as counselors, we must convince our counselees to take seriously their "high calling" and to submit completely to God's rigorous program of preparation for them. Healing of the soul resulting in death of the soul, is the first part of this preparation. The second part consists of the resurrection of the soul in Christ. Thus, our Deliverer died so that our souls might be cleansed, healed and sanctified, enabling us to die to our own wills. Our Victor rose from the dead so that our souls might be resurrected in Him, enabling us to do His will instead of our own. "I have been crucified with Christ; and it is no longer I who live, but Christ lives in me" (Gal. 2:20).

God's will is that we be conformed to the image of His Son. "For those whom He foreknew, He also predestined to become conformed to the image of His Son" (Rom. 8:29). We have learned that if our soul has truly been resurrected in Christ and conformed to His image, we will love our neighbor as ourselves and manifest the fruit of the Spirit in our lives, as Jesus did. In addition to this, we will take our positions as rulers and exercise dominion over all of the spiritual forces of darkness, as He also did. "The Son of God appeared for this purpose, that He might destroy the works of the devil" (1 John 3:8 NAS 1977).

Sad to say, the church of Christ is failing miserably when it comes to spiritual warfare. Because so many wounded saints have not been healed and delivered from Satan's grasp, they are too weak to exercise their authority over him or too blinded to even recognize his schemes. We cannot say, as Paul did, that no advantage can be taken of us by Satan because we are not ignorant of his schemes (see 2 Cor. 2:11). Satan is ripping off the body of Christ in every conceivable way because we are all so ignorant of his strategies.

The devil and his band of demons are doing an astonishingly good job of stealing, killing and destroying (see John 10:10). For example, experts estimate that at least 30,000 children and teenagers are being sacrificed to Satan yearly in America! This news is so shocking that most people recoil in horror, unable to believe it! Yet these same people, many claiming to be Christians, see nothing wrong with killing millions of precious babies in the womb!

The great deceiver is extremely clever, and the church is losing ground daily to him because it does not even recognize his schemes, let alone know how to combat them! Not only this, the few brethren who are attempting to teach the body how to do spiritual battle are attacked unmercifully by the rest of the church! If we, the saints of the church, do not wake up, see the "Big Picture" and join together in combating the devil and his evil forces, we are going to lose the horrendous war which is fast approaching!

But even though we are aware of the fast-approaching danger, each of us is only responsible for what God is calling him or her to do. As counselors, part of our responsibility to our counselees is to see that instructions on how to fight the enemy are fed into their Parent data. We are to encourage them to "fight the good fight of faith" so that, after soul healing, the evil one may never get control of their thoughts, emotions or wills again. "Be of sober spirit, be on the alert. For your adversary, the devil, prowls about like a roaring lion, seeking someone to devour. But resist him, firm in your faith" (1 Pet. 5:8, 9).

(1.) Identification of Enemy. One of the first principals of war is to locate and identify the enemy. What do we know about our enemy and his troops? Paul declares in his letter to the Ephesians that "...we wrestle not against flesh and blood, but against principalities, against powers, against the rulers of the darkness of this world, against spiritual wickedness in high places" (Eph. 6:12 KJV). Wow! The enemy camp certainly sounds impressive! This Scripture suggests that the satanic army is highly organized into ranks of ruling spirits who are subject to Satan as the head.

The word "principality" is described as "the territory or jurisdiction of a prince" by Webster's dictionary. Thus, ruling spirits must be assigned over certain areas, such as nations and cities. This is confirmed by the fact that while Daniel was seeking God, an angel appeared and explained to him that he had been delayed for twenty-one days in delivering God's message by the prince of the kingdom of Persia—a demon prince (See Dan. 10).

The word "powers" in this Scripture tells us that the ruling demon forces have power or authority to carry out whatever orders have been assigned to them. The phrase "rulers of the darkness of this world" informs us that the evil one and his hierarchy intend to control the world which is in their grasp. Satan is referred to in the Word as "the god of this world" (2 Cor. 4:4) and the "prince of the power of the air" (Eph. 2: 2).

The phrase "spiritual wickedness in high places" tells us that the devil has access to heavenly places where he also performs his wicked deeds. For example, our accuser presented himself to the Lord one day and informed Him that he had come from "roaming about on the earth." He then convinced God to allow him to touch all that Job had because he was sure Job would curse God if He would remove the hedge which He had placed around Job, his family and his possessions (See Job 1.). Another example relates that when Joshua, the high priest, stood before the angel of the Lord, Satan also stood at his right hand to accuse him (See Zech. 3:1,2).

Although Lucifer and his diabolical hosts have power and authority to practice wickedness on earth and in heaven, we know that we have power and authority over them all through the Blood of Jesus! Our Savior "...cancelled out the certificate of debt consisting of decrees against us" by "nailing it to the cross." He then "...disarmed the rulers and authorities, made a public display of them, and triumphed over them" (Col. 2:14,15). The Lord of Hosts then gave us authority over all the power of the enemy that nothing should injure us and made the spirits subject to us!! (See Luke 10:19,20). Praise the Lord!!!

(2.) Recognition of Enemy Tactics. How then, are we to take our authority over the power of the enemy? The leaders of an army always attempt to discover the battle plans of their enemy so that they will know how to avoid his traps and what tactics to employ against him. Paul says that we are to "wrestle" against the prince of darkness and his evil, controlling forces. Wrestling involves "hands-on" grappling with the enemy, implying that the battle is very personal and intimate. Wrestling also suggests pressure tactics; thus, our adversary's main tactic is to put pressure on us. What pressure tactics does he use, anyway? As we have learned from our study of soul development, the great deceiver is an expert at attacking our thoughts and emotions through the skillful utilization of our past programming. He is acutely aware of the particular word curses, judgments and inner vows that make up our individual programming which he cleverly manipulates to adversely affect our decisions, attitudes and behavior.

Satan's main tactic is to assign deceiving demons to bombard our minds with lies and seducing spirits to entice us to believe these lies. For example, if a highly abused individual is even slightly rejected, a deceiving demon can bring back all of the word curses and judgments recorded in this person's Parent data. Examples might be: "See, I told you nobody likes you;" "You are worthless, so why bother?" "You might as well give up on having friends; etc." The seducing spirit then entices him into believing these lies which hook his Inner Child, making him feel hurt, rejected and worthless just as he did when his parents abused him in childhood.

The deceiving spirit then replays an inner vow recorded in his Child data, such as, "Since I am no good, worthless and no one likes me, I will be a "loner" and shut everyone out of my life." The seducing spirit convinces him to believe this lie; so, he rejects and hurts the person whom he thinks has rejected him, setting himself up for more rejection. The deceiving demon may then plant the thought in this hurting individual's mind that he should turn to alcohol, food, drugs, or any one of the other symptomatic behaviors which have been discussed previously in an attempt to heal the hurt and find the love for which he is continually searching. In all probability, the seducing spirit will then be able to convince him to fall for this lie. Thus, these evil spirits have manipulated this emotionally scarred person's decisions, attitudes and behavior simply by planting lies in his thoughts. Once again, the enemy troops have won the battle by luring this unsuspecting individual into their trap!

There is no end to the "mind-control games" which Satan plays. He not only speaks lies directly to our minds, he also speaks lies through other people, often through fellow believers. Jesus said to the Pharisees, "You are of your father, the devil and you want to do the desires of your father. He was a murderer from the beginning, and does not stand in the truth, because there is no truth in him. Whenever he speaks a lie, he speaks from his own nature, for he is a liar and the father of lies" (John 8:44). Examples of some of the lies with which our adversary might try to control our minds and affect our actions might be:

"Boy, you can't pay your rent again this month. You are such a failure! You'll never amount to anything! What makes you think God gives a hoot about you anyway? Why don't you just give up trusting Him?"

"Listen, so what if there is a little sex and profanity in the movie. Lots of Christians are watching these movies, so there is nothing wrong with it;"

"Your husband is a louse! He's so insensitive! Why do put up with him anyway? I think you should divorce him. It would serve him right for putting you down all the time!" and

"All those TV evangelists are hypocrites! Look at all of the sin in their lives and the lavish lifestyles they live! How can you believe anything they say, anyway?"

Some examples of lies which Christian leaders, including Spirit-filled ones, are falling for nowadays are:

"Brother 'so-and-so' said something about Christians being 'little gods.' He has fallen from the faith and is now part of the New Age movement! Also, brother 'so-and-so' is now part of the 'Kingdom Now' camp, so we can't trust him anymore!"

"Speaking in tongues is from the devil! Deliverance, positive confession and inner healing are all from the devil! Healing and other miracles went out with the apostles. My denomination has the truth, so don't go to those other churches."

The list of lies goes on and on! The father of lies has been allowed to unleash a host of lying demons upon America because we, its citizens, have turned away from God. So many lies are flying around that it is almost impossible to find the truth anymore! Black is white—white is black! There is nothing wrong with homosexuality, fornication, abortion, etc. Nothing is considered a sin in this day and age! If an addiction, such as drugs or alcohol, is hurting a person, it is called a "sickness"—never a sin.

Recently on one of the national talk shows, a Catholic priest commented contemptuously, "Surely we are all beyond believing that the Garden of Eden was an actual place! We all know that the first eight books of Genesis, including the stories of the flood and the tower of Babel, were all Jewish mythology." None of the panelists, except the fundamentalist minister, believed that there was an actual hell because God would not be cruel enough to torture millions of people for all eternity. Several people in the audience believed that this life on earth was the "hell spoken of in the Bible." One panelist believed that everyone was going to heaven, while the New Age witch believed in reincarnation. Her theory was that "we come back until we get it right." I could not believe how many different lies these people had swallowed!

The prince of darkness will unleash the biggest pack of lying demons ever during the coming New Age Movement which Texe W. Marrs, in his illuminating book, *Mystery Mark of the New Age*, defines as the reestablishment of Mystery Babylon. Marrs states that the New Age Movement is a perverse and diabolical institution founded on lies which spans the globe and includes hundreds of millions of teachers and disciples. He describes how world-renowned financiers, corporate heads, diplomats, and politicians are now combining their efforts with New Age religious leaders to usher in a New Age World Order.

The first goal of the New Age World Religion is to join all religions and cults together which believe that man is himself "God," that sin and evil do not exist, that man should seek guidance directly from the spirit world, and that the "ancient wisdom" of Babylon, Egypt and Greece is the basis of all truth. The ultimate goal is to bring about "oneness," "unity," "peace," harmony," "sharing," "brotherhood," "love," etc., by establishing the New Age World Order, headed by the New Age "Messiah," or "Christ," whom the Bible calls the Beast. Satan will successfully seduce much of mankind with his New Age "gospel" which promises personal power, glory, prosperity, and even divinity—total gratification and glorification of the flesh! They will fall for this cheap substitute which can, of course, never take the place of the peace, love and joy to be found only in an intimate relationship with a personal, loving God—the priceless treasure for which they are really searching!

Thus, unimaginably, thousands of people will flock to receive the Mark of the Beast, spoken of in Revelation, viewing it as a "badge of distinction," a "symbol of pride." Christians will be the only holdouts! We will be regarded as narrow-minded, self-righteous bigots who must be extinguished because we will not join together in "unity, fellowship and brotherhood." Sadly, however, much of the church is completely unaware of the evil one's malicious scheme to trap all of mankind in these latter days. Thus, Timothy warns that "...the Spirit explicitly says that in the later times some will fall away from the faith, paying attention to deceitful spirits and doctrines of demons" (1 Tim. 4:1). Truly, Satan disguises himself as an "angel of light!" (2 Cor. 11:14).

Therefore, it is imperative that, as counselors, we teach our counselees how to discern the deceitful strategies of our malevolent adversary. Knowledge of Satan's battle plans will not only help them escape the colossal delusion of the end-times, it will also give them an understanding of the devices which he uses to attack them personally on a daily basis. Thus, each counselee should discover during his soul healing process what doors he has opened to demonic forces in the past, including the judgments and inner vows which he made as a child. Each counselee should become aware of his vulnerable areas and the lies that Satan uses to hook his Child in these particular areas. He should be encouraged to ask the Spirit to make him aware of the lies and other traps with which "ole' slew-foot" is trying to snare him every day.

I personally believe that one of the greatest needs in the church today is the ability to discern the wily tactics of the tempter, especially the snares which he lays for each believer individually. In eighteen years of counseling, I am in awe at the incredible diversity of the lies for which people have fallen! Satan has definitely earned the title of "The Great Deceiver!" Of course, after recognizing the enemy's battle plans, it is also essential for every saint to know how to engage in spiritual warfare through which he will gain the victory over his malicious foe.

(3.) Full Armor of God. Now that we are aware of the devices which the devil uses to trip us up, what strategies does the Word of God advise us to use to defeat our cunning enemy? Paul instructs us to first "...put on the full armor of God so that we might be able to stand firm against the schemes of the devil" (Eph. 6:11). In Ephesians 6:10-18, Paul compares the armor of God to the armor that the Roman soldiers wore in his day. The Roman warriors never went into battle without putting on their full suits of armor. Neither should we! Every piece of God's armor is absolutely essential for our protection and victory! But, as soldiers of God, every one of us is responsible for putting on each piece of his or her own armor. No one else can put it on for us. Without the covering of every piece of armor, we stand naked and unprotected on the battlefront, facing the enemy troops!

The first item of protection that we are to put on is "truth." We have learned that repression is the one defense mechanism which every one of us becomes very adept at applying. In the early years of our childhood we learn to cope with hurts by denying and repressing painful, undesired truths (sins, such as anger, hatred, unforgiveness, bitterness, etc.) about ourselves. We then bury these truths in our hearts, hoping that we will never have to face them again. "The heart is more deceitful than all else and is desperately sick; who can understand it?" (Jer. 17:9). Because our wounded hearts are so "deceived and sick," we become easy prey for the enemy's lies, causing us to develop negative attitudes and fall into sinful behavior.

Thus, the principal task of the counselor is to gradually and gently "persuade" his counselees to allow the Spirit to expose the painful truths hidden in their hurting hearts. "Would not God find this out? For He knows the secrets of the heart" (Ps. 44:21). Only as a counselee permits the Spirit to disclose the secrets buried in his broken heart (Child), will he be delivered from the lies with which Satan holds him in bondage. Therefore, bringing the truths repressed in childhood into the light where they can be dealt with is the only way we can be set free from slavery to satanic deception. The truth will indeed set us free!

As counselors, we are also responsible for eliminating deception from a counselee's mind by reprogramming his Parent with truth, especially the truths contained in God's Word, and for encouraging him to continue to diligently seek truth. Since our wily adversary's chief weapon is deceiving us through our thoughts, the more truth we have acquired, the easier it is to recognize the lies with which he tries to ensnare us. Knowledge of the truth will literally set us free, since only truth can disarm our opponent by exposing his lies. Simply stated, if we know the truth, we will not fall prey to the enemy's lies. This renders him helpless and harmless, since we have exposed his primary plot to gain control of our lives.

But we may ask, why do we "gird our loins with truth," rather than some other part of our bodies? One of the definitions given in Webster's dictionary for the word "loins" is "the seat of generation or procreation." God said to Jacob, "A nation and a company of nations shall be of thee, and kings shall come out of thy loins" (Gen. 35:11 KJV). Thus, when we gird our loins with truth, we are protecting our children and all of our descendants from the deceptive devices of the treacherous one. If we know the truth and walk in it, we will also raise up our children with a knowledge of the truth, so that they will not fall for the lies of Lucifer. Therefore, walking in truth ensures that blessings, rather than curses, will flow through the bloodlines of our future generations.

Also, the phrase "to gird up the loins" means to prepare for active work. People in the eastern countries commonly wore flowing garments; so, when they had active work to do, they would tuck them up out of the way. So, when we gird our loins with truth, we might say that we are preparing to actively work in the kingdom of God. We will not be able to fulfill the great commission which our Lord gave us to preach the gospel to all nations, open blind eyes and set the captives free unless we ourselves are well-grounded in the truth. Nor will we be prepared to do battle on the front lines with the enemy if we do not have truth because truth is the only defense which we have against Satan's lies.

Next, Paul says that we are to put on the "breastplate of righteousness." We have discovered that the righteousness of Jesus is legally transferred to everyone who accepts Him as their Redeemer. He became sin that we might become His righteousness. Thus, we are to put on His righteousness in the form of a breastplate because this piece of armor covers the heart which is the place where sin dwells. "For out of the heart come evil thoughts, murders, adulteries, fornications, thefts, false witness, slanders" (Matt. 15:19). Thus, our Savior's righteousness covers our sinful hearts, placing us in right-standing with God.

Hearing that Jesus' righteousness covers all of our sins, we might be tempted to say, "That's great because now we don't have to be concerned about sinning anymore!" But wait—the Word says that our Sacrificial Lamb "...bore our sins in His body on the cross that we might die to sin and live to righteousness; for by His wounds we were healed" (1 Pet. 2:24). Therefore, the cleansing, sanctifying Blood which Jesus shed for the healing of our souls makes it possible for us to stop sinning and live righteously. If we will allow our Deliverer to heal, cleanse, sanctify, and circumcise our hurting, hardened hearts and replace them with brand new, bright, shiny, pure hearts, we will then be able to walk in holiness and righteousness.

But, on the other hand, the Word of God is quite explicit about what will happen "...if we go on sinning willfully after receiving the knowledge of the truth" (Heb. 10:26). According to Hebrews 10:26-31, there will "...no longer remain a sacrifice for our sins, but a certain terrifying expectation of judgment." The writer asks the question, "If anyone who has set aside the Law of Moses dies without mercy, how much severer punishment do you think he will deserve who has trampled underfoot the Son of God and has regarded as unclean the blood of the covenant by which he was sanctified and has insulted the Spirit of grace?" The writer then warns that "it is a terrifying thing to fall into the hands of the living God." Thus, this Scripture passage leaves no doubt in our minds that we are to "die to self and live to righteousness" after donning the breastplate of Christ's righteousness!

After discovering the truth which frees us so that we can trust God and after accepting Christ's righteousness so that we can obey God, we are now ready to "shod our feet with the preparation of the gospel of peace." Again, we see that unless we allow the Spirit to expose the secrets of our hearts (Child), as well as the deceptions of our minds (Parent) and to heal, cleanse and deliver our hearts and minds, freeing us to trust and obey God, we will not be able to deliver the gospel to all mankind. Thus, it is mandatory that we put on the first two pieces of God's armor before we attempt to put on the third piece if we do not want to become casualties of war!

In Ephesians 4:21-29, Paul beautifully describes how truth frees us to walk in righteousness: "...just as truth is in Jesus, that, in reference to your former manner of life, you lay aside the old self (Child controlled by Parental programming) which is being corrupted in accordance with the lusts of deceit (Satan's lies), and that you be renewed in the spirit of your mind (Parent reprogrammed with truth), and put on the new self (Child resurrected in Christ), which in the likeness of God has been created in righteousness and holiness of the truth (Parent now contains truth which frees Child to die to self and live to righteousness).

We are told to "shod our feet with the preparation of the gospel of peace" because our Lord commissioned us to preach the good news of our salvation through His death and resurrection to all nations. We are not to sit at home with this good news, but to "put it on our feet" and walk, carrying it to all mankind. The only reason we, as soldiers in Christ's army, are willing to go forth into battle is to make sure that everyone hears the Gospel of Peace. The apostles risked their lives to take to the known world the good news that the Messiah had come, and "...reconciled all things to God, having made peace through the blood of His cross" (Col. 1:20).

Our primary purpose in life should also be to share the "glad tidings" with everyone so that they can have peace with God simply by accepting His free gift of redemption from their sins through the Blood of the Lamb. "Therefore, having been justified by faith, we have peace with God through our Lord Jesus

Christ" (Rom. 5:1). The more we make God's precious Son the Lord of our lives, completely submitting our wills to Him and allowing Him to search, heal and cleanse our hearts and minds, the more the "...peace of God, which surpasses all comprehension, shall encompass our hearts and minds" (See Phil. 4:7). "...Serve Him with a whole heart and a willing mind, for the Lord searches all hearts and understands every intent of the thoughts" (1 Chron. 28:9).

But why, we might ask, is the third piece of armor defined as the "preparation" of the gospel of peace? Webster's dictionary describes the word "preparation" as "the state of being prepared or ready for use or service." Many saints rush out and attempt to spread the gospel without taking the time or making the effort to be made ready for service in God's kingdom, making them easy targets for Satan to shoot down! Thus, the most common word used to describe us, as Christians, is "hypocrites" because our actions very often do not coincide with our message.

A glaring example of how our adversary can destroy us in battle if we are not prepared is the life of televangelist Jim Bakker, who attempted to spread the gospel by building a worldwide television ministry, as well as a Christian theme park. Although he was well-prepared as far as knowledge of the Bible goes, the fact that his soul had not been healed and delivered caused him to readily fall into the trap which Satan had set for him. On one of his programs I heard him say, "I vowed in high school that I would do anything to become popular." This vow, no doubt originally made in early childhood, propelled him to build a fantastic Christian "empire" which revolved around his wife and him. As thousands of people flocked to their glamorous Christian resort, the Bakkers did indeed become extremely popular, to the extent of becoming "idols."

I believe that, subconsciously, the Bakkers also began to view themselves as "idols," exempt from the principles and rules which must govern the life of every Christian. They bought the devil's lie that since they were doing such a "great work for God," they were somehow special, unique–"above the law," so to speak. This being the case, they truly believed that they deserved to live an exorbitant lifestyle, spending millions of dollars on luxurious homes, expensive cars, designer clothes, etc. I think that Bakker also truly believed that he deserved to "have a little sex on the side," rationalizing that the pressures of his job were greater than other men's.

My belief is that this deluded couple lived in subconscious denial of the facts, actually believing that they had done nothing wrong. Their tearful statements insisting that they were innocent and that no one understood what they were going through bears out this belief. It is further substantiated by the fact that Bakker experienced a mental breakdown on the second day of his trial when he was confronted with the truth. Since he had always surrounded himself with people who "idolized" him and always agreed with him, he never really had to face the truth about himself. Confronted by the hard, cold facts, the shock was too much for him, so he broke down emotionally. Therefore, Bakker walked right into the trap which Satan had set for him.

I am relating this story not to judge or condemn my brother. My heart cries for him as he is just another victim caught up in the snare which the evil one laid for him. The body of Christ should surely pray and grieve for this unfortunate brother. But we should also learn from his graphic story that we had better be prepared in all ways for battle before we rush out to deliver the gospel if we do not want to die on the battlefield! (NOTE: Jim Bakker has subsequently redeemed himself and is now conducting a humble, spirit-filled and productive ministry).

Next, we are to "take up the shield of faith with which we will be able to extinguish all the flaming missiles of the evil one" (Eph. 6:16 NAS 1977). A shield may be defined as a weapon which protects or defends the person carrying it from the arrows or other offensive weapons which his enemy is hurling at him. Thus, Paul is referring in this Scripture reference to the fact that the shields of the Roman soldiers were made of leather which they soaked in water so that they would extinguish the flame-tipped arrows of the enemy. Likewise, our shields should be "soaked in faith" because the only way we can "put out" the "flaming" thoughts with which our crafty foe bombards our minds is by having faith in God and His promises.

Why, we might ask, did Paul choose a shield to symbolize faith? Webster's dictionary defines the word "faith" as "that which is believed" or "complete confidence in someone or something open to question or suspicion." As Christians, we believe and have complete confidence that Jesus Christ, the Son of God, shed His precious Blood on the cross to cleanse us from our sins, that He rose from the dead, and that soon we will be taken to heaven to rule and reign with Him! Hallelujah! There should be no doubt about these facts in our minds! If we have no doubt that this statement is true, Satan cannot convince us that we are not saved, that Jesus is not the Son of God, our Redeemer, or that any other lie of his is true. Thus, a strong, unshakable belief in Christ Jesus and what He has done for us becomes the shield which protects us from being taken in by the enemy's deception.

Tragically, people who do not believe the truth about Jesus of Nazareth have absolutely no shield to guard them from falling prey to the great deceiver's delusions. Because of this lack of defense, in the coming decade many people will be hit by the "flaming missiles" of the New Age "gospel" only to discover at the Messiah's return that they are going to burn in hell for all eternity. Harsh as this statement may sound, it is indeed the truth! Therefore, anyone or anything in which we put our complete faith other than Jesus Christ of Nazareth can offer us absolutely *NO* safeguard from eternal damnation!

Although faith in Jesus Christ as our Savior is the first step in developing our shields, we should not be satisfied with just purchasing "fire insurance." The Spirit gave me a picture years ago of just how small the shields most of us carry really are. They barely afford any protection from Satan's attacks of deception! "But why," I asked, "are our shields so small?" "Because, He replied, "most of My people do not really know Me. You would not ask someone whom you did not know to take care of your child because you would not trust her. You would have to get to know that person first. In the same way, My people must get to know Me before they can trust Me!"

As we have discovered, very few people really know their heavenly Father, that is, have a deep, intimate relationship with God. Because we tend to view God in the same way that we see our earthly parents, we often believe that He is cruel, demanding, uncaring, nonexistent, weak, etc. Thus, until our souls are healed and liberated from their past programming, we are not free to really get to know God so that we can trust Him. As counselors, our foremost goal is to help our counselees develop an intimate, personal relationship with their Daddy so that their shields of faith will be able to grow larger and larger.

When we truly get to know God as our Father, we are able to hear His voice clearly and distinctly and obey His instructions without any reservations, even as our forefathers did. Hebrews 11, the "faith" chapter, lists many of the great men of God who heard and obeyed Him because they were assured and convinced that they would receive the "...things for which they hoped–things which they did not yet see" (See Heb. 11:1). "By faith they conquered kingdoms, performed acts of righteousness, obtained promises, shut the mouths of lions, quenched the power of fire, escaped the edge of the sword, from weakness were made strong, became mighty in war and put foreign armies to flight" (Heb. 11:33,34).

The only way we can obtain shields of faith as large as our forefathers is by spending many hours getting to know and become close to our Father. Only then will we be able to "know that we know that we know that we know" that our Daddy most certainly will fulfill all of the promises contained in His Word for us and that He will never leave us, nor forsake us! "In the day of trouble, He will conceal me in His tabernacle, in the secret place of His tent He will hide me" (Ps. 27:5). Only an enormous shield of faith held high will be able to ward off all of the demonic doctrines which our opponent is going to release upon all mankind in what I believe is the last decade before Christ's return!

The last item of protection which we are to put on is the "helmet of salvation." According to Webster's dictionary, a helmet is "a defensive covering for the head which guards against head wounds." As we know, "...there is salvation in no one else (except Jesus); for there is no other name under heaven that has been given among men by which we must be saved" (Acts 4:12). What better place for the good news that Christ saved us from our sins to be placed than upon our heads which enclose our minds? Here it forms a helmet, a defensive covering which protects our minds from "wounds" inflicted by the crafty one's lies.

As we have discovered, the priceless Blood which flowed from the Balm of Gilead's head sanctified our minds. The crown of thorns placed upon His head, soaked with His holy Blood, became our helmet of salvation, a Blood covering for our minds. This protective helmet "saves" each of our minds from the thoughts which the devil continually tries to implant in them, whether they are impure, negative or deceptive. As we become more intimate with our Father and more conformed to the image of His Son, our helmets of salvation will become larger and more encompassing.

The helmets of the Roman soldiers covered their heads completely, including their ears and some of them even had pieces which could be brought down to protect their eyes. Thus, a full helmet of salvation will protect us from hearing or even seeing anything which Satan might use to fill our minds with impure, negative or deceptive thoughts. Only a very large, snugly fitting helmet, entirely encircling our heads, will be able to guard our minds from not only the prevailing evil, but also the seductive devices which the father of lies will use to pull even the elect away from the truth of salvation in these latter days.

The more secure we are in God's love, the more grounded we are in His truth and the more changed we are into the image of His Son, the larger, stronger and more impregnable our suits of armor will be. Well-ensconced and sheltered by God's suit of armor, we are now ready to swing the "sword of the Spirit, which is the Word of God." The sword is an offensive weapon which is used to attack and destroy an enemy. One of the definitions in Webster's dictionary of a sword is "a symbol of power, such as judicial or legal authority."

As we have seen, Jesus won the authority over the devil with His living Blood which He then gave to His followers under the New Covenant. As children of the King of all the universe, our legal rights and privileges are laid down in the Word of God which is the written document of the New Covenant. Therefore, the Word of God, which is our only offensive weapon, gives us the legal authority and power to attack and destroy the strategies of our adversary and his forces.

John states in Revelation 19 that "Jesus' name is called the Word of God" and that "...from His mouth comes a sharp sword, so that with it He may smite the nations" (Rev. 19:13,15). Every time the devil tempted Jesus in the wilderness, our Lord "struck down" His diabolical opponent with the Word of God, the sharp sword which came from His mouth (See Matt. 4:1-11). "The Word of God is quick and powerful and sharper than any two-edged sword" (Heb. 4:12a KJV).

Since we are to be conformed to the image of Christ, thinking and acting like Him, we are to speak God's Word to Satan, just as our Master did, striking the fiend down with the sharp swords which come from our mouths! Since the Kings of Kings has given us the privilege to rule with Him and His Father, we also have the right and the authority to "call into being that which does not exist," even as God does (See Rom. 4:17). When we speak the Word from our mouths, we are calling into being that which does not exist. God told Jeremiah, "Behold, I have put My words in your mouth "...I am watching over My word to perform it" (Jer. 1:9,12). As children of the King, we may also claim this promise that if we speak God's Word, He will perform it for us.

Another promise, given in Job, declares that if we "...receive instruction from His mouth, establish His words in our hearts and remove unrighteousness far from our tents, we may decree a thing and it will be established for us" (See Job 22:22,23,28). This promise proclaims that if we fulfill the requirements of the New Covenant—trust and obedience—we may decree the Word of God and it will be established for us. Therefore, since God promises to fulfill His Word when we speak it forth in faith, we can rest assured that our enemy has been stabbed and felled, rendering him helpless, with the swords proceeding from our mouths! Praise the Lord!!

Unfortunately, just like our small shields of faith, most of us possess tiny, dull swords which usually hang limply at our sides, although we may occasionally take some half-hearted swipes at Satan! A Roman soldier would never have gone into battle with a small, blunt-edged sword which he had no idea how to use. In like manner, if we wish to conquer the prince of this world and his henchmen, we must first enlarge and sharpen our swords by meditating on and memorizing the Word, as discussed previously. The more Scripture we devour and digest, the larger, sharper and more deadly our swords will become!

(4.) Keys of the Kingdom. Each of us must also learn how to wield his or her offensive weapon. We cannot destroy Satan by brandishing our swords aimlessly. How then, can we use the Word of God effectively to strike down and annihilate our malicious adversary and his comrades? The Scripture states that our Redeemer gave us the keys of the kingdom of heaven" which He described as "the power to bind and loose" in regard to the devil and his cohorts. After Peter declared that Jesus was the Christ, the Son of the living God, our Savior replied as follows:

> "And I also say to you that you are Peter, and upon this rock I will build My church; and the gates of Hades shall not overpower it. I will give you the keys of the kingdom of heaven; and whatever you shall bind on earth shall have been bound in heaven, and whatever you shall loose on earth shall have been loosed in heaven" (Matt. 16:18,19).

Jesus repeated what He stated in verse 19 again in Matt. 18:18, revealing its profound significance.

One of the definitions given for the word "key" in Webster's dictionary is "that which affords or prevents entrance or possession." Thus, our Bridegroom is actually giving us the keys to enter and possess the kingdom of heaven! Unbelievable!! The keys given to us by our great High Priest are the authority and power to bind and loose. But what are we to bind and loose? Since our Lord's preceding statement was that the gates of Hades would not overpower the church, He must have been referring to binding and loosing Satan and his associates.

At an earlier time, Jesus answered the Pharisees, who were challenging His authority to cast out demons, by saying, "How can anyone enter the strong man's house and carry off his property unless he first binds the strong man? And then he will plunder his house" (Matt. 12:29). Therefore, the Overcomer was explaining that the demons had to obey Him because He had already bound the strong man—Satan. How can we possess the kingdom of heaven and rule with Christ unless He also gives us the authority to bind the power of the prince of darkness and to loose that which he has taken captive?

The Greek word for "bind" is "deo," which means "to fasten, tie or constrain—as with cords or chains." When we bind Satan, he is made inoperable, thus losing the ability to act against us. Hallelujah! After binding our antagonist, we no longer have to defend ourselves against his darts, so we are free to attack him and his vicious band with our swords—the Word of God!

Now that we know what to bind, what is it that we loose? The Prince of Life has given us the legal authority to loose the captives from the bonds with which the accuser has enslaved them. The Greek word for "loose" is "luo" which means "to set free one bound; to discharge from prison." "When Jesus saw a woman, who was bent over with a spirit of infirmity, He said to her, 'Woman, thou art loosed from thine infirmity'" (Luke 13:12 KJV). When His adversaries reprimanded Him for healing on the Sabbath, the Messiah replied, "Ought not this woman, being a daughter of Abraham, whom Satan hath bound, lo, these eighteen years, be loosed from this bond on the Sabbath day?" (Luke 13:16 KJV).

The Alpha and Omega, therefore, has given to every believer the keys to shackle the god of this world and his perverse partners and to set free anyone bound by these vile forces of darkness. As counselors, we must help our counselees grasp just what an awesome privilege and responsibility we saints have been granted to be entrusted with the keys of the kingdom by the God of all the universe!

But what, we might ask, is the meaning of the phrases "shall have been bound,"/ "shall have been loosed" in this Scripture verse? Bible translators point out that the verb form used is the perfect passive participle, so the reference is to things in a state of having already been bound or loosed. This means that whatever we bind or loose is done on the basis that it has already been bound or loosed in heaven. Once again, we see that Jesus has already won the victory over Satan in the eternal or spiritual realm, but His victory becomes a reality in the temporal or natural realm only when the church recognizes and exercises its God-given authority to bind and loose the powers of darkness! Simply stated, we are required to bind and loose on earth what has already been shackled or set free in heaven. Thus, as counselors, we must teach our counselees how to use their keys to unlock the power of Christ's kingdom so that His triumph over the prince of darkness and his wicked accomplices will also become a fact in their lives.

An example of how I recently used my keys of the kingdom concerns my neighbor, a young, single woman who enjoys playing music in her bedroom at ear-splitting levels. Since my bedroom is right next to hers, I could not pray, read or rest when she turned up the volume on her stereo. Speaking to her brought no results, so I decided to take my authority as follows:

"Satan, the Word of God declares that Jesus has defeated you by His Blood. The Word also states that the King of Kings has given me the authority to bind you and evil spirits in His name. I take that authority now and bind you and the demons of rebellion, persecution and loud pagan music in Jesus' name. I command that music to be turned off now in the mighty name of Jesus! I loose this woman from Satanic bondage so that she can accept Jesus as her Lord and Savior!"

"Lord Jesus, Your Word says that if I ask anything in Your name, You will do it. So, I ask You to make that music begin hurting her ears and getting on her nerves. Give her a hunger to know You, soften her heart, open her mind, and bring her into your kingdom. Then give her an overwhelming desire to play Christian music. In Jesus' name, I pray."

After binding the devil and his demons, loosing the captives and claiming the Word, the next step is to "place the whole situation on the altar" and begin praising and thanking God for the problem. The Scripture says, "...always give thanks for all things" (Eph. 5:20) and "...in everything give thanks; for this is God's will for you in Christ Jesus" (1 Thess. 5:18). The reasons why we are to thank God for every problem will be discussed in the next section.

So, after "nailing my rights to the cross," forgiving my neighbor, asking the Lord to bless her, and giving my problem to Him, I began praising and thanking Him for the loud music. Within a few minutes the music stopped! Thank God! I followed this plan of spiritual warfare every time my neighbor turned on her deafening music. Every time, it would quit within a few minutes until finally she no longer played it loud at all! I must add that I fully expect to be tested on this in the near future!

Now it would be wonderful if spiritual warfare worked this quickly and effectively in every situation. We can all attest to the fact that it does not! I have often said that if I had a nickel for every Bible verse I have claimed for my physical healing over the last twenty years, I would be rich! All of us have some area of our lives in which we will have to fight the old serpent "tooth and nail" in order to gain the victory.

The key to conquering our wretched foe is the ability to stand firm! Paul states that we are to "...stand firm against the schemes of the devil" (Eph. 6:11). This means that we are to persevere; to persist; to endure in our battle against our perverse adversary! We are not to give up until we have the victory which has already been won for us by our Lord and Conqueror! "Resist the devil and he will flee from you!" (James 4:7). "You are from God, little children, and have overcome them; because greater is he that is in you than he who is in the world" (1 John 4:4).

But what are we to do when we grow weary? I confess that I have grown extremely weary of the battle and have given in or been tempted to give in to discouragement and self-pity many times. The Lord has shown me that on these occasions, I must ask Him as quickly as possible to give me the strength to endure so that my antagonist will not pull me down into depression and despair, thereby winning the skirmish.

Since half the battle is won if an army discovers its opponent's plans, if we are aware of how Satan attacks us personally, we will be able to defeat him. Discouragement and self-pity are my warning signals that I am beginning to lose the present contest. I will admit that on occasion I (my Adult) have given myself (my Child) permission to wallow in self-pity for a short while. But being in the Adult, I am in control and know that I must soon ask my Father to send ministering angels to strengthen me just as they did Jesus in the Garden of Gethsemane. I claim Isaiah 40:29-31, which declares that "He gives strength to the weary, and to him who lacks might He increases power." I claim that "I can do all things through Christ who strengthens me" (Phil. 4:13).

My God is always faithful to strengthen me so that I can begin taking authority over Satan and binding the spirits of infirmity, discouragement and self-pity, breaking their hold over me, and commanding them to loose me in Jesus' name! I remind them that I am a child of God, covered by the Blood of the Lamb; therefore, they have no right to touch me! I then inform these spiritual forces of wickedness that, according to Luke 10:19, I have been given authority over all the power of the enemy that nothing should injure me! I then attack the enemy troops with my sword—the Word of God, claiming about ten or fifteen scriptures which promise healing and provision for my needs.

After this, I remind God that He promised to watch over His Word to perform it and that I stand steadfast in my belief that He has no choice but to fulfill His promises because He honors His Word above his name! I put my faith into action by picturing myself already healed and feeling fantastic! Then I begin thanking and praising God that, according to His Word which is reality, I am healed and delivered from every infirmity! As I have consistently applied this battle plan in dealing with physical problems over the years, my faith has grown, slowly but steadily. Rarely has a day gone by that I have not had to fight for victory over some bodily symptom.

My physical problems began when I became seriously ill with pneumonia during my senior year in high school. Being in bondage to my script of perfectionism, I (my Child) believed that I always had to excel academically in order to please my Internal Parent. Thus, throughout high school and college, I pushed my body beyond its limit in my attempt to perform perfectly. In addition to this, because I was addicted to products containing sugar and white flour, I put more stress on my body by eating poorly. Consequently, the depressed state of my immune system resulted in my contracting inner ear infection during my freshman year of college. I received large doses of Tetracycline for this and also for cervicitis which I developed several years later.

As a result of this antibiotic breaking down my immune system even further, I began experiencing many symptoms including extreme fatigue, headaches, abdominal bloating, and pain, dizziness and just plain, feeling "lousy" all over. Doctors had no answers, so I cried out to the Lord. All during my illnesses I had been praying that He would heal me. My supplications brought no immediate results, so I finally asked the Lord what else I should do. Even though I was not yet Spirit-filled, I heard the Spirit tell me that I would have to change my eating habits. Since those were the days before "health food," I argued with Him that I could not improve my eating habits because there was sugar, salt and white flour in everything in the supermarket. The Lord informed me that He would help me if I would submit to His will in this area, which I did. He then led me to information concerning nutrition, exercise, vegetable cleansing fasts, herbs, etc.

Although the condition of my general health improved as I worked on building up my immune system through nutrition and exercise, I still suffered from several symptoms. Eventually, I was diagnosed by Dr. Julian M. Whitaker, head of Whitaker Wellness Institute Medical Clinic in Newport Beach, CA, as having systemic Candida Albicans, an intestinal fungus which develops from yeast infections caused from receiving large amounts of tetracycline. This disease, which has many diverse symptoms, has only recently been discovered and is treated mainly through diet. Thus, Dr. Whitaker put me on a very strict diet consisting mainly of vegetables and protein with carbohydrate intake restricted to only eighty grams daily. After two years of attempting to adhere to this diet, the Lord recently healed me of Candida, although I still must stand in faith against "lying" symptoms rather frequently.

Many saints mistakenly believe that God only requires them to stand in faith for healing, not to employ effort and wisdom in disciplining their bodies, souls and spirits. I am relating my struggle with physical problems in order to point out the importance of, not only battling spiritually by patiently standing firm in faith for healing, but also obeying God's instructions in the physical and soulish realms. I could not presume that I would receive healing from Him if I had not diligently applied myself to following my prescribed diet and exercise program and to acquiring healing and liberation from my life-controlling Parental script.

My testimony would not be complete without including some examples illustrating how my Deliverer has come through for me as I have both obeyed His instructions and persevered in administering my warfare tactics. Although exercise was extremely difficult for me at first, I persisted in working at it until I was able to participate in such activities as aerobics, bodybuilding, hiking, bicycling, and skiing. For the past several years, my husband and I have spent almost every Saturday enjoyably riding our tandem bicycle. Satan has frequently tried to thwart our plans by laying various symptoms on me. Many times, I, feeling miserable, but determined not to let that wretched fiend ruin my fun, have taken my seat on the back of our bicycle. As I have resolutely executed my strategy of spiritual warfare, God has faithfully given me the victory!

I recall one time when I was feeling particularly rotten, I fought the good fight of faith with no results while pedaling fifteen miles. After napping on the grass for fifteen minutes, when I awoke, I felt somewhat better. Determined to keep going, I began feeling better and better as we rode. We ended up bicycling about forty miles that day!

My faith has also been sorely tried during several vacations. On the second day of a trip to Mammoth, I felt as though I was coming down with the flu which necessitated agonizing over whether we should drive further or not. Resolutely deciding that the destroyer was not going to rip me off, we drove on to Lake Tahoe. Although I felt worse as the day wore on and was in misery that evening, the next morning I woke up feeling absolutely great! We spent the day joyfully hiking while praising and thanking God for His abundant loving-kindness!

On another occasion, after hiking 1300 feet in elevation without allowing my body to become adjusted to the altitude, I became very ill with altitude sickness. After an agonizing hour of battling my vile attacker with my husband and wondering how in the world I was going to make it back down the trail, all of my distress suddenly lifted! Boy, did I ever praise God as I literally hopped over rocks and bounded back down that mountainside!

Another time while on vacation, the evil one struck me with insomnia one night, a problem with which he has often plagued me. Although I did not sleep one wink that night, but passed the long hours praying in tongues, the next day I felt wonderful! We spent that day glorifying the Lord Jesus while riding through the autumn leaves on our tandem bike! Praise the Lord for His marvelous miracles!

I am convinced that the principal way in which God builds our faith is by allowing the enemy to test and try us. Sad to say, most saints give up the battle if they do not win the war after a few encounters with their assailant during which their faith is greatly tested. Therefore, as counselors, we cannot stress enough to our counselees how vital it is that they remain strong in their faith, resisting the roaring lion so that he will not devour them! "Do not throw away your confidence, which has a great reward. For you have need of endurance so, that after you have done the will of God, you may receive what was promised" (Heb. 10:35,36).

Years ago, the Lord pointed out to me that when a vicious dog snarls and threatens to attack a person, this individual has two choices. On the one hand, he can cower, fearfully turn around and run as fast as he can; in which case, the dog will tear after him, biting and possibly ripping him to shreds! On the other hand, he can confidently stand his ground and command the dog in a strong, authoritative voice, saying, "You stop that right now; you go lie down and shut up! I don't want to hear any more out of you!" If the canine is convinced that this person means business, he will lower his head and slink off, whimpering, to lie down in the corner, obediently resting his head on his paws.

Since God gave man the authority to rule over animals (see Gen. 1:26), a vicious dog will obey if he is convinced that the person commanding him knows that he has power over him and is not afraid of him. Satan is exactly like this ferocious animal! He will attack us with a vengeance if he knows that we are afraid of him and that we are not aware of the authority which we have over him. But, if he is persuaded beyond a shadow of a doubt that we have no fear of him and that we are confident of the absolute power which we have over him, our wicked aggressor will slink off in defeat like the coward that he truly is!

Rev. Kenneth E. Hagin, Sr. relates that Jesus was talking to him in a vision one day when a hideous, perverse little demon came between them and proceeded to jabber and cackle so loudly that he could not hear his Master's words. He kept waiting for Jesus to banish this impetuous little imp, but his Lord and Savior just kept right on talking. Finally, Hagin got so frustrated at not being able to hear what Jesus was saying that he ordered the annoying, scraggy spirit to depart in Jesus' name. The demon immediately vanished, of course, and the Holy One then explained to Hagin that

He had given his followers authority over the power of the enemy. Therefore, Jesus pointed out that He could not command the evil spirit to leave because this was the job which He had turned over to Hagin, along with all his brothers and sisters in Christ!

Our Captain was, of course, well aware of the power which He had over the spiritual forces of darkness while He walked on earth. After He had allowed the devil to test Him in the wilderness, Jesus simply said, "Begone, Satan! For it is written, 'You shall worship the Lord your God, and serve Him only!'" The devil left immediately! (Matt. 4:10,11 ESV). Thus, the Prince of Life vanquished His vindictive tempter from His sight merely by ordering him to go and then striking him with the sword which comes from His mouth–the Word of God! The god of this world had no choice but to vanish!

The Pearl of Great Price never wavered in His faith. Whether He was changing water into wine or raising Lazarus from the dead, He gave no thought to his feelings or to the things going on around Him. God's Word, not His situation, was absolute reality to the Son of Man. He spent much of His time on earth discerning whether or not people had faith, praising those who had it and rebuking those who did not. A study of Christ's reactions to people in reference to their faith as recorded in three gospels revealed the following responses:

> "Truly I say to you, I have not found such great faith in Israel "...Let it be done to you as you have believed." And the servant was healed that very hour"' (Matt. 8:10,12).

> "Why are you timid, you men of little faith?" 'Then He arose and rebuked the winds and the sea, and it became perfectly calm"' (Matt. 8:26).

> "For they had not gained any insight from the incident of the loaves, but their hearts were hardened" (Mark 6:51).

> "...and Jesus, seeing their faith said to the paralytic, 'Take courage, My son, your sins are forgiven. Rise take up your bed and go home.' And he rose and went to his home"' (Matt. 9:2,6,7).

"And He said to the woman (Mary Magdalene), 'Your faith has saved you; go in peace'" (Luke 7:50).

"Daughter take courage! your faith has made you well." 'And at once, the woman was made well"' (Matt. 9:22).

"Then He touched their eyes, saying, 'It shall be done unto you according to your faith.'" And their eyes were opened'" (Matt. 9:29-30).

"Jesus said to the synagogue official, 'Do not be afraid any longer, *only believe* "...Little girl, I say to you, arise!' And immediately the girl got up and began to walk'" (Mark 5:36,41,42).

"And He did not do many miracles there because of their unbelief" (Matt. 13:58).

"But seeing the wind, he (Peter) became afraid "...he cried out, 'Lord, save me.' Jesus "...said to him, 'O you of little faith, why did you doubt?'" (Matt. 14:30,31).

"Then Jesus answered and said to her, 'O woman, your faith is great; be it done to you as you wish.' And her daughter was healed at once'" (Matt. 15:28).

"Jesus said, 'You men of little faith, why do you discuss among yourselves that you have no bread?"' (Matt. 16:8).

"Do you not yet see or understand? Do you have a hardened heart?" (Mark 8:17).

"Jesus said, 'O unbelieving and perverted generation, how long shall I be with you?' ... The disciples said, 'Why could we not cast it (demon) out?' And He said to them, 'Because of the littleness of your faith!'" (Matt. 17:20).

"All things are possible to him who believes!" (Mark 9:23).

"If God so arrays the grass in the fields "...how much more will He clothe you, O men of little faith." (Luke 12:28).

"Rise and go your way; your faith has made you well" (Luke 17:19).

"And Jesus said to him, 'Receive your sight; your faith has made you well.' And immediately he received his sight'" (Luke 18:42,43).

"However, when the Son of Man comes, will He find faith on the earth?" (Luke 18:8).

"Simon, Simon, behold Satan has demanded permission to sift you like wheat; but I have prayed for you, that your faith may not fail" (Luke 22:31,32).

"He reproached them for their unbelief and hardness of heart, because they had not believed those who had seen Him after He had risen" (Mark 16:14).

"O foolish men and slow of heart to believe in all that the prophets have spoken!" (Luke 24:25).

Thus, we can see that the foremost concern of our Savior when He walked the earth was the state of people's faith. Since He never changes, this is still His main concern almost 2,000 years later. It is interesting to note that the men who were the closest to Him, His disciples, were the ones whom Jesus had to rebuke for their unbelief and hardened hearts. This might discourage us except for the fact that, through the life-changing experience of receiving the Holy Spirit from their Master, "...they all became strong, steadfast stones in the foundation upon which the church of Christ was built" (See Eph. 2:20).

Thus, just as our Cornerstone and foundation stones did, we also must stand firmly upon the Word of God, unmoved by our feelings or the circumstances we might see with our natural eye. Regardless of what we feel or see, we must hold fast to God's promises–forever, if necessary! "But My righteous one shall live by faith; and if he shrinks back, My soul has no pleasure in him" (Heb. 10:38).

(5.) Exultation In Trials. Scripture makes it clear that if we want to please God and become sturdy, solid stones in His spiritual house, we must continuously walk in faith as we go through trials. But why is it necessary to praise Him when we are tested and tried? We have no problem, of course, praising God when everything is going well for us. It seems natural to thank our Maker when we are experiencing success, prosperity and physical and emotional health. It does not seem "normal" or "right" to praise Him when things are going wrong and we are hurting physically, emotionally or financially. But God's ways are not our ways, and many Scriptures exhort us to praise and thank the Lord when we encounter tribulation.

Paul E. Billheimer, in his inspiring book, *Destined for the Throne: How Spiritual Warfare Prepares the Bride of Christ for Her Eternal Destiny*, shares a key with us which he discovered in Hebrews 13:15. This verse says, "Through Him then, let us continually offer up a sacrifice of praise to God, that is, the fruit of lips that give thanks to His name." What is meant by "the sacrifice of praise?" Billheimer relates that a sacrifice involves death; so, in the "sacrifice of praise," it is "self" that dies. We must sacrifice, that is, die to our own opinions, judgments, needs, desires, and choices, when we offer up to God the sacrifice of praise. Since we cannot, humanly speaking, see any beneficial purpose in praising our Father for affliction or tragic circumstances, when we "give thanks always for all things," we are sacrificing or dying to self.

When we humbly offer up the sacrifice of praise, we are acknowledging that the great I Am is supreme; that He is still on the throne and has everything in the universe under His control, no matter how hopeless things may look to us. We are obeying His command to "...cease striving and know that I am God" (Ps. 46:10). We are relinquishing our difficulties and placing them in the hands of Jehovah, trusting that "...He will work our misfortunes together for our good," no matter how impossible this may seem to our finite minds (Rom. 8:28). When we immerse ourselves in worshipping God in the midst of our trials, our focus will automatically be shifted from ourselves and our troubles to the glory and majesty of Almighty God. The more we become enraptured by the infinite beauty and power of the "Most High," the more we will forget about ourselves and our preoccupation with our problems.

To illustrate this point, let me share a word of wisdom which the Spirit gave me for a couple whose son was on drugs and had run away from home. The Spirit explained to me that just as *my* husband likes to have his workmanship admired, so our heavenly Father enjoys having the creativity which He uses to answer our prayers admired. So, He said to tell this couple that He wanted them to "relax in His arms and relish with awe and excitement the awesome creativity which He was going to demonstrate in bringing their son to Him!" What a profound word!! It truly states the epitome of faith! This word from God should be "engraved in stone" upon the mind and heart of every counselee! If each one remembered nothing more about faith than this statement, it would be sufficient!

The Spirit revealed to me that when we apply this word to our difficulties, we are challenging the Lord—not arrogantly, of course, but in all humility, to apply all of His ingenuity to working everything out for our good. We sometimes forget that man was made in the image of God. So, just as man loves to take on a challenge, so does the King of Glory. Just as man enjoys an opportunity to display his ingenuity and receive admiration and honor for it, so does the Lord of Lords. Jehovah-Jireh is thrilled to accept our challenge because it "unties His hands," freeing Him to take over in our situation and make good things happen for us. When we are anxious and worried about our problems, just the opposite happens. We "tie God's hands" with our lack of faith and He cannot undertake for us because He is bound by our lack of faith.

Oh, that we could be like little children! A child who has a loving, understanding father trusts him to the ultimate. How pleased our heavenly Father would be if we would trust him like this little child! How excited our Daddy would be if we would joyfully anticipate how ingenuously He was going to work good out of all of our misfortunes! He will even work good out of the misery that we have brought upon ourselves through our wrong choices if we will repent, turn them over to Him and praise Him for them.

A poignant example illustrating why we should always praise God for everything was given in a recent issue of *Guideposts* magazine. The story told about a woman who had flown to New Mexico to speak at a Christian seminar. She was perturbed because the airlines had lost the suitcase containing the shoes which matched the outfit that she planned to wear. But she quickly recalled that the Word tells us to always give thanks for all things. At the close of the seminar, several people, including this woman, were at the speaker's stand when an ear-splitting "crack" and the sound of exploding glass was heard. As she saw a man brandishing a gun through the window, someone shouted, "Lie down!" Later she discovered that the projectile shot from the gun had struck the wall an inch over the spot where she had been standing! As she thought of a pair of two-and-a-half-inch heels in her missing bag, she realized just why we should make it a practice to always give thanks to God for everything!

Another reason we are to praise the Lord in tribulation is because there is power in praise! Praise is an offensive weapon to be used, along with the Word, in spiritual warfare. Jehoshaphat appointed singers unto the Lord to go before the army, saying, "Praise the Lord! For His mercy endureth forever." When the Israelites began to sing and to praise, the Lord set ambushments against their enemies, and their enemies destroyed themselves" (2 Chron. 20:21-23).

The power of praise is also illustrated in a story told by Billheimer which concerned a minister who went out into a field in order to be alone for prayer before a revival service. He did not see a bull charging him until it was too late to reach safety. He had no idea what to do! But just before the enraged animal reached him, he began shouting, "Praise the Lord!" The bull stopped short in his tracks, turned and fled. What is the explanation for this? Billheimer suggests that Satan sent evil spirits to enter the bull and incite him to attack the minister. But the shouts of praise foiled the plans of the demons inhabiting this beast in the same way that the praise of the Israelites discomfited the wicked spirits motivating their foes.

But just what makes praise an effective weapon against the forces of darkness? Psalm 22:3 says that God "inhabits the praises" of His people. Satan cannot operate in the presence of God because the presence of the Holy One of Israel always expels the devil and his malevolent accomplices. As Billheimer says, "Satan is allergic to praise, so where there is massive, triumphant praise, Satan is paralyzed, bound and banished" (pg. 120). Since Satan hates praise as well as the Word of God, worshipping the Giver of Life while claiming His Word is the most powerful weapon we can use against our vicious opponent! Thus, when we praise God when things go wrong, we are turning our problems over to Him, trusting that He will work good for us and expel any Satanic influence from our circumstances.

I learned the power of praise from Merlin R. Carothers' enlightening books which the Holy Spirit led me to read shortly after I became Spirit-filled. The only reason I was able to cope with all of my physical difficulties was because I learned how to praise and thank the Lord for them. My primary objective, as well as that of most believers, for praising God for every hardship is to win the victory over Satan in prayer so that my distress will be alleviated. But is God's purpose the same as ours? Not necessarily! We know that the ways and thoughts of the "Ancient of Days" are not the same as ours. In the matter of suffering, as in all things, His ways and thoughts serve a much higher purpose than ours.

My suffering has led me to thoroughly study the Word in order to discover what God's reasons are for requiring us to praise him for affliction and sorrow. As Scripture clearly reflects, the apostles understood the Lord's purpose for allowing misfortune and pain to enter their lives. They realized that our heavenly Father is much more interested in transforming us, His children, into the image of His Son than in alleviating our misery and distress. This is made evident in the following verses:

> "Consider it all joy, my brethren, when you encounter various trials, knowing that the testing of your faith produces endurance. And let endurance have its perfect result, that you may be perfect and complete, lacking in nothing" (James 1:2-4).

"In this you greatly rejoice, even though now for a little while, if necessary, you have been distressed by various trials, so that the proof of your faith, being more precious than gold which is perishable, even though tested by fire, may be found to result in praise and glory and honor at the revelation of Jesus Christ" (1 Pet. 1:6,7).

"...and we exult in hope of the glory of God. And not only this, but we also exult in our tribulations, knowing that tribulation brings about perseverance; and perseverance, proven character; and proven character, hope" (Rom. 5:2-4).

In the preceding verses the apostles exhort us to "...consider it all joy, greatly rejoice and exult in our tribulations!" Their words leave no doubt that we are to jump up and down and shout for joy when we are hit by various trials. They also tell us the reasons why. We are all naturally impatient when we encounter tribulation. The quicker we get out of it, the better! So, what better way for God to build our patience, endurance and perseverance than by allowing us to go through trials?

Webster's dictionary defines the word "endurance" as "the power of continuing under pain or hardship without being overcome." The verb "endure" is defined as "to bear up; to remain firm; to suffer patiently." The first definition of the word "perseverance" is "the quality of persisting steadfastly in an undertaking," while the second definition is, "continuance in a state of grace until it is succeeded by a state of glory." Praise God for a man whose dictionary reflects his Christianity!

When Elohim does not answer our prayers right away, we have no choice but to rely upon His grace and strength to help us bear up under pain or hardship without being overcome. The longer we are required to endure suffering, the more we must turn to Jehovah for help. The more we have to depend on God for assistance, the more our wills are broken, bringing us to repentance from going our own way. Even Jesus "...learned obedience from the things which He suffered; and having been made perfect, He became to all those who obey Him, the source of eternal salvation" (Heb. 5:8,9). If Jesus had to learn obedience and be perfected through suffering, surely, we must be required to!

Thus, our heavenly Father uses affliction to "melt us" and "mold us" into the image of His precious Son, Jesus. As we persist steadfastly, firm in our faith in the midst of our troubles, the fruit of the Spirit is developed in us; "...love, joy, peace, patience, kindness, goodness, faith, gentleness, self-control" (Gal. 5:22,23). Patience or long-suffering is formed in us as we tolerate suffering, calmly and contentedly, for long periods of time. I believe that the development of patience (endurance, perseverance, forbearance, long-suffering) is of major importance because it tends to perfect the rest of the fruit of the Spirit in our characters.

As we patiently put up with problems, standing firm on the Word until our prayers are answered, our faith grows. The greater our trust in God and His promises becomes, the more we will experience a deep sense of peace and harmony in our lives, regardless of our circumstances. Because we are convinced that God will always come through for us, we will be able to "be anxious for nothing" and to "exult in tribulations." The more pain and sorrow we undergo in life, the deeper our compassion, love and understanding becomes for other people. We are able to treat them with gentleness, kindness and goodness because we can relate so well to the grief and misery which they are feeling. Also, the more storms we patiently weather, the easier it becomes to exercise self-control and restraint over our actions.

We sometimes hear people say that a particular person has "mellowed" as he has grown older. According to Webster's dictionary, the word ''mellow" means "soft or tender by reason of ripeness; fully-developed, made sweet or gentle by maturity; easily worked—as in soil." Just as the word "mellow" accurately describes a beautiful, fully ripened piece of fruit, so it also correctly characterizes an individual in whom the fruit of the Spirit has been fully developed. This person is sweet, gentle, soft, tender, mature, and easily "worked" or "molded" into the image of Jesus.

Synonyms given by Webster's Thesaurus for the word "mellow" are "perfected, full-flavored, seasoned, aged, cured, well-matured." Just as these synonyms describe a food or beverage whose flavor, aroma and texture has been developed fully through the aging process, so they also rather precisely portray an individual whose character has been tried and proven through bearing the brunt with forbearance of many storms in his life.

Conversely, a person who does not "count it all joy when he encounters various trials" throughout life often becomes bitter as he grows older. Webster's dictionary defines the word "bitter" as "having a peculiarly acrid, astringent or disagreeable taste; piercingly harsh or cruel, stinging, caustic acrimonious." Synonyms given in Webster's Thesaurus for the word "bitter" are "acid, tart, sour, sharp, biting and severe." Just as the word "bitter" accurately describes a fruit which tastes tart, sour, sharp, and biting, so it, also correctly portrays the fruit of an individual who complains, murmurs, grumbles, and moans when life "deals him a bad hand." His character may be described as piercingly harsh, cruel, caustic, and severe. As he grows older, he becomes so hardened, unyielding and "set in his ways" that the Spirit is unable to "mold" him into Jesus' image. The thought of becoming like one of these bitter, hardened individuals ought to be enough to convince us to continually "exult in our tribulations!"

As we have seen, the person who yields to the Spirit's "molding" by "greatly rejoicing when distressed by trials" develops perseverance which brings about proven character. According to Romans 5:4, proven character then brings about hope. Hope in what, we might ask? Romans 5:2 declares that our hope is "of the glory of God." In what way does our character which is proven through our ability to joyfully endure suffering bring about hope of the glory of God? The apostles' writings reveal that they considered suffering to be the secret to receiving glory. The following scriptures reveal that they viewed glory as God's eternal compensation for the unjust suffering which believers experience (Refer back to 1 Pet. 1:6,7):

> "...our inner man is being renewed day by day. For momentary, light affliction is producing for us an eternal weight of glory far beyond all comparison" (2 Cor. 4:16,17);

> "...and if children, heirs also, heirs of God and fellow heirs with Christ, if indeed we suffer with Him in order that *we* may also be glorified with Him. For I consider that the sufferings of this present time are not worthy to be compared with the glory that is to be revealed to us" (Rom. 8:17,18);

> "...but to the degree that you share the sufferings of Christ, keep on rejoicing, so that also at the revelation of His glory, you may rejoice with exultation" (1 Pet. 4:13).

As a result of His unjust suffering, Jesus received the greatest glory of all by being crowned King of all creation. Through His suffering, He also brought many sons to salvation and glory. "For it was fitting for Him, '...in bringing many sons to glory, to perfect the author of their salvation through sufferings'" (Heb. 2:10).

Paul declares that if we suffer with Jesus, we will also be glorified with Him. Paul also seems to be saying that he has placed his sufferings on one side of a scale—the numerous times he was beaten, stoned, imprisoned, shipwrecked, hungry, thirsty, cold, falsely accused, etc. (2 Cor. 11:23-28). On the other side, he has placed the glory that is to be revealed when Christ appears. After measuring the two, he concludes that the weight of the glory to be revealed is far greater than that of his suffering.

Thus, to Paul and the other apostles, there was "no such thing as bad news." They literally believed that "...no evil could befall them, nor could any plague come near their tents" (Ps. 91:10). They believed that nothing but "good" could come to a child of God, no matter how "bad" a thing might seem. They perceived every misfortune as coming from the hand of an all-wise, all-loving, all-powerful God, who always used every difficulty which they encountered to form "Christ in them, the hope of glory" (Col. 1:27).

Our brethren knew that, as believers, we are all running an "obstacle course on life's track." As we gain the victory over the smaller obstacles which Satan is allowed to place in our paths, God permits somewhat larger obstacles to confront us. As Billheimer asks, "Whoever heard of an athlete, training for an obstacle race, pleading with his trainer to remove the obstacles?"

(pg. 129). God has promised rewards for those saints who overcome, and how can we be overcomers with nothing to overcome? "Blessed is he who perseveres under trial; for once he has been approved, he will receive the crown of life, which the Lord has promised to those who love Him" (James 1:12). "He who overcomes, I will grant to him to sit down with Me on My throne, as I also overcame and sat down with My Father on His throne" (Rev. 3:21).

Each obstacle that we overcome "proves" our faith and our characters a little more. As Peter says, we should greatly rejoice because our faith, which is more precious than gold, is proven by testing it with the fire of trials so that it may result in glory at Jesus' return. The process used to clarify gold is a perfect analogy for the method used by God to purify our souls and prove our characters. Dross is removed from gold by heating it up to extremely high temperatures. Each time the fire is turned up, more scum rises to the top of the gold and is dredged off. Finally, when all of the refuse has been burned out, the gold is so pure that it looks transparent. A pot of clarified gold is so pure and clear that a person looking into it can see a reflection of his face!

Just like gold, each of us, as sons of God, is also purified by being put through fire—the flames of tribulation. As we go through each trial, the fire is turned up higher and more dross is removed from our souls. The goal, of course, is to burn so much refuse out of our souls that they will become pure, clear and transparent, like clarified gold. According to Webster's dictionary, the word "transparent" is defined as "having the property of transmitting rays of light, so that bodies can be seen through; luminous, bright, guileless, free from pretense." Nathanael was so "transparent" that Jesus said that there was no guile (deceitful cunning, treachery, craftiness) in him (John 1:47).

Thus, when enough garbage has been burned out of our souls, we will become so transparent that Jesus will be able to see Himself—His light, love and glory—reflected in us! People will see the glory of Jesus illuminating our countenances as His light shines brightly through our faces! We will be so luminous that we will transmit the brilliant light of Jesus to others which will draw them to Him! Hallelujah!!

A beautiful illustration of this is given in Acts in connection with the conversion of Saul of Tarsus. Saul witnessed the stoning of Stephen, a man filled with the very life of Jesus. As the stones were crushing him, Stephen prayed for his enemies while gazing into heaven with a face reflecting the glory of his Savior who was about to receive his spirit. Thus, as Stephen joyfully endured his suffering, the true essence of Jesus was brought forth so that others could see its glory in him (Acts 7:54-60). I believe that when Saul saw that glory radiating from Stephen's face, he could not get away from it until, finally, he encountered that same glory on the road to Damascus and was transformed by it! (Acts 9).

Therefore, we can conclude that suffering is invaluable; not only does it benefit the one undergoing it, but it also profits others. The suffering of Stephen played a large part in the redemption of Paul because Paul was forever changed when he saw Jesus' resurrected life in this saint. Stephen had counted the cost and was willing to pay the price required for the salvation of others. How many of us have naively sung the words, "Melt me, mold me, fill me, use me," without considering what they really meant? We did not realize what it would cost us when we asked the Master Craftsman to "melt" the dross out of our lives, "mold" us into priceless golden vessels, "fill" us with the precious Holy Spirit, and "use" us to rescue others from perishing! When God tries to take us up on our offer, many of us rebel, saying, "Forget it! This is too hard! I can't take it!" I confess that I am certainly guilty of doing this!

Malachi 3:3 states that the Lord "...will sit as a smelter and purifier of silver and He will purify the sons of Levi and refine them like gold and silver, so that they may present to the Lord offerings in righteousness." Just like these Old Testament priests, we also, as a "royal priesthood," must be refined like gold before we can "...offer up spiritual sacrifices acceptable to God through Jesus Christ" (1 Pet. 2:5). Jesus Himself, advised us "...to buy gold refined by fire from Him so that we might become rich" (Rev. 3:18). As followers of Christ, those of us who do consent to allow God to mold us into golden vessels for Him must understand that we will have to joyfully persevere under greater and greater tests. Like Stephen, Paul and all of the apostles, "...we all, with unveiled face beholding as in a mirror the glory of the Lord, are being transformed into the same image from glory to glory, just as from the Lord, the Spirit" (II Cor. 3:18). Thus, if we are willing to rejoice in our suffering as we are being changed into Christ's image from glory to glory, our lives, like those of Stephen and Paul, can also serve a redemptive purpose. This truth is graphically presented by Paul in 2 Corinthians 4:8-12:

"We are afflicted in every way, but not crushed; perplexed, but not despairing; persecuted, but not forsaken; struck down, but not destroyed; always carrying about in the body the dying of Jesus, that the life of Jesus also may be manifested in our body. For we who live are constantly being delivered over to death for Jesus' sake, that the life of Jesus also may be manifested in our mortal flesh. So, death works in us, but life in you."

What the Spirit seems to be revealing through Paul is that the more a person dies to self, the more the glory of Jesus' resurrected life will be seen in him by others. Therefore, the pain with which God allows Satan to afflict us is not meant to destroy us, but to bring others to eternal life! Thus, the Spirit is saying that when we joyfully and patiently endure tribulation, He is able to change our nature into that of Christ so that others will be brought to salvation by seeing His light, life and glory reflected in us.

Since many counselees have been highly abused and rejected, it is most important for them to understand that the horrendous things which they have endured can serve a redemptive purpose. I often tell my counselees that the more pain and torture they have experienced, the more opportunity they have to allow the Spirit to use their agony for the salvation of others. I believe that the more traumatic the abuse for which a person has to forgive others, the "heavier the weight of glory that his affliction produces in him." The more the glory of Christ shines through him, the more the Spirit can use him to rescue lost souls from eternal damnation! Counselees that are able to grasp this truth can sincerely thank God from their hearts for all of the torment which they have experienced!

Some of the people who have embraced this truth and are cashing in on the redemptive purpose which their past anguish can now serve have written soul-piercing books. Counselees should be encouraged to read these books in order to discover not only that God can use their suffering for His glory, but that there are some people who have sustained more agony than they. Some of these books are listed as follows: *The Hiding Place*, ten Boom; *Satan's Underground*, Stratford; *Don't Waste Your Sorrows*, Billheimer; *Suffer the Children*, Spencer; *Michelle Remembers*, Smith & Pazder; *Tortured for Christ*, Wurmbrand; *Joni*, Eareckson; *Vanya*, Grant; *A Face for Me*, Fox; *Dear Mamma, Please Don't Die*, Horton; *Lay Up Your Treasures in Heaven*, Mead; *David*, Rothenberg; *More Than Survivors*, Friesen; *Babunia*, Basansky; *Angels in the Camp*, Markell; *The Normal Christian Life*, Nee, and *Beyond Betrayal*, Koons.

The authors of these inspiring books have all learned the secret that suffering is priceless because it develops the glory of Jesus in us which brings others to our Lord and Savior. They know that their lives and those of the saints depicted in their books cannot be shaken because they were formed out of lives that were shaken. They have discovered that cross-bearing and crown-wearing cannot be separated. If we wish to wear the crown with Jesus, we must also bear the cross with Him!

Someone has said that the love that chose us also chastens us; the love that purchased us also purifies us. The love that delivers us from death also disciplines us for life. We have also heard that "growth only takes place in the valleys, not on the mountaintops." We only grow stronger in faith, perseverance, courage, obedience, truth, and the fruit of the Spirit as we are tested and tried in the fires of adversity. Therefore, everything that God allows in the lives of His beloved children is because of His love for them. This is why a woman who was brought back to God through illness could triumphantly declare, "I have been richly blessed by cancer!" This is why Scottish minister Samuel Rutherford (1600-1661) stated, "When we come to the other side of the water, we will say, 'If God had done otherwise with me, I would never have come to this crown of glory.'"

When the Inner Child within each of us finally realizes just how invaluable suffering is, both to himself and to others, he will no longer rebel against it. Instead of getting angry at God and blaming Him for his misfortunes, he will truly be able to thank Him and be grateful for them. This is the kind of yieldedness, flexibility, softness, "meltedness," in which the Spirit delights so that

He may freely form each of us into the unique kind of vessel which He desires us to be.

Thus, we can understand the importance of reprogramming the Internal Parent of each counselee with the truth that he must always be prepared to offer up to God the sacrifice of praise, that is, to "give thanks always for all things." He will not be able to stand against the discouragement, anger, bitterness, self-pity, hopelessness, etc., with which Satan is sure to bombard him if he is not ready at all times to praise and thank God for every affliction and adversity.

The best way to prepare counselees to be able to offer up sacrificial praise is to encourage them to establish praise as a way of life—a habit pattern which pervades every area of their lives. Praise that overcomes is not merely occasional praise which fluctuates with moods or circumstances. It is continuous, rapturous praise and adoration which emanates from our hearts and floods every fiber of our beings! "I will bless the Lord at all times; His praise shall continually be in my mouth" (Ps. 34:1). "My mouth offers praises with joyful lips" (Ps. 63:5). "How blessed are those who dwell in Thy house! They are ever praising Thee" (Ps. 84:4).

Praise is so important that it constitutes the total occupation of the four living creatures who surround the throne of God. "Day and night, they do not cease to say, 'Holy, Holy, Holy is the Lord God, the Almighty, who was and who is and who is to come" (Rev. 4:8). God gave King David such a revelation of the power and importance of praise that, following the heavenly pattern, he set aside and dedicated four thousand Levites whose sole occupation was to praise the Lord. "And they are to stand every morning to thank and praise the Lord, and likewise at evening" (1 Chron. 23:30).

David, more than any of the other great men of the Bible, seemed to emphasize praise as a principle which permeated the very essence of his being. In Psalm 57:7 (KJV), he declares, "My heart is fixed, O God, my heart is fixed: I will sing and give praise." This suggests that he had made a decision with his Adult to always give praise to God, regardless of his circumstances or emotions. We chose to make praise a full-time occupation—a habit pattern which reflected the pattern of unceasing praise in the heavenly realm. Reading the Psalms certainly gives us a sense of the great significance which David placed upon praise as a way of life. He would whole-heartedly agree with Billheimer's statement that "to be most effective, praise must be massive, continuous, a fixed habit, a full-time occupation, a diligently pursued vocation, a way of life" (pg.121).

This type of praise does not happen spontaneously. It must be developed like any other habit pattern. After reading Carother's books, I made a strong decision in the Adult to praise and worship God throughout every day. I asked the Holy Spirit to come to me at different times during each day and remind me to magnify the Lord and exalt His holy name. There are so many things that demand our attention and occupy our minds during a typical day that it is extremely difficult to make the Lord our focal point. So, at first, I had to force myself to take time to concentrate fully on praising God. Remembering to offer up praises to the Lord during the day takes discipline in the same way that it takes discipline to remember to brush our teeth, exercise, drink water, etc. So, it required concerted effort at first to establish the habit pattern of praise. But the Spirit was faithful to remind me at intervals during every day, and soon I was spontaneously breaking forth into thanksgiving and praise without any reminders!

As counselors, we can help our counselees develop the habit of praise by encouraging them to read the Psalms out loud and also to pray and sing in tongues. Praying in the Spirit enables us to worship God beyond our own intellects because the Holy Spirit is praising through us. Counselees should be assured, however, that praise does not have to be expressed out loud to be "effective." We can praise God in our minds; in this way, our spirits are continually communing with God. When I am listening to a counselee, I am perpetually praying in tongues in my mind.

When I first began to counsel, being a perfectionist, I was constantly plagued with doubts and worries that I might say the wrong thing. So, after doing spiritual warfare, I would pray in tongues in my mind as I drove to the Teen Challenge center. After a short time of praying in tongues, I would involuntarily begin singing in tongues in my mind. I did not consciously switch from praying to singing; it was just something that the Holy Spirit caused to happen. As I sang in the spirit, all of my anxiety and doubt would leave, and I would be overwhelmed with joy and confidence! This blessing from the Lord was my reassurance that He was truly in control and would take care of everything!

Counselees may be instructed to enter into worship by praising and thanking God for the good things He has done in their lives. Meditating on the infinite divine attributes of the Almighty—His beauty, power, glory, majesty, splendor, wisdom, lovingkindness, faithfulness, righteousness, etc., will then bring them into the inner courts of praise and worship. "On the glorious splendor of Thy majesty, And on Thy wonderful works, I will meditate" (Ps. 145:5). "Thus, I have beheld Thee in the sanctuary, to see Thy power and Thy glory" (Ps. 63:2 NAS 1977). Counselees will be inspired to enter into deeper worship as thy read some of the examples of praise given in Revelation, such as, Rev. 4:8,11 and Rev. 5:9-13. "To Him who sits on the throne, and to the Lamb, be blessing and honor and glory and dominion forever and ever" (Rev. 5:13).

One practice that never fails to lift me into higher realms of worship is meditating on the innumerable names of Jesus. As I dwell on such names as the Rose of Sharon, the Lily of the Valley, the Image of the Invisible God, and the First-born of all Creation, I am swiftly transported into a state of ecstasy and bliss as the sweet presence of our Lord Jesus enfolds my entire being! In their delightful book, *The Wonderful Names of Our Wonderful Lord*, T. C. Horton and Charles E. Hurlburt list three hundred and sixty-five names and titles of our Savior—one for every day of the year!

Establishing praise as a way of life makes it easier to offer up the "sacrifice of praise" when we encounter various trials. Someone has said that thanksgiving and praise is the way to victory in every situation. This must be true because praise banishes Satan and frees God to work in a problem or misfortune. As Billheimer says, "The secret of answered prayer is faith without doubt. And the secret of faith without doubt is praise—continuous, massive, triumphant praise, praise that is a way of life" (pg. 126).

B. FAMILY OF GOD.

We can readily see that reprogramming the Internal Parent of a counselee with new judgments (beliefs) composed of God's truth is a never-ending job! It is such a huge task that it should not, of course, be the entire responsibility of a counselor. As we have discovered, a counselor becomes a "substitute parent" who is responsible for bringing the soul of his counselee through the "death and resurrection process." This process consists of healing the scars of the counselee's Inner Child with God's love and reprogramming his Parent with God's truth. After some initial soul healing, a counselor should be able, at least for the most part, to turn his counselee over to the body of Christ to complete the healing process by "loving him to resurrection life."

1. PRIMARY PURPOSE–REPARENTING.

Unfortunately, the family of God is failing miserably at the task of reparenting! Although we do a fairly good job of getting people born into the kingdom, we do not follow through, as the Sandfords say in their book, *The Transformation of the Inner Man*, by raising them up as sons and daughters in Christ. I will qualify this by saying that some parts of the body, for example, Paul Yonggi Cho's church in Seoul, Korea, are doing admirably well in this area. At last count, Pastor Cho heads approximately a thousand elders who are responsible for small cell groups which meet the spiritual, emotional and physical needs of the church members. Pastor Cho is said to have stated that in America the front doors of churches are wide open but, sad to say, so are the back doors! This "revolving door" problem simply means that the needs of the people are not being met.

When we are reborn in Christ, we are babies. We need to be nurtured and brought up spiritually by the family of God. I believe this is the real reason for the church's existence. Sadly, the primary purpose of the church is also its least understood function. But even if a body of believers does understand and is attempting to fulfill this function, it is much more difficult in this age of increasing divorces and rampant physical, psychological and sexual abuse to accomplish it. Not only must God's family nurture reborn babies spiritually, its members must also nurture them emotionally! This is made doubly difficult by the fact that we, the saints required to do this "reparenting" of the souls and spirits of baby Christians, have not been sufficiently healed and "loved back to life" ourselves. We cannot give what we have not received. Thus, if we have not received love and healing, we cannot give it.

a. INAPPROPRIATE METHODS. The sad fact is that we have a family which is hurting so badly that, for the most part, its members are unable to furnish the loving hands and hearts needed to touch and heal the souls and spirits of new believers. Therefore, the total burden of re-parenting baby Christians often falls on a few people—counselors, pastors and others—who are willing to be used by God for this purpose. Unfortunately, many of these volunteers have not been sufficiently healed or prepared by the Spirit to be able to accomplish this task effectually. Often these self-appointed parents in Christ are "rescuers" who are performance-oriented—still trying to please the Internal Parent by doing "good." They feel "good" when they have many people relying on them for wisdom, strength and support. They "need" to be needed.

The problem is that the "power, glory and honor" bestowed on them by their "dependents" can go to the heads" of these "saviors," causing them to become very controlling and directive. Since they have probably made judgments against their own critical, possessive parents, the inclination to become just like them is already there. Even though they mean well and may have a lot of love, these "rescuers" are very domineering and eventually end up directing every move which their "followers" make.

The end result is that, just like children, young Christians under the care of these controllers will either become "robots," obeying their every directive and possibly "idolizing" them, or they will become "rebels," insisting that they be allowed to make their own decisions. The "robots" will never feel like they are "good enough to meet the mark," while the "rebels" will, sooner or later, get "hit over the head with the Bible" for some infraction.

Whether they become robots or rebels, these young saints find themselves in the same type of "dominant-submissive" relationship which they had with their natural parents. Because of this frustrating situation, more anger, unforgiveness and bitterness is added to that which they have already built-up, causing them, in many instances, to leave the church and go back into the world.

(1.) Shepherding Movement. The most illustrious example of reparenting at its worst was found in the now-defunct "Shepherding" movement. Although I strongly believe that the intentions of these fine, well-meaning leaders in the Charismatic Christian community were strictly honorable, they were not aware of the pitfalls inherent in "shepherding" and thus, fell into Satan's traps. Fortunately, most of these sincere, upright men saw the error of their ways and repented of them, but sad to say, not before a lot of damage had been done.

The most flagrant violation committed by these and other leaders while reparenting is insisting that young believers follow their advice and obey their commands. One of the first things we were taught in counseling was never to give advice. If the client follows the advice and the results are "bad," he will blame the counselor and lose trust in him. If the results of following the advice are "good," the client will become dependent upon the advice of his counselor to run his life. If the client decides not to follow his counselor's advice, he will feel guilty and insecure, fearing that his therapist will reject him just as his domineering parents did.

The leaders of the Shepherding movement compounded the error of ordering their "sheep" to follow their advice by correcting and rebuking them when they failed to obey their commands. Some were even guilty of sharply rebuking their members in public, thereby crushing their self-esteem. Although these glaring errors of Shepherdship may no longer exist, many fellowships still practice some of the Shepherdship tactics. My husband and I were members of several churches whose leaders dominated and manipulated their flocks without realizing it. In one church, saints were not allowed to do anything major without checking with the shepherds first. If St. Peter had belonged to this church, he would have had to get the leader's permission before he went to the house of Cornelius to begin preaching the gospel to the Gentiles.

The main tactic used to keep the sheep in submission was to say we had a "rebellious attitude" if we disagreed with or did not obey our shepherds' commands. We were then told that if we refused to "submit," we would not be "covered" (spiritually protected) and Satan would have a "free hand" with us because we were "not in divine order." If a believer objected to all this, he was warned "not to touch God's anointed."

The Houses (Ronald K. and Judy) have written a very eye-opening book, *How to Recognize Shepherdship Error*, which exposes the mistakes being perpetrated, often unknowingly and innocently, in many churches today. They relate that 'Shepherdship Error' first began in the early church with the Nicolaitans who believed that ministers were set in authority over the laity whom they were to "rule over in the name of divine order" (all for the good of the laity, of course). The word "Nicolaitans" comes from "nikao" (to conquer) and "laos" (the laity). The Nicolaitans probably moved in the Spirit for a while, but before long the church became a dead, ecclesiastical entity ruled by the papacy and his hierarchy according to divine order.

b. APPROPRIATE METHODS. As spiritual parents—whether counselors, pastors or others—I would say that we are responsible to give advice and counsel based on the Word of God to our children in Christ, but that we should always allow them to make their own decisions. This is one of the "laws" of reparenting that should be "engraved in stone!" If we make the decisions for our spiritual sons and daughters, we take the place of God in their lives. This is the deadly trap into which the leaders of the Shepherding movement fell. By directing the lives of their members, they claimed responsibility for them. No one but the Lord should have the responsibility for directing people's lives! Only our Savior can handle the power and pressure involved in this awesome task!

However, we should be aware that our children in Christ will often, unknowingly, "push" us into making decisions for them. Passive dependents, especially, will try to get us to take over this responsibility for them. Thus, we must always be very careful to state, "This is just my opinion; you must seek the Lord for what He wants you to do." This cannot be stressed often enough! Foremost in our minds must be the fact that our primary goal is to help our spiritual youngsters get healed so they can trust their heavenly Father enough to bring every hurt, need, feeling, burden, and question to Him. We must be vigilant about getting their eyes off of us and onto their glorious Lord and Savior! We must be very careful never to replace God in their lives in the areas of guidance, attention, affection, or anything else! This is what made the Shepherding movement so very dangerous!

Thus, we can see that no one in the family of God has the authority to make the decisions or govern the life of anyone else in the body! Pastors, counselors, spiritual parents, and other leaders must forever keep this vital point foremost in their minds! Our tendency, like that of natural parents, is to take over and run the lives of our children in Christ, especially the new "babies," because, after all, we know "what is best for them." We must beware of what happened to the early church when man took over and ruled the laity! The same heresy of man taking over the Lordship of Jesus eventually led to the death of every church denomination and now threatens the Charismatic movement today as well!

(1.) Unconditional Love. Therefore, parents in Jesus must always be on guard to allow their spiritual child to make his own decision even if they discern that his decision is completely wrong. In this case, after imparting what they believe to be God's wisdom and exhorting their "child," in love, to seek the Lord's direction in the matter, they must place him on the altar as Abraham did Isaac. They should then pray fervently, taking their authority in the spiritual realm and then trusting God to deal with their "child." They must continue to stand by him, supporting, encouraging, loving, and accepting him unconditionally. This kind of unqualified love, which stands by a person even when he makes a mistake, will eventually convince this "child" that he can trust his spiritual parents because they are not controlling, domineering and possessive like his natural parents.

The kind of reception which the prodigal son received when he returned home after blowing it royally is what melts and heals hearts. Although this father must have been sorely disappointed and hurt by his son's behavior, he was overjoyed when he saw him and welcomed him with open arms! This young man must have felt overwhelmed by the fact that he was cherished just because he existed! He had certainly done nothing to earn his father's esteem and acceptance. On the contrary, he had done everything to destroy his father's faith in him, but he could not!

This is the kind of unqualified, unrestricted, unconstrained love, and acceptance that substitute parents need to have for their "children" in order to be the "bridge" that transports them to their heavenly Father. When the Internal Child of a person feels truly loved and cherished by the Lord through his substitute parents, just because he exists, God's healing balm and resurrection life flows freely through him. Then a person's Inner Child finally feels secure in knowing that God's love is his, never to be snatched away—no matter what he does—this individual is well on his way to wholeness because he can trust God to bring his soul to fullness of life.

This does not mean that a parent in Jesus must always do everything right as far as his "child" is concerned. He may fail to be understanding and supportive at certain times; he may be impatient or inattentive at other times. Nevertheless, as long as the Inner Child of his spiritual youngster feels the unconditional love and acceptance of Jesus flowing from his spiritual parent, the job of reparenting is being capably accomplished. As my mother delights in saying, "Love covers a multitude of 'sins," she is absolutely right!

How do we come to the place where the unrestricted, unqualified love of our Lord can flow freely through us? Sandford found the key which he shares in his book, *The Transformation of the Inner Man.* When his counselees began asking why they could not become more "whole" with him, he realized that no one could really become free of him (or anything else) because he needed people to be "sick" so he could help them. He acknowledged that he must die to his "performance script" and his image of himself as a "rescuer" (parenthesized words are mine), but he knew that something was still missing. The Lord revealed to him that a person could place every sinful practice on the cross and still remain a functionally incapable person. More important than death to the negative was resurrection of the soul to new life.

The Lord made him aware that people were "latching onto" his wife and him because they seemed to be "promising something that they were withholding." "Paradoxically," God said, "If you will open up and give all of yourselves, they will be satisfied, and not drain you anymore" (pg. 387). He explained that some counselees were seeking the nurturing love of parents which they had never received. The Spirit then told Sandford that if he and his wife would give themselves wholly to be used as vessels for the Father's love, He would so satisfy the hearts of their "children" that they would become whole.

This dedicated couple was then able to overcome the fear that they would be risking too much of themselves if they obeyed the Spirit. As they gave all of themselves, they immediately began to see people take hold of their lives and grow up more quickly. Incidentally, if more husbands would apply this key and risk giving all of themselves to their wives, they would find, to their delight and amazement, that their wives would be satisfied and would make their mates' lives sheer bliss in return! My husband has found that this key has worked remarkably well in our marriage!

(2.) Burden-Bearing. St. Paul seemed to understand the tremendous importance of the task of re-parenting. Consequently, he devoted all of himself to being the spiritual father of many "children." As we read his letters to the churches, we can feel Paul's heart-rending concern as he painfully struggles to birth and raise up his many "children" spiritually and, most probably, emotionally, in most cases. In my opinion, it is practically impossible to separate spiritual from emotional reparenting. "My children, with whom I am again in labor until Christ is formed in you." "I fear for you, that perhaps I have labored over you in vain" (Gal. 4:19, 11). "...for in Christ Jesus, I became your father through the gospel" (1 Cor. 4:15). "...just as you know how we were exhorting and encouraging and imploring each one of you as a father would his own children" (1 Thess. 2:11). "You are our letter, written in our hearts "...cared for by us" (2 Cor. 3:2,3). Anyone who has done any reparenting at all can really relate to what Paul is saying!

Just as Paul proclaims, when we offer ourselves to be spiritual parents, we will carry our "children" in our hearts. We will feel their pain, loneliness, anxiety, doubt, insecurity, etc., and also experience their joy in our hearts. Often, I have felt some anxiety or pain or sensed some burden and been drawn to telephone one of my "children." Invariably, this "Child" will say, "Oh, I'm so glad you called! How did you know that I needed you?" Of course, I must be very sensitive to the Spirit's leading as He may tell me not to call because this person now needs to go to the Lord directly. I know that the Spirit is drawing me to a particular "Child" when I "can endure it no longer." As Paul said, "When I could endure it no longer, I also sent to find out about your faith, for fear that the tempter might have tempted you, and our labor should be in vain" (1 Thess. 3:5).

Although we are called to bear our spiritual children's burdens and empathize with their feelings, we must be able to release any anxiety or fear concerning their situations to the Lord. As with our own progeny, we must have faith that Jesus will see them through regardless of how desperate the circumstances may seem. I have found this to be the most difficult part of reparenting. Trusting the Father for my children in Christ's physical provisions is extremely difficult for me. Since I counsel mostly divorced women with children, I have reparented many who have had to trust God for finances daily and several who have had to leave their homes because they were unable to pay their exorbitant rent. But I have seen God do so many miracles over the years for my "children" that my faith has grown immensely! Perhaps I am now ready to retire and become a "grandmother in Christ." Now that sounds like fun!

Everyone that we counsel will not need reparenting in the "full" sense of the term. Some individuals have received enough love from their parents that, after some initial soul healing, they will be able to come to fullness of life through the love of their pastor or others in the body of believers. As we might suspect, those counselees who have been highly rejected and deprived of love by their natural parents are the ones who are most in need of reparenting. It has been my experience that they will usually "force" their counselors into the role of substitute parents whether they are aware of what is happening or not! Possibly it is better this way because if we knew what was going to be required of us in a particular reparenting job, we might not sign up for it!

No one can determine how much will be required when a reparenting relationship is established. As is the case with our own offspring, some children in Jesus require a lot more patience, dedication and forbearance on our part. Those who have been under some form of mind control, whether from parents who gave them "double-bind" messages or dominated or subjected them to SRA, are particularly difficult to reparent because they do not trust anyone to love them or help them discern truth. They often put their spiritual parents through many trials with their double-minded behavior; one minute they see the light of God's truth and realize how much He loves them and the next, Satan has again overcome their minds with lies, confusion, doubt, and unbelief.

The Lord may ask us to invite a child in Christ to live with us for a time. This will usually be a teenager or young adult who needs "intensive care." This young person will undoubtedly be harboring an excessive amount of anger because he is so wounded and starved for love. Most likely, he will test his spiritual parents to the limit with all kinds of obstinate, rebellious behavior before he is satisfied that they love him just as he is. In our case, the Lord asked my husband and me to take in our fourteen-year old niece. My husband's divorced sister was not functioning well emotionally and had placed her daughter in a state facility after stating that she just "could not live with teenagers." I could empathize completely with her because our two children were thirteen and fifteen years old at the time. I, of course, did not have the luxury of kicking our teenagers out, although I am sure the thought crossed *my* mind several times! Since I happened to be counseling parents with incorrigible children at Teen Challenge at this time, I believe the Lord allowed me to be tested in this same area with our niece.

Our niece, whom I would classify as an active ambivalent personality type, proved to be a real challenge! Naturally, she had built up a lot of anger and resentment due to the emotional wounds which she had sustained. Although she was generally obedient, for which I thank God, she had developed an internal resistance pattern, typical of her particular personality type, which resulted in stubborn, negativistic, moody behavior. She would be very compatible and sweet and then, for no apparent reason, become very angry and defensive. She would then act as though nothing had happened, expecting everyone to love her again without even apologizing for her behavior.

Our children became extremely frustrated with her changeable moods, especially our daughter, a "people pleaser," who bore the brunt of most of them. Since our niece was barely five feet tall, while both of our children were six feet and over, they nicknamed her "Mighty Mite!" I struggled to love and accept her no matter how she behaved, but I, of course, "blew it" at times. The Lord always insisted that I apologize for the slightest bit of anger, while expecting no apology from her. After two years of spiritual warfare and "hanging in there" on our part, she was invited to a little Church of God by a precious Christian girl. Our niece accepted Jesus at this church, and the change in her was dramatic! She became much more cooperative, sweet and loving.

Our little niece moved out when she was twenty years old, and although she backslid for a time, she is now serving Jesus again. She is an excellent mother of two active little boys, and we are very proud of her! We love her very much and would definitely say that she was worth every bit of effort and love which we put into her! We all grew as much as she did through the experience.

I would caution a spiritual Parent, however, to make very sure it is God's will before he invites a child who needs reparenting to live with him. Only God knows if the experience will be too disruptive to his home life or if he will have enough time and love for his own children so they will not feel neglected. We can rest assured, however, that whatever reparenting task God calls us to, He will be faithful to supply everything we need to accomplish it, provided we do it in His strength and not our own!

(3.) Cord-Cutting. We need to adopt a "hang loose" attitude with our spiritual offspring and let maturation occur as naturally as it does with our own children. God—not ourselves, should be in charge of "cutting the emotional umbilical cord" because only He knows when the time is right. While they are going through the process of soul healing, we should see our children in Christ once every week, if possible. There is no set schedule for breaking free, but we will feel them begin to pull away when they do not need us as much. They will begin telling us how well they handled a certain situation—how excited they felt when they did not react with anger or fear like they used to and how they were able to trust their own discernment. As one counselee put it, "I don't feel any anger anymore! I feel all warm and loved inside!" These are all signals that we should allow our children in Christ to break free of us emotionally even as we gave this same opportunity to our own children.

Our spiritual progeny may still need us to answer a question or counsel about some specific problem at times, just as our natural children do. In this case, they should be treated as mature and not be subjected to a lot of "counseling wisdom" which they already know. They will feel insulted if we do not relate to them on the level to which they have grown, just as our own children feel "put down" when we treat them as though they were still our little ones. Even if a child in Christ regresses and behaves rather childishly, his spiritual parents should still treat him as the adult he is.

As we have seen, the key to helping a spiritual child mature is to always treat him with utmost respect as an adult. Although we are touching the Inner Child when we pray for or give affection to a child in Christ, we must always speak and relate to him respectfully in the Adult, not the Parent ego state. In this way, we fill his Inner Child with God's love for which he is hungering, while at the same time, we encourage him to behave in the Adult ego state. We truly become the nurturing, understanding, considerate parents for which he has always longed.

2. CHURCHES—HEALING CENTERS.

I believe the greatest need in the body of believers today is wise, loving parents in Christ who have been healed and trained sufficiently to raise up mature, strong, honorable spiritual sons and daughters who thrive on intimacy with their heavenly Father. The soaring divorce rate, the acceptance of sexual promiscuity and the increasing mobility in this nation have all contributed to destroying family relationships. No longer do children grow up surrounded by the love and support of their extended family members. The security and strength which they derived from being supported by a strong foundation of close-knit family ties no longer exists.

I understand the tremendous importance of strong extended family relationships because I grew up in a very close-knit, loving, extended family. As a youngster, I spent almost as much time at my grandparents' home as I did at my own. My fondest memories consist of Sundays and holidays filled with laughter, love, games, and food, shared by my relatives of German descent. Feelings of security and warmth still envelope me when I recall these "good old days." I thank God that I was blessed so richly with such a beautiful family!

My grandmother, aunts and uncles abundantly filled the needs which my mother and father did not or could not fill. As I have shared, although my mother loved me dearly, I perceived that she expected a "perfection" from me which I was not able to give her. But I knew my hurts would always be healed by my grandmother, as well as my aunts, who were only five and seven years older than I, because they all accepted me just as I was. Being the first-born grandchild, my relatives doted on, pampered and spoiled me. This provided a balance in my upbringing–a "safety valve," so to speak–since I was able to go from being the "uptight first- born" in *my* immediate family to being the "carefree baby" in my extended family.

As I became older, one of my uncles helped me with my homework and provided "intellectual stimulation," a need which my father was unable to fill. I also had the advantage of spending summers with another aunt and uncle on a farm where I churned butter, gathered eggs, played in the hayloft, and rode the combine. Needless to say, I experienced total freedom here as "perfection" was a state that did not exist, evidenced by the "sandy" bed in which I slept. Since all the water had to be pumped, a nightly bath was out of the question. Staying at the farm, I was truly in "seventh heaven!"

Not only are there fewer extended families today, many children grow up without a father's care. Thus, the family of God must also fill the void created by divorce which shatters family relationships, forever scarring children's souls. Churches should be healing centers where spiritual family members come together not only to worship and feast on the Word of God, but to fill the needs created by this void in family relationships. One way in which this can be accomplished is to place spiritual parents who have been healed and trained in reparenting and developing intimacy over home care groups. Group leaders can be trained in ways to help people "open up" and share deep feelings, hurts and problems and in how to minster to these needs.

Home-care fellowships should constitute small, intimate families where members can be healed, nurtured and loved to life by their parents and sisters and brothers in Christ. Oozing love and acceptance, grandparents in Jesus can stimulate saints to fullness of life simply by lavishing hugs, smiles and kisses upon them. Groups which meet special needs, such as those of divorced women, children without fathers, couples with marriage problems, and survivors of SRA, suffering with MPD, can also be formed.

Pastors can do certain things during services which bring healing and life to their members, while building intimacy among them. The more healed and freer the shepherd is, the more open he will be to receiving creative ideas from the Spirit for meeting the emotional needs of his flock. Our former pastor established the beautiful custom of gathering the children around him, laying hands on and praying for each one before they were dismissed to go to children's church. The little ones loved to receive this blessing and sometimes came up even before he called them.

Several times during a service, Pastor Randy would ask us to go around the room, hug our brothers and sisters, tell them we loved them or build them up in some way. He often asked us to pray in groups of two or three, pray "power" into the person next to us or repeat a soul-cleansing, life-building prayer after him. He sometimes had us sing a song of Jesus' love to another person while looking into his or her eyes. This nurturing gesture is especially healing and life-giving, while it also develops intimacy between the saints.

The desire of my heart is that our churches would become healing centers filled with God's love so that believers would truly feel like they were part of a large, loving, accepting spiritual family. If only we could understand how desperately people are searching for a "family" who would sincerely cherish, comfort and protect them, thereby fulfilling their lifelong dreams and desires! Only we, the family of God, can end their quest and satisfy the cry of their hearts because we alone have the lifeline through which God's healing compassion, security and acceptance flow.

Oh, that we would all understand how vital it is that we allow our Father to make us conduits of His love! I firmly believe that if the shepherd and elders of a fellowship determine to lay down their lives for their flock, their church will soon be bursting at its seams with people starving for love! "Greater love has no one than this, that one lay down his life for his friends" (John 15:13). Oh, that we had more pastors and leaders in the body of Christ willing to lay down their lives for the saints!

C. RESURRECTION OF THE INNER CHILD.

If our churches truly were the soul healing centers that God has called them to be, the Internal Parent of wounded, scarred people would be reprogrammed with God's love and truth much more quickly. Usually, however, it takes a long time for the outdated tapes of a rejected person's Parent to be reprogrammed with new judgments based on God's love and His Word. The more thoroughly the Parent (mind) of a wounded person is reprogrammed, the easier it will be for his Inner Child (heart) to trust his Internal Parent. The more he trusts his renewed Parent, the more healing the hurting Child (heart) of this scarred person will receive. As his healing progresses, his wounded Child, which was controlled through fear and anger by the cruel judgments of his archaic Parent, will gradually "die" (death of self) and be "resurrected."

The resurrected Child of this rejected individual will finally feel loved, secure, confident, and worthy because he knows that his renewed Parent loves and accepts him just as he is. What freedom, joy and peace his resurrected Child now feels! As a result, his "reborn" Child will now be able to relinquish his control of this wounded person's will to the Adult because he knows that his Parent will no longer deceive or hurt him. Thus, the "will" of this individual will finally be returned to the Adult which can now exercise its full reasoning capabilities without the interference of the Child's emotions. His Child will now be able to trust that the Adult will make the right choices for him because he feels cradled in the protective arms of a loving Parent. Thus, the self-will of this emotionally damaged person has been broken and "the eyes of his heart have been enlightened."

What is the final outcome of all this? Since this person's Child no longer feels threatened by his Parent, his Child will be able to allow his Adult to choose to let his Parent (mind renewed by the Word of God) judge him. "The Word of God "...is able to judge the thoughts and intentions of the heart" (Heb. 4:12). This means that this individual will finally be able to allow the Holy Spirit to examine and cleanse his heart (resurrected Child). As we have learned, none of us are able to freely do this because we are all subconsciously controlled by the Parental tapes of our outdated scripts.

Since this person's resurrected Child no longer feels dominated by his Parent, the inner vows contained in his Child will at long last lose their control. Now that his Child sincerely believes that his renewed Parent knows what is best for him, his Child will at last be able to hear, understand and accept the directives of his Parent and to allow his Adult to choose to follow them. This means that this individual will finally be able to hear the Holy Spirit's instructions clearly and to obey them without any hesitation. The final outcome will be that the Child of this scarred individual will, at long last, be able to develop an intimate love relationship with his heavenly Father! Praise the Lord!

Because his Inner Parent-Child conflicts have been resolved, many of his defenses, that is, the walls and barriers that have prevented him from pursuing this intimacy will begin to crumble. Thus, the promise that he is, from an eternal perspective, "a new creature in Christ," "conformed to His image," "dead to sin and alive to God in Christ Jesus," that he has "put on the new self," and "grown up in all aspects into Him" is finally becoming a reality for him in the temporal realm! Of course, we must always bear in mind that this process of sanctification will never be totally completed here on earth since "our inner man is being renewed day by day." "But I am confident of this very thing, that He who began a good work in you will perfect it until the day of Christ" (Phil. 1: 6).

Since Jesus' Internal Parent was composed primarily of His Father's Word, His Inner Child was able to wholeheartedly trust and yield itself to His Internal Parent. He was completely devoid of His own will; He had no self-will. Unbelievable! "I can do nothing on My own initiative." "...I do not seek My own will, but the will of Him who sent Me" (John 5:30). As a result, he suffered no Inner Parent-Child conflicts and consequently, built up no defenses. This absolute freedom from conflicts and defenses which His Inner Child enjoyed, in turn, enabled His personal spirit to delight in continual, intimate communion with the Holy Spirit. Likewise, as the Inner Child of a person yields itself (self-will) to God, his personal spirit will be set free to perform all of its functions. As we have seen, these functions include the ability to worship God, to commune with Him in an intimate way, to hear and receive His guidance and to comprehend His Word.

Thus, when the soul of a wounded person is healed enough to allow his spirit to be released, his spirit is at last able to become the energizing force which God intended it to be. As this person's spirit breathes God's life into his soul, his Inner Child comes to life. In the same way that a bulb bursts into light when and electric current flows through it, "...his light breaks out like the dawn (Child is 'turned on')!" (Isa.58:8). Thus, we might say that his Inner Child has now been resurrected in the full sense of the term. Oh, that we could all be like King David, whose Inner Child was so free that his spirit soared and he leapt and danced before the Lord! "And David was dancing before the Lord with all his might." 'Michal "...saw King David leaping and dancing before the Lord'" (2 Sam. 6:14,16).

1. BREAKING OUR SCRIPTS.

In the fullest meaning of the term, however, the resurrection of a person's Inner Child takes place over a lifetime through the process of sanctification. As we have discovered, when a counselee breaks life-controlling judgments and inner vows during the process of soul healing, they are "broken" only in the spiritual realm. The task of the Holy Spirit is to bring about freedom from them in the natural realm. I have discovered that God's ways of breaking our scripts, that is, the life-controlling plans written for us during childhood by our parents and other authority figures, are definitely not our ways!

During the "good old days" of the Charismatic Renewal, many of us found that God's ways were not our ways when we naively prayed for patience or humility. We discovered, to our dismay, that God did not reach down from on high and sovereignly endow us with patience and humility. Rather, He brought forth the fruit of patience and longsuffering in our lives by putting us through many trials and tribulations. Likewise, we received the fruit of humility by going through humbling circumstances. For example, one Spirit-filled priest shared that, after praying for humility, he caught his foot in his robe and fell flat on his face while approaching the altar during the solemn procession before high mass! Most of us are still reaping the consequences of those innocent prayers of our "honeymoon" phase!

In this same manner, when an individual decides to pay the price of sanctification and allow God to break his old script, His method of accomplishing this task seems to consist of allowing circumstances to come into this person's life which will test his sincerity. How he handles these situations will show just how serious this individual is about not allowing his former judgments and inner vows to dominate and control his life any longer. Thus, breaking our old scripts definitely does not take place automatically, but involves a tremendous battle on our part against the evil forces who are determined to keep our souls imprisoned by our outdated scripts!

a. PASSIVE DEPENDENT PERSONALITY. To illustrate this point, according to **Table 4**, the life-controlling self-judgment of a passive dependent person is that he counts only when he avoids conflict. He has vowed during childhood that he must get approval from others for everything he does. So how does God go about breaking his life-controlling script? You guessed it! This individual will encounter many circumstances in which he will risk the disapproval of others if he chooses to obey God.

I am delighted and honored to share the example of one of my three "special" counselees, who later became a very compassionate, devoted and dedicated counselor. Having been raised in a very close-knit, Italian, Catholic family dominated by an extremely controlling, possessive mother, she developed a passive dependent personality. Intimidated by both her mother and the Catholic religion, she succumbed to an inordinate fear of disapproval. Haunted by the fear that she would never be "worthy enough" to make it to heaven, any small infraction would drive her to the window of the confessional. Convinced that she was not scrupulous enough to meet the demands of both her mother and the Catholic Church, she was continually plagued by feelings of anxiety, guilt, self-condemnation and unworthiness. Unable to cope with these overwhelming feelings, she denied, repressed and buried them.

The "idol" in her Italian family around which their lives revolved had always been food. Plying her children with enormous amounts and varieties of food was her mother's way of showing "love." It was also the way she subconsciously controlled her daughter. After urging my counselee to, "Eat, eat, already," her mother would often insinuate that she was really putting on weight. This double bind message, coupled with her insatiable desire for approval, led this counselee to become bulimic, a symptom with which she struggled for fifteen years until she met Jesus.

The deep-seated fear of God which she had acquired from Catholicism made it impossible for her to even think of approaching the Lord on a personal level. The Spirit began to heal her of this fear by giving her a beautiful vision of Jesus kneeling before her. Needless to say, she was awestruck that the King of the Universe would actually be so humble as to kneel before her! Jesus showed this fear-ridden lady by His humble gesture that He truly was approachable and desired to demonstrate His love for her through a personal relationship. "Perfect love casts out fear."

After more soul healing in which she also acquired a greater understanding of her behavior, God began to break her script. He set about accomplishing this task by giving this counselee, who was so extremely dependent on the approval of others for her self-image, the gift of prophecy. Her prophecies did not elaborate on the fabulous gifts God was planning to bestow on people or the marvelous callings He had for them. No, indeed! On the contrary, the Spirit gave this timid, gentle lady prophecies for strong-willed people which revealed the darkened condition of their hearts and strongly exhorted them—in love, of course—to seek the soul healing which they so desperately needed!

Needless to say, most of these stubborn people did not believe or accept their prophecies because of the hardened condition of their hearts. Many attacked this sweet, sensitive prophetess—some even viciously! After receiving a prophecy from her, one pastor informed her that her prophecies were from Satan and that she needed to beg forgiveness from the elders of his church! Then the pastor who was the covering for our prayer group at that time received one of her "loving, but truthful" words from God; he would not allow my husband to minister in music because I believed her prophetic words! In each case, she was besieged with devastating feelings of rejection, anxiety, unworthiness, and doubts concerning her ministry. Although God had healed her of the symptom of bulimia, she still had to fight the overwhelming desire to indulge in self-pity and give in to her addiction to food at these times.

Twice God asked this prophetess to speak at city council meetings, warning the city "fathers" that God was not pleased with their actions. The first time concerned their denial of a church's request to lease a building in the industrial area of their city, while the second dealt with their decision not to allow pastors to mention the name of Jesus when opening the council meetings with prayer. Both times she spoke out boldly, testifying in love that they must be careful to embrace an awesome fear and respect for Almighty God. Several friends even "rebuked" her the next day for speaking out so strongly about God, claiming that her speech was disrespectful to the council members. Again, she fought not to give in to the overwhelming desire to gorge herself with food which resulted from her feelings of rejection, fear, condemnation, doubt, and self-pity. Ways to "walk in our healing" and gain control over the temptation to give in to our compulsions and other symptoms will be discussed in the next section.

The hardest test for this counselee was to confront her dominating mother on many issues and break the "ties that bind." She had to learn to say "no" lovingly and respectfully and accept the inevitable disapproval and rejection of her mother. This was extremely difficult since her mother has few interests of her own and tends to live her life through her children. This brave counselee also had to obey God and lovingly confront several close friends, who were very controlling, with the truth. They also rejected her and, in some instances, harshly mistreated her.

Recently, God sent her and one of my other "special" counselees to a city in another state to minister to a large group of women. Once again conquering her fear of rejection and disapproval, she shared her testimony and the longing of the Lord's heart that His bride be cleansed and spotless to usher in His second coming. Many women experienced healing of their souls as they were touched by God during prayer. Now a confident counselor, this once timid counselee also, lovingly but firmly, confronted an extremely controlling friend with words of truth from God.

Thus, I am thrilled to say that this courageous woman passed every one of her monumental tests with flying colors! She learned to fight the overpowering temptation to indulge in food by recognizing and dealing with her oppressive feelings of self-doubt, self-condemnation_ and guilt. Since she had been a bulimic for fifteen years, only God knows how difficult these temptations were for her to overcome!

Winning the victory in every battle has made her bolder, stronger, more courageous, and confident of who she is in Christ! She no longer fears confrontation because she knows that she "counts" when she chooses not to avoid conflict, but to obey God, even if it means facing rejection, disapproval and persecution from others. It has been exciting to watch her change from a passive-dependent person who felt inferior, unworthy, anxious, and guilt-ridden to a strong, bold prophetess and prayer warrior who knows that she is a conqueror through Christ! Praise God for her indomitable spirit!

Not everyone passes their ''script-breaking tests; however. The passive-dependent counselee mentioned previously who discovered that her aunt had given birth to her had no problem accepting healing for this trauma. But she failed when God expected her to break her script by standing up for the truth and refusing to be part of the "family lie" any longer. When faced with her mother's rejection and disapproval, she caved in and clung to her outdated script.

During the time this counselee was attending our prayer group, she also received healing of a thyroid problem and the Lord told her to quit taking her medicine. Consequently, her family accused our group of being a cult who not only lied to her about her birth, but also told her to stop taking her medicine (which, of course, we would never do). So, even after many loving, sweet prophecies in which God called her His "shining star" and asked her to lead her family out of the darkness of denial into the light of truth, she still chose to disobey the Lord because she could not live without her family's approval. Thus, she was not able to break her life-controlling judgment—"I only count when I avoid conflict."

b. PASSIVE AMBIVALENT PERSONALITY. In my own case, since I have a passive ambivalent personality, my life-controlling judgment is, "I only count when I perform perfectly." Therefore, as a child I vowed that I must always earn approval by performing perfectly or I would be put to shame. My first test came when I chose to marry a Catholic, although my Lutheran parents were adamantly opposed to my decision. Fortunately, I did make sure that my husband was also the Lord's choice for me! I continued to break free from my script when, in obedience to God, I became a Catholic, even though my mother had said, "You may have married a Catholic, but don't you ever become one!" The fact that I was not "performing perfectly" for my mother was very painful for me and I struggled with feelings of failure, shame, guilt, and condemnation. In fairness to my mother, I am delighted to say that she now thinks my husband is the greatest!

However, the Lord set about breaking my script in earnest when I began counseling. Circumstances began to occur which made it appear that I had performed poorly, putting me to shame. It is important to note here that the breaking of my script would not require circumstances to take place in which I would actually perform poorly, but only for situations to occur which would tempt me to feel that my performance was somehow inferior. My test would be whether or not I (my child) would realize that I count even when my performance is or appears to be less than perfect.

To illustrate, I had been counseling for about seven years at Teen Challenge under a pastor who then started his own counseling center. He was happy to have me counsel there until a young man with a master's degree offered his services. I had not completed my master's at the time. I soon noticed that no new counselees were being referred to me. The secretary, who was my friend, informed me that her orders were to refer all new counselees to this young man. I (my Child) felt very hurt, angry, betrayed, jealous, and ashamed, although I (my Adult) knew that I had done my best. I fought these feelings, however, and determined not to give in to self-pity, but to die to my flesh. Although I left this center, I heard later from the secretary that the young graduate just up and disappeared after only two weeks on the job because he could not handle his heavy counseling load!

My real "refining in the fire" tests, however, came later when I counseled at a large church of several thousand. While completing my master's degrees, I spent long, exhausting hours counseling several days a week. Due to the "political problems" at this church, about five consecutive pastors headed the counseling department during my stay there. The fourth pastor was very interested in learning about soul healing and asked to sit in on my counseling sessions. But then he received a call from a friend who was a social worker in northern California. Because her recent divorce had drained her emotionally, she was planning to take a sabbatical from counseling.

Since this pastor was exhausted and harbored strong desires to move back to his hometown in the south, he invited her to come for a visit, subconsciously wishing, I believe, that she would take over his job. Possessing an active dependent personality, she tended to use flirtation to manipulate in her rather bold attempt to take over the counseling department. Once again I was "ignored" and soul healing took a back seat as this "southern gentleman" pastor was taken in by her provocative ways. As before, I felt hurt, angry, betrayed, rejected, jealous, and put to shame as I watched her attend the pastor's meetings and go out to lunch with them. At one point, she even told me things would be much better when she was in charge!

But I was determined to die to myself, so I fought to stay in the Adult and gain the victory over all of my negative feelings (my Child). Satan tempted me to give in to my life-controlling judgment and feel ashamed that somehow, I had not performed well enough. Realizing that this judgment was not realistic since I was still carrying the "lion's share" of counseling, I struggled to break free of my old script. In the next section, ways to win the victory over negative feelings, thereby crushing our outdated scripts, will be discussed.

The southern pastor moved back to his hometown and a young man who had just become a pastor was appointed as head of the counseling department. This particular church did not require pastors to have any type of formal training. Although it was humbling to have a pastor who had no training or experience in counseling and was young enough to be my son as head over me, I chose to obey God and submit to this young man. Although the social worker had become "friends" with this young pastor and his wife, he said that she would not be involved with the counseling department because his wife had discerned that she had a "seductive" spirit. So, God removed this "thorn in my side" from the counseling department.

Then the Lord did a beautiful thing which reassured me that He was still on the throne and that He was honoring my attempts to "...present my body a living and holy sacrifice, acceptable to God" (Rom. 12:1). The young pastor called me into his office one morning shortly after he had been appointed. Visibly shaken, he began to tell me that he was going to "put all of his apples in my cart." He said that God had come to him during the night and told him that he was to make me supervisor, that I was to train other counselors and that he was to sit under my teaching. Needless to say, I was shocked! I could not believe what I was hearing! When I realized that he really meant it, I told him that several women whom I had been counseling had expressed desires to become counselors. I wish I could say that my story ended happily here, but that would be too good to be true!

Two weeks after appointing me supervisor, this youthful pastor informed me that he was "sending me home to rest for three weeks because I was tired." I realized that "politics" had entered the scene once again, making him look "bad" because I was supervising the counselors. I explained to him that I had appointments scheduled and that, professionally, I had an obligation to see these people. So, he agreed to let me counsel, but I could not come to the weekly counselors' meeting for three weeks. I was told later that he announced to the counselors that I was no longer supervisor and that he would now be in charge of the meetings. So, once again, I fought feelings of hurt, betrayal, anger, and being put to shame.

It was, of course, very humbling to obey such a foolish order from a young man who was disobeying God. But God gives grace to the humble and He honored my attempt to walk in His ways by submitting to the head which He had placed over me. When I was allowed to return to the meetings, this insecure pastor would open them with a few comments and then defer to me. After a while he did not attend the meetings at all. It seemed like he was more than happy to let me supervise as long as the leaders "thought" that he was in charge. This really became evident when an article about my ministry was written for the church paper, but he then substituted this for one about his "accomplishments" as head of the counseling department.

Choosing to stay on the road to Calvary, I was determined to go all the way to the cross and die to myself. The fact that many people were able to receive soul-healing from God during this time is all that was really important. In fact, so many people were coming for counseling, not only from our church, but from many others, that we had to refer many people to other counseling centers. Illustrating God's marvelous sense of humor, I discovered that the secretary was referring most of the people to the same center I left earlier! Ironically, the minister who would not assign new counselees to me even asked the young pastor heading our counseling department to come and share our "secrets of success" with him! God is so ingenious! Of course, this minister did not know that I was now counseling at this particular fellowship. The young pastor did go and share with him; as to what he told him, I have no idea!

Unfortunately, the stress generated by my increasing responsibilities gradually took its toll and my health began to suffer. Although I knew I would be risking my ministry at this church, I boldly asked the head minister if I could train more counselors. Even though he seemed to be in favor of the idea, he closed the counseling department several months later. Although he was teaching about inner healing on his television program at that time, his "vision" for the church was that it should function primarily as an evangelistic center. Thus, this ambivalent pastor was basically opposed to having a large counseling department, even though he was partially responsible for it!

At any rate, his closure of the department helped me understand why the Spirit had given me the scripture, Micah 4:6-8, one month before this took place. Since people were upset by his move, the head of this fellowship defended his behavior by saying that the counseling department was costing too much (hard to believe since we were all volunteers), that the counselees were becoming dependent on the counselors who were seeing them too many times, that "rumors" were being spread to other churches, etc.

The exciting thing about all of this was my response to his actions! Although I "tried" to feel hurt, angry, betrayed, and put to shame because he was obviously saying that my performance had been "less than perfect," I just felt sad because this leader had failed to "...walk in a manner worthy of God and to please Him in many respects" (Col. 1:10). This was a tremendous victory in smashing the outdated script which controlled my life! To God be the glory!

I had one more major test to pass before God released me from this church. After resting for a while, the Lord led me to begin praying with several other women. Soon He began bringing more women to our group, some of whom received soul healing. Knowing that I would be in "trouble" if the leaders heard about our group, my husband and I asked an elder to inquire of the pastors if they would be a "covering" over our prayer group. Sad to say, the leaders of this fellowship had become more controlling as time passed. The elder was excited about our group as the Lord revealed to him that He would heal the souls of many who came to it.

He changed his tune when we were asked to meet with him and the pastor who was currently the head of counseling. We could not believe the treatment which we received at this meeting! This young man who had just recently been made a pastor asked me point blank, "Don't you know that you are not supposed to be counseling anymore?" He and the elder then informed me that I was not to counsel and that I must disband my group immediately!

One of the women whom I had taken through soul healing and also trained was leading a group at this time, but we were told that hers had been approved because it had been "raised up" in the church. We were then told that if I did not obey, we would be considered rebellious. When we said that we would have to pray about it, this rude young pastor informed us that we must obey him now or turn in our "prayer team badges." Of course, we turned them in because this church had definitely fallen into shepherd error!

Once again, my reaction, thanks to Jesus, was exciting to me! Amazingly, I did not feel angry, hurt or ashamed that I had failed. After leaving the meeting, the Lord blessed me unbelievably! An overwhelming feeling of grief and sorrow enveloped me, and I cried out to the Lord to "forgive them for they did not know what they were doing!" God had truly given me His heart of compassion and understanding for them and I was thrilled!

The next Sunday the Lord confirmed that I had "passed the test" through a vision. Every Sunday during worship, I envisioned myself pouring costly perfume from a large bottle over the beautiful feet of Jesus and wiping them with my hair just as Mary Magdalene had done (Luke 7:37,38). This particular Sunday, the Spirit gave me a vision of one last drop of liquid falling from an empty bottle onto Jesus' beloved feet. Jesus then told me that my "alabaster vial" had been filled with my tears. They represented my life which I had "poured out" on Him. What precious words these were to me! The empty vial indicated that my job was done, and He was well-pleased with me. Did I ever rejoice while breathing a long sigh of relief when I heard this!

Since then the Lord has allowed many more tests to come my way to see if my childhood self-judgment and inner vow still controlled my life. I am happy to say that I had no difficulty staying in the Adult and handling my emotions during these tests. The ability to control our emotions, rather than permitting them to control us, is a sure sign that our old scripts have—at least to a great extent—been "burned up." Incidentally, the church where I was "tried in the fire" has since come to be known as the "place where God sends believers to 'die!'"

c. ACTIVE DETACHED PERSONALITY. Because God's ways are not our ways, I shared in detail the "ways" God used to break the control which my script had over my life. Since it is important that we become thoroughly familiar with His ways, I would like to share one more example. According to **Table 4**, the life-controlling self-judgment of the active detached person is, "I am the only one who counts." Since we have learned that this individual has suffered extreme rejection during childhood, we know that this is not a judgment stemming from high self-esteem or pride. Rather, this belief is based strictly on survival.

Since this person discovered early in life that no one cared about him, he knew that he would have to fend for himself if he was going to survive. It follows that the only conclusion to which he could come was that he could not afford to let anyone else "count" in his life but himself. If he did, he would not survive! Consequently, he vowed that he would look out for himself and whoever got in his way would be sorry! Sad to say, these days we are seeing more and more people locked into this hardcore script in our society.

The deeply ingrained distrust stemming from the scars which this battered individual bears makes this tragic script the most difficult one for God to destroy. However, the more wounded a person is, the greater is the sacrifice which he has to offer his Lord and Master. Thus, the one who has received the least of this life's blessings has the greatest opportunity to please God and thrill His heart! "The Lord is near to the brokenhearted and saves those who are crushed in spirit" (Ps. 34:18). Therefore, the active detached individual who allows God the privilege of "setting fire" to his script will receive the greatest blessing because he has given up the most! "I will make the lame a remnant and the outcasts a strong nation, And the Lord will reign over them in Mount Zion" (Micah 4:7).

From our discussion of the ways God uses to break our scripts, you may have already guessed that He will eradicate this one by allowing circumstances which make it appear that the active detached person is the only one who does not count. Keep in mind that God does not actively begin stripping away our scripts until after we have received a generous amount of soul healing. Subsequently, after he has received some emotional healing, the person who was so rejected that he decided he did not need anyone to survive will realize that he does not want to be alone any longer. By accepting and working through situations which give the impression that he is the only one who does not count, he will discover that he no longer has to be the only one that counts in order to survive. In fact, he will decide that he really does need people to survive; therefore, other people do count!

Simply stated, the method which God uses to demolish the script of the person who outwardly rebelled when he was rejected during childhood is to allow him to experience what appears to be a rejection after he has received some soul healing. By working on accepting rejection and forgiving those who seem to be rejecting him, his Inner Child no longer finds it necessary for his survival to rebel when he feels that he is being rejected.

With great admiration and pleasure, I would like to share the example of another of my "special" counselees, a woman with an active detached personality, with whom I have worked over the years. This determined lady has worked hard, sacrificed much and paid a high price to overcome her childhood of rejection, deprivation and abuse! I previously described her as the counselee who defiantly informed me that "she had no parents" when I asked her about her childhood. After much soul healing in which we used her sister as a "substitute" for her mother, God began breaking her script by putting her in situations in which it appeared that she was the only one who did not count.

First, God placed a man in her life who had been separated from his wife for eight years but was still very much in love with her or so he thought. Actually, he was controlled by his wife's demanding, manipulative behavior. Having been spoiled and pampered all of her life, she was used to getting her own way. You guessed it! Her personality profile was that of a Passive Independent. She exploited him in every way and he always gave in to her demands. If she spent all of the support money which she received from him on a vacation, phone bill or pedicure, she knew that he would always come through with more!

When he could no longer afford his dingy, rundown apartment due to his wife's exploitation, my counselee took him in. Although my counselee had feelings for him, it was strictly a plutonic arrangement because she was a strong Christian. She washed and ironed his clothes, cooked for him and, even though she was raising three children on welfare, loaned him money when his wife had spent all of his. Once in a while, her "roommate" would give my counselee a little money for expenses, but essentially, he paid nothing on a regular basis for room and board.

She encouraged, supported and was always there for him emotionally when he felt discouraged about his lack of relationship with his wife. She even offered many suggestions concerning how he might get her back! Even though his wife had a boyfriend, she would phone her "husband in name only" whenever she needed emotional support or experienced her "version" of an anxiety attack. He would always drop everything and soothe and comfort her until she calmed down. Thus, my counselee "gave her all" in this relationship while receiving very little in return.

When this man did not respond to God's calling, the Lord brought another one into her life. He lived in his controlling, manipulative mother's home with his two teenage daughters who had him "wrapped around their little fingers." Although he and his mother had split the money which they received when she refinanced her house, he was required to pay off the entire mortgage. Since his daughters had been "deprived" while living with their mother, he informed my counselee that they came first and proved it by buying them whatever their hearts desired.

When this man's car broke down, my counselee was required to drive the whole family everywhere because he could not afford another one. He rarely bought gasoline and like the other gentleman, even borrowed money from her, even though his income was twice as much as hers. Enough said! Again, this devoted lady "walked the extra mile" and met this man's needs while hers went begging.

In both of these situations, it definitely seemed like she was the only one who did not count. In the "natural," I would have counseled her to leave these seemingly selfish men as she had received enough rejection in her lifetime! Not that she did not threaten many times to do just that! But her heavenly Daddy would not allow her to break off these unfulfilling relationships. Much of the time she felt angry, rejected, deprived, used, and abused. Many times, she would declare, "Who needs men anyway! I was getting along just fine without any male companionship!" She would then be tempted to withdraw in rebellion and cut off all relationships.

Fortunately, she would allow me to minister to her, although at times, it took much patience, compassion and time to bring her to the point of releasing her hurts to Jesus. Faithfulness, dedication and endurance were required on my part as her counselor. But "hanging in there" with the Lord paid off! We became close friends and I think of her as my precious "little sister!"

Eventually, after much practice, my counselee became so adept at "visualizing her Inner Child" that, during prayer, she would instantly get a picture of just how her "little girl" was feeling. Often, she would see her Inner Child standing defiantly before Jesus with her arms crossed, informing Him that "she wanted nothing more to do with men because they were mean, and she hated them!" Often, she would get a vision of herself as a little girl "protecting herself as a baby" from Jesus. This meant, of course, that her Inner Child did not trust Jesus because He was also a "man."

After I prayed that Jesus' love would melt the walls of distrust separating them, her little girl would eventually let Jesus hold "her baby." This act of submission indicated that she was willing to release her hurts to Jesus. He would then give her a vision which revealed to her the prison of performance, denial and double-mindedness in which the wounded little boys of her male companions were locked. Jesus would explain that only she, using the "key" of her love, patience and understanding, could help Him unlock the prison doors and release them. Since her Inner Child loved a challenge, she would always "accept the key!"

Only about seven years after we began working together did the Holy Spirit reveal to this dedicated counselee that her father had molested her. She had repressed, buried and denied the horror of this trauma so completely that she did not remember anything concerning her father's behavior. This explained the root of her deeply ingrained hatred for men. It also points out how crucial it is to allow the Spirit complete freedom to surface traumas since only He knows when the time is right!

This determined counselee has chosen time after time to "walk in her healing" and gain the victory over Satan. It has been a long, slow, draining process for her, but I am proud and thrilled to say that she has met every challenge that God has presented to her! Through continually choosing not to rebel, but to "accept rejection in the form of being used and taken advantage of," her Child discovered that she did not have to be the only one who counted in order to survive. It *was* possible for her to "lay down her life for another" and still "survive!"

This courageous counselee has won a greater victory than most of us because her past is, by far, the most difficult one to overcome. It has been exciting to see her make the right choice every time and allow God to "set fire" to her old script and change her from a defensive, suspicious, hostile, self-centered person into a trusting, compassionate, generous lady who would joyfully lay down her life for her brothers and sisters!

Recently, the Spirit revealed in a dream that my three special counselees had "graduated" from soul healing "boot camp." All three had truly gone through the "school of hard knocks," chosen to die to their flesh, allow God to circumcise their hearts and had thus, paid the "price" for the ministry of soul healing. "To this end also we pray for you always, that our God may count you worthy of your calling" (2 Thess. 1:11). I have described in detail how God broke the scripts of two of these counselees. Since the personality profile of the third counselee is similar to that of one of the other two, I will not share the details of how God dealt with her script. I do want to give her recognition, however, because like the other two, she passed her many tests and triumphed over Satan!

In many ways, her trials were much more difficult than mine and the other counselees. Married to an alcoholic who continually verbally abuses her, she is the mother of two rebellious teenagers and five younger children. Her first husband, the father of her teenagers, physically and verbally abused her so brutally that she asked God to remove him from her life. Within several days, he was put in jail where he remained for seven years.

Her oldest child, his son, was taken to juvenile hall when he was only thirteen and he has been there many times since. This brave, persevering young woman is weary from spending so many hours in court with him and paying all of the bills he has incurred. He and his sister both drink, take drugs and have refused to go to school. The Lord has recently informed this counselee, whose youngest child is only one year old, to get prepared because her daughter will soon be pregnant at the age of fifteen.

Her five younger children are very insecure, and she has great difficulty controlling them. Her husband rejected the fifth child, pounding on his wife's stomach while insisting that she get an abortion. Consequently, this child refused to leave her mother's side, would not sleep at night and was not weaned until she was four years old. Her father did accept her, however, after she almost died of pneumonia as a baby. Unfortunately, her little soul had already been damaged by his rejection of her in the womb.

Thus, at the young age of thirty-three, this courageous counselee has endured much suffering and given a great deal more than she has ever received. I have always greatly admired her because even in the depths of despair she was more concerned about friends whose needs she considered more urgent than her own! In counseling sessions, we often ended up praying more for them than for her! Although she often felt angry, used, abused, condemned, and unworthy, she continually chose not to give in to these feelings, but to gain the victory over them with Jesus' help. With great joy, I have watched her quietly persevere in her trials, allowing God to destroy her old script and change her from an anxious person who felt inferior and weak to a strong saint who knows who she is in Christ!

2. WALKING IN HEALING.

If you have concluded from the testimonies which I have just shared that "walking in healing" is the most difficult part of the soul healing process, you are absolutely correct! Each of these women, including myself, had (and still have) to decide, day by day, sometimes minute by minute, whether to rebel or continue to walk in healing. As the tests get harder, the choice also gets more difficult. Often, through "gritted teeth," we had (and still have) to pray for strength to make the right choice as we were (and still are) tempted to fall back into our old rebellious attitudes and behavior patterns. Each decision to walk in our healing is a choice to allow God to sanctify and change us into the image of His Son.

As counselors, we must explain to our counselees how God will go about accomplishing the task of breaking their individual scripts after they have received some soul healing. Then we must be prepared to go through this part of the soul healing process with them. Since they may fail their tests many times, much dedication, compassion and faithfulness is required of us as we help our counselees learn how to win the victory over their scripts and walk in their healing.

a. CONQUERING NEGATIVE FEELINGS. Just how can we, as counselors, help our counselees go through the script-breaking process and begin walking in healing? As we have discovered, the culprit that draws us into destructive, symptomatic behavior is always negative feelings. However, most people are not even vaguely in touch with their feelings, and even if they are, they have no idea how to deal with them. For example, usually when an addictive person feels hurt and rejected, he immediately begins drinking, eating, taking drugs, or indulging in some other type of compulsive behavior. He is usually not at all aware of the negative emotions churning within him.

However, the counselee who has received some healing of his past wounds, freeing his Inner Child from the control of his old parental programming will now be able to develop constructive behavior patterns. His Inner Child will now be free to choose to allow his Adult to make decisions based on the love and truth contained in his renewed Parent. However, a person's Inner Child can make this choice only if this individual is able to recognize the feelings contained in his Child.

Therefore, we must train our counselees to recognize negative feelings the moment they arise within them. We can encourage them to ask the Spirit to make them aware of the first sign of a destructive emotion. The secret is that the sooner a person becomes aware of a harmful feeling rising up within him, the easier it will be for him to gain control over it. In the language of Transactional Analysis, when a negative emotion comes up in an individual, it is said that his "Child is hooked." Rather than allowing his Inner Child to nurture the feeling, thereby letting it control him, the "healed" person will be able to choose to "get into the Adult."

As we have seen, if a person's Inner Child is allowed to nurture a harmful feeling, he will either express it toward others, exhibiting the symptoms of a victimizer or he will repress it and turn it toward himself, displaying the symptoms of victim. The more healing a counselee has received, the easier it will be for his Child to release a destructive emotion to his Adult, thereby relinquishing his right to nurture it. We have studied in detail what happens when an individual's Child hangs onto a negative emotion, but just what happens when this feeling is turned over to the Adult? Since anger is the most basic, recognizable, hurtful feeling which arises within us, let us consider first how to handle this destructive emotion.

(1.) Anger. According to Webster's Dictionary, anger is defined as "the strong emotion of displeasure and usually antagonism, excited by a sense of injury or insult." We may try to rationalize our anger by saying it is justified, but very little anger is truly justified. Anger resulting from seeing injustices and suffering is the only anger that is warranted. Jesus displayed justified anger when He cleansed His Father's house of the moneychangers. Even anger that appears to be warranted is often displaced anger. For example, the man who is angry about the government spending so much money is usually really angry at his wife for spending so much money.

Actually, anger is the healthiest of all the negative emotions. It only becomes harmful when we handle it incorrectly. As Paul said, "Be angry, and yet do not sin; do not let the sun go down on your anger" (Eph. 4:26). As we have discovered, we usually handle anger in one of two ways: we either express it or repress it. We express anger when we explode violently, scream, use force, etc. We repress anger when we refuse to accept the fact that we are angry and admit it. Many Christians think that anger is not a legitimate emotion for them to have, so they ignore it and bury it. As we have seen, this is the worst response because the anger will come out later in one or more emotional and/or physical symptoms.

So, we need to share with our counselees the fact that, even after soul healing they will, of course, get angry at times. The important thing is that a counselee recognize as soon as possible that his Child is hooked. He should then choose to get into the Adult and handle his anger correctly. The next step is to confess his anger in the Adult in a way that the person with whom he is angry can accept. He can do this by admitting that he is the one with the problem. Instead of saying, "You are making me angry," he might say, "I am beginning to feel angry." Another one of those facts to engrave in stone is: Each of us is responsible for our emotional reaction to another person. No one can make us angry, no matter what they are doing to us! A hard fact to swallow, but true nevertheless!

The next step for the counselee is to try to discover what other feelings he is experiencing underneath his anger. He may feel abused, frustrated, taken advantage of, betrayed, belittled, ignored, shamed, made fun of, etc. Hurt is usually the feeling underneath all of the others. The third step is to recognize that he has judged the person with whom he is angry because this individual has violated his rights, not fulfilled his expectations and blocked his goals.

For example, you may be angry with your husband because he always has his eyes glued on the television set. You discover that you feel ignored, unloved, rejected, hurt, etc. You have judged him as being insensitive, uncaring, lazy, and violating your right to have a husband who is attentive, caring and sensitive to your needs. So, what do you do with all of your emotions and judgments? It helps to ask the Spirit to show you how He sees the situation, what is really happening and to reveal to you the other person's point of view or how his Inner Child is feeling. Since the Spirit is completely objective, He can clarify the situation and help you see it in a new light which often dissipates your anger.

For example, when my husband and I first received the baptism in the Spirit, in our enthusiasm, we foolishly gave more money to a man in need than we should have. When his teenage daughter announced that her father had bought her three pair of the latest style pants, I became angry because I had bought my daughter only two pair of these pants. When I asked the Spirit to show me this father's feelings, He revealed that he had never been able to afford to buy his daughter any clothes that she wanted, so he had gotten carried away. This insight helped dissolve my anger and I was able to forgive him.

The next step for the counselee is to release his rights to the Lord—"nail them to His cross"—and rescind his judgment of the person with whom he is angry. The last step is to ask Jesus to heal his hurts, help him forgive the offending person and, if possible, allow him to share his feelings in love with this individual. Using the example given above, you might ask the Spirit to show you your husband's point of view and how his Inner Child is feeling, which hopefully, would help you release your right to have a caring, attentive husband. You would then rescind your judgment and forgive him for being insensitive and ignoring you. You might say to your mate, "I feel ignored and unloved when you spend so much time watching television. Can we talk about it?" He may not respond favorably to your request, but at least you have dealt with your anger in the way God wanted you to.

Formulas depicting how anger develops and how to dissipate anger might be expressed as follows:

VIOLATED RIGHTS + JUDGMENT + HURT FEELINGS = ANGER CONFESS ANGER + DISCOVER FEELINGS + RELEASE RIGHTS + RESCIND JUDGMENT HURTS HEALED + FORGIVE + SHARE FEELINGS = ANGER DISSIPATES

As every woman who has an abusive husband knows, handling anger correctly is no easy task! My experiences with my niece and the church which I have shared were just "warm-ups" in dealing with anger for me. The real test came with our son-in-law. Although she was warned in a prophecy to stay away from this young man, because our daughter had always felt inferior concerning her appearance, she was captivated by his good looks, charming ways and "silver tongue."

Because he had received so much rejection and abuse in his past, he was also a very hostile, controlling, self-centered, manipulative, possessive young man—the classic Active Detached personality. Drinking beer and smoking marijuana, he had lived on the streets and in jail since the age of fourteen. Although he professed the desire to follow the Lord when he married our daughter, he gradually slipped back into drinking. After much verbal abuse and a night of physical abuse, our daughter asked us to come get her and our five-month-old grandson.

Our son-in-law threatened, berated and harassed us all on the phone, damaged our daughter's car, spent her money, sold their wedding gifts and other items we had purchased for their house, and even kidnapped the baby one afternoon! We all worked long and hard on "nailing our rights to the cross" and forgiving him! After four months during which drinking took over his life, he called, crying, admitted that he was an alcoholic and apologized for everything that he had done. The Lord asked me at that time to take him in. He even gave me an "excited" feeling about it, so I know it had to be the Lord!

Running a "drug rehab house" was definitely not real easy though, as there was still some drinking and smoking pot. There was still a lot of verbal abuse, climaxing the week before Christmas with our son-in-law shouting obscenities at my daughter because she would not move to Las Vegas with him so he could skip out on his court date!

Continuously releasing our rights to the Lord, we have relied on Him to help us forgive, love and accept this young man just the way he is. We also read the Word over him daily, plus prayers which "call those things that be not as though they were" (Rom. 4:17, KJV) from the book, *Prayers That Avail Much* by Germaine Copeland, Founder of Word Ministries, Inc. (WMI). God has worked in him, slowly but surely, healing his past wounds and scars as we have attempted to "overcome evil with good, thus heaping burning coals upon his head" (Rom. 12:19-21). Stating that he now realizes that he can live a different lifestyle, his attitudes and behavior are slowly changing. He is gradually becoming more sensitive and caring, less controlling and demanding, more secure and trusting, and less defensive and hostile.

I have shared our story so that you will know that I realize how extremely difficult it is to handle anger the way God wants us to, especially when we are faced with some sort of persecution every day. I wish to give *my* daughter maximum credit for dealing with anger better than anyone I have ever known! She has taken more abuse, given her rights to Jesus and forgiven her husband more times than I can begin to count! I am sure the Lord has used her working so hard to accept her husband when he rejects her to help heal the scars from his past.

Always a happy child, she has remained her joyful, "bubbly" self through all of her trials. She will admit, however, that this is due, in large part, to the fact that God has blessed her with the most beautiful, happy, extra-special baby in the whole world! Not being at all prejudiced, my husband and I would agree that our precious grandson has been a special gift from God—the JOY of our lives—to help us through our hard times! Naturally, the Lord made him look exactly like his father so that we would always have something for which to thank our son-in-law!

In addition to this blessing, our son-in-law delivered our second grandson in the car on the way to the hospital! The doctor had just informed us the morning of the day our daughter delivered that the umbilical cord was wrapped around the baby's neck twice.

Our son-in-law told us later that he had never been so scared in all of his life and that he desperately called on God for help the whole time, especially when the baby was not breathing! The Lord told me that He allowed Neal to deliver his son in order to show him how helpless he was and that he could do nothing without Him. So, this beautiful, healthy grandson is definitely a miracle for which *we* also thank God and our son-in-law!

Thus, I have felt totally blessed and privileged to be able to have my daughter and grandsons so close to me and to share the joy of caring for them during their early years. As we know, God truly works all things together for our good. I thank God that He has blessed our family by using tribulation to bring our daughter close to Him and to deepen our relationships with her and with each other!

I also wish to thank God at this point for blessing me with such a fabulous husband! I felt honored that God gave me such a precious gift which I will always treasure! Since my husband received the baptism in the Spirit, he has steadily and quickly grown in the Lord. He has become more and more caring, compassionate and sensitive to my needs. I feel cherished and highly esteemed when he calls me his "princess." Indeed, I feel like a princess as he often senses and fulfills my needs without my saying a word! Many times, I have felt Jesus loving, comforting and strengthening me through my sweet husband's tender, loving care. Thus, the Lord has used him to nurture me and fulfill the needs which my father was not capable of filling.

During my problems with church leaders and our son-in-law, my wonderful husband was always there to help me sort out and struggle through my feelings. Without his understanding, support and concern, I can honestly say that I would not have been able to release my rights to God and forgive the people with whom I was angry.

My faithful husband has also grown tremendously in the ability to do spiritual warfare for my physical health. I thank God that he heeded a certain pastor's vision and Word from the Lord for him stating that he saw two rams butting horns which meant that God wanted him to start butting horns with Satan. He asked my husband if he would just sit there if some man was hurting me and trying to kill me. My husband realized at this time that he had better get serious about spiritual warfare! He had to work at it as he is a passive person and not a fighter by heart. I am happy to say that he has risen to the occasion, however, and is now attacking Satan with his full armor on. Praise God for more husbands like mine!

Sad to say, though, many women patiently endure living with husbands who abuse them—verbally and in many other ways. Needless to say, any woman who is being physically abused should be counseled to separate from her husband. Most of these hurting wives are not able to handle anger as well as our daughter because they did not receive the love and acceptance in childhood which she did. Many, if not most, were brought up by very abusive parents. In many instances, these victimized women repress their anger and as a result, suffer from many debilitating emotional and physical symptoms. However, those victims who have been healed enough to recognize their anger should be encouraged to apply themselves diligently to the task of handling it in a healthy manner. They should be counseled to spend as much time as possible with the Lord, asking Him to surface every emotion which they may be experiencing and to give them word pictures to illustrate their feelings. For example, a victim may feel rejected, used, persecuted, maligned, violated, defiled, debased, harassed, berated, desecrated, and tortured—depending on the extent of the abuse.

She may feel hopeless and helpless, like a slave who, even though he obeys every command of his master, is constantly being beaten and thrown into the dungeon if he displeases him in any way. She may feel like an old worn-out drudge, like a bag lady, haggard and spent, unable to drag herself through another day. One counselee said she felt like a threadbare carpet, always getting stomped on and dirt drug all over her.

I might add a note of caution here. As counselors, when we hear the heartbreaking stories of victimized wives, we must be careful not to do the Holy Spirit's job, no matter how tempting this may seem. This means that we must advise our counselees to seek the Lord on whether or not they should separate from their spouses. Only if the counselee is being physically abused or on the verge of having an emotional breakdown should she be advised to leave her mate.

Surprisingly, I have found in my experience of counseling many victims that after just one session of expressing their feelings and allowing Jesus' love to heal their emotional bruises, they were able to forgive their husbands and once again love and accept them unconditionally. The Lord would then gently and sweetly encourage them to be patient with their spouses and to remain with them, knowing that "His grace would be sufficient."

To comply with the Lord's request, victimized wives must continuously work hard on getting in touch with and releasing their feelings to Him. Before they are able to do this, it may be necessary for them to get out some of their anger by beating on pillows, banging doors or screaming out to God just what they think of their husbands–all in private, of course. Contrary to secular opinion however, these techniques tend to build anger if dwelt on for very long. Consequently, counselees should be encouraged to move quickly on to the next step.

Applying the exercise discussed previously, they might write down all of their feelings, "wrap them as a beautiful gift and place them on the altar as a sacrifice to their heavenly Father." After placing her emotions on the altar, one counselee saw a vision of a crown in which there were many precious jewels, each representing a feeling which she had sacrificed to God!

Likewise, victims must work diligently at giving up all of their rights and expectations. Just as our sweet Savior gave up all of His rights and died for us on the cross, so we must also die to our rights. "For whoever wishes to save his life shall lose it; but whoever loses his life for My sake shall find it" (Matt. 16:25).

To illustrate this point, during one of our marriage workshops, we had our daughter calligraphy the following "Bill of Rights" on a sheet of parchment paper. After burning the edges, we nailed this paper to a rugged wooden cross which my husband had made:

BILL OF RIGHTS

I have a right:

1. to be treated fairly;
2. to have my needs met;
3. to be accepted as I am;
4. to be respected;

5. to be loved and nurtured;
6. to be listened to;
7. to be understood;
8. to get angry with my mate;
9. to pout if my mate hurts me;
10. to blame my mate if things go wrong.

Counselees may add their own rights and expectations to this list and nail it to a cross also. When they are tempted to hang onto a right, they will have this visual aid to remind them that they have nailed that right to the cross. After breaking the judgments and any word curses which they have placed upon their husbands, counselees should ask the Lord to forgive them for their anger.

Next, emotionally battered wives should be encouraged to seek healing for their wounds from their Savior. Picturing themselves as they looked as little girls, they can curl up in Jesus' lap while He rocks them. As He gently embraces them, enfolding them next to His bosom, they will feel His love and comfort flowing tenderly through them. "In His arm He will gather the lambs and carry them in His bosom" (Isa. 40:11). It is important that they spend as much time as possible everyday soaking up His love as He heals their deepest hurts and fills them with the love and affection which they are not receiving from their husbands.

Many of the victimized women whom I counseled had been so degraded by the vulgar names which their spouses had called them that they felt worthless, contemptible and guilty. Many felt defiled and corrupted by the vile language which constantly streamed from their husbands' mouths. Thus, the more abused and debased victims have been, the more time they should spend picturing Jesus cleansing them with His priceless blood from all defilement, depravity and desecration. As He snuggles them close to His bosom, He will nurture, encourage and build them up, telling them how special and precious they are to Him and how much He cherishes and treasures them.

Jesus will then show each woman how hurt and maimed the little boy inside her mate is and that he is striking out at her from his pain. He will help her realize that he is still trying to punish his parents for rejecting and abusing him. Putting down his wife is just a desperate attempt to make himself feel better. Actually, he is projecting on his spouse exactly how he feels about himself.

Our precious Redeemer will fill these suffering wives with His compassion, long-suffering, tenderness, and empathy for their husbands. Thus, His insight and love will help them forgive and accept their mates just as they are. Our beloved Bridegroom will then give them a vision of their husbands as He sees them by faith—sensitive, compassionate, nurturing, considerate, understanding, supportive, spiritual leaders. The ultimate objective for which all wives, not just abused, should strive is to treat their mates as if they were already living up to this faith image. The idea is, of course, that the attitude and behavior of a faith-filled wife might inspire her spouse to become more like Jesus' vision of the ideal husband.

According to scripture, wives are to be subject to their husbands as to the Lord, respect their husbands, and have a gentle and quiet spirit. They are to be submissive to their husbands, obey them, and call them lord, even as Sarah did (Eph. 5:22,33); (1 Pet. 3:1-6); (Col. 3:18). During one of our marriage workshops, the Spirit revealed to me in a vision that wives are to put their husbands "on a pedestal," call them "lord," respect and honor them even if they in no way, deserve this privileged treatment!

Wives are to submit to their husbands even as Jesus submitted to His Father. We often feel that we may lose our identity if we submit to our husbands. But God bestowed upon His precious Son a name above all names because He submitted to the point of death on a cross (Phil. 2:5-11). Likewise, we can submit to our husbands and trust God to establish our identity. God highly honors submission because we are respecting the order which He established and obeying His Word. Through submission, wives free God to work in a powerful way in their husbands' lives, changing them into the image of Jesus. A wife's lack of submission literally prevents God from working in her husband's life. Of course, she cannot submit to anything that is against God's Word.

It stands to reason, of course, that abused wives will have great difficulty respecting, honoring and submitting to their husbands. Only after being reconstituted and refilled with Jesus' love, strength, long-suffering, and all the fruit of the Spirit will they be able to attempt to accomplish this feat. Likewise, only by faith and the grace of God will these battered victims be able to praise God for their spouses just as they are, put on the full armor of God, take up the sword of the Word and continually do spiritual warfare for them! The Bible has many scriptures which they can claim daily for their husbands' salvation and sanctification. **Table 14** gives the formula relating how anger develops and how to dissipate it, plus our Bill of Rights which we must nail to the cross.

(2.) Fear. Unfortunately, as we have noted, many, if not most, victims are unable to get in touch with their anger. As a result, they experience fear, the negative emotion which emerges when they repress and turn their anger against themselves. Unbeknownst to them, this behavior takes place on a subconscious level, often beginning in the womb and continuing throughout their lives. We have discovered that even in the womb, when a person is emotionally hurt, his first reaction is a feeling of displeasure or anger. But, due to his lack of power to do anything about this wound, he often feels helpless and afraid. However, when fear overtakes him during his life, he is unaware that it usually stems from anger which he subconsciously repressed in his early years.

It is reasonable to assume that the more situations a person encounters in which he feels helpless, the more anger he will repress and the more fear he will experience. Therefore, the more critical and demanding his parent is, the more fear a child will experience. As an adult, he may displace his fear on a variety of external objects or situations or on a vague "everything," which is defined as "free-floating" anxiety. Thus, fear of animals, disease, heights, airplanes, etc., may be due to an actual traumatic experience or to displacement.

The more a person has "opened the door" to demons of fear by burying his anger, the more objects and situations he will find on which to displace his fear. The end result is often the ultimate incapacitation of agoraphobia (fear of open places) in which a person is so bound by fear that he cannot leave his home. It is said that before he died, Howard Hughes was so afraid of germs that he was forced to lie naked in bed, while insisting that everything with which he came in contact be sterilized.

Thus, fear is such a debilitating emotion that it is critical that we ask the Spirit to show us all of the root causes of a counselee's fear. As a counselee goes through the soul healing process, fear and anxiety resulting from repressed anger dissipates as Jesus heals the emotional scars of his Inner Child, enabling him to forgive those who have hurt him. The Savior will also heal any trauma and diffuse any fear of objects or situations resulting from frightening childhood experiences. In addition, he will lead us, as counselors, to break any generation curses of fear by which a counselee may be bound.

Having dealt with the root causes of his fear, the counselee should now be free from any incapacitating fear, such an anxiety attacks, phobias, etc. While the Lord is breaking this individual's script, however, Satan will still attempt to bind and oppress him with fear. Therefore, it is important that we teach our counselees how to handle fear so that "ole' slew-foot" will not win the victory over them.

First, a counselee should be encouraged to ask the Spirit to show him immediately when fear has hooked his Child. He should then choose not to give in to his fear, but to get into his Adult and deal with it God's way. His next step would be to ask the Spirit to reveal the cause of his fear. The Spirit may show him that he has buried some anger instead of handling it in the correct way. The Spirit will then point out the source of his displeasure since he may have displaced the fear resulting from his repressed anger on some object or situation far removed from the cause of it. The counselee would then proceed to handle his anger in the healthy way previously outlined.

Understandably, only a counselee who has received enough soul healing and understanding concerning the causes of fear will be able to hear such precise information from the Holy Spirit. For example, the passive dependent "graduate" who had been bulimic stated that even after she had received soul healing, she would find herself eating compulsively when suddenly she would hear the Lord's voice. He would bluntly state, "What do you think you are doing?" This would shock her back into the reality that she was giving in to her life-controlling script once again.

As she sought insight from the Spirit, He would point out that her Child had been hooked with negative feelings, and that she must get into the Adult and deal with her emotions. While in the Adult, the Spirit would help her discover that her Inner Child felt fearful, anxious, unworthy, guilty, ashamed, condemned, and hurt. While investigating the origin of these emotions, she might recall an earlier conversation in which her controlling mother had made it quite clear that she was very displeased with her because she was not calling or coming to see her often enough. She would then realize that her Adaptive Child, still controlled by her old parental programming, had been hooked with fear, anxiety, guilt, etc., which had led her to fall into her old destructive behavior pattern.

The Holy Spirit would then help her get in touch with the anger which she had repressed and turned against herself, resulting in feelings of fear, guilt and shame that her actions had displeased her critical mother, causing her mother to reject her. She would then recognize that these emotions had led her to try to heal her emotional wounds and replace her mother's love through eating since this was the primary way in which her mother had given her love during her childhood. She would also realize that at the same time she was subconsciously punishing herself through compulsive eating which would destroy her body and could lead to bulimia again.

Thus, her aching Inner Child was attempting to fill its emotional needs by nurturing itself, on the one hand, while punishing itself, on the other, through the harmful behavior of compulsive eating. This dichotomous behavior pattern, leading to anorexia-bulimia disorders, is an all too common way of life which Satan uses to destroy people in a nation with high-performance expectations plus an abundance of food. These particular food disorders are especially common among women from upper and middle socioeconomic groups raised with an overcontrolling style of parenting. Unfortunately, food disorders of all kinds are especially prevalent among Christian women. I believe that these symptoms could be eliminated, to a great extent, through the anointed ministry of soul healing.

Insight concerning the origin of her feelings and the reasons for her behavior would enable this former bulimic to gain control over her actions. Realizing that she had repressed her anger toward her dominating mother, she would ask the Lord to help her face and deal with it in the appropriate manner. Revealing that she was angry because she was still allowing her mother to control her life, He would show her that she must once again confront her mother with this issue if she wished to eliminate the cause of her fearful, guilty and unworthy feelings. Risking her mother's disapproval, she must "draw her boundaries" and explain to her, in a loving way, that she must live her own life now and "be about her Father's business."

To implement the drawing of her boundaries, she must inform her mother that she will call or see her once a week, a month or whatever the Lord tells her. When her mother realizes that her daughter means business, she will stop trying to run her life. When a victim stops playing his victimizer's "game," the source of the victim's repressed anger and consequent fear and guilt is made "null and void."

In order to eliminate his fear, a person must face and confront its source, whether it is an individual, a situation, object, or memory. Often in childhood, things happen to us that "open the door" to fear. We may fall off a bed when newborn, get bitten by a dog, injured in an accident, beaten up by a gang, see a horror movie, etc. During the soul healing process, Jesus will heal the wounds and trauma of these events, but the counselee will still have to break his script by facing the person, object or situation which caused his fear. For example, if he is afraid to fly in an airplane, he will eventually have to get on one and fly in order to conquer his fear of flying.

We learned that the only way to gain the victory over fear in our dreams is to confront it. Likewise, the only way to render fear powerless when awake is to face it. The Bible says, "the devil goes about like a roaring lion seeking whom he may devour." This sounds really scary, but Tammy Faye Bakker shares an interesting fact about lions in her book, *Run to the Roar: The Way to Overcome Fear*.

A missionary to Africa told her that when a lion gets old and has no teeth left, his "roar" is still used by the herd. When the young lions go hunting, they hide in the bushes on one side while the old lion stands on the other side. When an antelope comes along, the old ferocious-looking lion roars and scares it so much that it runs the other way—right into the waiting jaws of the young lions who tear him to pieces! If that poor little animal would have run toward the roar, he would not have been hurt because the old lion was too old and weak to attack him.

What a lesson this is for us! Satan was defeated by the King of Kings at the Cross of Calvary! All he has left is a scary roar! The big mistake that we make as Christians is that we run away from "ole' slew-foot instead of attacking him with the sword of the Word. As a result, we run right into all of the imps of hell who destroy us with fear! When David set out to kill the giant, the Bible says that he ran toward him. Obviously, this small shepherd boy, having only five pebbles and a slingshot, must have been afraid of the enormous giant! But he ran toward his fear and God gave him the victory over the giant.

Praise God that when we run toward the "giants" in our lives, they will be destroyed! Running toward whatever we fear shows that we have faith that the Lord will take care of us. Thus, when we run toward our fear, Jesus will give us the victory over it. As one leader said, "We have nothing to fear but fear itself."

Long before I knew there was any such thing as soul healing, I had to face my fear of heights and run toward it. I had no choice because my husband enjoyed skiing and if I wanted to share this sport with him, I had to ride the chair lift. My husband used to say I "white-knuckled it," meaning that I clutched the poles of the chair so hard that my knuckles turned white! While riding the chair lift, I often heard "voices" telling me to jump. But the old devil and his demons did not win because I continued to ride chair lifts even though some of them rose so high off the ground that I shivered with fear! I had pretty much conquered my fear of heights before the Lord taught me about soul healing.

If I would have had the benefit of receiving soul healing during this process, the Spirit would have revealed that this fear came in when, as a newborn, the doctor purposely "dropped" me to show my mother that I would not "break." Jesus would then have healed the trauma of this memory for me. Revealing that my fear of heights was dramatically increased when my father unknowingly insisted that I ride a chair lift alone one summer at Aspen, the

Lord would have healed the shock of this memory also. Although healing these traumatic situations should have helped dissipate my fear, I still would have had to face and deal with any remaining fear by getting on a chair lift.

To prepare me to accomplish this feat, the Spirit might have given me a vision of Jesus sitting next to me on a chair lift with His arm around me, holding my hand. Most likely, my Savior would have reassured me not to be afraid because he would be right there beside me all the way and He would not let me fall. I would have felt security, peace, comfort, and assurance flowing from him into my little Child. After spending ten or fifteen minutes several times a week visualizing Jesus beside me on a chair lift, I would have been ready for the real thing. While actually riding the chair lift, it would have been essential for me to continue "practicing the presence of Jesus," as Brother Lawrence would say, while binding the spirit of fear, claiming the Word and praising God for the situation!

As counselors, we can ask the Holy Spirit to give our counselees a vision of their "Victor" taking care of them in any situation which causes them to be afraid. For example, if a counselee is afraid to fly in an airplane, the Spirit might give him a vision of Jesus sitting next to him on a plane, holding his hand and reassuring him that nothing bad can happen to him because the King of Kings will be right there beside him during the whole trip. The counselee will feel confidence, serenity and surety flowing from the Master into his soul. The more time he spends visualizing this scene, the more secure and calm he will feel. His anxiety will melt away because "perfect love casts out fear."

On family vacations, we often rode the rapids on the Rogue River in Oregon in a small two-man rubber canoe. Our daughter would ride in the canoe with my husband while I would drive downstream with our son to meet them. After bringing the canoe back upstream, our son, who was only thirteen at the time, would steer me through the "troubled waters." Although the rapids were only medium-sized and my son exuded great confidence, I was quite scared! While contemplating whether or not to "chicken out," the Spirit suddenly gave me a vision of our little tiny canoe cradled in the enormous hand of God. I felt so protected, secure and safe that I was never again afraid to "shoot the rapids" with my son!

Thus, the Spirit will give the counselee the exact vision he needs to help him overcome his fear. If he is afraid to go on a job interview, he may see his Protector sitting beside him at the interview, calming him and giving him all of the "right" answers. Or the Spirit may give him a picture of Jesus as the interviewer, treating him with great compassion and tenderness. If a counselee is afraid to give birth, the Spirit may give her a vision of Jesus as her doctor or friend, gently rubbing her back and stomach and coaching her through her delivery in a soothing, comforting manner.

Even though imagining Christ in a fearful circumstance will help dispel his anxiety, the counselee must still be prepared to fight satanic forces when he confronts the actual frightening situation. Putting on the full armor of God, he must bind the spirit of fear in the name of Jesus and break its hold on him. He must then pray the Word of God over himself, claiming some of the promises given in **Table 12**. Many of the Old Testament scriptures listed reveal that God was constantly telling the Israelites not to fear because he would fight for them and save them from their enemies. Even so today, our omnipotent God will save us from Satan and his hordes of demons. When we continually "resist the devil, he must flee," for "greater is He that is in us than he that is in the world!"

The counselee must then rivet his eyes on Jesus while praising and thanking Him for "setting the captives free." The double-edged sword of praising and practicing the presence of the Lord of Lords will slay the devil every time! As we have learned, Satan must flee when we praise because God inhabits our praises and His presence always expels the adversary. The god of this world and his rogues have no choice but to go! As long as the counselee has the eyes of his heart (Child) fixed firmly on Jesus, His perfect love will deliver him from fear. The minute he looks at his frightening circumstance, fear will once again enter his heart and overtake it. As long as Peter had his eyes fastened on Christ, he was able to walk on the water. "But seeing the wind, he became afraid, and beginning to sink, he cried out, saying, 'Lord, save me!' His Master responded, "O you of little faith, why did you doubt?"' (Matt. 14:30, 31).

As we know, fear is the opposite of faith. If we are afraid, we are not trusting God. Daniel found himself in a terrifying position when he was placed in a den full of lions. But the next morning, "...no injury whatever was found on him because he had trusted in his God" (Dan. 6:23). Likewise, Shadrach, Meshach and Abednego found themselves in an appalling situation when they were thrown into the fiery furnace still tied up. All of the king's high officials were amazed when these three children of God walked out of the fire unharmed without even the smell of smoke on them! The king declared, "Blessed be the God of Shadrach, Meshach and Abednego, who has sent His angel and delivered His servants who put their trust in Him" (Dan. 3:28). Praise God for the tremendous faith of these Old Testament saints!

God not only hopes that we New Testament saints will have this type of faith—He demands it of us! "Without faith it is impossible to please Him" (Heb. 11:6). "But My righteous one shall live by faith; and if he shrinks back, My soul has no pleasure in him" (Heb. 10:38). Many times, the Lord reprimanded his disciples for their little faith, while He praised many people who were healed for their great faith. Therefore, our Messiah insists that we "...not be of those who shrink back to destruction, but of those who have faith to the preserving of the soul" (Heb. 10:39). If we let the perfect love of Jesus envelop us and have total faith in His promises, our fears will evaporate, and our souls will be preserved!

(3.) Guilt. Just as counselees often experience the negative emotions of anger and fear while going through the script-breaking process, some will also be attacked with feelings of guilt. Since the root causes of a counselee's guilt have been dealt with during the soul healing process, in all probability, these "guilt-attacks" will have no basis in reality. Counselees who have been brought up with one of the overcontrolling parental patterns, especially the perfectionism and overprotective patterns, are the most prone to experience unrealistic guilt. This is to be expected since the perfectionist parent is never pleased with his child's efforts, no matter how well he does. Therefore, as an adult, this person may be plagued with pervading feelings of guilt if his Inner Child is still trying to gain the acceptance of his Internal Parent.

Since the overprotective parent tends to make his child dependent on him for his emotional needs, in adulthood, this person's Inner Child will feel pangs of guilt if he tries to break away from his smothering Internal Parent. The vile individuals who abuse children during satanic rituals and those who molest them often brainwash these little ones to believe they asked for it because they are bad, evil, dirty, etc. Thus, when these youngsters grow up, they also will be plagued with intense feelings of guilt. Along with guilt feelings, adults who have endured such traumatic abuse or have overcontrolling parents often experience emotions of unworthiness, inadequacy and self-condemnation. These counselees must be given a plan of action to help them combat the demonic forces attacking them through these feelings.

First, a counselee should be instructed to ask the Holy Spirit to help him recognize when feelings of guilt, inadequacy and unworthiness have hooked his Inner Child. He should then be encouraged not to give in to these emotions, but to get into the Adult and handle them God's way. Next, the counselee must ask the Spirit to show him if there is any unconfessed sin in his life which might be causing his guilt feelings. If not, the Spirit will reveal that the person's Internal Parent is once again "beating on" his Inner Child. This is readily detected by what psychologists term the "self-talk" that is taking place in his mind. I believe negative self-talk is induced and fed by demons who simply replay our outdated parental tapes.

For example, if someone does not speak to us, we may say to ourselves, "I wonder why Joe didn't say 'hello' to me. I must have done something to offend him. He probably doesn't like me. Nobody else likes me; why should he?" Negative self-talk might also occur if we think we did poorly on a test. We might say to ourselves, "I know I failed that test. I'm such an idiot! Why didn't I study harder? I'm never going to amount to anything. I don't know why I bother! I think I'll just quit school."

Evil spirits have a field day playing our archaic parental tapes which simply replay what our parents said to us when we were children, such as, "You are so stupid! You never get anything right! You'll never amount to anything! You are so stubborn and selfish! Who would want to be your friend, anyway?" As we have seen, these tapes most often consist of negative parental judgments of us which are the basis of the negative evaluations which we make of ourselves. Our negative self-judgments lead to feelings of guilt, unworthiness, self-doubt, self-condemnation, and self-pity. The prince of darkness and his cohorts use these emotions to oppress us and drag us down into hopelessness and depression and, eventually, self-destruction!

If a counselee has adequately reprogrammed his internal Parent with God's truth, his Adult will be able to see that his negative self-talk is based upon programming from his past which is no longer true. His Adult will also recognize that Satan is using these lies to pull him down into discouragement and despair. Thus, this person's next step would be to break the self-judgments on which these lies are based that he is stupid, no good, unlikeable, selfish, etc., and to ask his heavenly Father to forgive him for rejecting His creation. He must then bind the spirits of guilt, unworthiness, inadequacy, self-condemnation, and self-pity and break their hold over him. As he resists the devil, Lucifer must flee as he has no choice!

The counselee's next step should be to reaffirm the positive self-judgments based on God's Word with which he reprogrammed his Internal Parent, such as, "I am a child of the King, a joint heir with Jesus, a new creature in Christ, a worthy, intelligent, confident, special, and cherished person made in the image of God!" Positive self-talk leads to a positive self-image! He might visualize Jesus' worthiness, righteousness, intelligence, confidence, and self-acceptance flowing into him. He should reaffirm his acceptance of himself just as he is and forgive himself for not performing as well as he thought he should have.

The counselee should be encouraged to declare daily who he is in Christ Jesus according to the truths of God's Word. Praying the Word of God over himself, believing that the promises are speaking about him and accepting them by faith, will help him realize that he is indeed "in" Christ, not just in the spiritual realm, but also in the soulish realm. If a counselee diligently performs these steps whenever his Inner Child is hooked by guilt and unworthiness, his image of himself will eventually become firmly grounded "in" the image of Christ. Thus, "he (will finally be) a new creature; old things (will truly be) passed away; behold all things (will finally be) new" in the soulish, as well as the spiritual realm!

Negative feelings can control us if we let them, especially through our Parental "shoulds" and "musts." Our attempts to shape up our mate (anger), reshape our past (guilt) or shape our future (worry) through "if onlys" and "what ifs" paralyze us and block the restorative work God desires to accomplish in our souls.

D. RESURRECTION OF THE PERSONAL SPIRIT.

As we have discovered, the more emotional healing a counselee has received, enabling his Inner Child to forgive those responsible for hurting him, the less his Child will be controlled by his parental programming, freeing him from destructive attitudes and behavior patterns (symptoms). The more freedom his Inner Child enjoys, the easier it will be for a counselee's Child to trust his Adult to make constructive choices based on the love and truth now contained in his renewed Internal Parent. Simply stated, the counselee's Inner Child will finally be able to allow his Adult to handle the negative emotions that hook it in the correct manner. His Inner Child will no longer feel compelled to handle his feelings or fulfill his emotional needs by resorting to one of the destructive symptoms previously discussed.

The counselee's Internal Parent-Child conflict having finally been resolved, his Inner Child will now be able to relinquish its self-centered hold on this person's will and trust his Adult with it. As a result, the will of the counselee will no longer reside in his Inner Child, but in his Adult where it belongs. The rebellious, self-will of his Adaptive Child having, at long last, been broken, the counselee's Adult will feel free to encourage his Natural Child to come forth, be creative, spontaneous, joyful, and enjoy the abundant life his renewed Internal Parent wishes to bestow on him. His Natural Child will be able to release his problems to his heavenly Father, relax in His arms and allow Him to nurture, protect, encourage, and fill him with His perfect love and peace.

1. INTIMATE COMMUNION WITH THE FATHER.

As we discovered when discussing the personal spirit, a counselee's spirit may be wounded, imprisoned or slumbering due to the rejection, abuse, neglect, or trauma which his soul suffered in utero or during his formative years. Having healed the wounds inflicted upon the counselee's soul and spirit through the process of soul healing, the Lord Jesus, by the power of the Holy Spirit, is now able to bring this person's Natural Child into intimate communion with his heavenly Father. Secure in his Daddy's perfect love at long last, the counselee's resurrected spirit is now free to perform each of its duties with fullness of life. Hallelujah! Recalling that the personal spirit is comparable to the electric current which illuminates a light bulb, we can say that his resurrected spirit has become the energizing force which is now able to "light up his life (soul)!"

Blessed with an alert, functioning personal spirit, the counselee will now be able to enter more fully into fellowship with the Holy Spirit, one of whose tasks is to help him gain much deeper insight into God's Word. Illuminated by the Holy Spirit, the Word will truly come alive, taking on thrilling new dimensions! The counselee will declare with David, "How sweet are Thy words to my taste! Yes, sweeter than honey to my mouth! My eyes fail with longing for Thy word," and with Job, "I treasure Thy words more than my necessary food."

With the counselee's personal spirit having been liberated and revived, the Holy Spirit will also be able to lead him into a much deeper realm of worship. His Natural Child will feel the elation of entering into his Father's presence, of basking in His love and peace and thrilling to His awesome glory, power and majesty! "God is spirit, and those who worship Him must worship Him in spirit and in truth" (John 4:24). With all the host of heaven, he will ecstatically proclaim, "Amen, blessing and glory and wisdom and thanksgiving and honor and power and might, be to our God forever and ever!" (Rev. 7:12). Like David, he will joyously declare, "O magnify the Lord with me, and let us exalt His name together!" (Ps. 34:3). As David did, he will also freely leap and dance like a little child before the Lord! "Whomever then, humbles himself as this child, he is the greatest in the kingdom of heaven" (Matt. 18:4).

King David is an excellent example of a man who was blessed with an intimate love relationship with his heavenly Father. He not only relished God's Word and knew how to enter into deep worship, he was able to humble himself and be open and honest with his Daddy. Unencumbered by inhibitions, he was always willing to share his innermost thoughts and feelings with Him. He let God know when he felt hurt, frustrated, disappointed, or angry with Him. He shared his fears, failures and feelings of shame, guilt and unworthiness boldly and with abandon.

David was able to be this forthright with his heavenly Father because he totally trusted Him with his emotions. He was secure in his Daddy's unconditional love, knowing that he would never be rejected, shamed or ignored by Him. His loving, nurturing, compassionate Father would always accept and heal his emotions, then reassure him that He was still in charge of everything. As a result, David would always release his burdens to the great I Am in thanksgiving, praise and worship.

David's Psalms are perfect examples of what intimate communion with Jehovah really consists of. Many of his Psalms begin with David openly sharing his deepest feelings with his Father and close with him joyfully exalting his Lord and Master's mighty power and glorious splendor! The greatest desire of our Daddy's heart is that we would all know Him as intimately as David did! No wonder God said David was a man after His own heart!

Intimate communion with his heavenly Father will enable the counselee to hear and receive clear guidance and counsel through the still, small voice of the Holy Spirit, along with the correct interpretation of dreams and visions. His liberated personal spirit will "turn on" his Natural Child so that this person will be able to think creatively, receive inspiration from the Holy Spirit and give birth to original ideas.

The counselee's newly vitalized spirit will enable him to empathize deeply and identify with other people's pain. He will become a brilliant golden vessel from which God's agape love will abundantly flow. He will be able to feel God's compassion and unconditional love for each individual as the Holy Spirit reveals the scarred, little Child within each one. Having received the heart of God, his foremost desire will then be to gather Jesus' cherished, wounded lambs in his arms and allow the healing balm of Gilead to flow through him, touching their pain.

Thus, the counselee will have finally discovered his true identity in the security of God's love and the freedom of His truth. By trusting God to fully develop his potential in Jesus, his Lord and Savior, he will, at long last, discover the true meaning and purpose of his life! He will no longer struggle to obey God's Word out of religious duty (try to please his internal Parent). Finally, he will truly understand what it means to "...love the Lord his God with all his heart, and with all his soul, and with all his mind, and with all his strength, and to love his neighbor as himself" (Mark 12:30,31). His heart will now be bursting with desire to fulfill the greatest commandment our adored Redeemer ever gave!

The counselee will at last be able to follow Paul's directive: "... that in reference to your former manner of life, you lay aside the old self, which is being corrupted in accordance with the lusts of deceit, and that you be renewed in the spirit of your mind, and put on the new self, which in the likeness of God has been created in righteousness and holiness of the truth..." (Eph. 4:23-32). "But we all, with unveiled face beholding as in a mirror the glory of the Lord, are being transformed into the same image from glory to glory, just as from the Lord, the Spirit" (2 Cor. 3:18). Hallelujah!

2. THE HOLY OF HOLIES.

Therefore, as counselors, we are called to be the instruments the Lord uses to apply His healing love to the crushed, broken hearts of our counselees and His truth to their distrusting, deceived minds. Through the soul healing process, their souls are brought to death and resurrection in Christ which frees their spirits to commune intimately with their heavenly Father.

These truths are exquisitely illustrated in an analogy given to Pastor Sherman by the Holy Spirit. The Spirit revealed that the holy place of the tabernacle symbolizes the soul, while the outer court represents the body and the Holy of Holies symbolizes the Spirit. As we know, the soul is composed of the emotions, the mind and the will. Contained in the holy place are the lampstand, the table of showbread and the altar of incense. The Spirit disclosed that the lampstand symbolizes the healing and comforting of the emotions. Its seven lamps contain oil which is produced by the crushing of the olive from the olive tree which represents love. Thus, this healing oil, representing our heavenly Father's love, heals the wounded emotions (heart).

After our hearts (Inner Child) have been healed, the light from the seven lamps illuminates the holy place (our souls), giving us insight concerning the reasons for our attitudes and behavior. We then partake of the showbread which symbolizes the renewing of our minds (Internal Parent) with God's truth. After our hearts have been healed and our minds renewed, we are able to approach the altar of incense which symbolizes the releasing of our wills to God.

As we have seen, the most treasured gift that we can give our Savior who gave everything for us, is our wills. Sacrificing our wills on our Father's altar means that we are laying down our rights to hold onto all of the pain and hurts we have nurtured over many years, resulting in bitterness, anger, hatred, and unforgiveness being locked in our hearts. Thus, the only truly meaningful gift that we can give to our Daddy is all of the pain we have suffered over the years. He is thrilled beyond belief when we willingly embrace our pain and suffering and freely offer it up to Him as a sacrifice of praise, knowing that our sacrifice will produce in us an eternal weight of glory! As we lay our wills on our beloved Father's altar and burn them as priceless incense, the sweet fragrance of our sacrifice of love and praise symbolically splits the veil between the Holy Place and the Holy of Holies!

Our Heavenly Father, reeling to and fro as He inhales the heady aroma ascending from our supreme sacrifice, lovingly beckons us with outstretched arms! Covered by the blood of the Lamb, we eagerly bound into the Holy of Holies, curl up on our Daddy's lap, snuggle into His bosom and soak up His nurturing caresses as He wipes away every tear from our eyes! He delights in our fellowship as we laugh, play and frolic with Him in complete abandonment among the fragrant flowers blooming abundantly in His luscious, verdant meadows! Our liberated souls and spirits soar to new heights as we are finally able to fully experience intimate communion with our adored Daddy!

Thus, after the emotions in our hearts (Inner Child) have been healed with God's love using the oil of the lamps and our minds (Internal Parent) have been renewed with God's truth by partaking of the showbread, our souls are free! Hallelujah!! Since the Inner Child is no longer controlled by the programming of the Internal Parent, we are free to place our wills, embodying all of our rights, pain, bitterness, etc., on the altar of incense, offering them up as a sacrifice. We have, therefore, died to ourselves and been resurrected in Christ whose will was totally surrendered to His Father. "...The words that I say to you I do not speak on My own initiative, but the Father abiding in Me does His works" (John 14:10).

Having sacrificed our wills on the altar of incense, our resurrected souls and spirits are now able to enter the Holy of Holies and delight in the ecstasy of an intimate love relationship with our beloved Daddy! "...And as the bridegroom rejoices over his bride, So your God will rejoice over you" (Isa. 62:5). Thus, the small Child within each of us has, at long last, realized the most cherished desire of his heart—to experience a deep intimate relationship with someone (the only One) who loves and accepts him exactly as he is!

As counselors, we are called to put our hand to the plough and not look back," becoming spiritual parents whose love, long-suffering, gentleness, and empathy will help bring healing and deliverance to God's little wounded lambs, enabling them to enter the Holy of Holies. Our job is only to be faithful bondservants, consistently doing our small part, while our Lord and Master performs the major task of "healing the brokenhearted and setting the captives free." "For I am confident of this very thing, that He who began a good work in you will perfect it until the day of Christ Jesus" (Phil. 1:6). May Jesus help us rise to the occasion and be strong, sturdy "bridges" which carry His little "wounded lambs" to their Heavenly Father.

Part IV. TABLES *and* ILLUSTRATIONS

Table 1.

CONTENT OF THE EGO STATES

PARENT – **BELIEF SYSTEM**
(mind)
Parental Beliefs, Judgments, Opinions, Prejudice, Myths, Laws, Rules, Morals, Standards, Values
Admonitions (shoulds, should nots; musts, must nots)
Parental Patterns of How to Do Things
Parental Behavior (accepting, loving, nurturing, protecting)
Parental Behavior (rejecting, abusing, critical, neglecting)
Child's Perceptions of Parental Behavior
Child's Judgments (Beliefs Formed from Perceptions of Parental Behavior—usually negative)
Verbal: you should, should not; you always, never, you must; you ought to; lazy, stupid, absurd
Physical: pursed lips, pointing index finger, hands on hips, foot-tapping, tongue-clucking, patting another on head, arms folded across chest

ADULT – **THOUGHT SYSTEM**
(will)*
Rational Executive
Data Processor - Parent (Belief System)
- Child (Motivation System)
- Reality (Truth, Knowledge, Wisdom)
Verbal: why, what, when, how, where, who, possible, I think, I feel, in my opinion, true, false
Physical: interested, alert facial expression; continual movement of face, eyes, body; allows curious, excited Natural Child to show his face

CHILD – MOTIVATION SYSTEM

(heart) Emotional Reactions to Parental Behavior

(Feelings = love, joy, anger, hatred, fear, guilt, shame, unworthiness)

Inner Vows (Life-controlling Decisions Resulting From Judgments)

Self-will*

Natural Drives, Desires, Needs, Wants, Dreams, Goals

Creativity, Curiosity (desires to know, experience, express)

Rights, Expectations

Verbal: I want, I need, I must have, I don't care, I have a right, I don't want to, I can't

Physical: Tears, temper tantrums, quivering lip, pouting, high-pitched whining voice, downcast eyes, giggling, laughter, squirming, teasing, delight

*A person's "will" is controlled by the Child (self-will) until he is healed enough emotionally to be set free from his Parental programming, enabling him to trust the Adult to take charge of his "will."

Table 2.

PATHOLOGICAL SOUL DEVELOPMENT

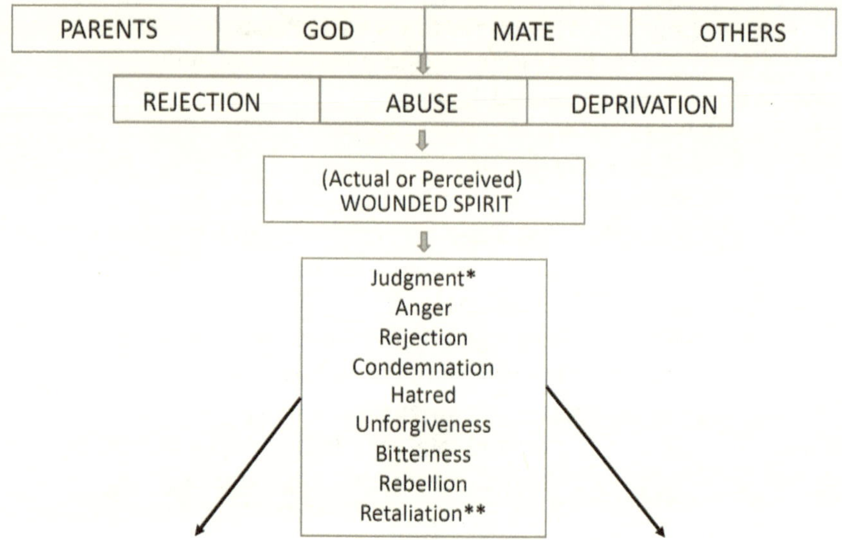

Expressed Toward Others **VICTIMIZER** (Symptoms)	Repressed – Turned Toward Self **VICTIM** (Symptoms)
Abuse-Verbal & Physical, Selfishness, Jealousy, Dishonesty, Gossip, Martyr, Neglect, pride, Sabotage, Control, Manipulation, Seduction, Sadism, Homicide Lust	Fear, Guilt, Self-pity, Depression, Psychosomatic Illness, Overwork, Accident proneness, Indulgence, Phobias, Anorexia-Bulimia, Delusions-Hallucinations, Promiscuity, Masochism, Suicide, Psychoneurotic Disorders
*1. JUDGMENT : You hurt me, so you deserve to be punished	*1. JUDGMENT : You hurt me, and since you are bigger and stronger, it is safer to agree with you that I deserve to be punished
**2. INNER VOW : I will punish you (Retaliation)	**2. INNER VOW : I will punish myself (Retaliation)

Table 3.

PARENTAL PATTERNS AND PERSONALITY PROFILES

UNDER-CONTROL PATTERNS	OVERCONTROL PATTERNS	REJECTION PATTERNS
Security through manipulation	Security through obedience	Security through power or withdrawal
<u>OVER-SUBMISSION</u> (Active Dependent) manipulating attention seeking impulsive gregarious relative conscience <u>OVERINDULGENCE</u> (Passive Independent) spoiled self-loving superior feelings irresponsible relative conscience	<u>AUTHORITARIAN</u> (Active Independent) dogmatic competitive task-oriented insensitive authoritarian conscience <u>OVER-COERCION</u> (Active Ambivalent) negativistic procrastinating vacillating moody conflicted conscience <u>PERFECTIONISM</u> (Passive Ambivalent) conforming guilt-prone inhibited compulsive oversensitive conscience <u>OVERPROTECTION</u> (Passive Dependent) dependent inadequate fear of rejection self-pity relative conscience	<u>ACTIVE REJECTION</u> (Active Detached) hostile defensive self-centered suspicious hardened conscience <u>PASSIVE REJECTION</u> (Passive Detached) withdrawing aloof unresponsive apathetic underdeveloped conscience

TABLE 4-a.

COMMON LIFE SCRIPTS

The most influential authority figure in a child's life, usually the strongest, most dominating parent, "writes the script" or plan for his life. The child responds to a particular pattern of parenting by making judgments and inner vows which control his behavior, attitudes and choices the rest of his life. Thus, a person's life is controlled by his script, i.e., his inner child is controlled by his Parental programming until Jesus sets him free!

Some of the more common scripts of life-controlling plans, resulting from the eight patterns of parenting are as follows:

PERSONALITY OF CHILD	PARENTAL PATTERN	SCRIPT CHARACTERISTICS
1) ACTIVE INDEPENDENT*	***AUTHORITARIAN***	
(victimizer, excluded Child)	(overcontrol)	(dogmatic)

PARENT-JUDGMENT:	My parent is stern, controlling, dominating, mean, strict, impatient, rigid, critical, demanding.
SELF-JUDGMENT:	I count only when I am in control.
INNER VOW:	I am out for "number one;" I will get ahead even if I have to step on a few people!

2) ACTIVE AMBIVALENT	***OVER-COERCION***	
(victim, dominant Parent)	(overcontrol)	(negativistic)

PARENT-JUDGMENT:	My parent is inconsistent, irritating, confusing, frustrating, unpredictable, double-minded.
SELF-JUDGMENT:	I count only when I keep people off-guard!
INNER VOW:	Since I never know what to expect from people, I am going to give everyone a real hard time!

PERSONALITY OF CHILD	PARENTAL PATTERN	SCRIPT CHARACTERISTICS
3) PASSIVE AMBIVALENT	***PERFECTIONISM***	
(victim, dominant Parent)	(overcontrol)	(conforming)

PARENT-JUDGMENT:	My parent is critical, controlling, particular, impatient, never satisfied.
SELF-JUDGMENT:	I count only when I am perfect!
INNER VOW:	I must always perform perfectly and strive to earn the approval of others or I will be put to shame!

4) PASSIVE DEPENDENT	***OVERPROTECTION***	
(victim, dominant Parent)	(overcontrol)	(dependent)

PARENT-DEPENDENT:	My parent is smothering, possessive, overly concerned, controlling, dominating.
SELF-JUDGMENT:	I count only when I avoid conflict!
INNER VOW:	I must get support and approval from others for everything I do or I will feel anxious, rejected and guilty!

5) ACTIVE DEPENDENT	***OVER-SUBMISSION***	
(victimizer, dominant Child)	(under-control)	(manipulating)

PARENT-JUDGMENT:	My parent is weak, easily manipulated, spineless, inept, undisciplined, flighty.
SELF-JUDGMENT:	I count only when I am noticed.
INNER VOW:	If I am cute and clever enough, people will like me, and I can get whatever I want!

TABLE 4-b.

COMMON LIFE SCRIPTS
(cont.)

PERSONALITY OF CHILD	PARENTAL PATTERN	SCRIPT CHARACTERISTICS
6) PASSIVE INDEPENDENT	***OVERINDULGENT***	
(victimizer, dominant Child)	(under-control)	(spoiled)

PARENT-JUDGMENT: My parent is powerless, easily controlled, stupid, unworthy of respect, undisciplined.

SELF-JUDGMENT: I count only when I get my own way!

INNER VOW: I am so great, and people are so stupid that I can always get my own way just by demanding it!

PERSONALITY OF CHILD	PARENTAL PATTERN	SCRIPT CHARACTERISTICS
7) ACTIVE DETACHED**	***ACTIVE REJECTION***	
(victimizer, excluded Parent)	(rejection)	(hostile)

PARENT-JUDGMENT: My parent is cruel, brutal, harsh, hostile, punitive, belittling, demanding, critical.

SELF-JUDGMENT: I am the only one who counts!

INNER VOW: Since people are no-good, I don't care about anyone but myself; whoever gets in my way will be sorry!

PERSONALITY OF CHILD	PARENTAL PATTERN	SCRIPT CHARACTERISTICS
8) PASSIVE DETACHED	***PASSIVE REJECTION***	
(victim, excluded adult)	(rejection)	(withdrawing)

PARENT-DEPENDENT: My parent is uncaring, nonexistent, unloving, negligent, indifferent, absent.

SELF-JUDGMENT: I am the only one who doesn't count.

INNER VOW: Since no one cares about me, including myself, I am going to drop out of life!

* If his temperament tends to be introverted, the Active Independent person may decide to repress his anger and become a victim instead of a victimizer. In this case, his script would be similar to that of the Passive Ambivalent or the Passive Dependent person.

** If his temperament tends to be introverted, the Active Detached person may also decide to become a victim instead of a victimizer. His script would then be like that of the Passive Detached individual. Often the Detached person is schizophrenic, meaning that he may switch back and forth from the Active Detached to the Passive Detached script. This is probably due to the fact that he was rejected by his parents in both an Active and Passive manner on different occasions.

Table 5.

DEFENSE MECHANISMS

REPRESSION:	denying painful, undesired truth about ourselves.
PROJECTION:	attributing one's own undesirable actions, motives and attitudes to others.
RATIONALIZATION:	giving socially acceptable explanations for behavior while hiding true motives.
EMOTIONAL WITHDRAWAL:	withdrawing into passivity to protect oneself from hurt.
REGRESSION:	retreating to an earlier developmental stage involving less maturity.
DISSOCIATION:	separating from the memory of a painful event and creating a new person, or alternate personality (alter), to whom the trauma did not happen.
SUBLIMATION:	gratifying frustrated aggressive or sexual impulses by channeling them into socially-approved activities.
FIXATION:	persisting in a behavior pattern or stage of development after the time has come to move to a more advanced level.

FANTASY: gratifying frustrated desires by imaginary achievements.

INTELLECTUALIZATION: sealing off the emotions of the heart from the mind; ability to deal with emotional matters without stirring up one's own fragile emotions.

REACTION FORMATION: expressing actions and attitudes which are directly opposite to the true feelings repressed in the heart, e.g., kindness instead of cruelty.

IDENTIFICATION & INTROJECTION: increasing feelings of self-worth by adopting and internalizing personality, characteristics and values of a highly regarded person

DISPLACEMENT: discharging emotions, usually hostile, on a source less dangerous than the one which initially aroused the emotions.

UNDOING: engaging in ritualistic behavior in an attempt to atone for immoral desires or acts.

Table 6-a.

SYMPTOMS OF PATHOLOGICAL BEHAVIOR

1. PUNISHING OTHER

A. ANTISOCIAL PERSONALITY DISORDER

1. Emotional Abuse	2. Physical Abuse	3. Sexual Abuse
4. Homicide		

B. MANIPULATION

1. Control	2. Withdrawal	3. Joking
4. Sabotage	5. Martyr	6. Seduction
7. Jealousy	8. Sarcasm	9. Gossip

2. PUNISHING OURSELVES

A. PSYCHOSOMATIC DISORDERS

1. Hypertension	2. Peptic Ulcer	3.Colitis
4. Asthma	5. Migraines	6. Amenorrhea
7. Impotence	8. Arthritis	9. Hyperventilation

B. INDULGENCES

1. Alcohol	2. Drugs	3. Food
4. Work	5. Sex	6. Gambling
7. Material Goods	8. Cult & Occult	9. Entertainment

C. SEXUAL DEVIATIONS

1. Homosexuality	2. Fetishism	3. Voyeurism
4. Pornography	5. Transvestism	6. Pedophilia
7. Exhibitionism	8. Sado-Masochism	9. Zoophilia

D. PSYCHONEUROTIC DISORDERS

1. Anxiety
2. Hysteria
    a. Conversion
        i. Sensory Symptoms
        ii. Motor Paralyses
        iii. Disordered Movements
    b. Dissociative
        i. Amnesia
        ii. Fugue
        iii. Somnambulism
        iv. Multiple Personality
1. Phobias
2. Obsession & Compulsions
3. Depression
4. Hypochondriasis
5. Depersonalization
6. Neurasthenia

E. AFFECTIVE DISORDERS

1. Manic-Depression
    a. Depression
        i. Simple
        ii. Acute
        iii. Depressive Stupor
    b. Manic
        i. Hypomania
        ii. Acute
        iii. Delirious

Table 6-b.

SYMPTOMS OF PATHOLOGICAL BEHAVIOR
(cont.)

F. SCHIZOPHRENIA

1. Paranoid
    a. Loosening of Thought Associations
    b. Autistic Withdrawal
    c. Ambivalence
    d. Inappropriateness of Affect
    e. Hallucinations
    f. Delusions
        i. Delusions of Grandeur
        ii. Delusions of Persecution
        iii. Delusions of Reference
        iv. Somatic Delusions
2. Disorganized
    a. Above Symptoms
    b. Incoherent Babbling
    c. Strange Gestures
    d. Bizarre Appearance
3. Catatonic
    a. Above Symptoms
    b. Motor Disturbances
        i. Excessive Activity & Excitement
        ii. Stupor, Rigidity, Mutism

G. PARANOIA

1. Delusions of Persecution, Grandeur, Reference
2. Egocentric, Narcissistic, Introverted, Suspicions

H. BRAIN SYNDROMES

1. Acute
    - i. Reversible Symptoms
    - ii. State of Stupor or Coma
    - iii. Delirious (incoherent, tremors, hallucinations, delusions, disorientation)
2. Chronic
    - i. Irreversible Symptoms
    - ii. Dementia (progressive intellectual deterioration)

I. OTHER SYMPTOMS

1. Bulimia-Anorexia
2. Accident proneness
3. Procrastination
4. Suicidal Tendencies
5. Masochistic Tendencies
6. Self-Pity Fantasy

Table 7.

THE DELIVERANCE PRAYER

Lord Jesus Christ, I believe You died on the cross for my sins and rose again from the dead. You redeemed me by your blood, and I belong to You, and I want to live for You. I confess all of my sins—known and unknown—I am sorry for them all. I renounce them all. I forgive all others as I want You to forgive me. Forgive me now and cleanse me with Your precious blood. I thank You for the blood of Jesus Christ which cleanses me now from all sin. And I come to You now as my Deliverer.

You know my special needs—the thing that binds me, that torments, that defiles, that evil spirit, that unclean spirit. I claim the promise of Your Word. "Whosoever that calleth on the name of the Lord shall be delivered." I call upon You now. In the Name of the Lord Jesus Christ, deliver me and set me free. Satan, I renounce you and all of your works! I loose myself from you, in the name of Jesus, and I command you to leave me right now, in Jesus' name! Amen!

—Derek K. Prince

Table 8-a.

COMMON DEMON GROUPS

1. **BITTERNESS**
   Resentment
   Hatred
   Unforgiveness
   Violence
   Temper
   Anger
   Retaliation
   Murder

2. **REBELLION**
   Self-will
   Stubbornness
   Disobedience
   Anti-submissiveness

3. **STRIFE**
   Contention
   Bickering
   Argument
   Quarreling
   Fighting

4. **CONTROL**
   Possessiveness
   Dominance
   Witchcraft

5. **RETALIATION**
   Destruction
   Spite
   Hatred
   Sadism
   Hurt
   Cruelty

6. **ACCUSATION**
   Judging
   Criticism
   Faultfinding

7. **REJECTION**
   Fear of Rejection
   Self-rejection

8. **INSECURITY**
   Inferiority
   Self-Pity
   Loneliness
   Timidity
   Shyness
   Inadequacy
   Ineptness

9. **JEALOUSLY**
   Envy
   Suspicion
   Distrust
   Selfishness

10. **WITHDRAWAL**
    Pouting
    Daydreaming
    Fantasy
    Pretension
    Unreality

11. **ESCAPE**
    Indifference
    Stoicism
    Passivity
    Sleepiness
    Alcohol
    Drugs

12. **PASSIVITY**
    Funk
    Indifference
    Listlessness
    Lethargy

Table 8-b.

COMMON DEMON GROUPS
(cont.)

13. **DEPRESSION**
    Despair
    Despondency
    Discouragement
    Defeatism
    Dejection
    Hopelessness
    Suicide
    Death
    Insomnia
    Morbidity

14. **HEAVINESS**
    Gloom
    Burden
    Disgust

15. **WORRY**
    Anxiety
    Fear
    Dread
    Apprehension

16. **NERVOUSNESS**
    Tension
    Headache
    Nervous habits
    Restlessness
    Excitement
    Insomnia
    Roving

17. **SENSITIVENESS**
    Self-awareness
    Fear of man
    Fear of disapproval

18. **PERSECUTION**
    Unfairness
    Fear of judgment
    Fear of condemnation
    Fear of accusation
    Fear of reproof
    Sensitiveness

19. **MENTAL ILLNESS**
    Insanity
    Madness
    Mania
    Retardation
    Senility
    Schizophrenia
    Paranoia
    Hallucinations

20. **SCHIZOPHRENIA**
    See Chapter 21 of Hammond book

21. **PARANOIA**
    Jealousy
    Envy
    Suspicion
    Distrust
    Persecution
    Fears
    Confrontation

22. **CONFUSION**
    Frustration
    Incoherence
    Forgetfulness

23. **DOUBT**
    Unbelief
    Skepticism

24. **INDECISION**
Procrastination
Compromise
Confusion
Forgetfulness
Indifference

25. **SELF-DECEPTION**
Self-delusion
Self-seduction
Pride

26. **MIND-BINDING**
Confusion
Fear of man
Fear of failure
Occult spirits
Spiritism spirits

27. **MIND IDOLATRY**
Intellectualism
Rationalization
Pride
Ego

28. **FEARS** (All kinds)
Phobias (All kinds)
Hysteria

29. **FEAR OF AUTHORITY**
Lying
Deceit

30. **PRIDE**
Ego
Vanity
Self-Righteousness
Haughtiness
Importance
Arrogance

31. **AFFECTATION**
Theatrics
Playacting
Sophistication
Pretension

32. **COVETOUSNESS**
Stealing
Kleptomania
Material lust
Greed
Discontent

33. **PERFECTION**
Pride
Vanity
Ego
Frustration
Criticism
Irritability
Intolerance
Anger

34. **COMPETITION**
Driving
Argument
Pride
Ego

35. **IMPATIENCE**
Agitation
Frustration
Intolerance
Resentment
Criticism

36. **FALSE BURDEN**
False Responsibility
False compassion

Table 8-c.

COMMON DEMON GROUPS
(cont.)

37. **GRIEF**
    Sorrow
    Heartache
    Heartbreak
    Crying
    Sadness
    Cruel

38. **Fatigue**
    Tiredness
    Weariness
    Laziness

39. **INFIRMITY**
    (May include any disease or sickness)

40. **DEATH**

41. **INHERITANCE**
    (Physical)
    (Emotional)
    (Mental)
    (Curses)

42. **HYPERACTIVITY**
    Restlessness
    Driving
    Pressure

43. **CURSING**
    Blasphemy
    Coarse jesting
    Gossip
    Criticism
    Backbiting
    Mockery
    Belittling
    Railing

44. **ADDICTIVE & COMPULSIVE**
    Nicotine
    Alcohol
    Drugs
    Medications
    Caffeine
    Gluttony

45. **GLUTTONY**
    Nervousness
    Compulsive eating
    Resentment
    Frustration
    Idleness
    Self-pity
    Self-reward

46. **SELF-ACCUSATION**
    Self-hatred
    Self-condemnation

47. **GUILT**
    Condemnation
    Shame
    Unworthiness
    Embarrassment

48. **SEXUAL IMPURITY**
    Lust
    Fantasy lust
    Masturbation
    Homosexuality
    Lesbianism
    Adultery
    Fornication
    Incest
    Harlotry
    Rape
    Exposure
    Frigidity

49. **CULTS**
Jehovah's Witnesses
Christian Science
Rosicrucianism
Theosophy
Urantia
Subud
Latihan
Unity
Mormonism
Bahaism
Unitarianism
(Lodges, societies and social agencies using the Bible & God as a basis but omitting the blood atonement of Jesus Christ)

50. **OCCULT**
Ouija Board
Palmistry
Handwriting analysis
Automatic handwriting
ESP
Hypnotism
Horoscope
Astrology
Levitation
Fortune telling
Water witching
Tarot cards
Pendulum
Witchcraft
Black magic
White magic
Conjuration
Incantation
Charms
Fetishes
Etc.

51. **RELIGIOUS**
Ritualism
Formalism
Legalism
Doctrinal obsession
Seduction
Doctrinal error
Fear of God
Fear of Hell
Fear of lost salvation
Religiosity
Etc.

52. **SPIRITISM**
Seance
Spirit guide
Necromancy
Etc.

53. **FALSE RELIGIONS**
Buddhism
Taoism
Hinduism
Islam
Shintoism
Confucianism
Etc.

Table 9.

JUDGMENTS AND INNER VOWS

COGNITIVE BELIEFS imparted by ritual abuse and mind control, seen in both adult and child survivors, include the following:

1. **THERE IS NO ESCAPE**

   "The cult members are everywhere. The spirits, monsters, demons, devils, etc. that the cult controls, surround me, too. They know if I violate any of the rules of the cult, and they will punish me. I can never leave."

2. **THE CULT COMPLETELY CONTROLS ME**

   "I am controlled by the cult and by the demon which the cult has placed in me to both control and monitor my behavior. I have no freedom and must follow the orders of the cult leaders in all things. I must be ready to assault others and neither trust nor make any close associations with anyone outside the cult."

3. **I AM INCAPABLE OF PROTECTING MYSELF**

   "I am inadequate. I have no control and no power. I am paralyzed."

4. **THE CULT IS MY ONLY TRUE FAMILY**

   (In extrafamilial cases)—"My family is dangerous to me and only the cult members accept me. I will eventually live with them forever because they are my true family."

5. **MEMORIES ARE DANGEROUS**

   "I must hurt myself if I begin to remember. I must cut myself, beat myself or kill myself if I remember what happened. Terrible things will happen to me and my family if I remember."

6. **DISCLOSURES ARE DANGEROUS**

   "The cult will know if I tell anyone. If I do tell, I or my family will be hurt by them, or I will be compelled to hurt myself."

RELIGIOUS BELIEFS imparted by ritual abuse and mind control, seen in both adult and child survivors, include the following:

1. **SATAN IS STRONGER THAN GOD**

   "Satan has all the power. He is stronger than god. God has not been able to do anything to protect me from what has happened."

2. **GOD DOES NOT LOVE ME**

   "I am despised and rejected by God. I am guilty of crimes that God could never forgive. I am evil and beyond hope for redemption or restoration."

3. **GOD WANTS TO PUNISH ME**

   "I am profoundly afraid of God who must want to destroy me."

4. **MY LIFE IS CONTROLLED BY SATAN**

   "I belong to Satan irrevocably. His power lives inside me and has taken over my life. I am possessed by an evil spirit or demon that controls my life."

5. **MY LIFE IS DEDICATED TO SATAN**

   "I have taken vows to serve Satan throughout my life. I will serve him by willingly committing acts of evil and destruction. In turn, he will protect me from harm and allow me to gratify all of my desires."

Table 10

HE KNOWS MY PAIN

Life is never as simple as it seems;
It seems a run of endless dreams,
A maze of scenes that ebb and flow...
How they'll work out, you never know.

Time is a guardian; it stands at the gate.
Oftentimes our master, sometimes it seems our fate,
To go on and on in an endless dream,
Till in a moment, by coincidence... it may seem....

All of a sudden, I realize You're there,
Conducting the music, directing the scenes,
In control of everything, even my dreams.
Then, like pages of a book unfolded,

I finally realize; I really see,
All along You were there with me,
Right from the start, molding and making me over,
Changing the strings of my heart.

Like a fine-tuned instrument,
Or a portrait painted over and then scraped,
To reveal something more beautiful inside...
No matter what the cost, it's futile to hide.

You battle my long-time enemy, pride.
I cringe, and I cover; I run and sit;
I busy myself, thinking, no... it's too hard...,
I mustn't see the pain but oh, it's all in vain!

Sovereignly, You lift me out of the dust,
Brush off the fear and crumble the crust,
Of mountainous walls I've built to defend,
A life full of hurt and rejection, at last at an end!

An end to pretense, defensiveness, and pain...
I look at the loss,
But there's so much more to the gain.
Eternity, at a glimpse, as I call out Your Name!

Jesus, I love, Defender of the lame...
I cry out to You in my shame.
You answer, "I'll never leave you or forsake you;
I know all your pain!"

—Priscilla Van Sutphin

Table 11.

TRAUMAS IN THE WOMB

Healing the Wounded Spirit
Clues for Identification of In Utero Wounds

The Condition In Utero	*Commonly Observed Patterns of Attitude and Behavior after Birth*
In Utero Encounters	
A child is not wanted.	Striving, performance orientation, trying to earn the right to be, inordinate desire to please (or the opposite, rejecting before he can be rejected), tension, apologizing, anger, wishing death, frequent illness, problems with bonding, refusing affection (or having insatiable desire for same).
A child is conceived out of wedlock.	Having deep sense of shame, lack of belonging.
The parents face a bad time financially.	Believing "I'm a burden."
The parents are too young, not ready.	Believing "I'm an intrusion."
The mother has poor health.	Guilt for being; child may take emotional responsibility for mother.
A child being formed is what one or both parents consider to be the wrong sex.	Sexual identification problems, sometimes one of the causes of homosexuality, striving to please to be what the parents want, futility, having a defeatist attitude, "I was wrong from the beginning."
This child follows other conceptions that were lost.	Being over-serious, over-achieving, striving, trying to make up for the loss, anger at being a "replacement," not getting to be "me."
Mother has inordinate fear of delivery.	Fear, insecurity, fear of childbirth.
Fighting in the home.	Nervousness, uptightness, fear, jumpiness, jumping in to control a discussion when differences of opinion emerge, feeling guilty: "I'm the reason for the quarrel," parental inversion: taking emotional responsibility for the parents.

The Condition In Utero	*Commonly Observed Patterns of Attitude and Behavior after Birth*
In Utero Encounters	
Father dies or leaves.	Guilt, self-blame, anger, bitter root expectation to be abandoned, inordinate hunger to find that one, having a death wish, depression.
Mother loses a loved one and is consumed by grief.	Deep sadness, depression, having a death wish, fear of death, loneliness, imagining "no support for me; I will have to depend on myself."
Unwholesome sexual relations, father's approaches to mother are insensitive or violent—or more than one sexual partner.	Aversion to sex, fear of male organ, general unhealthy attitude.
Mother is afraid of gaining too much weight, does not eat properly.	Insatiable hunger, anger.

These observations are those we have discovered during many years of counseling. Many are very much the same as reported in Dr. Verney's research. He added several more, among which are:

Mother is a heavy smoker.	Predisposition to severe anxiety.
Mother consumes much caffeine.	Baby likely to have poor muscle tone and low activity level.
Mother consumes alcohol.	More than the chemical effect, the baby absorbs the negative feelings which caused the mother to drink.
Breech delivery.	Higher risk of having learning problems.
Unusually painful delivery.	Anger, lacking an acceptable outlet, having ulcers, depression.
Relatively normal delivery.	Fury if pain, mother's or child's, seems to confirm rejection or ambivalence in utero.

Table 12-a.

"HEART" SCRIPTURES

"The intent of man's heart is evil from his youth" (Gen. 8:21).

"The Lord has led you in the wilderness ". . . testing you, to know what was in your heart, whether you would keep His commandments or not" (Deut. 8:2).

"Moreover, the Lord your God will circumcise your heart and the heart of your descendants, to love the Lord your God with all your heart and with all your soul, in order that you may live" (Deut. 30:6).

"God sees not as man sees, for man looks at the outward appearance, but the Lord looks at the heart" (1 Sam. 16:7).

"Thou alone dost know the hearts of all the sons of men" (1 Kings 8:39).

"Let your heart therefore be wholly devoted to the lord our God, to walk in His statutes and to keep His commandments" (1 Kings 8:61).

"Serve Him with a whole heart and a willing mind, for the Lord searches all hearts -and understands every intent of the thoughts" (1 Chron. 28:9).

"Would not God find this out? For He knows the secrets of the heart" (Ps. 44:21).

"Create in me a clean heart, O God" (Ps. 51:10).

"A broken and a contrite heart, O God, Thou wilt not despise" (Ps. 51:17).

"Pour out your heart before Him; God is a refuge for us" (Ps. 62:8).

"Do not harden your hearts" (Ps. 95:8).

"His heart is upheld; he will not fear" (Ps. 112:8).

"He heals the brokenhearted and binds up their wounds" (Ps. 147:3).

"Watch over your heart with all diligence, for from it flow the springs of life" (Prov. 4:23).

"Deceit is in the heart of those who devise evil" (Prov. 12:20).

"The heart knows its own bitterness" (Prov. 14:10).

"A tranquil heart is life to the body" (Prov. 14:30).

"A joyful heart makes a cheerful face" (Prov. 15:13).

"The plans of the heart belong to man" (Prov. 16:1).

"Everyone who is proud in heart is an abomination to the Lord" (Prov. 16:5).

"A joyful heart is good medicine" (Prov. 17:22).

"Many are the plans in a man's heart" (Prov. 19:21).

"Who can say, 'I have cleansed my heart, I am pure from my sin?"' (Prov. 20:9).

"For as a man thinks within his heart, so he is" (Prov. 23:7).

"Apply your heart to discipline" (Prov. 23:12).

"Do not let your heart envy sinners" (Prov. 23:17).

"Give Me your heart, My son" (Prov. 23:26).

"Does He not consider it Who weighs the hearts?" (Prov. 24:12).

"He who hates disguises it with his lips, but he lays up deceit in his heart" (Prov. 26:24).

"When he speaks graciously, do not believe him, for there are seven abominations in his heart" (Prov. 26:25).

"He who hardens his heart will fall into calamity" (Prov. 28:14).

"He who trusts in his own heart is a fool" (Prov. 28:26).

"Circumcise yourselves to the Lord and remove the foreskins of your heart" (Jer. 4:4).

"The heart is more deceitful than all else and is desperately sick; who can understand it?" (Jer. 17:9).

"I, the Lord, search the heart; I test the mind" (Jer. 17:10).

"And I will give them a heart to know Me, for I am the Lord; and they will be My people, and I will be their God, for they will return to Me with their whole heart" (Jer. 24:7).

"Moreover, I will give you a new heart and put a new spirit within you; and I will remove the heart of stone from your flesh and give you a heart of flesh" (Ezek. 36:26).

"Return to Me with all your heart, and with fasting, weeping and mourning" (Joel 2:12).

"And rend your heart and not your garments" (Joel 2:13).

Table 12-b.

"HEART" SCRIPTURES
(cont.)

"Blessed are the pure in heart, for they shall see God" (Matt. 5:8).

"Where your treasure is, there will your heart be also" (Matt. 6:21).

"I am gentle and humble in heart" (Matt. 11:29).

"This people honors Me with their lips, but their heart is far from Me" (Matt. 15:8).

"For the mouth speaks out of that which fills the heart" (Matt. 12:34).

"But the things that proceed out of the mouth come from the heart, and those defile the man" (Matt. 15:18).

"For out of the heart come evil thoughts, murders, adulteries, fornications, thefts, false witness, slanders" (Matt. 15:19).

". . . pondering them in her heart" (Luke 2:19).

"His mother treasured all these things in her heart" (Luke 2:51).

"But because of your stubbornness and unrepentant heart you are storing up wrath for yourself" (Rom. 2:5).

"But he is a Jew who is one inwardly; and circumcision is that which is of the heart, by the Spirit, not by the letter" (Rom. 2:29).

"He who searches the hearts knows what the mind of the Spirit is" (Rom. 8:27).

"The secrets of his heart are disclosed" (1 Cor. 14:25).

". . . strengthened with power through His Spirit in the inner man, so that Christ may dwell in your hearts through faith" (Eph. 3:16 -17).

". . . because of the hardness of their hearts" (Eph. 4:18).

". . . making melody with your heart to the Lord" (Eph. 5:19).

". . . slaves of Christ, doing the will of God from the heart" (Eph. 6:6).

"May the Lord direct your hearts into the love of God and into the steadfastness of Christ" (2 Thess. 3:5).

"The Word of God ". . . able to judge the thoughts and intentions of the heart" (Heb. 4:12).

"Let us draw near with a sincere heart in full assurance of faith, having our hearts sprinkled clean from an evil conscience" (Heb.10:22).

Table 13-a.

THE CRY OF OUR FATHER'S HEART

My arm is not shortened that it cannot reach—even into the depths of the pit—it can reach, for wherever there is a hand lifted up, I will meet it and I will help, and I will uphold by my righteous right hand. Even in times of turmoil when things have seemingly reached their darkest, 'I AM' is there ready to answer the call of a heart unto me. In my wisdom and my grace, I will allow destruction, if necessary, to run its natural course to reach someone—to get them to a place where they will look up and acknowledge my presence in their life and allow me entrance into their heart; for indeed, there are those who will allow me into their life and then push me further and further from their heart. What good can I do for them if they continue to push me away? Can I comfort them? Can I heal them? Yes, they cry unto me with their minds, but their hearts are not open to receive their answer; for I do not speak of head knowledge, for their minds are enmity unto me, but when I want to reach someone, I speak to their inner being—to their heart—to their spirit—and if this inner person has closed me off, wherefore am I to get in? How can I answer their prayers? These are their own worst enemy and the enemy is so willing to help in their defense.

Denial is ruining the hope of my people. These walls of denial must be brought down. Spiritual warfare must be done to uproot these walls and cause them to crumble and turn to dust. Walls of denial—even for the true Christian—have kept many from walking intimately with me. For I desire to walk with and fellowship with my people—to taste the sweetness of an intimate relationship with my children, but too many deny their hurts. They bury them because they feel they are too painful to deal with and that shuts off my power to heal and this causes a roadblock in our relationship—our walk can only go so far and my people can't understand why they feel dry and empty, why they can only remember my anointing instead of experiencing it afresh and anew.

Table 13-b.

THE CRY OF OUR FATHER'S HEART

(cont.)

My heart cries out to these who have shut me off. I am reaching and will continue to reach out to them, but they must respond. Relationship goes two ways. I cannot have a relationship with them on my own. They must take off their masks, tear down their walls and allow my spirit to permeate their hearts. Once I have healed the hurts and removed the scars, then they must choose daily to walk with me and not in their flesh. Walking in denial is walking in the flesh. Walking in the flesh profits nothing. It has no solutions or answers. It brings misery and confusion and idleness and will eventually, if left undealt with, bring a falling away from the faith when all becomes dry and meaningless. These will find themselves on the road to destruction before long and there will seemingly be no way out. But oh–even then, if they will but look up to me, I will reach down even into the very pit of destruction and lift them out, but only if they call upon me and trust me enough to let me into their heart of hearts–to the very seat of their existence. Once they allow my Spirit to do His continuous work, they will never be the same again.

In My Great Love for You,

Jesus

Jesus Christ of Nazareth

Table 14.

HOW ANGER DEVELOPS AND IS DISSIPATED

Violated Rights + Judgment + Hurt Feelings = ANGER

Confess Anger + Discover Feelings + Release Rights +
Rescind Judgment + Hurts Healed + Forgive + Share Feelings =
ANGER DISSIPATES

Since we have been bought with a price, the priceless Blood of Jesus, we are His bondservants. Since bondservants have no rights, we must nail all of our rights and expectations to the cross of Jesus, that is, release them to Him. We must put all of our rights and expectations on the Lord's altar as a sacrifice of love and praise to Him.

Give up your Bill of Rights—put it on the altar and nail it to the cross! Burn up your Bill of Rights!

BILL OF RIGHTS

I have a right:

1. to be treated fairly;
2. to have my needs met;
3. to be accepted as I am;
4. to be respected;
5. to be love and nurtured;
6. to be listened to;
7. to be understood;
8. to get angry when people hurt me;
9. to feel self-pity when people hurt me;
10. to blame others if things go wrong.

Illustration 1.

CHARACTER TREE

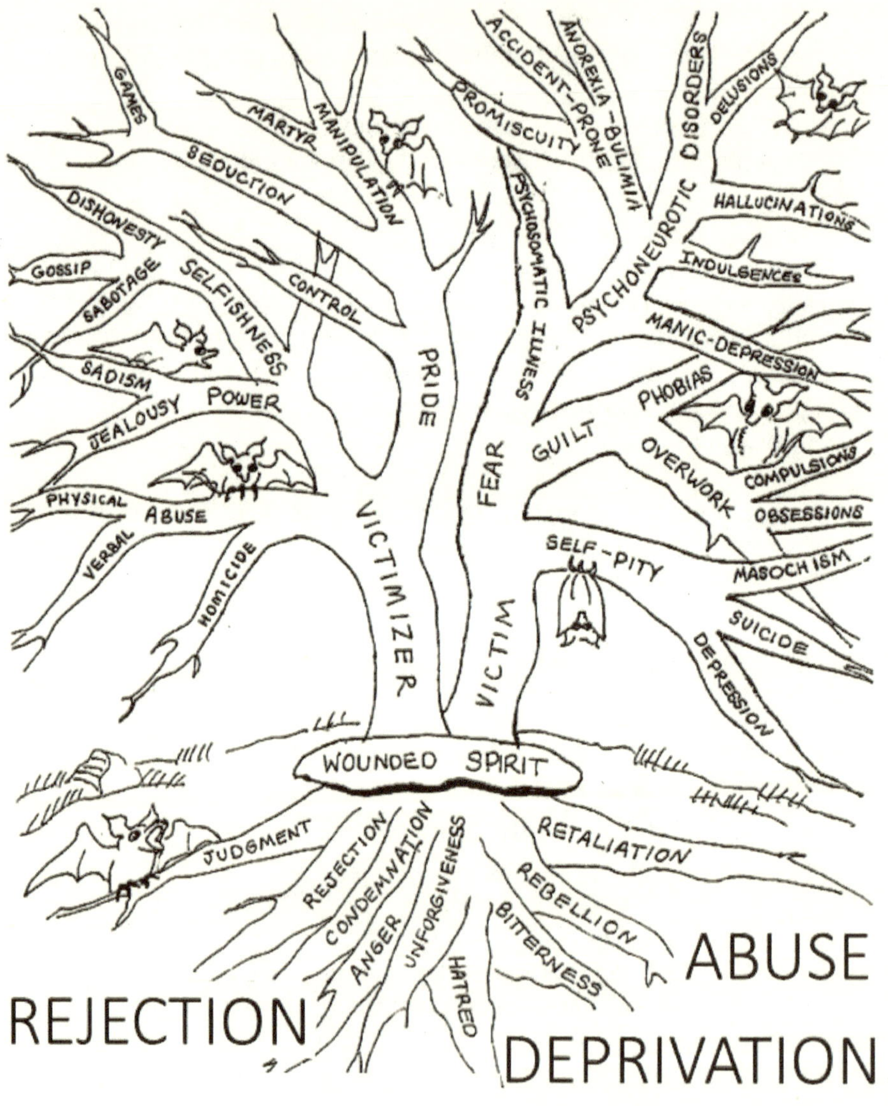

BIBLIOGRAPHY

Alsobrook, David, *The Precious Blood* (Tulsa: Custom Graphics, 1979)

Bakker, Tammy, *Run to the Roar* (Harrison: New Leaf Press, Inc., 1980)

Basansky, Bill, *Babunia* (Plainfield: Logos International, 1976)

Bennett, Rita, *You Can Be Emotionally Free* (Old Tappan: Fleming H. Revell Co., 1982)

Billheimer, Paul, *Destined for the Throne* (Fort Washington: Christian Literature Crusade, 1975)

Billheimer, Paul, *Don't Waste Your Sorrows* (Fort Washington: Christian Literature Crusade, 1977)

Cho, Paul Yonggi, *Holy Spirit, My Senior Partner* (Lake Mary: Strang Communications Co., 1989)

Conner, Kevin J., *Interpreting the Symbols and Types* (Portland: Bible Temple Publishing, 1980)

Copeland, Germaine, *Prayers That Avail Much* (Tulsa: Harrison House, Inc., 1989)

Eareckson, Joni, *Joni* (Grand Rapids: Zondervan Publishing House, 1976)

Fox, Debbie Diane, *A Face For Me* (Old Tappan: Fleming H. Revell Co., 1978)

Friesen, James G., *Understanding the Mystery of MPD* (San Bernardino: Here's Life Publishers, Inc., 1991)

Friesen, James G., *More Than Survivors* (San Bernardino: Here's Life Publishers, 1992)

Grant, Myrna, *Vanya* (Lake Mary: Creation House, 1974)

Hammond, Frank & Ida Mae, *Pigs in the Parlor* (Kirkwood: Impact Books, Inc., 1973)

Harris, Thomas, *I'm OK—You're OK* (New York: Harper & Row, 1967)

Horton, Marille, *Dear Mamma, Please Don't Die* (Nashville: Thomas Nelson Publishers, 1979)

Horton & Hurlbert, *The Wonderful Names of Our Wonderful Lord* (Los Angeles: Grant Publishing House, 1925)

House, Ronald & Judy, *How to Recognize Shepherdship Error* (Jacksonville: Living Word Ministries, Inc., 1983)

Hunt & McMahon, *Seduction of Christianity* (Eugene: Harvest House Publishers, 1985)

Leman, Kevin, *The Birth Order Book* (Old Tappan: Fleming H. Revell Co., 1985)

Markell, Jan, *Angels in the Camp* (Wheaton: Tyndale House Publishers, 1979)

Marrs, Texe W., *Mystery Mark of the New Age* (Westchester: Crossway Books, 1988)

Mead, Eleanor Tyler, *Lay Up Your Treasures in Heaven* (Plainfield: Logos International, 1977)

Millon, Theodore, *Disorders of Personality: Introducing a DSM/ICD Spectrum from Normal to Abnormal* (New York: John Wiley & Sons, Inc., 1981)

Nee, Watchman, *The Normal Christian Life* (Gospel Literature Service, 1957)

Nee, Watchman, *What Shall This Man Do?* (Wheaton: Tyndale Publishers, 1961)

New American Standard Bible (La Habra: Foundation Press Publications, 1960)

Nielsen, Lawrence, *The Liberation of the Soul* (Self-published, 1980)

Philpott & Kalita, *Brain Allergies: The Psychonutrient Connection* (New Canaan: Keats Publishing, Inc., 1980)

Riffel, Herman, *Your Dreams: God's Neglected Gift* (New York: Ballantine Books, 1981)

Rosen, Fox, & Gregory, *Abnormal Psychology* (Philadelphia: W.B. Saunders Co., 1965)

Rothenberg, Marie, *David* (Old Tappan: Fleming H. Revell Co., 1985)

Sandford, John & Paula, *The Transformation of the Inner Man* (South Plainfield: Bridge Publishing Inc., 1982)

Sandford, John & Paula, *Healing the Wounded Spirit* (South Plainfield: Bridge Publishing, Inc., 1985)

Smalley & Trent, *The Language of Love* (Pomona: Focus on the Family Publishing, 1988)

Smith & Pazder, *Michelle Remembers* (New York: Pocket Books, 1980)

Spencer, Judith, *Suffer the Child* (New York: Pocket Books, 1989)

Stratford, Lauren, *Satan's Underground* (Eugene: Harvest House Publishers, 1988)

Sumrall, Lester, *Demons: The Answer Book* (Nashville: Thomas Nelson Publishing Co, 1979)

ten Boom, Corrie, *The Hiding Place* (Uhrichsville: Barbour & Co., 1971)

Verny & Kelly, *The Secret Life of the Unborn Child* (New York: Dell Publishing Co., Inc., 1981)

Webster's New Collegiate Dictionary (Cambridge: The Riverside Press, 1956)

Wurmbrand, Richard, *Tortured for Christ* (U.S.A.: Diane Books, 1967)

RECOMMENDED READING

Bennett, Rita, *Making Peace With Your Inner Child* (Old Tappan: Fleming H. Revell, 1987)
Bennett, Rita, *How to Pray for Inner Healing for Yourself and Others* (Old Tappan: Fleming H. Revell, 1987)
Hinn, Benny, *Good Morning, Holy Spirit* (Springdale: Whitaker House Publishing, 1992)
Joyner, Rick, *The Harvest* (Charlotte: Morning Star Publications, 1989)
Koons, Carolyn, *Beyond Betrayal* (San Francisco: Harper & Row, 1987)
Kraft, Charles H., *Deep Wounds, Deep Healing* (Ann Arbor: Servant Publications, 1993)
Kraft, Charles H., *Defeating Dark Angels* (Ann Arbor: Servant Publications, 1992)
Larson, Bob, *Satanism: The Seduction of America's Youth* (Nashville: Thomas Nelson Publishers, 1989)
Littauer, Fred, *The Promise of Healing* (Nashville: Thomas Nelson Publishers, 1994)
McGhee, Geri, *Clearing the Land: Preparing for Deliverance* (Richardson: Abiding Life Ministries, 1985)
Michaelson, Johanna, *Like Lambs to the Slaughter* (Eugene: Harvest House Publishers, 1989)
Michaelson, Johanna, *The Beautiful Side of Evil* (Eugene: Harvest House Publishers, 1982)
Payne, Leanne, *The Healing of the Homosexual* (Westchester: Crossway Books, 1985)
Peck, M. Scott, *People of the Lie* (New York: Simon & Schuster, 1983)
Pruitt-Salem, Cheryl, *Abuse: Bruised But Not Broken* (Tulsa: Praise Books, 1989)
Seamands, David, *Healing of Memories* (Wheaton: Victor Books, 1985)

Spencer, James R., *Heresy Hunters* (Lafayette: Huntington House Publishers, 1993)

Stapleton, Ruth Carter, *The Experience of Inner Healing* (Waco: Word Books, 1977)

Stapleton, Ruth Carter, *The Gift of Inner Healing* (Waco: Word, Inc., 1976)

Tapscott, Betty, *Inner Healing Through Healing of the Memories* (Kingwood: Hunter Books, 1975)

White, Thomas R., *A Believer's Guide to Spiritual Warfare* (Ann Arbor: Vine Books, 1990)

ACKNOWLEDGMENTS

Thanks goes to John Allen who was a great help in publishing this book and provided much guidance and many hours of work getting the cover and manuscript ready. The original manuscript was not in electronic form and had to be read by Optical Character Recognition software. This process produced very many reading errors, many of which John corrected.

Thanks also goes to Steve Durham who spent a very large amount of time proofreading, editing, checking references, and adding information as appropriate. He took a personal interest in getting the book published and his help and dedication is greatly appreciated.

Lastly, thanks goes to Douglas Friedman who provided encouragement along the way and was the one who recommended John Allen as a guide for publishing the book.

ABOUT THE AUTHOR

JUDITH GIESING has served the body of Christ in the Spirit-anointed counseling ministry since 1975. Through her ministry, the Holy Spirit has touched and healed the hidden wounds and scars of many hearts, even those of memories that had been buried since childhood. Her credentials include a M.S. in Pastoral Counseling and a M.A. in Marriage, Family and Child Counseling.

Judith is director of **Wounded Lamb Ministries**, a ministry dedicated to training Christian laymen to bind up the broken-hearted and set the captives free. The need for trained, anointed, Spirit-led counselors far exceeds the supply. Thus, she is eager and excited to share the wisdom and insight which the Spirit has given her during many years of experience and training. Her heart's desire is to pass down her "mantle" to those whom God has called to minister to the emotionally wounded, lame, and outcast "lambs" in the body of Christ.

wake-
robin
PRESS

www.ingramcontent.com/pod-product-compliance
Lightning Source LLC
LaVergne TN
LVHW101320110826
845152LV00015B/158/J

9781946970046